VOLUME 83

Denmark

Revised Edition

LeeAnn Iovanni

Compiler

CLIO PRESS

OXFORD, ENGLAND · SANTA BARBARA, CALIFORNIA
DENVER, COLORADO

© Copyright 1999 by ABC-CLIO Ltd.

British Library Cataloguing in Publication Data

LeeAnn Iovanni
Denmark – Rev. Ed. – (World bibliographical series; v. 83)
1. Denmark – Bibliography
I. Title
016.9′489

ISBN 1–85109–305–2

ABC-CLIO Ltd.,
Old Clarendon Ironworks,
35A Great Clarendon Street,
Oxford OX2 6AT, England.

———————

ABC-CLIO Inc.,
130 Cremona Drive,
Santa Barbara,
CA 93117, USA.

Designed by Bernard Crossland.
Typeset by Columns Design Ltd., Reading, England.
Printed in Great Britain by print in black, Midsomer Norton.

Denmark

WORLD BIBLIOGRAPHICAL SERIES

General Editors:
Robert G. Neville (Executive Editor)
John J. Horton

Robert A. Myers   Hans H. Wellisch
Ian Wallace   Ralph Lee Woodward, Jr.

John J. Horton is Deputy Librarian of the University of Bradford and was formerly Chairman of its Academic Board of Studies in Social Sciences. He has maintained a longstanding interest in the discipline of area studies and its associated bibliographical problems, with special reference to European Studies. In particular he has published in the field of Icelandic and of Yugoslav studies, including the two relevant volumes in the World Bibliographical Series.

Robert A. Myers is Associate Professor of Anthropology in the Division of Social Sciences and Director of Study Abroad Programs at Alfred University, Alfred, New York. He has studied post-colonial island nations of the Caribbean and has spent two years in Nigeria on a Fulbright Lectureship. His interests include international public health, historical anthropology and developing societies. In addition to *Amerindians of the Lesser Antilles: a bibliography* (1981), *A Resource Guide to Dominica, 1493-1986* (1987) and numerous articles, he has compiled the World Bibliographical Series volumes on *Dominica* (1987), *Nigeria* (1989) and *Ghana* (1991).

Ian Wallace is Professor of German at the University of Bath. A graduate of Oxford in French and German, he also studied in Tübingen, Heidelberg and Lausanne before taking teaching posts at universities in the USA, Scotland and England. He specializes in contemporary German affairs, especially literature and culture, on which he has published numerous articles and books. In 1979 he founded the journal *GDR Monitor*, which he continues to edit under its new title *German Monitor*.

Hans H. Wellisch is Professor emeritus at the College of Library and Information Services, University of Maryland. He was President of the American Society of Indexers and was a member of the International Federation for Documentation. He is the author of numerous articles and several books on indexing and abstracting, and has published *The Conversion of Scripts and Indexing and Abstracting: an International Bibliography*, and *Indexing from A to Z*. He also contributes frequently to *Journal of the American Society for Information Science*, *The Indexer* and other professional journals.

Ralph Lee Woodward, Jr. is Professor of History at Tulane University, New Orleans. He is the author of *Central America, a Nation Divided*, 2nd ed. (1985), as well as several monographs and more than seventy scholarly articles on modern Latin America. He has also compiled volumes in the World Bibliographical Series on *Belize* (1980), *El Salvador* (1988), *Guatemala* (Rev. Ed.) (1992) and *Nicaragua* (Rev. Ed.) (1994). Dr. Woodward edited the Central American section of the *Research Guide to Central America and the Caribbean* (1985) and is currently associate editor of Scribner's *Encyclopedia of Latin American History*.

THE WORLD BIBLIOGRAPHICAL SERIES

This series, which is principally designed for the English speaker, will eventually cover every country (and some of the world's principal regions and cities), each in a separate volume comprising annotated entries on works dealing with its history, geography, economy and politics; and with its people, their culture, customs, religion and social organization. Attention will also be paid to current living conditions – housing, education, newspapers, clothing, etc. – that are all too often ignored in standard bibliographies; and to those particular aspects relevant to individual countries. Each volume seeks to achieve, by use of careful selectivity and critical assessment of the literature, an expression of the country and an appreciation of its nature and national aspirations, to guide the reader towards an understanding of its importance. The keynote of the series is to provide, in a uniform format, an interpretation of each country that will express its culture, its place in the world, and the qualities and background that make it unique. The views expressed in individual volumes, however, are not necessarily those of the publisher.

VOLUMES IN THE SERIES

For Christian

Contents

Contents

Contents

Contents

Introduction

Denmark is the smallest and southernmost of the Scandinavian countries. The oldest monarchy in the world, Denmark consists of the Jutland (Jylland) peninsula, which forms almost two-thirds of the country's territory, and over 400 islands, fewer than one hundred of which are inhabited. Zealand (Sjælland) and Funen (Fyn) are the largest islands, and the capital city of Copenhagen is situated on the eastern coast of Zealand. Other important islands are Lolland, Falster and Møn which are just off the southern coast of Zealand, and the isolated island of Bornholm which lies in the Baltic Sea, between Poland and Sweden.

Jutland is bounded on the north by the Skagerrak Sea, which separates it from Norway, and on the west by the North Sea. The Kattegat Strait and the Sound (Øresund) lie to the east, dividing Denmark from Sweden, and the Baltic Sea extends east of Bornholm. The Little Belt Bridge links Jutland with Funen and the Great Belt Bridge and Tunnel connects Funen and Zealand. Ferry service is also vital to linking various other parts of the country.

The kingdom of Denmark has two self-governing possessions in the North Atlantic Ocean: Greenland, the world's largest island, and the Faroe Islands, a group of eighteen islands located midway between Norway and Iceland. Greenland's colonial status ended in 1953, when Denmark adopted a new constitution; in 1979, it was finally granted internal self-government. A strong nationalist movement in the Faroe Islands resulted in home rule in 1948.

Denmark is a small country with a total land mass of 43,093 sq. km. (16,638 sq. miles), but with a coastline of 7,000 kilometres (4,500 miles). The Jutland peninsula forms Denmark's only land border (68 kilometres or 42 miles) with Germany to the south. Nowhere in Denmark is further than 52 kilometres or 32 miles from the sea. The surrounding seas and the Gulf Stream ensure a generally mild, coastal climate. There are no mountains in Denmark. It is a low-lying country, the highest elevation being only 173 metres or 568 feet above sea level. Wilderness areas account for only ten per cent of the country's territory. Two-thirds of Denmark's land is devoted to agriculture, which consists primarily of cereal production used in livestock fodder.

The 1996 population of Denmark (excluding the Faroe Islands and Greenland) was about five and one-quarter million, one-third of whom are resident in the greater Copenhagen area. Around one-third live in towns of more than 10,000 residents, and another one-third live in smaller towns and rural areas. In addition to metropolitan Copenhagen, the greatest concentrations can be found in the three other large urban areas of Odense (on Funen), and Aalborg and Aarhus (on Jutland).

Denmark has few natural resources, but the extraction of oil in the North Sea, since 1972, and natural gas, since 1984, have helped to improve the situation. The country still must rely on imports for nearly all essential raw materials, and its economy is heavily dependent on exports. But what Denmark lacks in natural resources, it makes up for in its greatest resource, namely a well-educated, highly skilled, and flexible workforce. Industrialization came relatively late to this once agrarian economy, not getting into full swing until after the Second World War. The processing and export of agricultural goods, especially pork and dairy products now accounts for a significant proportion of Denmark's industry. Fishing remains an important industrial sector, and the retail and service industries have become increasingly profitable. Denmark exports a variety of products that attest to the skilled workmanship of its workforce such as ships, medical products, electrical and mechanical goods, and furniture, as well as Danish beer, which is considered to be among the world's best.

Denmark has always been a trading nation, and was once a much larger kingdom. The story of its economic and political history is one of a rather violent struggle to acquire and hold on to its territory, coupled with a relatively peaceful internal path to democracy and modernization.

There is evidence of human presence in what is now modern Denmark as early as 100,000 years ago, prior to the last Ice Age. Evidence of more continuous habitation can be traced to around 10000 BC, during the Old Stone Age, when nomadic hunters moved up from central Europe, following the northern migration of the reindeer as glacial ice receded. The New Stone Age, which lasted until about 2500 BC, saw the introduction of agriculture and the domestication of animals, which were accompanied by the formation of permanent settlements and the erection of stone monuments. The Bronze Age (1500 to 500 BC) was marked by progress in shipbuilding, and prosperous trade relations with other European lands, particularly in the

Mediterranean. Artistic crafts, flint weaponry, and the much sought-after amber or 'sea gold' were important exports.

The migration of the Celts across central Europe around this time resulted in a barrier of sorts between the north and south, cutting off trade routes with southern Europe. The Celts eventually fell to Rome, and while the Romans never made it to Scandinavia, evidence of the 'Roman Iron Age' has been found in Denmark. After 100 AD, peaceful trade links with a Europe now under Roman rule were re-established, the Danish population increased after a period of decline, and small kingdoms existed. Denmark was able to defend itself against much of the large-scale migration occurring throughout Europe after the fall of Rome, but did experience a period of cultural decline with local tribal migration and invasions.

The Danes had also spread their influence into northern Germany and parts of France. But the transfer of the capital of the Roman Empire from Rome to Constantinople, as well as the growing power of Germanic tribes to the south, forced Denmark once again to abandon southern trade routes in favour of east–west trade to the Baltic, making sea-faring an even more important profession. Indeed, struggles for commercial power in the Baltic and in Russian rivers would characterize much of the relationship between Denmark and Sweden.

The Viking Age, a period of intense Scandinavian expansion, is usually placed between 800 and 1050 AD, although there is evidence of Viking presence in Denmark as early as the 700s. Peaceful trading and settling gave way to plundering and conquering. Danish armies engaged in series of attacks and invasions over much of western Europe, and major campaigns were waged against England. Thousands of Danish immigrant peasants settled in the area of central and eastern England, establishing an independent Viking kingdom known as the 'Danelaw' in 878, an area that was eventually reconquered by Alfred the Great (871-901).

Harald Bluetooth (c.950-c.986), a son of Gorm the Old, succeeded in uniting Denmark and Norway as one kingdom. Attacks on England continued during the reign of Harald's son Svend Forkbeard (c.986-1014), who took control of all the English provinces. England, Denmark, and at times, southern Norway, eventually all came under the rule of Svend's son Knud (Canute the Great, 1018-35). After a series of power struggles following Knud's death, the Danish empire eventually collapsed. Denmark itself became united under Svend Estridsen (1047-74), and the Vikings living in Denmark gradually decreased in number.

The Vikings had brought Christianity back with them from western Europe, and for a time, Christianity and belief in the Norse gods coexisted in Denmark. Despite an early conversion by Harald

Bluetooth in 960, Christianity did not become firmly established until the reign of Svend Estridsen when regular dioceses were designated. It was not until 1104, when a new archbishopric was created in Lund, in the Scania province, which was Danish territory at this time, that the Church assumed more power.

A period of internal strife and civil war between various contenders for the throne in the late 11th and the early 12th centuries gave way to stability beginning with Valdemar I (1157-82) and ending with Valdemar II (1202-41). The 'Age of the Valdemars' was considered a time of expansion of Danish influence both in Scandinavia and the Baltic, and a period of economic prosperity, with the founding of new villages and farms, and increased shipping and trade. It was during a Crusade led by Valdemar II to the Baltic lands in 1219 that, legend has it, the Danish standard, the Dannebrog, fell from heaven during a surprise attack by Estonians, inspiring the Danes to victory.

The Valdemar era gave way to economic decline and political unrest, in the late 13th and early 14th centuries, due in part to conflicts between the sons of Valdemar II, who had been made dukes in various parts of the country, and proceeded to vie for the throne. It was also a time of growing class differences and a rise in the power of a politically ambitious and organized nobility, keen on limiting the power of the Crown. The nobles succeeded in forcing King Erik Klipping to sign the country's first Royal Charter in 1282, which, among other things, limited the king's judicial authority and obligated him to an annual national assembly. Future elected kings would sign such an accession charter (håndfæstning) limiting their powers until the establishment of absolute monarchy in 1660.

During the 14th century, Denmark was also facing the growing threat of German cultural and economic domination. Powerful Holstein counts – to whom estates in Scania, northern Jutland, Funen, Zealand had been mortgaged in the course of various uprisings – actually controlled all of the Danish kingdom for an eight-year period (1332-40), during which the country was without a king. German merchants of the Hanseatic League had control of fiefdoms on the coast of Sweden, as well as a stronghold on Norwegian trade. A strong German presence in the upper classes of Copenhagen was also a concern. Valdemar IV (1340-75) succeeded in returning some degree of stability to the country, gradually liberating, confiscating, and reuniting all of Denmark. He reconquered Scania, which had rebelled against Holstein and aligned with Sweden in 1332, and took the Swedish island of Gotland from control of the Hanseatic League.

When Valdemar died without leaving a male heir, his daughter Margaret, married to the king of Norway, took the throne of Denmark.

After her husband's death, she ruled Norway as well, and succeeded in uniting the three Scandinavian kingdoms of Denmark, Norway, and Sweden in the Kalmar Union of 1397, a union that may have been driven in part by the common fear of German infiltration. Erik VII of Pomerania (1396-1439), the grandson of Margaret's sister, was proclaimed King of Scandinavia. The Kalmar Union lasted until 1523 at which time Sweden, who had periodically asserted her independence from the richer and more powerful Denmark, broke away for the last time. Denmark and Norway would remain united until 1814.

The first signs of the Reformation had appeared in Denmark when Christian II (1513-23) began to favour Lutheran reforms, although he eventually reverted to Catholicism. A popular movement also spread, carried by the preaching of a young student, Hans Tavsen, who had heard Martin Luther preach in Wittenberg. Upon his return to Denmark, Tavsen began preaching in the provincial towns and in Copenhagen, under the protection of Frederik I (1523-33), who, although a Catholic, attempted to remain neutral in the religious debate in an effort to maintain popular support for his place on the throne.

Compared to other European countries the Reformation in Denmark took place peacefully, but the Reformation would also see Denmark embroiled in one last civil war. During the savage Counts' War that was motivated primarily by economic and political concerns, Catholic bishops gave in to Protestant nobles, and Christian III (1534-59), Frederik's son and himself a Lutheran, was proclaimed king. At a national assembly in Copenhagen, King Christian summarily imprisoned all the Catholic bishops, with their release contingent upon their giving up resistance to the Lutheran Reformation. The Catholic Church was abolished and the Reformation became law. A new church constitution established a state Church with the King as its head.

The following century saw Denmark flourish as a trading nation with her position at the gateway to the Baltic ensuring her dominance in the north. A series of rivalries took place between Denmark and Sweden for control of the Baltic, but little changed even after the Northern Seven Years' War (1563-70), which also involved Poland and Russia. Denmark emerged as the greater power, but rivalry with Sweden continued for mastery of the Baltic. An ambitious Christian IV attempted to reassert control over Sweden in the Kalmar War (1611-13), but made little headway, obtaining only Sweden's surrender of territory to the far north of Norway. Twelve years of peace followed with Denmark still the strongest Scandinavian power.

Denmark's position as a great territorial power was seriously weakened when Christian IV, who was also Duke of Holstein, involved the country in the Thirty Years' War in 1625, both to satisfy his territorial ambitions, as well as to stop the advancing army of the Catholic League, in northern Germany. Danish troops were defeated at the Battle of Lutter the following year. Sweden joined the war with Germany in 1630, making both territorial and political gains. Worsening relations between Denmark and Sweden culminated with Sweden occupying Jutland and acquiring some of Denmark's provinces in the Sound.

Denmark, now under Frederik III (1648-70), saw an opening for revenge with Sweden's involvement in war with Poland in the mid-1650s. After an initial Danish attack, Sweden again occupied most of Jutland and moved on to take the large Danish islands. In a temporary peace, Denmark was forced to surrender central Norway, the island of Bornholm, and all her provinces in Scania, to the east of the Sound.

Still wary of Denmark, Sweden attempted again to take Zealand and the capital city of Copenhagen, but was defeated with the help of her other enemies who came to Denmark's aid. The end result of the Danish-Swedish War (1657-60) was the return of Bornholm and central Norway to Denmark, but the permanent loss of Scania provinces to Sweden. The Sound was now divided between Sweden and Denmark, who never regained her control of the Baltic. Relations between the two countries would remain stable for a time.

The wars with Sweden and the loss of territory had deleterious effects on Danish agriculture and trade, as well as on the Crown's resources. With the economy seriously weakened, Frederik III summoned together the commoners' Estates, and representatives of the burghers and of the clergy. These groups united against a nobility who had been enjoying tax-exempt status in return for military service during wartime, a practice instituted under Valdemar I. The nobles, who were now themselves weakened by economic difficulties, as well as by their own exclusionary policies in force since the late 16th century, agreed to a limited tax burden, but hesitated on full tax equality for all citizens.

A check on the power of the nobles was a situation that was favoured by all, both as a way to more evenly distribute the tax burden and to defend against social upheaval. The Estates were in fact keen on expanding the power of the monarchy, as they were already enjoying increasing royal privileges and sympathy, and supported a resolution making the monarchy hereditary, similar to the majority of the other European crowns. Frederik III also saw a chance to break free of the power of the nobles, who often had the upper hand in a shifting balance of power. He accepted the proposal of hereditary monarchy, and took the further step of removing all restrictions on his authority. The monarchy was decreed absolute in 1661, and an absolutist constitution (Kongeloven) was drawn up in 1665. The king now had absolute power as head of state and church, and the accession charter was rendered obsolete.

It was absolutism of a rather peculiar character, however, the result being a radical reorganization of central and local administration, which would assume a structure that would be retained for nearly two hundred years. This centralized bureaucracy saw a new governing body with a collegiate structure formed in Copenhagen, and a remodelling of the treasury and judiciary. In the provinces, the fiefs were abolished and replaced by a county system under the direction of salaried civil servants drawn from the local aristocracy, and tax collection was further delegated to those of lower social status. Salaried civil servants were eventually granted titles, becoming a new aristocracy loyal to the Crown. The weakened traditional Danish nobility faded into the background.

After a failed attempted on the part of Denmark and Norway to regain the Scania provinces in the Scanian War (1675-79), Frederik IV in 1699, in an alliance with Russian and Poland, saw a chance for revenge against Sweden's young inexperienced king, Charles XII. In the Great Northern War (1700-20), Sweden's initial victories gave way to defeat by Russia in 1709. Denmark attempted unsuccessfully again to regain the Scania provinces. Sweden's Charles XII was slain in 1718 in an unsuccessful attempt to take Norway. Peace finally came in1721, with Denmark acquiring control of the duchy of Schleswig from the Duke of Holstein-Gottrop, Sweden's ally. Sweden also lost her exemption from payment of Sound dues. The war left Russia a dominant power in the Baltic for the first time, and Denmark's economy damaged. In 1720, Denmark's territory consisted of Denmark proper, the duchies of Oldenburg and Delmenhorst in northwest Germany, Schleswig, and the royal portion of Holstein, Norway, Iceland, the Faroe Islands, Greenland, and the West Indian islands, posts in India, and forts on the coast of Ghana. With the exception of one brief war with Sweden in 1788, entered into only as part of a Dano-Russian defence agreement, the country was at peace until the end of the 18th century.

It was during the reign of Frederik IV (1699-1730), that the effects of European Enlightenment began to be felt in Denmark. Scandinavia had been slow to take part in European artistic and literary culture, but Norwegian-born Ludvig Holberg, educated at the University of Copenhagen, and the most celebrated of Danish playwrights, began to attract public attention with his comedies and satires, which would be performed at Copenhagen's Royal Theatre founded in 1748.

Frederik IV was known for taking an active part in government and for his concern over the welfare of his subjects. He re-established a national militia in 1701, rather than be dependent on inadequate foreign mercenaries, and it was on his initiative that the institution of vornedskab, a form of serfdom which bound a tenant's heir to the tenant's holding, was abolished in 1702. Frederik's son, Christian VI (1730-46) abolished the national militia, and while not re-instituting vornedskab, in 1733 reconstituted the militia via adscription (stavnsbånd). This form of serfdom ensured that able-bodied males would remain with their estates in order to fulfil military duty, and in practice it could not be distinguished from the earlier vornedskab. Christian agreed to adscription under pressure from military leaders, who opposed the abolition of the militia, and from landowners, who had been feeling the effects of a decrease in the number of serfs.

The latter half of the 18th century brought an upheaval in the government when the reign of Christian VII (1766-1808), who suffered from schizophrenia, was taken over by German Court physician Johann Friedrich Struensee in 1771. Struensee ran a virtual dictatorship for a sixteen-month period, zealously instituting a wave of Enlightenment-inspired administrative reforms, but was eventually overthrown by conservative forces and beheaded. For the next several years, Denmark was ruled by a triumvirate consisting of Queen Dowager Juliane, her son Frederik and bourgeois minister Ove Hoegh-Guldberg, who ultimately held sway over the other two. The triumvirate was forced to relinquish power to Crown Prince Frederik in 1784, who would rule as Regent until King Christian VII's death in 1808.

Frederik and his reform-minded ministers would wisely use their power to improve the lives of Danish peasants. Although there was some conservative opposition, reforms were generally supported by intelligent landowners in light of the current improvements in market conditions. In 1786 the Great Land Commission was formed, chaired by Christian Reventlow, resulting in a series of reforms: in 1786 landlords were deprived of the right to punish tenants, and in 1787, tenants were granted the right to compensation for improvements. In 1788 it was decreed that adscription would be abolished in stages, freeing all peasants by 1800. Landlords were also encouraged to make labour contracts with their tenants. It was often more profitable for a landlord to sell land to tenants, and by 1820 over half of Denmark's farmers owned their own land, which ultimately led to improvements in agricultural methods. These land reforms were a remarkably peaceful change in comparison to the social unrest in much of Europe.

After the Great Northern War, Denmark had managed to remain neutral in European conflicts, and because of this her trade and shipping industries had prospered. But at the end of the 18th century,

Denmark was drawn into maritime conflicts, motivated primarily by a concern for preserving Mediterranean trade. Armed neutrality alliances, first with Russia, Prussia and Sweden and then with Sweden and Russia, ultimately did not protect Denmark, and neutrality was no longer an option in the wars between Britain and France. After two attacks by Britain on the Danish fleet in Copenhagen in 1801 and 1807, a weakened Denmark was forced to align herself with Napoleonic France against England. Denmark was now part of Napoleon's Continental system, which forbade trade with England, and Denmark and England would be at war for seven years.

Sweden, which in 1812 had come under the rule of Karl Johan (formerly Marshal Bernadotte under Napoleon), aligned with Russia against Napoleon, with designs on Denmark and the surrender of Norway. The anti-French coalition had promised Norway to Karl Johan partly in compensation for the loss of Finland to Russia, and partly due to the fact that England favoured the breakup of the Dano-Norwegian kingdom. Frederik had been offered other territory for Norway if he would also turn against Napoleon. But convinced that Napoleon would ultimately triumph, and perhaps would even aid him in a last bid for the Swedish throne, Frederik reaffirmed the alliance with France in 1813, snubbing the European Great Powers.

After Napoleon's defeat at the battle of Leipzig, Karl Johan invaded Denmark and forced Denmark to make peace at Kiel in January 1814. In the Treaty of Kiel, Denmark surrendered Norway to the Swedish crown in exchange for Swedish Pomerania and the island of Rügen. Denmark also surrendered the island of Heligoland to England. Iceland, Greenland, and the Faroe Islands remained with Denmark. Denmark would later exchange Pomerania and Rügen with Prussia in return for Lauenberg, a territory which bordered on Holstein. Prussia also paid Denmark, which had declared bankruptcy in 1813, a large sum of money for the difference in size of these territories.

After having been on the losing side in the Napoleonic wars and having suffered the loss of Norway, Denmark would lose even more territory in the latter half of the 19th century in what would be the final phase of its transformation from a major European power to the very small nation that is modern Denmark. Interestingly, the violent conflict over Schleswig-Holstein became entangled with the peaceful transition from absolutism to democracy.

King Christian I had been elected Duke of Schleswig and Holstein in 1460, with a promise that they should forever be united. In 1806, Holstein became incorporated under the Danish crown with the dissolution of the Holy Roman Empire. The duchy had been granted a provincial consultative assembly by the Congress of Vienna in 1814, and was allowed by Frederik VI to become part of the German Confederation, formed in 1815. Holstein was German in its composition, language and sympathies. Schleswig belonged to the Danish crown, but had been administered as an independent duchy since the Middle Ages, with the Danish king as both king and duke. North Schleswig was Danish-speaking, while the German influence predominated in South Schleswig.

The clash of German and Danish nationalistic feelings in the region gradually led to the formation of two camps. The Schleswig-Holstein party consisted of liberals as well as conservative German landowners with their own interests, who wanted unification of the two duchies and separation from Denmark. The other group consisted in large part of Danish-speaking farmers from north and central Schleswig, fearful of German influence and of the spread of the German language. This group favoured separation from Holstein and closer ties with the Danish kingdom. In 1831, in the wake of the July Revolution in France in 1830, news of which was enthusiastically received by many Danes, Frederik VI agreed to provincial assemblies in Schleswig, Holstein and Denmark proper. The king knew well that this action did not bode well for his absolute rule, but feared any revolutionary activity, although there were no real indications of such tendencies.

When Frederik VII came to power in 1848, the Schleswig-Holsteiners demanded a constitution for the united duchies and entry into a united Germany. The newly formed National Liberal Party, in solidarity with the farmers, countered with a demand for a constitution valid for Schleswig and the kingdom, and a new National Liberal government. On 22 March 1848, Frederik VII yielded, declared himself a constitutional monarch, and a National Liberal government took over. Danish absolutism peacefully came to an end. Rebellion had, however, broken out in Holstein, where the Schleswig-Holsteiners formed a provisional government of their own and seized the fortress of Rendsborg, an act of civil war. Prussian troops came to the aid of the rebels, but Russian pressure secured an armistice. Hostilities would be renewed several times between Danish and Prussian-backed rebel troops before peace was finally secured with British and Russian pressure in 1850, and the rebel army was disbanded.

Frederik VII and the new National Liberal government ratified Denmark's first free constitution on 5 June 1849 (the June Constitution), where power would be shared by the crown and a legislative body, the Rigsdag, which would consist of a lower and an upper chamber, the Folketing and the Landsting. The king maintained the right to choose his own ministers. The constitution also guaranteed religious freedom, freedom of speech, and the general liberty of the individual. But under this 1849 constitution, with further international agreements in 1851-52, Denmark still existed as three parts: the kingdom proper, Schleswig, and Holstein-Lauenberg, the latter being free to continue membership in the German Confederation. The 1849 constitution was limited to Denmark proper. The duchies' provincial assemblies were preserved. There was in effect a return to the original situation. Denmark had to agree not to unite Schleswig to the kingdom. It would have no closer tie to Denmark than did Holstein. In 1855 a plan for a new constitution was adopted for the duchies and Denmark that would establish a Rigsraad, a council empowered to discuss matters that would affect all the territories such as foreign policy, general finance and defence. It was felt that this arrangement would in effect be a constitution for the Helstat (the kingdom proper and the duchies) but would not breach the 1851-52 agreements. Opposition from the Holsteiners, with support from the German states, resulted in a suspension of the Helstat plan. Negotiations dragged on for the next five years with no satisfactory conclusion.

In March 1863 the National Liberal government issued a 'patent' for a separate constitution for Holstein (and Lauenberg) separating them from the kingdom, a move that was opposed by the German Confederation. A further proposal in November of that year provided for a new constitution incorporating Schleswig and Denmark proper, in outright disregard for the 1851-52 international agreements. Prussia and Austria issued an ultimatum for withdrawal of the November Constitution, threatening Denmark with invasion of Schleswig. Denmark responded too late and Prussia invaded on 1 February 1864. German troops had already moved into Holstein on 24 December 1863, despite Denmark's revocation of the March Patent. With no outside support, Denmark was forced to sue for peace. At the Peace of Vienna in October 1864, she had to renounce all rights to the duchies, thereby losing about one-third of her territory and of her population, many of whom were Danes who now lived under foreign rule.

It is noteworthy that, although revolutionary events in France and other parts of Europe did not go unnoticed by the Danish population, revolution was an unnecessary element in the change-over from absolute monarchy to a representative government. The final action, which took place quite peacefully, can be viewed as the culmination of a gradual process that actually began soon after the 1665 adoption of the absolutist constitution. The convergence of a number of factors such as increased literacy in the provinces, a rise in nationalism and liberalism, and a resurgence of economic and agricultural prosperity provided the backdrop for the ratification of the first free constitution. All these events were part of a larger reform spirit present at the end of the 18th century through the mid-19th century, informed by Enlightenment principles.

This era witnessed a social and economic revolution with far-reaching implications for the formation of modern Denmark. Among these were peaceful land reforms that were both profitable to landlords and significant for the personal and economic freedom of peasant farmers. In addition to the land reforms, this era also saw the institution of a system of poor relief, improvement of prison conditions, and a lifting of import prohibitions. In a crusade that began in 1789, education was made compulsory for all children between the ages of 7 and 14 (the age of confirmation) by the Education Act of 1814. The constitutional process was also directly spurred on by the joining of forces of the National Liberals demanding a constitution, and farmers' leaders seeking general military conscription and the transfer of tenure deeds to land ownership. These groups came together in 1846 in the Society of the Farmers' Friends.

It should also be noted that in the early 1800s, Danish liberalism and nationalism were inspired in no small measure by the teachings of the noted theologian, historian and poet, N. F. S. Grundtvig and his innovative blend of Christianity, Norse myth, and patriotic principles. Influenced by civil and religious freedom in England, Grundtvig came to believe that parliamentary representation could truly succeed only with an enlightened public, and advocated a liberal education ('Education for Life') for the common people in which they would be taught history and poetry in addition to practical subjects. His ideas regarding the connection between education and democracy formed the basis of the Folk High School movement, the first school being opened in 1844 in Rødding.

During the remainder of the 19th century, Denmark was occupied with a constitutional struggle between conservative forces and proponents of reform. Wealthy landowners and a contingent of disgruntled National Liberals organized as the 'Right party' who held a majority of the upper house, the Landsting, squared off against reformers consisting of farmers, organized as the 'Left party' (also referred to as the Liberal Democrats or the United Left). The Right party maintained that the king could choose ministers freely, while the Left party favoured a basic principle of parliamentary democracy, whereby the king would choose his ministers from the party with a majority in the lower house, the Folketing. (Indeed, the Left party achieved a majority in the Folketing in 1872.)

Conservatives had put forth a new constitution in 1866 that abolished universal suffrage and introduced a privileged franchise in the Landsting. The king agreed to this, and continued to choose his ministers from the Right majority in the Landsting. This set in motion a struggle that would last 29 years. In the final outcome, the Right party yielded amidst other voter dissatisfaction, and the king was forced to submit to the demands of the Left. In 1901 the 'change of system' brought representative democracy, whereby, according to the principle of 'cabinet responsibility', the king was bound to appoint a government with a majority in the Folketing behind it. Soon thereafter the four major parties of the modern system would be in place: Social Democrats, Radical Liberals, Liberals, and Conservatives.

In the second June Constitution of 1915, a much more progressive form of government based on universal suffrage was put in place. The privileged franchise of the Landsting was abolished, women and servants were given the vote, and the principle of proportional representation was introduced, which replaced the earlier system of plurality elections. The constitution was not implemented until 1918, after the First World War. Reforms to the legal system, separating the executive from the judiciary, were passed in 1916, but were not enforced until 1919.

The principle of cabinet responsibility, which had been a political reality, was officially incorporated in the 1953 constitution, when the Landsting was also abolished and a single-chamber parliament, the Folketing, was introduced, with provisions for referendums to be held on controversial legislation. The Folketing would also appoint an ombudsman to allow for the investigation of complaints by individuals against public authorities, a feature borrowed from the Swedish system.

The latter half of the 19th century was also a time of economic and social change. Industrialization increased rapidly during this time with the advent of free internal trade through the passing of the Free Trading Act of 1862, which resulted in the disappearance of the guild system. Although many small companies were already in existence, by the 1870s the formation of limited companies had begun. Commercial activity increased with improvements to the railway system, the advent of the steam engine, and a new harbour in Copenhagen. A growing working class began organizing themselves into independent trade unions, freed from association with the Social Democrats. Perhaps in response to the employers having organized themselves in 1896 as the Employers' Association (Arbejdsgiverforeningen), various unions coordinated their efforts in the Association of Trade Unions (Det Samvirkende Fagforbund) in 1898. Health insurance societies connected with individual trades were also formed at this time.

Although industrialization was taking hold, the basis of the economy was still primarily agrarian. In the 1880s, however, Danish farmers found that they could not compete with cheap grain from the American and Russian markets. Danish grain production and export was forced to give way to animal husbandry and the export of animal products, particularly to meet demands from the British and German markets.

There was an enormous increase in cattle and pig farming, dairying, and poultry raising at the end of the 1800s and the beginning of the 1900s. Problems of distribution and quality control led to the formation of agricultural cooperative societies, which allowed small farmers to gain the economic advantages of large-scale production, while still retaining their individual proprietorships. These democratic societies, which began in the dairy industry, have been fundamental to the agricultural sector ever since, and have become a distinguishing feature of the Danish way of doing business generally.

Denmark declared her neutrality in the First World War, and although she successfully stayed out of the war, she could not entirely escape the economic repercussions. Although the outset of the war benefited certain sectors of the economy, by the end Denmark was suffering shipping losses, shortages of raw materials, factory shut-downs, rising unemployment, and inflation. However, she still maintained a favourable economic position compared to other countries.

Germany's collapse in 1918 and the nationality principle adopted at the Treaty of Versailles, whereby national borders would be chosen by the people, were the basis for an appeal from the Danish-speaking inhabitants of North Schleswig that they be allowed reunification with Denmark. After much debate about where to draw the border, the re-incorporation of North Schleswig passed in a referendum in the northern part, while the southern and primarily German part voted to remain with Germany. The law was made official in June 1920. The occasion was marked with celebration, and King Christian X made his dramatic crossing of the old border on horseback, promising not to forget the Danes who still remained south of the new borderline under German rule.

Denmark experienced other territorial changes at this time. The Danish West Indies (the Virgin Islands) were sold to the USA for $25 million in 1916, and in 1918, Iceland became an independent state, though still sharing monarchy and foreign policy with Denmark. (It would declare full independence in 1944, with the occupation of Denmark by German troops.)

As did many countries after the war, Denmark experienced a period of economic and political instability, faced with shortages of goods, inflation, trade problems, depleted financial reserves, and general discontent among workers. Political problems came to a head in what became known as the Easter Crisis of 1920. Amidst tensions, stalemates, and a desire for a revision of electoral laws in the Rigsdag,

King Christian dismissed a government he felt no longer had a majority behind it and appoint a caretaker government of specialists in its place.

The Social Democrats and the trade unions responded with a demand for the reinstatement of the government and issued a strike ultimatum. After much heated negotiation and fear of revolution, the crisis was finally resolved. A fresh caretaker government whose members were approved by the political parties was appointed, and new elections were held soon after. The Easter Crisis marked the one occasion where a king interfered with the elected majority principle of government. This action was within the king's legal rights, but was one that flouted the spirit of the constitution. The crisis also demonstrated the power of the Social Democratic Party.

The governments of the next decade were characterized by alternating Social Democrat and Liberal minority cabinets until a 1929 coalition of Social Democrats and Radical Liberals came to power. This government was opposed to the laissez-faire philosophy of the Liberals and pledged to more state intervention in economic life and a reform of social legislation. It remained in power until 1940 and saw Denmark through the economic crises of the 1930s.

The Wall Street crash of 1929 reverberated in Europe in 1930. The Danish economy was not spared: firms were liquidated, unemployment rose dramatically, grain and livestock prices fell, and farmers declared bankruptcy. Many farmers and workers saw the devaluation of the krone as one solution that would help exports, improve the overall economy, force up prices, and stall wage reductions. In 1933, the Social Democrat–Radical Liberal government reached a compromise with the Liberal Party with the aim of counteracting the economic crisis. In the Kanslergade Agreement, so named for the street in Copenhagen where Prime Minister Stauning resided, the Liberals agreed not to oppose the one-year ban on strikes and lockouts and would not oppose a new social reform bill, in exchange for the devaluation of the krone, a reduction of the taxation on farms, and other agricultural protections.

That same year, and as part of the Kanslergade Agreement, Minister of Social Affairs Karl Kristian Steincke instituted a social reform package that rationalized piecemeal social legislation over the previous 40 years. Four statutes addressed labour exchanges and unemployment insurance; social insurance including sickness, disability, and accident insurance, and old age pensions; and public welfare including child welfare services, general public welfare, and care of the blind, deaf and other special groups. The autonomy of local authorities was reduced in favour of close cooperation between the state and local authorities.

By the end of the 1930s, Denmark's economy was gaining ground. When Germany attacked Poland in September 1939, Denmark immediately declared her neutrality, but this declaration did not protect Denmark from being occupied by Germany on 9 April 1940. The Nazis had decided that Denmark was essential to their war effort, not only for its economy, but also as a stepping-stone to the occupation of Norway.

The occupation was a curious one as Germany wished to hold Denmark up as a model protectorate. Initially, the Danish government was allowed to remain in office, the armed forces remained intact, and the press carried on freely covering Danish affairs (but voluntarily censored themselves where it was deemed necessary). A constitutionally required election was allowed to take place in 1943, although the results, which confirmed the previous Folketing, were a foregone conclusion.

As time went on, however, many Danish citizens became dis-illusioned with what they saw as politicians' efforts to appease the occupying forces, particularly the actions of the apparently pro-German Erik Scavenius, whom the Germans had insisted on as prime minister in 1942. A resistance movement developed, loosely at first and later quite organized, engaging in sabotage and producing anti-German propaganda and illegal newspapers. As the movement grew in strength and number, German policies became more stringent and increasingly repressive. The resistance, willing to risk a German takeover rather than have Denmark classified as a German ally, responded with stepped-up activity, strikes and sabotages. The Danish government did little to quell the resistance.

On 29 August 1943, Germany introduced a state of emergency, after the Danish government refused to do so on its own, thus beginning the second and less tolerable phase of the occupation. The Danish cabinet was forced to resign, the armed forces were demobilized, and the media was more strictly censored. Danish civil servants were eventually allowed to continue running the administration. Not surprisingly, the German takeover was soon followed by orders from Berlin to begin the deportation of Danish Jews. This information was leaked by the German political leader in Denmark, Werner Best, making it possible to warn the Jews. By the time the arrests were to begin, approximately 7000 Danish Jews had been hidden by friends, and were then safely smuggled to neutral Sweden, in what became a well-organized rescue effort.

As a result of the takeover, the resistance movement became more organized, forming the Freedom Council in September of 1943, which functioned both as a type of illegal government, as well as working in conjunction with the political leadership. The Council also received support from the Allies in the form of arms supplies and assistance in bombing raids. Resistance activity increased, and some periods during the last months of the occupation were quite violent and bloody. When

German capitulation was announced on 4 May 1945, lighted candles appeared spontaneously in Danish windows.

After the immediate issues of punishing war criminals and balancing finances, the first steps toward economic recovery and expansion began with Marshall Plan aid in 1948. The 1950s brought slow improvement as Denmark was still heavily dependent on exports; other countries, who had not fared as well as Denmark, were also in the process of economic recovery. But in the early 1960s, light industry for the production of consumer goods – furniture, radios, televisions – flourished, and the number of white-collar, service, and retail employees increased. There was an overall rise in the standard of living and Denmark became a consumer society.

Postwar security concerns also led to a focus on international alliances. Denmark quickly joined the United Nations with the setting up of that organization in 1945 and also abandoned her neutral status. When attempts to form a Nordic Defence Alliance with Sweden and Norway failed, Denmark joined the North Atlantic Treaty Organization (NATO) in 1949, a founding member with Norway and Iceland who also favoured alliance with Western allies. Sweden and Finland remained neutral. Aside from defence and foreign policy issues, Nordic efforts at cooperation that had begun before the war led to the formation of the Nordic Council in 1952, where members of parliament from the five countries and their territories began meeting at regular intervals to coordinate internal legislation. The efforts of this group continue today and have fostered cooperation in many spheres such as education, research, welfare, trade, and the labour market.

The idea of a formal Nordic economic cooperation took a back seat to efforts at European integration, and Denmark joined the European Free Trade Association (EFTA) in 1960, an association that was initiated by Britain and Sweden, and a step that brought an end to the idea of a Nordic Common Market. Denmark had already become a member of the Organization for European Economic Cooperation in 1948 (OEEC, renamed in 1961 as OECD, the Organization for Economic Cooperation and Development) and the Council of Europe in 1949. Industrial and financial recovery were also aided by Denmark's membership in the International Monetary Fund (IMF) and the International Bank that were formed after the war.

In the decades after the war, the Social Democrats, the largest party, but never with a majority, cooperated with other parties, usually the Radical Liberals, to bring about economic recovery and social reform. Newly set-up lending institutions granted building loans that had previously been provided by the state, resulting in a building boom, particularly in apartments. Free education beyond the primary stage for all social classes had been available since 1903. New educational legislation in 1958 provided for universal comprehensive education for seven years, up to the age of 14, after which a student was free to leave, to continue two more years voluntarily, or to take a three-year course leading to middle school examination, or take an extended academic course ending with the Student Examination, which would give access to a university. Today, nine years of education is compulsory, from age seven to sixteen, and is available to all in public school, or parents may opt for private or home schooling. The system is administered chiefly under the Folkskole Act of 1975 and its subsequent amendments.

The 'second social reform' also got underway at this time. Indicative of humanitarian modern Denmark, social security as a right for all was written into the 1953 constitution. In 1956, the 'people's pension' (folkepension), a general retirement pension, was introduced. In an effort meant to address a sudden change in circumstances, disablement benefits and widows' pensions were increased in 1965. Social services were reviewed in the light of the 1970 restructuring of local government, and former flat-rate contributions to health insurance were replaced by taxation based on income.

The early 1970s brought uncertain economic times on both the domestic and foreign fronts, with such problems as the rise in oil prices, recession, trade deficits, inflation, and increased taxation to maintain the welfare state. The political system experienced a period of party fragmentation with new special-interest parties springing up. A general dissatisfaction among the Danish electorate with divisions over the issue of taxes and growth of the welfare state brought about what has been referred to as the 'political earthquake' election of 1973. This election saw the doubling of the number of parties represented in the Folketing from five to ten, with the old established parties suffering heavy losses.

This began an era in Danish politics of weak minority coalitions and frequent elections, where politicians faced increasing economic difficulties. The 1982 election saw its first Conservative prime minister since 1901 in Poul Schülter, who followed the neo-liberal line of England's Margaret Thatcher, Germany's Helmut Kohl, and the United States' Ronald Reagan. Schülter's bourgeois government, a Liberal–Conservative minority coalition with support from small centre parties sought to curb government spending, while maintaining the welfare state. Under the Schülter government, the economy generally improved. The tighter fiscal policy included taxed pension savings and public sector cutbacks. A fixed exchange rate helped check inflation and reduce interest rates, and loan reforms increased consumer savings. Unemployment was somewhat checked, but remained high.

Forced to resign in 1993 amidst an administrative scandal, Schülter was replaced by Poul Nyrup Rasmussen, who headed a Social Democratic-led government. A majority coalition of Social Democrats and Radical Liberals, with support from small socialist parties, has managed to keep the economy in the 1990s for the most part on a positive footing, with increases in public spending and services (as well as taxes), and a measure of success in reducing structural unemployment.

Denmark had not entirely abandoned her efforts at Nordic economic cooperation, but in 1971, when further attempts at forming the economic bloc known as Nordek, met with resistance, Denmark once again faced the issue of European economic integration. After a long and intense debate in the Folketing, a bill was passed with a clear majority in favour of membership of the European Economic Community (EEC). It was confirmed by a national referendum in 1972, with nearly two-thirds of those voting favouring membership. Denmark joined the EEC (now known as the European Union) on 1 January 1973, the first Nordic country to do so.

The pace of European integration gained speed when the Single European Act (SEA) passed in a 1986 referendum. The SEA further specified the conditions for creating a common market, such as the reduction of trade barriers, harmonization of legislation and taxation, and cooperation in monetary affairs. Events took a different turn, however, when it came to the Treaty on European Union (TEU) which was negotiated in 1991, at Maastricht, The Netherlands. The TEU called for the creation of a European Union (EU) with political and economic cooperation in the areas of monetary policy, foreign and security policy, justice, and internal affairs. It contained specific criteria for the creation of a common economic policy, central banking institutions, and a single currency by the year 1999. It also called for stronger cooperation in defence policy, a common legal basis for European citizenship, and cooperation in asylum, immigration, combating drug trafficking, organized crime and fraud, and the creation of a European-wide police information-exchange system. In addition, it called for European-wide cooperation in many other areas such as competition and taxation; social, educational, and environmental policy; consumer protection; and research and technology.

At the parliamentary level, consensus was building for fuller integration, but popular attitudes leaned towards the view that fuller monetary and political union was a threat to Danish internal affairs and the welfare state. A 1992 referendum failed to approve the TEU by a slim 'No' majority of 50.7 per cent. That same year Denmark negotiated four 'opt-outs' at the Edinburgh Summit in the areas of currency union, security policy, regulations for common citizenship, and regulations for juridical and internal affairs. In the light of these compromises, the treaty was approved in a 1993 referendum by a comfortable majority.

The Danes have made it clear that they wish to remain a sovereign and distinct nation, voluntarily participating in wider economic cooperation. Of utmost concern is the preservation of the essential elements of the Nordic model, namely democracy, egalitarianism, and the efficient delivery of quality welfare services. Egalitarianism is probably the word that is most often used in discussions of the Scandinavian or Nordic model. However, the nature of that egalitarianism is not only the welfare state provision of social security and services, although that is a large part. It is worthwhile to point out that other elements of Danish society have contributed significantly to promoting equality among its citizens.

As mentioned above, the folk high school movement, which began as an effort to ready the peasant class for democracy, can be traced back to the theologian, philosopher, and poet N. F. S. Grundtvig in the 1830s. Today, the number of folk high schools exceeds one hundred, and all manner of curricula are offered, including arts and sports. They are residential schools with courses of usually three to six months' duration, and they have retained the notions of community fellowship, and dialogue between and among lecturers and students. It is a defining feature that there are no tests, no exams or diplomas. The concept of adult education (folkeoplysning) has expanded to include many variations of labour market training, evening and continuation schools, and open education. These efforts receive extensive state grant support and are considered key to Denmark's ability to compete on the international level.

Another aspect of Danish society that has fostered equality is the unusually high number of farmers' and consumers' cooperative societies. This democratic style of doing business can now be found in numerous economic sectors including dairies, bacon factories, egg exporters, and producers of butter, cheese, cattle, poultry, fish, and fruit. Consumer cooperatives include bakery associations, fuel purchase associations, and cooperative building enterprises.

High rates of union organization, and the unity of the trade unions – although there has been some decentralization in recent years – are defining features of the Danish labour market. Union organization with its system of collective bargaining, where legislation is the exception not the rule, also serves as a societal leveller. Approximately three-quarters of all employees are members of a trade union, with rates being highest among manual workers. Today, the major umbrella organization of trade unions is the Danish Federation of Trade Unions or LO (Landsorganisation i Danmark) and includes mainly craft unions. Among the affiliated unions are the Metal Workers' Union, the Commercial and Clerical Employees' Union, and the Specialized Workers' Union. There are other unions outside the Federation, but which work closely with it, such as the Public Servants' Union, and the Professional Workers' Union, in addition to constituent organizations such as the Teachers', Nurses', and Bank Employees' Unions. These various groups engage in negotiations with the Confederation of Danish Employers or DA (Dansk Arbejdsgiverforening), and central and local government. Settlements between LO and DA generally set the patterns for the entire manual labour market.

Egalitarianism is also manifested in Denmark's firm adherence to consensus-style democracy, which has allowed corporatist arrangements to flourish. This close relationship between interest groups and government, where interest groups have institutionalized access to and participation in policymaking, is considered right and proper in a democratic society. Corporatism can be traced to the change in the world economic order after the First World War and the Depression of the 1930s, when Danish government intervention in the economy drew the major economic organizations into close cooperation. Today, all cabinet and parliamentary committees have representatives from the major business and labour market sectors such as agriculture, industry, and commerce.

Finally, the core of Danish egalitarianism is the social security system based on citizenship, financed mainly by the state through general taxation. It comprises a comprehensive system of cash benefits and an extensive public system for delivery of free services in the areas of health care, education, and general welfare. It provides free medical treatment, free public schooling and higher education, low-cost day care and other child care institutions, as well as social services for the sick, disabled, and elderly. It is a decentralized system administered at the local and regional levels in order to allow for the most efficient delivery of services and the most effective use of resources. Although not without its problems and criticisms – words like poverty, social exclusion, marginalization, and privatization have crept into discussions of the welfare state in recent years – the system strives to ensure equality and fairness in its treatment of all individuals.

It must also be mentioned that gender equality in the welfare state is still somewhat elusive, although Danish and other Scandinavian women fare significantly better in terms of social and economic position in international comparisons. However, while low-cost day care has freed many women to participate in the labour market, thus giving them personal economic independence, women dominate in care work.

Introduction

Although women comprise approximately half of the work force, they often end up as employees in public sector care work. The labour market is indeed sex-segregated. A significant proportion of women work in female-dominated occupations which tend to be lower paying jobs – clerical, retail sales, cleaning, nursing, day care, and home help staff. Women also spend more time on unpaid work in the home and are more likely to hold part-time positions.

Although not without its economic problems, Denmark is one of the richest countries in the Western world. Its welfare model ensures a comfortable standard of living for all its citizens, and it boasts a healthy free-market economy, having made up for what it lacks in natural resources by becoming a successful trading nation. Throughout the latter half of the twentieth century, it has demonstrated the ability to assume a more activist role in international relations, albeit sometimes with reluctance and caution. Indeed, Denmark has sent troops to war zones in Yugoslavia, has generously opened its doors to refugees (although this action is not without significant domestic controversy), and has shown a commitment to supporting new democracies in the Baltic, and Central and Eastern Europe, as well as to aiding developing nations. Like any other proud and prosperous nation, Denmark must continually balance domestic concerns with international ones. Two key features of Danish society – its welfare model and its economy based on trade – will continue to occupy policy debates, especially in the light of the stepped-up pace of European integration and harmonization. The new century will witness Denmark as it struggles to further define its role and identity in an increasingly open and integrated Europe.

The bibliography

This revised, annotated bibliography includes a considerable number of works published in English in the years since the original 1987 volume. Entries are organized within the chapters and sections by author surname or organizational author. Items which have no author are alphabetized by title. Of the total 682 works represented here, fewer than ten per cent have been retained from the first edition. The works retained are either seminal or one-of-a-kind books, many of which have been recently reprinted, or they are an annual publication or other periodical that continues to be available. For older works on Denmark, readers are referred to the first edition.

This volume seeks to provide a selective coverage of sources on all aspects of Denmark. Certain aspects of Danish culture and society command a great deal of attention. Topics such as the Vikings, and famous Danes such as Isak Dinesen and Søren Kierkegaard continue to be popular subjects for analysis. Translations of Danish fiction are becoming increasingly plentiful; the issue of European integration floods discussions of foreign and domestic politics; and N. F. S. Grundtvig, the folk high schools and their like remain a subject of international interest. These trends are reflected in the bibliography, but given the plethora of literature on these, I have sought to provide a representative range of selections. Other topics such as the agricultural cooperatives have receded in popularity in recent years. Since the World Bibliographic Series offers a separate volume on Greenland, works on this self-governing possession are not included. A limited number of works on the Faroe Islands have been included. Finally, I have sought to emphasize books, book chapters, and journal articles. The Danish government ministries and many non-governmental organizations offer numerous publications in English. I have included a select number that I found to be especially informative or which offered information not available elsewhere, and I have provided mailing addresses where I felt they would be needed. Many of the ministries, as well as the non-governmental organizations, can now be found on the World Wide Web, where they often list their publications.

The research for compiling this bibliography could not have been carried out without the cooperation of the Aalborg University Library, particularly those staff who work with interlibrary loan materials. Were it not for their professional, efficient, and courteous service, my task would have been much more difficult and a lot less pleasurable. I would also like to thank my husband, Christian, for his comments and encouragement. Any errors or oversights in this research are mine alone.

LeeAnn Iovanni
May 1999

The Country and Its People

1   **Danmark: land og by.** (Denmark: town and country.)
    I. Aistrup.   Copenhagen: Høst & Søns Publishers, 1974. Reprinted 1986;
    1988. 72p.
This is a lovely picture-book with sixty-four, full-page colour photographs of scenes
from all over Denmark during different times of the year. Each photograph is briefly
captioned, and extended captions are presented in one section at the end of the book.
The location of each photograph is referenced on a numbered map of the country. The
captioning is in Danish, English, French, Spanish, and German.

2   **Xenophobe's guide to the Danes.**
    Helen Dyrbye, Steven Harris, Thomas Golzen.   Horsham, England:
    Ravette Publishing, 1997. 64p.
A humorous, irreverent look at the Danes, written by non-Danes who have re-located
to Denmark. Among the topics discussed are nationalism and identity, customs and
traditions, government, business, language, culture, and attitudes. This is an entertaining
little book peppered with facts, but primarily designed 'to cure xenophobia'.

3   **We are a little land: cultural assumptions in Danish everyday life.**
    Judith Friedman Hansen.   New York: Arno Press, 1980; North Stratford,
    New Hampshire: Ayer, 1981. 229p.
An older work, this research now in book form was originally presented as the
author's thesis in 1970. It is an exploratory study and not a particularly rigorous piece
of research, but it offers some interesting insights into Danish life. The American
author identifies five cultural values that she found to be especially indicative of the
differences between Danish and American culture: festiveness, cosiness, egalitarianism,
moderation, and inclusion. Through participant observation and content analysis of
media sources conducted during a one-year stay in Denmark, the author describes the
ways these five concepts affect behaviour at both the individual and societal level. The
general reader may prefer the descriptions of small group interactions which allow one
to step into the Danish living-room, and to pick up some vocabulary along the way.

4   **Discover Denmark: on Denmark and the Danes; past, present and future.**
Edited by Per Himmelstrup, translated from the Danish by Vivien Andersen.   Copenhagen: The Danish Cultural Institute; Herning, Denmark: Systime Publishers, 1992. 240p. map. bibliog.

This work is a collection of essays built around various themes that explore how Danes organize their society and how they live. The topics include the country and its people, agriculture, industry, education, work and leisure time, the living environment, the social system, cultural policy, literature, and the arts. There are also character sketches of the Danish people by non-Danes, and a look at the country's political and economic future. The contributors represent such fields as history, geography, engineering, social science, journalism, law, political science, economics, and the arts. The work is not meant to be a systematic textbook. Rather, the essays are meant to provide 'glimpses of life' in this small, homogeneous nation-state. Nevertheless, there is a wealth of information here that is clearly and enjoyably presented. Many photographs and illustrations are included, as well as a helpful bibliography arranged by topic.

5   **Civilized Denmark.**
Garrison Keillor, photographs by Sisse Brimberg.   *National Geographic*, vol. 194, no. 1 (July 1998), p. 50-73.

A light-hearted piece by the well-known American writer and humorist, based on his personal relationship with the country. The author offers his impressions of Danish society through reminiscences and anecdotes that are related in vivid descriptions. There are also enough factual details to allow the article to serve as a short introduction to the country and the culture, and the author strives for a balanced portrait. This is a worthwhile and enjoyable read, one that is beautifully illustrated with sixteen full pages of colour photographs of the high quality for which *National Geographic* is famous.

6   **Of Danish ways.**
Ingeborg S. MacHaffie, Margaret A. Nielsen.   Minneapolis, Minnesota: Dillon Press, 1976. Reprinted, 1979. 250p. bibliog.

This work is an overview that truly gives the reader a sense of the people and the country. The authors are two sisters who were born of Danish parents, raised in a Danish environment, and have visited and resided in Denmark numerous times. The chapters are short, yet they are informative and cover a wide range of topics including history, world and social consciousness, the media, industry, education, the national character, and the arts. This is an enjoyable book, and it is written in an easy-to-read, anecdotal style. A chapter on food provides recipes for ten of the most well-known Danish dishes. Included in appendices are descriptions of twelve of the most famous Danish castles, the lyrics to three traditional songs in both Danish and English that are still sung today, and one page of common expressions and signs for the traveller.

7   **Definitely Danish: Denmark and Danish Americans: history, culture, recipes.**
Compiled by Julie Jensen McDonald.   Iowa City, Iowa: Penfield Press, 1993. 136p. map.

Pays homage to the Danish culture through short essays of a page or two by various contributors who share stories about growing up Danish, and emigrating and settling in America, and describe the Danish communities and institutions of Iowa, Minnesota, Nebraska, and California. There is also information on the country's history, legends, folk arts, festivals and holidays, as well as profiles of some famous Danes. A description of the Danish Immigrant Museum in Elk Horn, Iowa includes a list of the initial names on the Danish-American Wall of Honour. There is even a chapter with instructions for tracing your Danish roots. Twenty-two pages of recipes offer classic Danish favourites. This is a charming book that provides plenty of information.

8 **There is something wonderful in the state of Denmark.**
Arne Melchior, translated from the Danish by Esther Aagaard Tapelband. Secaucus, New Jersey: Lyle Stuart, 1987. 136p.

A heartfelt profile of the country and its people written by a member of the Danish Parliament. The book is written in an easy-to-read style, and the chapters are brief. Among the topics covered are 'the Danish model', democracy and politics, social services and education, the monarchy, foreign relations, and tourist attractions. There is also special mention made of the country's Jewish citizens. (The author's father, Marcus Melchior, was once Chief Rabbi of Denmark.) The various topics are examined to show how they reflect Danish values, culture, and behavioural norms. The text is enhanced by eight pages of black-and-white photographs. This book provides an overview and should be considered introductory.

9 **Peasants and Danes: Danish national identity and political culture.**
Uffe Østergård. Aarhus, Denmark: Centre for Cultural Research, Aarhus University, 1990. 55p.

This work analyses the role played by agricultural society and its peasant traditions of community and solidarity in the development of modern Danish society. The author explains that due to the formation of agrarian cooperatives, Denmark had market exchange mechanisms in place well before the industrial revolution; capitalistic values and peasant values became enmeshed. Further, the author discusses how this synthesis occurred in large part through the influence of the teachings of N. F. S. Grundtvig. This work is also a commentary on national identity in general and the meaning of 'Danishness'. It is an academic paper but well within the reach of a general audience. A version of this paper also appears in *Becoming national: a reader*, edited by Geoff Eley and Ronald Grigor Suny (New York: Oxford University Press, 1996, p. 178-201), and in *Contemporary Studies in Society and History*, vol. 34, no. 1 (January 1992), p. 3-27.

10 **Culture shock! Denmark: a guide to customs and etiquette.**
Morten Strange. London: Kuperard, 1996. 228p. bibliog.

Conveys information about most aspects of Danish life in an entertaining style. The author, who was born, raised, and educated in Denmark, spent most of his adult life abroad, but returned to his homeland to find his roots. With this book he aims to aid the foreigner who wants to integrate into this homogeneous society that also values individual freedom. The book gives a great deal of factual information, but combines it with personal experiences that give the reader an insider's view. There are sections on geography, history, language, transport, and the media, as well as practical information on travelling and settling in Denmark. Many personal anecdotes are offered to highlight and inform. There are also sections on socializing with the Danes and the rules of etiquette in both social and professional situations. The book is rich in commentary on the attitude and character of the Danish people, how they behave in various situations, as well as how others are viewed by the Danes.

11 **Facts about Denmark.**
    Jens Stubkjær.   Copenhagen: Danish Ministry of Foreign Affairs:
    Aktuelle Books, 1995. 12th ed. 112p. map.

A pocket-sized book in which the author briefly covers over twenty topics and
includes many colour photographs. The reader can find information on the land and
nature, the people, sports, government, history, the monarchy, Denmark's place in the
world, its contributions to science, architecture and design, literature, and the arts.
This is a handy introduction to the country and the society.

12 **Americans in Denmark: comparisons of the two cultures by writers,
    artists and teachers.**
    Edited by F. Richard Thomas.   Carbondale, Illinois; Edwardsville,
    Illinois: Southern Illinois University Press, 1990. 156p. bibliog.

A collection of essays written by Americans who have chosen to live in Denmark. The
essays were written in response to an eleven-point questionnaire distributed by the
editor while in Denmark on a Fulbright grant in 1985-86, and offer an intimate
glimpse into the experience of 'otherness' that results from living in a foreign country.
The contributors comment on everything from the food and the weather to the effect
of the expatriate experience on their identity and creativity. The essays vary in length
and detail and are primarily impressionistic. Taken as a whole, the collection provides
an informative and unique portrait of life in Denmark.

13 **Hello Denmark: a handbook for foreigners, immigrants and
    refugees in Denmark.**
    Edited by Peter Villads Vedel, Torben Thuesen.   Herning, Denmark:
    Stout, 1993. 176p.

This book is intended as an aid to foreigners who are planning to stay in the country
for an extended time. It contains basic information on the first steps one should take
upon arrival such as obtaining residence and work permits or a health insurance card,
and finding a place to live. There is also a wealth of information about the country and
about how society is organized. Among the topics covered in individual chapters are
law, politics, the media, education, the labour market, the social safety net, religion,
culture and leisure, and family life. The factual information is interspersed with
comments from immigrants who have lived in the country for a while. The book is
written in easy English and supplemented with many pictures. Clear chapter divisions
and an extensive index make this a handy reference. Each chapter provides referrals
for further information.

14 **Signposts to Denmark.**
    Anne Warburton.   Copenhagen: Hernov Publishers, 1992. 183p.

The author served as Britain's ambassador to Denmark for seven years beginning in
1976, and has written this book in order to help others find the happiness she
experienced. The work is described as 'a book of miscellaneous information about
Denmark' and is further referred to as part memoir, part guidebook, and part mono-
logue on a favourite subject. The chapters generally discuss early and contemporary
history and foreign policy, present-day political and economic structure, the monarchy,
the people, education and language, and the arts. There is also a chapter called 'enjoying
life in Denmark' that describes the Danes' love of outdoor activities and sports, party

traditions and etiquette, and food. Concluding sections offer tourist information on some of the author's favourite places. The personal knowledge and subjective style make for pleasant reading, but the author herself admits this work is introductory and selective.

Denmark.
See item no. 43.

Denmark: a troubled welfare state.
See item no. 276.

Denmark.
See item no. 649.

Geography

General

15 **Norden: man and environment.**
Edited by Uuno Varjo, Wolf Tietze.   Berlin; Stuttgart, Germany:
Gebrüder Borntraeger, 1987. 535p. maps. bibliog.

A general reference work that covers the major geographical aspects of the Nordic
countries in chapters by various contributors. The sections that relate to Denmark
include the historical shaping of the Nordic countries from the Stone Age to contemporary times; the seas of 'Norden'; the area's general climate and biogeography;
Denmark's geology and geomorphology; the settlement of Denmark and its population;
and Danish industries such as farming, forestry, fishing, manufacturing, and services.
There is also information on the Faroe Islands and Greenland. The book contains 387
illustrations and 110 tables.

Maps and atlases

16 **Denmark: Køge 1500-1950.**
Marie Bach, Ole Degn, Poul Stømstad.   Copenhagen: Danish
Committee for Urban History, 1993. 106p. (Scandinavian Atlas of
Historic Towns, no. 7).

An atlas and portfolio with twenty-seven leaves of plates for this medium-sized town
on Zealand. The aim of the Danish atlas volumes is to bring to light factors concerning
area, development, population, and the social topography of the urban community. The
information is based on both older and newly drawn maps, and on revised tax-
lists. This data is used to describe the economically active population within a number

of professions, and the numbers and types of houses and buildings. The point of departure for all the data is the 're-executed cadastral map' of 1870.

17 **Danmark færdselskort 1:200, 000 1997.** (Traffic Map of Denmark 1997.)
Copenhagen: Directorate for Maps and Land Registry, 1996. 8th ed.
60p. (Available from Directorate for Maps and Land Registry, Rentemestervej 8, DK-2400 Copenhagen NW).

A road atlas of eighteen two-paged maps and an index of 11,000 place-names. There are also enlarged maps of the four largest cities (Copenhagen, Odense, Aarhus, and Aalborg) and a distance table for selected cities and towns. Brief descriptive information of interest to travellers is provided in Danish, English, and German. This is a paperback book available in most bookstores throughout the country. It is updated regularly.

18 **Danmark 1:100, 000 topografisk atlas.** (Topographical Atlas of Denmark.)
Copenhagen: Directorate for Maps and Land Registry, 1995. 4th ed.
159 p. (Available from Directorate for Maps and Land Registry, Rentemestervej 8, DK-2400 Copenhagen NW).

An atlas of sixty two-paged maps showing topographical areas. There is a 22,000 place-name index and a distance table for selected cities.

19 **Denmark: Ribe 1500-1950.**
Ole Degn. Copenhagen: Danish Committee for Urban History, 1983.
90p. (Scandinavian Atlas of Historic Towns, no. 3).

An atlas and portfolio with twenty-eight leaves of plates for this large town in the southwest corner of the country on Jutland. The aim of the Danish atlas volumes is to bring to light factors concerning area, development, population, and social topography of the urban community. The information is based on both older and newly drawn maps, and on revised tax-lists. This data is used to describe the economically active population within a number of professions, and the numbers and types of houses and buildings. The point of departure for all the data is the 're-executed cadastral map' of 1870.

20 **Denmark: Stege 1500-1950.**
Poul Tuxen. Copenhagen: Danish Committee for Urban History, 1987.
56p. (Scandinavian Atlas of Historic Towns, no. 5).

An atlas and portfolio with twenty-four leaves of plates for this small town on the island of Møn which is off the southern tip of Zealand. The aim of the Danish atlas volumes is to bring to light factors concerning area, development, population, and the social topography of the urban community. The information is based on both older and newly drawn maps, and on revised tax-lists. This data is used to describe the economically active population within a number of professions, and the numbers and types of houses and buildings. The point of departure for all the data is the 're-executed cadastral map' of 1870.

Tourism and Travel Guides

21   **Access in Denmark: a travel guide for the disabled.**
Copenhagen: Danish Tourist Board, 1989. 4th ed. 100p.

A comprehensive and detailed information source. Provides practical information on hospitals, doctors, dentists, pharmacies, ambulances, the availability of medicine, wheelchair rental and repair, and accessibility to public toilets on motorways. There are also sections on transport both to and within Denmark by rail, ferry, air, bus and car; accommodation in hotels, hostels, and camping sites; and restaurant listings, sights, and general tourist information. Every section addresses wheelchair accessibility (with or without a companion) as well as other types of assistance such as lifts, toilets, and parking. The information is detailed and contains both positive and negative commentary. Every section also includes numerous listings for all the major geographical regions of the country, with full addresses and telephone numbers.

22   **Baedecker's Denmark.**
New York: Macmillan, 1994. 281p. maps.

A fully revised and updated guide for all of Denmark, i.e., the Jutland peninsula and the islands including Bornholm. There is also brief information on the Faroe Islands and Greenland. The book is divided into three parts. The first part provides general information on topics such as landscape, climate, flora and fauna, population, government, economy, history and art history, and famous people. Part two is the main section and describes the places and features of tourist interest – cities, towns, villages, islands, and scenery. This section is presented in alphabetical order, rather than by region. Part three is a very thorough presentation of practical information in terms of the number of topics and various listings. It is complete with addresses and telephone numbers. The accommodation section, for example, lists hotels, inns, guesthouses, and motels, and includes the number of beds. The restaurant listing, however, does not include descriptions. The book is small, but not quite pocket-sized. It is printed on glossy paper with colour illustrations.

23 Bed and breakfast in Denmark.
Hellerup, Denmark: Dansk Bed and Breakfast, 1997. 6th ed. 63p.

This work is presented as a list. There are no pictures or tourist information. Inexpensive places to stay and their hosts are listed in a fully keyed guide. The keys include information regarding the number of rooms, heating, bathroom facilities, cooking facilities, location in terms of surrounding towns and landscape, recreation, child and disabled traveller facilities, and prices. Addresses, telephone numbers, a town index, and a numbered map are provided.

24 Denmark: a Lonely Planet travel survival kit.
Glenda Bendure, Ned Friary. Hawthorne, Australia; Oakland, California; London; Paris: Lonely Planet Publications, 1996. 369p. maps.

The authors of this comprehensive and detailed travel guide visited Denmark four times in the four years prior to the book's publication, twice touring by car and twice by public transport. The book is divided into regions which include Copenhagen and its environs; North and South Zealand; the three main islands of Zealand – Møn, Falster, and Lolland; Funen; South, Central, and North Jutland; and the island of Bornholm. Each chapter provides extensive information on the important sights, places to stay, places to eat, entertainment, and local transport. Price information is given along with addresses, telephone numbers, and opening hours. All locales are noted on detailed numbered maps. The book's opening sections offer general background and factual information about the country and its people. The chapter on practical facts for the traveller is very extensive and includes information for women, children, the disabled, gays and lesbians, seniors, and travellers with special dietary needs. Sixteen pages of colour photos and a one-page glossary of key words and phrases are included.

25 Scandinavia: Denmark, Norway, Sweden and Finland: the rough guide.
Jules Brown, Mick Sinclair. London: Rough Guides, Ltd, 1994. 3rd ed. 656p. maps.

A comprehensive travel book with lots of essential information. Part One introduces the reader to Scandinavia with basic general information and also includes sections pertinent to women, gays and the disabled. Part Two is devoted to Denmark. Opening sections provide detailed practical information, a brief history and a brief language guide. There are separate chapters for the regions of Zealand, Funen, and Jutland. In each chapter, both the major cities and the lesser-known areas are described. Information is provided on the important sights, restaurants and nightlife, hotel and youth hostel accommodation, and 'getting around'. Addresses, telephone numbers, and opening hours are provided throughout.

26 Copenhagen: city guide.
Barbara J. Campbell. Glasgow: HarperCollins Publishers, 1991. 126p. maps.

A little travel guide that is easy to use as each section is alphabetized and includes cross-references. The listings include buildings, cafés, churches, museums, nightlife, parks and gardens, and squares. There are also suggested excursions and walking tours, and a very detailed section on practical information for the traveller. The restaurant guide is arranged by price, and the shopping section tells you where to go and what to buy. All entries include information on getting there, cost, and opening hours. All sections provide a map with explanatory notes. There is also a special emphasis on travelling with children. This is a small, pocket travel book that is printed on glossy paper with colour photographs.

27 The visitor's guide to Denmark.
Pat and Hazel Constance.   Ashbourne, England: Moorland, 1989; Ashbourne, England: Landmark, 1997. 2nd ed. 256p. maps.

This guide is particularly helpful for its itinerary approach. The authors divide the country into ten geographical areas, the tenth chapter covering five of the smaller islands. Each chapter designates motoring routes, as well as walking tours in the cities, which are intended to take the traveller a bit off the beaten track. Each section also provides maps which point out the main towns, villages, and places of interest; they are not intended as road maps. Places of interest are also listed in each chapter and described in the text. A total of thirty-three different itineraries are provided.

28 Denmark.
Jo Hermann.   Singapore: APA Publications, 1993. 93p. maps. (Insight Pocket Guides).

This guide is prepared and presented by a native Dane who emphasizes local recommendations. The guide covers the areas of Copenhagen and its surroundings, Aarhus and around, and North Jutland. For each section, the author has created special itineraries, which are either half-day or full-day excursions with suggested sights and activities. Recommendations are also provided for restaurants and accommodation in each section. There is also shopping and nightlife information, a calendar of events, a section on practical information, and an introductory chapter on history and culture. All sections include maps and colour photographs.

29 Blue guide: Denmark.
W. Glyn Jones, Kirsten Gade, maps and plans by John Flower. London: A. & C. Black; New York: W. W. Norton, 1997. 2nd ed. 383p. maps. bibliog.

This guide is divided into twenty-four routes or chapters, with tourist information given within the route. Many tours include excursions off the main route. The chapter on Copenhagen includes a brief tour by car, and is further divided into seven walking tours. Improvements over the first edition include mention of two hotels each and the nearest youth hostel for the larger towns, as well as mention of a small number of restaurants. Listings of tourist offices with addresses and telephone numbers are also provided. As far as possible, new attractions have also been detailed. The first chapter provides detailed practical information, and concluding sections give a brief history of the country, a chronology, and a description of Danish churches and church artists.

30 **Bornholm: the green guide.**
C. H. Kibsgaard, P. Nørgaard, translated from the Danish by Hamish
Barclay. Rønne, Denmark: William Dams Boghandel, 1992. 80p.
maps.

A guide to this Baltic Sea island which is the only remaining part of the old East
Denmark that is still Danish. Given that Bornholm geologically belongs to a different
part of Europe, it offers the traveller unique scenery, flora, and fauna. The book
includes several walking tours. There is also a detailed description of the island's
sights. Arranged alphabetically, this section offers an outline of the island's noteworthy collection of runic stones. There are sections with background information of
the island's history, natural history, vegetation, and wildlife. A list of museums with
opening hours is provided. The section on practical tourist information is brief, but
does include addresses and telephone numbers. The text is enhanced with numerous
illustrations and photographs.

31 **Insight compact guide: Denmark.**
Hans Klüche. Singapore: APA Publications, 1995. 104p. maps.
(Insight Compact Guides).

A quick-reference guide that is pocket-sized and easy to use. An introduction provides
general background information and lists the historical highlights. The body of the
text is divided into eleven travel routes for the four largest cities, and for the main
regions of the country. Each has a corresponding map with numbered sights. A rating
system for the importance of the main attractions is used throughout the text. Other
sections provide information on art history, festivals and folklore, food and drink, and
recreation. There is also practical information on travel to and within Denmark,
important facts for visitors, and accommodation information including price ratings
and telephone numbers. The book is printed on glossy paper with colour photographs.

32 **Historic inns of Denmark.**
Ingeborg S. MacHaffie, drawings by Ellen McCumsey. Tigard,
Oregon: Skribent Press, 1988. 190p. maps.

Provides descriptions of seventy-seven of the 113 'royally privileged inns' that were
established along the 'King's Highway'. Some of these inns date back to the Middle
Ages, but only a few are the same as they were originally. The author, who is of
Danish descent and able to speak Danish, researched and personally visited many of
these inns. She describes their location, history, present accommodation and surroundings. Mailing addresses and telephone numbers are provided. The inns are scattered
throughout the countryside, and the book covers the regions of North and South
Zealand, North and South Funen, and North, South and Central Jutland. This book is
of interest to tourists who are looking for the charm and quaintness of an inn vacation,
and who want to experience some traditional Danish hospitality. Numerous black-and-
white photographs are included.

33 **A guide to medieval Denmark.**
Brian Patrick McGuire. Copenhagen: C. A. Reitzels Publishing, 1994.
240p. maps.

Aims to make the country's medieval heritage accessible to the person who has no
professional knowledge of this period. The opening chapters orient the traveller to

'Denmark as a medieval experience' and provide a brief historical sketch. The tour chapters cover all of the major regions of Denmark, and each describes a tour that can be covered in a single day. These tours are meant to be taken by car, since most medieval sites are not accessible by bus or train. The tours consist mainly of church architecture and art, but are not confined to these. Given that most mansions and castles seldom exist in their original form, ruins of medieval castles are included. Further, this guide emphasizes aspects of medieval life at their original sites; museums are only occasionally mentioned. Sites are clearly described and their significant features are noted. The book is written in a personal style, as if your guide is standing beside you. The entire text is presented in both English and Danish.

34 Cruising guide to Denmark and Germany.

Brian Navin.   St. Ives, England: Imray, Laurie, Norie & Wilson, Ltd, 1994. 208p.

Provides seven cruising routes throughout the North and Baltic Seas, an area of deeply indented coastlines and scattered islands. A pilotage overview is given for the general area, and passage and harbour information is given in sequence along each of the seven routes. This is a navigation and pilotage guide for the yacht skipper, but the author advises that the text needs to be supported with actual navigational charts. A list of the main chart series available, with corresponding diagrams for the areas they cover, is provided in an appendix. A list of water levels in the Southwest Baltic harbours and a list of harbour telephone numbers is also included. There are also recommendations for chart agents and bookshops, and for official hydrographic charts and small-craft yachting charts. This book is not a tourist guide, but brief references are made to major local features and scenery of interest where it is appropriate.

35 Denmark and the Danes.

David E. Nye.   Copenhagen: The Danish Society for the Advancement of Business Education, 1995. 3rd ed. 41p.

A concise and informative guide for visitors to Denmark, written by an American educator who has lived and worked in Denmark for several years. Written primarily with exchange students and new residents in mind, this handy booklet introduces the reader to the cultural background and national character of the Danes, dispelling a few stereotypes along the way. The author provides a glimpse into class structure, every-day family life, social customs, and leadership styles. There is also information on the educational system, the economy, employment, taxes and the welfare state, and politics. Two pages of practical advice cover such issues as meals, housing, the weather, the price of textbooks and what to pack in your suitcase. A short reading list of works written in English is provided.

36 Fodor's Denmark.

Edited by Karina Porcelli.   New York; Toronto; London; Sydney; Auckland: Fodor's Travel Publications, Inc., 1998. 176p. maps.

Includes chapters on the major regions of Zealand and its islands, Funen and its islands, Jutland, Bornholm, Greenland, the Faroe Islands, and the city of Copenhagen. Each section contains information on well-known sights as well as those off the beaten path. All sights are keyed on numbered maps. There are also recommended walking tours, and detailed information on dining, lodging, outdoor activities and sports, and transport. All entries include opening times and prices. The 'Gold Guide' section is an alphabetical listing of practical travel information that includes addresses and telephone numbers of organizations and companies that provide specific destination-related information, offer services, and other publications. This section is detailed and thorough. The main emphasis of this book is information and good maps; travellers will have to look elsewhere for photographs.

37 Live and work in Scandinavia.
Victoria Pybus, Susan Dunne. Oxford: Vacation Work, 1995. 319p.

This volume consists of separate sections for each Scandinavian country with the first section being devoted to Denmark. It is a detailed survey of information and opportunities for living and working in Denmark and covers such areas as entry and residence regulations, setting up a home, the educational system, the media and telecommunications, driving regulations, transport, banking, taxes, and health care. The employment information section addresses permanent and temporary work, and starting one's own business. The rules of employment, social security and unemployment benefits are discussed. A directory of the country's major employers, as well as British and multinational companies with subsidiaries or affiliates in Denmark is provided. Every section offers useful addresses and publications. This work is written from a British perspective and is particularly helpful to those readers who would be travelling from the United Kingdom.

38 A guide to Jewish Denmark.
Edited by Karen Lisa Goldschmidt Salamon, illustrated by Joseph Salamon. Copenhagen: C. A. Reitzel Publishing, 1994. 79p. maps.

Jews have lived in Denmark for nearly 400 years, but the most notable event surrounding their existence in Denmark is the famous rescue of 1943. The aim of this small guide is to shed more light on the story of Danish Jewish life. It is both a mini-history and travel book, and consists of a collection of short articles that discuss the following topics: Danish-Jewish history between 1622 and 1945; the Danish Jews today; the Jewish Collection of the Royal Library in Copenhagen; Danish painters in the 19th century; and Jewish cemeteries, sights and sites, and institutions and organizations throughout the country. This is a very informative, one-of-a-kind book. The contributors have backgrounds in history, sociology, anthropology, and journalism.

39 Essential Denmark.
Judith Samson. Basingstoke, England: AA Publishing, 1993. 128p. maps.

This is a thin, handy pocket-sized book packed with 'essential' information. Individual chapters cover Copenhagen; Funen and its surrounding islands; Jutland and its islands; the island of Bornholm; and Zealand and its north coast and islands. There is a special chapter on 'wildlife and the country side in Denmark'. There are road maps for each major area and street maps for the major cities. Each chapter describes the main attractions and uses a rating system for attractions that tells you whether something is: 'top ten; 'do not miss'; 'see if you can'; and 'worth seeing if you have time'. One chapter is devoted to practical information in a directory format. The work is printed on glossy paper and includes many colour photographs. If you are looking for one small travel book, this may be the one.

40 Drive around Denmark: a handy guide for the motorist.
Robert Spark. Cobham, England: Trafton Publishing, 1993.
4th rev. ed. 144p. maps.

This book is designed to lead the motorist to some of the country's most attractive areas, especially off the main roads to smaller, lesser-known places. There is a comprehensive discussion of the road system, driving rules and regulations, parking, fuel availability, what to do in the case of breakdowns and accidents, and important road sign translations. The itineraries are divided into numbered days, and there is a between-city mileage guide. Nearly all the itineraries have been personally checked by the author. Suggested overnight stops and selected excursions for short stays are designated. All routes originate in Esbjerg and take the traveller through South Jutland and Funen, Central Jutland, Zealand, Bornholm, Copenhagen, and the smaller islands where appropriate. This is a very small, pocket book and consequently the road maps are small. The reader is advised to supplement this with better maps.

41 2 to 22 days in Norway, Sweden, and Denmark: the itinerary planner.
Rick Steves. Santa Fe, New Mexico: John Muir Publications, 1994.
rev. ed. 184p. maps.

This guide aims to give the traveller the best two- to twenty-two-day tour, and suggests ways to use the time most efficiently. Designed for the independent traveller with limited time, this guide is meant for travel by rental car, but can be adapted to train travel. The author has over sixteen years of travel experience as a guide, writer and lecturer, and has tested and refined his itineraries. The book provides an overview for each day with an hour-by-hour suggested schedule, the most important sightseeing highlights (major attractions as well as out-of-the-way sights), transport tips, and food and lodging recommendations for the best budget places. All recommended locations are noted on maps. The book is pocket-sized and does not include any photographs.

42 Denmark.
Martin Symington. Basingstoke, England: AA Publishing, 1996. 192p.
maps. (Thomas Cook Travellers).

This is a good basic travel book with good maps and colour photographs. The five colour-coded sections include background on the country and the culture; an alphabetical listing of sights with opening times and a total of ten suggested walks and bike tours; places off the beaten track; a directory of practical information with recommendations for shopping, entertainment, activities for children, and restaurant listings for the major cities. There are individual chapters on Copenhagen, Odense, Aarhus, Aalborg, Zealand, Bornholm, Funen, and Jutland. The book is interspersed with many highlighted special features.

43 Denmark.
Edited by Doreen Taylor-Wilkie. Singapore: APA Publications, 1991.
342p. maps. (Insight Guides).

More than the average travel guide, this book offers lots of background information with an in-depth look at Denmark and the Danes. The work is a compilation of writings by professionals who have lived or worked in Denmark, and who are able to provide differing perspectives on Danish society and cultural life. The work is divided into three main sections: history, special features, and places. Within these sections, the reader will find chapters on such topics as the Vikings, the monarchy, Danish design, the Danish penchant for bicycles, and chapters on every major city and geographical region. The contributors have managed to combine an abundance of facts with a highly readable writing style. Each chapter is also splendidly illustrated with colour photographs, some featured as two-page spreads. Throughout the work are many special inserts detailing some of the country's most famous people and places. Concluding sections provide more basic and detailed travel information.

44   **Discover Scandinavia.**
     Doreen Taylor-Wilkie.   Oxford; New York: Berlitz Publishing, 1996.
     351p. maps.

An overall travel guide for Denmark, Norway and Sweden. The first section deals with Scandinavia as a whole, and contains both general and detailed practical information for the three countries. This section is where you find the necessary addresses, telephone numbers and opening hours. There is also background information on the region, its history, and its people, and mapped leisure routes and themes for each country are provided. The second section is devoted to Denmark and covers the areas of Northwest Zealand and Copenhagen; South Zealand and the islands; Funen; and North, Central and South Jutland and its west coast. This part of the guide describes, somewhat superficially, the important sites to see and these are in boldface type throughout the text. A final section contains restaurant and hotel listings for the major cities in each country. The book is printed on glossy paper with colour photographs. There are also many special highlight essays and inserts.

Danmark færdselskort 1:200, 000 1997. (Traffic Map of Denmark 1997.)
See item no. 17.

Strolls in the Golden Age city of Copenhagen.
See item no. 125.

Guide to Danish landscape architecture 1000-1996.
See item no. 438.

Historical gardens of Denmark: a guide to historical gardens of museums, castles and manors.
See item no. 593.

The Faroes: the faraway islands.
See item no. 673.

Flora and Fauna

45   **Where to watch birds in Scandinavia.**
Gustaf Aulén.   London: Hamlyn, 1996. 216p. map.

This guide provides practical information on the best birdwatching sites presented in individual chapters for Denmark, Finland, Iceland, Norway, and Sweden. In each chapter a brief introductory section is followed by detailed sections about the most significant birdwatching sites. Information is provided for each site on the timing for seasonal birdwatching, the various species likely to be found in the given area, and further details on whether the species is a resident species or present only during the breeding season, the winter, or passage. There is also practical information on access to the site. Although the text is quite complete, the country maps are admittedly not very detailed due to space considerations. Serious birdwatchers are advised to supplement this guide with a better map. The chapter on Denmark includes contact information for the Danish Ornithological Society.

46   **The Icones . . . florae Danicae . . . (1761-1883) as a source of names for flowering plants.**
Ib Friis.   In: *The Nordic flora – towards the twenty-first century.*
Edited by Ulla-Maj Hultgård, Karin Martinsson, Roland Moberg.
Uppsala: Acta Universitatis Upsaliensis, 1996, p. 7-22. (Symbolae Botanicae Upsalienses 31:3).

Examines the Flora Danica project, the systematic enumeration of all plants which was directly supported by the Danish crown, as a source for valid and legitimate names for flowering plants. Specifically, the author examines the various disputes and transitions in botanical nomenclature and taxonomy. The opening sections, however, offer some background information on the different components of the Flora Danica project itself and the floral areas it was meant to cover. The article concludes with an annotated list of new names published for flowering plants by some of the later editors on the project. This work is probably most valuable to readers with an interest in botany and botanical nomenclature.

16

47 **Scandinavian ferns: a natural history of the ferns, clubmosses, quillworts, and horsetails of Denmark, Norway, and Sweden.**
Benjamin Øllgaard, illustrated by Kirsten Tind.   Copenhagen: Rhodos, 1993. 317p. bibliog.

Describes 108 different kinds of ferns and 'fern-allies' in terms of their biological characteristics along with keys to identifying them. For each species the work also provides information on reproduction, geographical distribution, variation, ecology, practical and ritual uses, and the origin and meaning of names. The scientific (Latin) names are provided along with the English, Danish, Norwegian, and Swedish names. Species information is presented in systematic order according to prevailing current classification. The extent of information given on each species varies with the availability. Literature references are given where relevant. The 114 colour plates were all painted from living plants, most in their natural habitat, making this a beautifully illustrated scientific work. A glossary of terms is also provided.

Norden: man and environment.
See item no. 15.

Prehistory and
Archaeology

48 **Developments around the Baltic and the North Sea in the Viking Age.**
Edited by Björn Ambrosiani, Helen Clarke. Stockholm: The Birka Project, 1994. 320p. (The Twelfth Viking Congress, vol. 3).

A collection of conference papers by various Viking Age scholars that describe current archaeological evidence in the areas of urbanization and settlement, numismatics, and linguistics. Three papers specifically address Denmark. One of these reports deals with the current archaeological excavations in the city of Ribe, particularly the market-place. Another is a more general overview of Viking Age archaeology in Denmark, which describes some examples of investigations into settlements, ships, art, burial mounds, rune stones, and the Danevirke. The third examines recent coin finds and their effect on the current state of knowledge about monetary circulation.

49 **Sarup.**
Niels H. Andersen. Højbjerg, Denmark: Jutland Archaeological Society, 1997. 404p. bibliog.

An account of the funnel beaker culture of the Sarup enclosures. The work provides a description and comparison of the two enclosed sites, examining their characteristic features and providing an interpretation of their uses. Descriptions of artefacts including pottery, flint, stone tools, bones, and burial and votive finds are provided. The author notes that the account is general in that not every individual find and feature is described. A primary focus of the work is the relationship of the sites to contemporary settlement in southwest Funen and to other enclosed sites in Europe. Approximately half of this work comprises the comparison of the Sarup sites with European enclosed sites. A list of these European sites, which number nearly 800, is provided in an appendix. The book is extensively illustrated with photographs and diagrams.

50 **On the track of a prehistoric economy: Maglemosian subsistence in
early postglacial south Scandinavia.**
Hans Peter Blankholm.   Aarhus, Denmark: Aarhus University Press,
1993. 315p. bibliog.

Reports the results of an archaeological excavation and contributes to theoretical
development of the Mesolithic period, the last major prehistoric period in European
archaeology. Through detailed spatial analysis of fauna, the author examines the subsistence economy of the hunter-gatherer Maglemosians, and interprets the relationship
of the economy to other aspects of the society, such as settlement patterns, in time and
space. This researcher claims a novel theoretical and methodological approach, with
the integration of zoological material and its bearing on the economy, to provide a
cultural-historical treatment of the Mesolithic period. One chapter is devoted to a
multicausal model for hunter-gatherer development from the late Palaeolithic to the
introduction of farming. This work is, however, primarily a technical report. One half
of the book consists of appendices which contain the database of raw data gathered
from the excavation of ten sites included in the study.

51 **The ship as symbol in prehistoric and medieval Scandinavia.**
Edited by Ole Crumlin-Pedersen, Birgitte Munch Thye.   Copenhagen:
National Museum of Denmark, Department of Archaeology and Early
History, 1995. 196p. (Studies in Archaeology & History, vol. 1).

A collection of seminar research papers by archaeologists and religious historians that
have been edited for inclusion in this volume. The papers bring together physical
evidence with religious and social interpretation. The research covers the Stone Age,
the Bronze Age, the Iron Age, the Viking Age, and the Middle Ages. Among the
archaeological finds discussed are boat burials, ship pictorials on bronze objects, and
ships found in bogs, that provide especially favourable preservation conditions. Of
particular interest in Denmark are the 'Roman Iron Age' boat graves at Sebbesund in
Northern Jutland, and those of the early Christian period at Slusegaard on the island of
Bornholm. The significance of boat grave customs is discussed throughout the book.
The volume stands as an example of the state of the research on boat graves. Very
recent evidence is presented, as well as fresh interpretations of earlier evidence. The
text is enhanced with numerous photographs and diagrams.

52 **The Maglemose culture: the reconstruction of the social
organization of a Mesolithic culture in northern Europe.**
Ole Grøn.   Oxford: Tempus Reparatum, 1995. 99p. bibliog. (British
Archaeological Reports International Series 616).

Presents the results of the author's PhD research on the Maglemose culture, a hunter-
gatherer culture. The research focused on the study of the spatial organization of the
activities on Old Stone Age sites by attempting to distinguish patterns (random versus
non-random) in the position of items and the scatter of artefacts. The premise of this
type of research is that spatial relations are an ancient means of communicating social
relations, and can be considered more important than spoken messages. The analysis
concentrates on the position of microlithic pieces, the distribution of lithic waste, the
position of hearths, and the preserved structural remains of dwellings. The research
sites, which are noted on a map, are primarily located in Denmark, although a few are
in Sweden and Germany. Conclusions regarding social organization are presented.
A catalogue of items is also provided.

53 The earliest settlement of Denmark.
Jørgen Holm. In: *The earliest settlement of Scandinavia*. Edited by
Lars Larsson. Stockholm: Almquist & Wiksell International, 1996,
p. 43-59. bibliog.

A summary commentary on the later 20th-century archaeological breakthroughs, both
professional and amateur, in the study of Late Palaeolithic settlements. These breakthroughs establish that cultures associated with other parts of northern European
lowlands existed in Denmark as well. Recent finds have confirmed evidence of the
Bromme culture, which is regarded as southern Scandinavian and northern German,
on Funen, Jutland and Zealand. There has also been confirmation of the Hamburgian
culture at sites and in single finds at the Jels sites. Settlements from the Federmesser
culture have been confirmed at Slotseng's 'kettle hole', and sites of the Ahrensburgian
culture have been found at Sølberg. The chapter contains some detailed description of
some of this evidence, and some speculation on rates of expansion, as well as on
migration and communication routes.

54 Digging into the past: 25 years of archaeology in Denmark.
Edited by Steen Hvaas, Birger Storgaard. Copenhagen: The Royal
Society of Northern Antiquaries; Højbjerg, Denmark: Jutland
Archaeology Society, 1993. 312p. bibliog.

This volume celebrates the tremendous growth in the field of Danish archaeology
since the late 1960s. The editors note that this growth can be attributed to university
expansion and increased academic rigour, the increased soil displacement due to
infrastructure development and the harvesting of raw materials, and the passage of the
Nature Protection Act in 1969. The work takes stock of developments in the field,
with contributions from seventy-six authors in seven major areas: man and the
environment; the late Palaeolithic and Mesolithic; the Neolithic; the Bronze Age;
the Iron Age and the Viking period; the Middle Ages and more recent times; and the
archaeological institutions. This is a comprehensive volume with numerous photographs, drawings, diagrams, and maps.

55 The Vikings of Ribe.
Stig Jensen. Ribe, Denmark: Den Antikvariske Samling, 1991. 71p.

Ribe is the first Danish city to be named and its origins can be traced to the 700s. This
book tells the story of the discovery and excavation of Ribe's antiquity, which has
taken place at various intervals since 1973. Excavations of workshops provide a
description of the various handicrafts, not only the objects themselves, but also the
process by which they were made. These crafts include combs, textiles, leather goods,
tools and household items of iron and bronze, beads, and amber jewels. The founding
of the city is described, and a chronological account of Ribe's development from the
800s to the 1200s is provided. Graveyards have been excavated and burial practices
are described. The book, which is printed on glossy paper, includes black-and-white as
well as colour photographs of excavation sites and artefacts. The text is geared to a
general readership.

56 Analyses of medieval plant remains, textiles and wood from Svendborg.
Grethe Jørgensen, Lise Bender Jørgensen, Kirsten Jespersen, Else Ostergaard, Kjeld Christensen. Odense, Denmark: Odense University Press, 1986. 126p. (The Archaeology of Svendborg, Denmark, no. 4).

This is a scientific report that presents the results of an archaeological dig and is part of a series documenting the Svendborg Project, carried out from 1972 to 1985. In addition to the archaeological finds in the general Svendborg area, there is a preliminary report on the excavation of a plot on Møllergade, the city's most important medieval street. This excavation uncovered layers of evidence of houses and their foundations dating from 1150 to 1580. Throughout the work the authors detail how their excavations were carried out, catalogue the items that were found, and attempt to interpret the finds for what they reveal about everyday human life. The report includes black-and-white photographs, diagrams, sketches and summary tables.

57 Sites and monuments: national archaeological records.
Edited by Carsten U. Larsen. Copenhagen: The National Museum of Denmark, 1992. 250p.

A collection of papers, many of which were originally presented at the First National Archaeological Records Conference in 1991 and were revised for this book. The papers reflect the state-of-the-art in various countries' efforts to computerize archaeological history. Part one is devoted to Denmark and the topics include the organization and systematization of the prehistoric archives; the structure of the archive database and the process of retrospective data recording; the administrative and research uses of the records along with some search examples; how the database tracks inspections which are of key importance for the protection of sites and monuments; and the complex information management system required for excavation recording. This book is evidence of the country's significant technological advances in this area, which are necessary for archaeologists to keep pace with the rate at which modern machinery is used to develop land.

58 Denmark: introduction, prehistory.
Bent Rying, translated from the Danish by Reginald Spink. Copenhagen: Royal Danish Ministry of Foreign Affairs, 1981. 112p. map. (Danish in the South and the North, I).

Drawing on archaeological evidence, this volume presents Denmark up to the Viking Age, beginning with evidence of the very first 'Danes' some 80,000 years ago. The various ancient peoples of the Stone, Bronze and Iron Ages are discussed, and their occupations, customs, tools, handicrafts and religion are described. The book is extensively illustrated with sketches, diagrams and photographs, all of which are accompanied by detailed captions. This volume is filled with facts, but is written in an enjoyable and sometimes anecdotal style. The opening chapter provides an overview of the country's geography, natural history, and legendary origins.

59 **Building customs in Viking Age Denmark.**
Holger Schmidt, translated from the Danish by Jean Olsen.
Copenhagen: Poul Kristensen, 1994. 178p. bibliog.

Gives a general account of settlements, house sites, building constructions, and
designs based on archaeological evidence from Viking building sites excavated during
the previous fifty years. The work provides descriptions of selected settlements and
house sites, and attempts to form generalizations and typologies about Viking building
customs. The research focuses on the more usual buildings of the period, versus
wooden churches or sunken-floor pit-houses, and additionally examines the construction
of some Viking fortresses. Noting the transition from the prehistoric long-house to the
open medieval building cluster during the Viking period, the author argues that
prehistoric forms gradually evolved into medieval forms, although they appear quite
different. It is also observed that different forms of construction evolved concurrently.
At the same time, the author makes clear the need for caution in making conjectures
about above-ground layout and construction from limited archaeological evidence.

60 **An ethnography of the Neolithic: early prehistoric societies in
southern Scandinavia.**
Christopher Tilley.   Cambridge, England: Cambridge University Press,
1996. 363p. bibliog.

The author describes this work as an attempt to write an 'interpretative narrative of the
past' that spans a period of 3,000 years. The study first examines the shift from late
Mesolithic hunting, gathering and fishing to early Neolithic adoption of agriculture,
and then looks at monument and construction use in the middle Neolithic. Throughout
the book, the symbolic and political connotations of the evidence are stressed. The
evidence includes burial sites, tombs, and artefacts. The significance of the evidence
for everyday life, gender role differences, and social stratification is discussed. For
example, the author discerns a primitive communism in the late Mesolithic and the
growth of social inequality in the early and middle Neolithic. The work includes
numerous maps, diagrams and illustrations.

61 **From stone to bronze: the metalwork of the late Neolithic and
earliest Bronze Age in Denmark.**
Helle Vandkilde.   Højbjerg, Denmark: Jutland Archaeological Society,
1996. 495p. bibliog.

This comprehensive work examines early Danish metal artefacts for the period 2350
to 1500 BC through various quantitative and qualitative analyses. The work is divided
into two main parts. The first part discusses previous research and the present method-
ology, and details the features of the archaeological evidence. The empirical research
is presented, and issues such as chronology, classification, origin, and regionality are
addressed. The shorter second part provides some social interpretation of the archaeological evidence in the areas of technology, innovation, and society. This part attempts
to define the social structure of the period and to address the issue of social inequality.
The text is supplemented with numerous maps, graphs, and illustrations.

Towns in the Viking age.
See item no. 83.

Vikings!
See item no. 91.

The Vikings.
See item no. 94.

From Viking to crusader: the Scandinavians and Europe 800-1200.
See item no. 95.

The lost beliefs of northern Europe.
See item no. 221.

Myths and symbols in pagan Europe: early Scandinavian and Celtic religions.
See item no. 222.

Scandinavian mythology.
See item no. 223.

History

General histories

62 A short history of Denmark.
Stig Hornshøj-Møller.   Copenhagen: Aschehoug Publishing, 1998.
72p. map.

This pocket-sized overview of the events which have shaped modern Denmark aims to provide insight into 'why Danes are as they are'. The fact-filled book covers the Stone Age to the present day and features defining events from each period. Topics, in concise chapters, include the Vikings, the introduction of Christianity, medieval churches, the Reformation, the Swedish wars, the agricultural reforms, the English wars, the Golden Age of art, the loss of Schleswig-Holstein, the Constitution, the agricultural cooperatives, labour relations of the 20th century, the rescue of the Danish Jews, the build-up of the welfare state, the youth revolt of the 1960s, European Union membership, and the modern monarchy. The book includes numerous illustrations and photographs.

63 Denmark: a modern history.
W. Glyn Jones.   New York: Praeger, 1970; London: Croom Helm, 1986. 2nd rev. ed. 248p. bibliog.

Provides an account of modern Denmark which emerges in the beginning of the 19th century. After a brief account of the Viking period, the Reformation and the Enlightenment, the author, who is a literary historian, takes the reader through the dissolution of the absolute monarchy, the adoption of a constitution, the emergence of political parties and parliamentary democracy, the Depression, the Second World War, and post-Second World War political, economic and social developments. In this second edition there is less emphasis on political elections and social legislation, and more discussion of cultural history. Two appendices on Greenland and the Faroe Islands have been expanded. What is unique and interesting about this historical account is that each chapter discusses the effect of political and social history on literature, art, and music for the period under review. This work is written in a very clear and readable style.

64 **A history of Denmark.**
Palle Lauring, translated from the Danish by David Hohnen.
Copenhagen: Høst & Søn, 1968. 3rd ed. 274p. maps.
This is a fact-filled history book written in a highly readable narrative style. The
author aims to define Denmark and the Danes specifically for English readers in
the light of the fact that Denmark and England parted ways around 1,000 years ago.
The work is devoted primarily to the historical periods prior to the First World War.
Only the final chapter deals with the 20th century up to the 1970s. More detail is given
on the Middle Ages, the Reformation, and the period of the absolute monarchy. The
text is enhanced by thirty pages of black-and-white photographs and numerous
drawings. A comparative chronological list of the kings and queens of England and
Denmark is provided in an appendix. A similar, more concise history entitled *An
outline history of Denmark* by Helge Seidelin Jacobsen (Copenhagen: Høst & Søn,
1986. Reprinted 1993. 120p.) focuses primarily on post-Viking age Denmark up to the
20th century.

65 **Denmark: history.**
Bent Rying, translated from the Danish by Reginald Spink.
Copenhagen: Royal Danish Ministry of Foreign Affairs, 1988. 416p.
map. (Danish in the South and the North, II).
This volume of Denmark's history begins with the consequences of the Viking Age
and closes with the post-Second World War era. Among the highlights in this account
are the civil wars that followed the Viking Age, the travails of the various monarchs,
the revolt against the Catholic Church, the absolute monarchy and its decline, relationships with Norway and Sweden, the land and educational reforms and the peasant
emancipation, the various border wars, the two World Wars, and the German
occupation. This account is filled with facts and names, yet is highly readable. It is
also extensively illustrated and captioned.

Dictionary of Scandinavian history.
See item no. 650.

Historical dictionary of Denmark.
See item no. 654.

Miscellaneous

66 **Aalborg: a Danish port and its history.**
Per Bo Christensen, Lars Tvede-Jensen.   Aalborg, Denmark: The Port
of Aalborg Authority, The Historical Archives of the City of Aalborg,
1989. 52p. map.
The city of Aalborg is situated on the narrowest section of the Limfjord, which cuts
off the top of the North Jutland peninsula from the remainder of the mainland.
Because of this strategic location, the city is home to one of the most important ports

in Denmark. This book provides a brief history of this harbour city with descriptions of its importance during the Viking Age, the Middle Ages, the Renaissance, the revolutionary era, the industrial era, the time between the World Wars, and modern times. The port's growth is discussed, as well as threats to its survival. The text is enhanced with numerous black-and-white photographs and illustrations.

67   **A manorial world: lord, peasants and cultural distinctions on a Danish estate 1750-1980.**
      Palle Ove Christiansen, translated from the Danish by Kenneth Tindall.
      Copenhagen: Scandinavian University Press, 1996. 596p. bibliog.

Through archived historical materials and present-day interviews, the author aims to understand the cultural variation existing today in the region of Giesegaard, a former estate in mid-Zealand. This study is based on the premise that a modern cultural form can trace its formation to a past social system. The manorial estate/peasant relation is examined as a feature of the estate system, where relations between peasants and lords left behind forms that could later be found in new contexts. The author contends that the changing conditions of existence, shifts in the economic framework, and redefined political dependencies can all be viewed as a reorganization of their preconditions. This research can be categorized as historical anthropology/sociology. It might be most appreciated by those with a specific interest in peasant studies, but more generally, it is an example of how researchers approach the explanatory link between history and the present day.

68   **The historical evolution of the Danish constitution.**
      Ib Martin Jarvard.   Roskilde, Denmark: Institute for Economics and Planning, Roskilde University, 1992. 52p. (Research Report no. 2/92). (Available from Institute for Economics and Planning, Roskilde University, P.O. Box 260, DK-4000 Roskilde).

Presents the significant historical facts about the current Danish constitution of 1953. Among the topics examined are the transition from an absolute monarchy to a constitutional monarchy in 1848-49; the structuring of the resulting government; the introduction of universal suffrage and the formation of a popular political culture; the civil liberties granted by the constitution; the development of parliamentarism; and the pluralist party system and constitutional ideology. There is also brief coverage of Denmark's geo-political history, as well as commentary on present-day constitutional developments. This factual report is concise and informative. It was written to foster international comparisons and would be a good starting point for background on this topic.

69   **Technology in Denmark.**
      Henry Nielsen, Michael F. Wagner.   In: *Technology & industry: a Nordic heritage.*   Edited by Jan Hult, Bengt Nyström.   Canton, Massachusetts: Science History Publications/USA, 1992, p. 1-28.

A brief historical survey of the main developments in technology and industry from the mid-1600s up to the present day. The chapter is divided into historical periods, in which the authors chronologically examine developments in agriculture, infrastructure, crafts and manufacturing. The authors observe that Denmark was a latecomer to the industrial age, and a significant portion of the chapter discusses the country's agricultural past and the organizational and technological changes in the farming and dairy industry. Large-scale industrialization did not take place until the mid-1800s, and some of this is discussed in terms of short narratives of key figures and industries during that time. The book's editors acknowledge the limitations of the chapters, and so this chapter should be considered an overview.

70 **Lovers of learning: a history of the Royal Danish Academy of Science and Letters 1742-1992.**
Olaf Pedersen.   Copenhagen: Munksgaard, 1992. 348p. bibliog.
A general survey of the country's first learned society with emphasis on the period before the 20th century. The work is a history of the society's administration and structure as well as of its scholarship. The society's origins are described and its founding fathers profiled. The work gives information about some of the more prominent members and also describes the society's significant publications and research. The society was open to all scientific and scholarly disciplines. Given the wide membership and the breadth of the work these members produced, this book contains much factual information about Denmark's scientific and scholarly development. Parts of the book discuss how the society fared during various historical periods, such as the fall of the absolute monarchy. The society's leadership, administrative statutes, by-laws, finances, and membership statistics are also described. A list of the royal protectors, presidents, secretaries, and editors of the society since its inception is provided. The bibliography contains only Danish works.

71 **From fettered to free: the farmer in Denmark's history.**
Knud Ravnkilde.   Hurst, England: Danish Language Services, 1989. 128p.
Provides an account of the country's agricultural history from the Viking Age to the present day. The author divides this story into four phases: a period of development and expansion around the time of the Vikings; a period of decline that began around 1350 and endured for 400 years; a period of pioneering and progress sparked by the land reforms of the 1800s and the birth of the cooperative system; and modern-day Denmark at the end of the millennium. Although it is one of the smallest countries in the global marketplace, Denmark is today one of the world's largest exporters of animal products, admired worldwide for its efficiency and quality in dairy and pork production. This work is a thorough account that illustrates the effect of social, political, and environmental conditions on the agricultural economy. In that respect, it is not only an agricultural history, but also a history of the country as a whole. The author demonstrates how Denmark's modern-day success in agriculture is built on its unique historical struggle.

72 **Denmark.**
Henning Sørensen.   In: *The political role of the military: an international handbook.*   Edited by Constantine P. Danopoulos, Cynthia Watson.   Westport, Connecticut; London: Greenwood Press, 1996, p. 88-107. bibliog.
A short historical description of civil-military relations comprising security policy, defence policy, the organization of the armed forces, public opinion on defence matters, and a profile of the officer corps. The discussion covers the Viking era to the present day. In terms of security policy, six chronological periods are described: the universalistic, the northern European, the Nordic oriented, the German dominated,

the American oriented, and the new universalistic. Defence is discussed in terms of the deployment of armed forces within and outside national borders, and the relationship between the armed forces and politicians. The management, structure, recruitment and expenditures of the military are described. Public opinion is described in terms of opinion on expenditures and the military's role as a peace-contributor. The recruitment, education, occupation, esprit de corps, career pattern, and political orientation of the officer corps are described. As part of a 25-country handbook, the chapter is admittedly 'painted with a broad brush'. It provides a textbook-style overview of the facts.

73   **Denmark: the vanguard of conscientious objection.**
      Henning Sørensen.   In: *The new conscientious objection: from sacred to secular resistance*.   Edited by Charles C. Moskos, John Whiteclay Chambers.   New York; Oxford: Oxford University Press, 1993, p. 106-13.

Provides an historical perspective of the country's relative permissiveness towards conscientious objectors. The author describes how Denmark evolved from an official recognition of conscientious objection in 1917, based on religious or ethical pacifism, to a more liberal stance in 1968, where conscientious objector status was automatically granted, and selective and politically based objections were recognized. Civilian alternative service requirements and opportunities are discussed. The management of the conscientious objector system and public opinion regarding conscientious objection are also discussed. The author also attempts to account for the increase in conscientious objectors since the 1970s. One table reports the absolute and relative number of conscientious objectors for each year for the 1945-89 period.

The Viking Jews: a history of the Jews in Denmark.
See item no. 171.

Denmark in Scandinavian history

74   **Scandinavia in the revolutionary era, 1760-1815.**
      H. Arnold Barton.   Minneapolis, Minnesota: University of Minnesota Press, 1986. 447p. map. bibliog. (The Nordic Series, vol. 12).

Analyses the impact on Scandinavia of the era between the Seven Years' War and the Napoleonic defeat, which saw such transformations as the Enlightenment, political revolution in France, and economic revolution in Great Britain. Although the region was not yet experiencing industrialization and was not invaded or occupied, Scandinavia underwent the great changes of the era, as did other parts of Europe, in the form of geopolitical reorganization and ethnic consolidation, political and administrative developments, and economic growth. This work's focus is on these internal and inter-Nordic developments. It draws parallels and comparisons between the different Scandinavian countries, as well as between the region and the West as a whole. It is a comprehensive work that is detailed and well documented.

75   **The Scandinavian Reformation: from evangelical movement to
      institutionalization of reform.**
      Edited by Ole Peter Grell.   Cambridge, England: Cambridge
      University Press, 1995. 218p.

Examines the Reformation of the Nordic region as a whole given that national division
was in many ways a product of the Reformation itself. Various contributors provide a
detailed account of the political and theological struggles that characterized this
period, breaking it down into the early days of the movement beginning in the 1520s,
to the institutionalization of Protestantism in the first half of the 17th century. Two
chapters provide specific accounts of events in Denmark, where the Reformation
spanned the reigns of Frederik I, Christian III, and Frederik II. The early reformation
of royalty, and of the towns and cities where there were clashes between Catholics and
Protestants, is examined. The Reformation's effects on church-state relations, education, law, and the economy are discussed. In the later period, the consolidation of
Lutheranism and the formal union of state and church is examined.

76   **Scandinavia.**
      Tony Griffiths.   Kent Town, South Australia: Wakefield Press, 1991.
      212p. bibliog.

A short history of Scandinavia from the Napoleonic era, when the area comprised two
nation-states, Denmark-Norway and Sweden-Finland, to the present day. This author
claims to take a somewhat unconventional approach and analyses the relationship
between cultural and political change. The work examines artists, intellectuals, and
theorists not as individuals, but in their cultural context, and in their relation to political
events. The book is factual and informative, but written in a narrative style, that is at
times humorous.

77   **Scandinavia and the United States: an insecure friendship.**
      Jussi Hanhimäki.   New York: Twayne Publishers, 1997. 223p. bibliog.
      (Twayne's International History Series).

Examines Scandinavian-US relations since 1945. The early Cold War years are
discussed with a focus on Nordic integration, and a particular emphasis on the Nordic
security structure. Cultural developments during the 1950s are described. The Nordic
countries' role as 'bridge-builder' between the Soviet bloc and the West during
détente is examined, and the Nordic model or the Scandinavian 'middle way' between
capitalism and socialism is discussed. The economic and political crises affecting
Nordic unity during the 1970s, as well as the implications of the end of the Cold War,
are examined. The book is clearly written and serves as a concise contemporary
history of Scandinavian affairs.

78   **Scandinavia in the European world-economy, ca. 1570-1625: some
      local evidence of economic integration.**
      John P. Maarbjerg.   New York: Peter Lang, 1995. 300p. maps. bibliog.
      (American University Studies, Series IX, History, vol. 169).

Provides an overview of the influence of geography, socio-economic conditions, and
political structures on responses to economic integration. The author discusses the
general development of Scandinavian and Baltic trade, examines the effects of this
development on Danish society, discusses the situation of the Danish nobility and its

response to a growing international market, and offers a detailed analysis of the impact of economic changes on the southern Scandinavian region and Denmark in general, and on Funen-Langeland, in particular. (Other sections of the book examine these issues for the Bothnian region of what was then Sweden.) This work is significant because it approaches its topic from a general Scandinavian point of view, while it also deals with the local impact of economic change. The author compares his findings to those of extant research. The work is thoroughly documented and the ideas are clearly presented.

79   **Scandinavia and the great powers 1890-1940.**
      Patrick Salmon.   Cambridge, England; New York; Melbourne:
      Cambridge University Press, 1997. 421p. maps. bibliog.
This work is a detailed and wide-ranging examination of relations between the Nordic states and the European great powers – Britain, Germany, and Russia – during the first half of the 20th century. The book deals with the Nordic region as a whole, examining how the region managed for the most part to avoid international conflict even as it became more internationally integrated, and how domestic conditions interacted with foreign policy. Specific topics include economic modernization and the end of Scandinavian isolation; Scandinavian neutrality during the First World War; and Nordic security, foreign policy, and economic relations between the World Wars. Although the work examines the Scandinavian region, there is also much discussion of events as they involved or affected the individual countries. The book is well researched and the information is presented clearly.

80   **Medieval Scandinavia: from conversion to Reformation, circa 800-1500.**
      Birgit Sawyer, Peter Sawyer.   Minneapolis, Minnesota; London:
      University of Minnesota Press, 1993. 265p. bibliog. (The Nordic Series, vol. 17).
Traces the development of the region from the beginnings of Christianization to the rejection of Rome and the final collapse of the effort to form a united Scandinavian kingdom. The opening chapter discusses the limitations of the source materials which include the Icelandic sagas, law codes, runic inscriptions, archaeological evidence, coin evidence, and place-names. Other chapters discuss the geographical areas and the people; political history; government and law-making; Christianization and church organization; the distribution of landownership; the development of trade and towns; society and kinship systems; and the role of women in medieval Scandinavia. The authors observe that Scandinavia had more in common with other European regions than previously supposed, and at the same time, the unity of the region has been greatly exaggerated.

81   **Scotland and Scandinavia 800-1800.**
      Edited by Grant G. Simpson.   Edinburgh: John Donald Publishers, 1990. 154p.
Although the point of departure of this book is Scotland's relations with other lands, this collection of twelve papers is devoted to exploring the links between Scotland and Scandinavia as they are both part of the world of Northern Europe. The papers comprise both parallel studies and studies of direct contact between the two areas, and the volume aims to fill historical gaps and to examine little-researched areas. Two

papers examine Scoto-Scandinavian relations during the Viking Era. Other contributions look at trade, military, and intellectual contacts between the two areas. One chapter compares the two economies with an examination of the distribution of landed wealth. Two papers compare and contrast medieval castles in the two national contexts. The Scandinavian example here is Denmark, where, in 'Kings, nobles and buildings of the later Middle Ages: Denmark', Rikke Agnete Olsen (p. 48-59) examines the role of the castle in Denmark's political history and what castles tell us about the relationship between kings and the nobility, their closest rivals for power. The significance of building and fortification statutes for the balance of power between king and aristocracy is discussed in detail and is well documented.

82   **Northern crowns: the kings of modern Scandinavia.**
      John Van der Kiste.   Stroud, England: Sutton Publishing, 1996. 164p.
      bibliog.

Describes the lives of the kings of Denmark, Norway, and Sweden, who are considered the most popular of European royalty. The emphasis in this work is on the biographical and the personal, rather than the historical, in that these kings were constitutional monarchs who were rarely directly involved in the political process. The information relating to Denmark begins with the birth of Christian IX in 1818 and covers the period up to the reign of his great grandson, Frederick IX, who died in 1972. The author explores how these various monarchs maintained neutrality through the wars, and how they adapted to a democratic world while retaining the respect of their subjects. The work is quite detailed and draws upon unpublished sources. Genealogical tables and twenty-four pages of photographs are included.

Viking Age

83   **Towns in the Viking Age.**
      Helen Clarke, Björn Ambrosiani.   Leicester, England: Leicester
      University Press, 1995. 2nd rev. ed. 210p. bibliog.

This is a significant work in the Viking literature because it discusses a neglected aspect of their culture – the Vikings as town dwellers and urban founders. Further, this work provides a general survey of Viking towns in Scandinavia and the Baltic region, rather than focusing on an individual town. These authors rely extensively on archaeological evidence, but aim to set the physical evidence in context in order to show how early medieval Scandinavian people assimilated aspects of urbanization from other regions in Western Europe, how they converted to Christianity, and how they evolved into members of the wider European society. Patterns of early medieval urban growth and development are traced, and regional similarities and differences are highlighted. The physical structure and the economy of Viking towns are described. Chapter four focuses on Scandinavia, 'the real homeland of the Vikings', and contains descriptions of specific Danish Viking towns which are accompanied by detailed maps.

84 **Cultural atlas of the Viking world.**
Edited by James Graham-Campbell. Abingdon, England: Andromeda
Oxford; New York: Facts On File, 1994. 240p. maps. bibliog.

This fully illustrated atlas is presented in four parts by various contributors. Part one
provides an account of the physical background of Scandinavia and its settlement
through the Viking Age. Part two is an account of Viking civilization and covers
society, warfare, kingship, daily life, trade, crafts, religion, and literature. Part three
examines the Viking expansion into Western Europe, the North Atlantic, and Russia
and the East. Part four discusses the later Viking Age and beyond. There are special
features on the Viking ships, art, runes, and sacrifice and burial practices. A glossary
of important terminology, as well as numerous maps and photographs, are included.

85 **The Viking art of war.**
Paddy Griffith. London: Greenhill Books; Mechanicsburg,
Pennsylvania: Stackpole Books, 1995. 224p. bibliog.

Concentrates specifically on the military attributes of the Vikings in an effort to
redress the balance of the 'war and society' approach, which aims to portray the entire
Viking culture and way of life. The author observes that this general historical (and
politically correct) approach has dominated much of the later Viking literature, and
that no other recent military analysis of the Vikings exists. The work describes and
analyses the causes of the Viking expansion beginning in the 700s, evaluates the
Vikings as sailors and navigators, describes their various types of warfare, battle
strategies, arms and armour, and describes the composition, structure and types of
troops. The author defends the military focus with the point of view that marauding
and economic activity were closely associated in the Viking civilization and the secret
of Viking success lay in their qualities as warriors. The opening chapter offers a
thorough discussion of how the definition of 'Viking' has varied throughout the literature,
in terms of who Vikings were, and when and where they lived.

86 **The Danelaw.**
Cyril Hart. London; Rio Grande, Ohio: The Hambledon Press, 1992.
702p. maps. bibliog.

A work of Anglo-Danish studies that sketches some of the major features of the history
of Eastern and Northern England during the two centuries following the Danish settlement in the second half of the 9th century. The Danelaw refers to those parts of
England where customary law exhibited this Danish influence. The book is series of
essays by one author, half of which were published elsewhere but have been greatly
revised for inclusion in this volume. Although the author attempts to draw the essays
together in a cohesive review, the book appears rather disjointed. The various chapters
cover the geographical divisions and the administration of the Danelaw; its manorial
organization; charters and wills of the 10th century, five significant battles; and family
histories as they influenced national policy. The work includes an abundance of tables
and maps in order to convey the substantial variation in landscape, economy, and
custom from region to region within the Danelaw. This is a scholarly work that
assumes familiarity with the subject matter and requires patience with the vocabulary
of the period.

87 The Penguin historical atlas of the Vikings.
John Heywood.   London; New York: Penguin Books, 1995. 144p.
maps. bibliog.
Aims to provide a continuous series of maps covering the history of the Viking Age
from its prehistoric origins to the end of the 12th century. The accompanying text is
meant to highlight major issues and is not meant to be a comprehensive coverage of
the subject matter. This author notes that while recent works on the Vikings try to
emphasize their more civilized nature and their constructive contributions, this work
focuses directly on the warring aspect of Viking civilization and the causes of the
attacks. The chapters cover Scandinavia, the far north – Iceland, the Faroes, and
Greenland – and the raids in the United Kingdom. A list of Viking kings and rulers
from 800 to 1100 is also provided.

88 Women in the Viking Age.
Judith Jesch.   Woodbridge, England: The Boydell Press, 1991. 239p.
bibliog.
This book is based on the notion that the myth of the raiding and plundering Viking
'male' is simplistic in that it excludes one half of the Viking population, ignoring a
more complex history. This work represents another step in the recent research in
Scandinavian culture that has shown that the Vikings were not without a domestic life,
and they can be credited with achievements in many areas. The research contained
here is a multidisciplinary survey that finds that, in addition to domestic life, women
played a role in the settlement of uninhabited lands, trading and raiding, voyages to
explore North America, and Christian pilgrimages. Women were also subjected to
male violence, capture, and enslavement. The author brings together evidence from a
variety of sources – archaeological evidence; runic inscriptions; Scandinavian and
non-Scandinavian Viking Age documents; Scandinavian art, myth and poetry; and the
Icelandic sagas – to show the variety and diversity of women's experience in the
Viking Age. This is a well-researched, clearly written book.

89 Cnut: the Danes in England in the early eleventh century.
K. Lawson.   London; New York: Longman, 1993. 290p. bibliog.
Cnut became the most powerful monarch of Northern Europe (England, Denmark,
Norway and part of Sweden) following the invasion of England in 1013 with his
father, Swegen [Svend] Forkbeard, then king of Denmark. This historiography, which
is the first full-length study of Cnut since 1912, documents Cnut's importance as a
European monarch from written sources including the *Anglo-Saxon Chronicle*, law
codes, letters, and various charters and writs. Although the author tries to show the
extent of Anglo-Scandinavian contact, the work concentrates primarily on the English
aspects of Cnut's reign, the Scandinavian source materials being neither as extensive
nor as reliable as the English sources. Three maps and two genealogical tables are
included. (In some literature this Cnut is sometimes referred to as 'the Old' or 'the
Great'. The name is also spelled 'Knut' and 'Knud'.)

90 The Vikings in history.
F. Donald Logan.   London: Hutchinson, 1983; London: Routledge,
1992. 224p.
Represents a radical reassessment of the role of the Vikings in history. The traditional
focus in the story of Europe in the 9th to the 11th centuries has been on Francia and

the empire of Charlemagne and his successors. The Vikings have been considered only a peripheral, destructive force. This author argues that if there is to be a single focus, it should be on the Scandinavian peoples. The book documents the Viking civilization's strong impact on the rest of Europe and beyond. Chapters five and six of this book deal specifically with the role of the Danes during this period. The attacks on Western Europe in the south and in England were predominantly Danish. Although at times this culture was a destructive one, the Viking raids should be viewed as part of a larger movement of people from Jutland and the neighbouring islands. The work draws upon archaeological, literary, and historical evidence to tell the story of the Viking influence on European civilization.

91 **Vikings!**
Magnus Magnusson.   London: The Bodley Head, 1980. Reprinted, 1992. 320p. bibliog.
Tells the story of the Viking Age, bringing together archaeological and literary evidence. The opening chapter is an introduction to Viking myth and the civilization of 'raiders and traders' aboard Viking ships. Subsequent chapters specifically cover the raids on England and Ireland from Norway, Denmark and Sweden, as well as the Viking presence in Iceland, the Faroe Islands, and North America. The accounts are very detailed, with many references to the archaeological and literary evidence, and they include commentary from other experts in the field as part of the narrative. The story is told through accounts of events and the key players. For Denmark, these include the adventures of Guthorm, Harald Bluetooth, Svein Forkbeard, and Knut the Great. The book is based on a BBC television series by the same name, which was written and presented by Magnusson, who is considered to be a leading authority on this topic.

92 **Chronicles of the Vikings: records, memorial and myths.**
R. I. Page.   Toronto; Buffalo, New York: University of Toronto Press, 1995. 240p.
This book is not meant to be a formal history, but instead is a broad account of various aspects of Viking society. It is noteworthy in its striving for historical rigour as it is based on translations of primary written sources that come either directly from the Vikings themselves, or from those who observed them at first hand. It relies less on the Icelandic sagas and other secondary sources. The opening chapter discusses the source material, and the problems of use, translation, and interpretation. The nature of the runic inscriptions – the only direct communication from the Vikings, the Eddic verse passed down orally and recorded later in the 13th century, the skaldic poems themselves, and Snorri Sturluson's interpretation of them are all discussed. Subsequent chapters describe the Viking people and their homelands; the settlement process; the overseas journeys outside Scandinavia; the heroic as well as the unheroic life; the law and its importance; myth, religion and superstition; and the conversion to Christianity. A list of the quoted texts is provided.

93 **Knytlinga saga: the history of the kings of Denmark.**
Translated by Hermann Palsson, Paul Edwards.   Odense, Denmark: Odense University Press, 1986. 197p. bibliog.
This work chronicles the reigns of the Danish kings from the 10th century to the end of the 12th century, and is the first English translation of this early Icelandic saga. The saga's authorship and precise date are unknown, and the content is suspected to derive

from both oral anecdotes and written sources. At the centre of this saga is Knut the Saint who ruled for a relatively short period (1080-86), but whose reign receives significant attention in the saga. Filled with battles, conquests, and family feuds, the work is divided into 130 short sections. The reader is aided by an introduction which provides a chronology of the reigns of the eighteen kings who ruled during this period and a corresponding genealogical chart in that seventeen of these rulers are in the same family beginning with Harald Bluetooth. Two indexes of personal names and place-names are also included. The bibliography lists works that are primarily in Danish.

94   **The Vikings.**
     Else Roesdahl, translated from the Danish by Susan Margeson, Kirsten
     Williams.   London; New York: The Penguin Press, 1991. Reprinted,
     1998. 323p. maps. bibliog.
Surveys the Viking Age, which this author places from the mid-8th century to the second half of the 11th century. The primary purpose of this book is to counter the classic one-sided description of the Vikings as barbarians and warlords. This work testifies to fact that their culture achieved a high level of technological and organizational development, and that it was a complex civilization characterized by a strong class system and diverse social achievements. The author draws upon written sources, place-names, and archaeological finds to describe the Viking culture in Scandinavia and its eastward and westward expansion, tracing its activities and their significance. Details are provided about the people, language, social organization and norms, political development, transport, trade and commerce, warfare and weaponry, religion, and art and poetry. The various sources of knowledge are also discussed. The text is supplemented with numerous illustrations and photographs.

95   **From Viking to crusader: the Scandinavians and Europe 800-1200.**
     Edited by Else Roesdahl, David M. Wilson.   Copenhagen: Nordic
     Council of Ministers, 1992. 429p. maps. bibliog.
Half history book and half travelling exhibition catalogue, this work surveys Scandinavia from the Viking Age to the Middle Ages. Essays by various contributors, along with illustrations of historical objects, discuss such topics as the Viking culture in their homelands as well as in their conquered territories; the formation of nation-states in Scandinavia; the region's technological, social and economic developments; and pre-Christian religion and the introduction of Christianity. The exhibition was an international collaborative effort and included objects from numerous European museums such as runestones, weapons, jewellery, sculpture, coins, parts of ships and churches, manuscripts, animal bones, and burial artefacts. This book features over 600 objects in black-and-white and colour photographs. A five-page chronology of significant dates is also provided.

96   **The reign of Cnut: king of England, Denmark and Norway.**
     Edited by Alexander Rumble.   London: Leicester University Press;
     Rutherford, New Jersey: Fairleigh Dickinson University Press, 1994.
     341p. (Studies in Early History of Britain Series).
An interdisciplinary and international approach to the study of the reign of Cnut, this work is broad, in-depth, and not merely a chronological account of this powerful ruler. The work is a collection of essays by various scholars that brings together historical, literary, documentary, numismatic, and onomastic evidence, examining coins, skaldic

poetry, runic inscriptions and religious relics. We see, for example, that the study of coins can shed light on Cnut's economic policies. This work goes beyond the primarily English aspects of Cnut's reign, and takes into account the extensive geographical range of his influence and power. Three chapters deal directly with the Scandinavian and Danish aspects. This work is rich in detail and includes twenty-seven photographs, nineteen figures, eleven tables, and two appendices.

97   **The Oxford illustrated history of the Vikings.**
     Edited by Peter Sawyer.   Oxford; New York: Oxford University Press, 1997. 298p. maps. bibliog.

A comprehensive and authoritative account of the Viking Age from the end of the 8th century to the beginning of the 12th century, covering the different geographical areas of the Viking world. The work draws not only on the written sources on this subject, but also on the latest research in archaeology and numismatics. The book's contributors offer different interpretations of this evidence. Chapter seven is specific to Danish history where Niels Lund discusses the various Danish kings who dominated much of Scandinavia before the 11th century in 'The Danish empire and the end of the Viking Age' (p. 156-81). The book includes 150 black-and-white and colour illustrations and a nine-page chronology of significant dates.

Middle Ages

98   **The works of Sven Aggesen: twelfth century Danish historian.**
     Eric Christiansen.   London: Viking Society for Northern Research, 1992. 174p. bibliog. (Viking Society for Northern Research Text Series, vol. IX).

An English translation of the Latin works of this medieval Danish historian. According to the author and translator, the works of Sven Aggesen existed in two, rather inaccurate versions. This new version attempts to treat some of the previous problems of misinterpretation, and to place Sven's work in an international context (rather than merely Nordic) in terms of the 12th-century Western church. Included here are two of Sven's works: a law treatise and a history of the Danish monarchy. The book offers an extensive introduction that provides some background on Sven's life and on the existing texts, as well as a detailed discussion of this translator's interpretation. There is also an extensive section of explanatory notes for the translations. A genealogical chart appears in an appendix.

99   **Saxo Grammaticus: the history of the Danes, books I-IX.**
     Edited by Hilda Ellis Davidson, translated from the Latin by Peter Fisher.   Cambridge, England: D. S. Brewer, 1979-80, 2 vols; Woodbridge, England; Rochester, New York: Boydell and Brewer, 1996. Reprinted, 1998. 406p. maps. bibliog.

Saxo Grammaticus wrote his complex Latin account of Denmark's 'glorious past' in the early part of the 13th century. The first part of this work is a full English edition of the first nine books (out of the total sixteen books) of Saxo's account of the country's legendary kings and heroes. Each of the nine books is preceded by an introductory summary. The second part of the work is a detailed annotation and commentary on each of the books that rounds out the translation with information on the folklore, life, and customs of twelfth-century Denmark. Also included is a genealogy of Saxo's royal line.

100   **The birth of identities: Denmark and Europe in the Middle Ages.**
       Edited by Brian Patrick McGuire.   Copenhagen: C. A. Reitzel
       Publishers, 1996. 363p.

This book is a collection of revised conference papers concerned with the relationship between history and the construction of national identity. Eight of the sixteen papers are devoted to Denmark and the medieval origins of Danish nationalism. Among the issues addressed are the very question of the existence of a national identity during the Middle Ages; the central role played by historian Saxo Grammaticus in Danish history; the contributions by other scholars and philosophers to the creation of national identity; and links between Denmark and other European countries, particularly France. This is a scholarly work, but its presentation is suited to both general readers and specialists. The editor's afterword provides a sort of anchor to this rather diverse group of papers.

101   **The Cistercians in Denmark: their attitudes, roles, and functions in
       medieval society.**
       Brian Patrick McGuire.   Kalamazoo, Michigan: Cistercian
       Publications, Inc., 1982. 421p. bibliog.

The Cistercian monks appeared in Denmark around 1150, one hundred years after the end of the Viking Age and two centuries after the introduction of Christianity in Denmark. Indeed, prior to the Reformation, the Danish countryside was dotted with various monasteries. The author describes the intellectual, social and economic development of these monks, who, although they chose isolation, maintained a bond to the society around them. The Cistercians lead their lives in the ascetic tradition of isolation, simplicity, manual work and intellectual study as a means to spiritual growth, yet monasteries became centres of knowledge, proficiency and wealth with a wide cultural influence. This work is meticulously researched and included in the source material are original abbey chronicles and annals that take both the form of narrative as well as legal and property documents. This volume is a significant contribution to the study of medieval religion and to the history of monasteries in Scandinavia. A comprehensive list of Danish medieval bishops and Cistercian abbots is provided.

102   **Music aloft: musical symbolism in the mural paintings of Danish
       medieval churches.**
       Dorthe Falcon Møller.   Copenhagen: Falcon Publishing, 1996. 192p.
       bibliog.

Murals can be found in around 1,000 churches in Denmark and its former provinces in Sweden and Northern Germany; two hundred of these murals include musical imagery. This work provides a chronological overview of musical iconographical imagery from the 1100s through to 1600, a period which covers late and early Romanesque and Gothic murals, and Renaissance murals. Musical imagery is broadly defined and includes musical instruments, singers, and dancers. The author examines musical imagery's biblical roots and aims to determine why a musical ingredient is incorporated into a mural. A conclusion of the research is that although musical ingredients were not added to murals at random, the imagery is often tradition-bound and based on earlier designs. Such a conclusion cautions against using medieval pictures as a basis for conclusions about medieval reality and religious beliefs. This book includes over 150 illustrations of church murals in medieval Denmark. It would be of interest to historians with an emphasis on religion, art, and medieval Scandinavia.

103 **Queenship in medieval Denmark.**
Inge Skovgaard-Petersen, with Nanna Damsholt. In: *Medieval queenship.* Edited by John Carmi Parsons. New York: St. Martin's Press, 1993, p. 25-42.

Discusses various topics related to the lives of medieval queens, such as the patriarchal system, the backgrounds of Danish queens, the conditions of royal marriage, and the duties of medieval queens. Three queens receive specific focus: Thyra, married to Gorm the Old; Margaret Sambiria (of Pomerania), married to Christopher I; and Margaret I, married to Hakon of Norway. The concluding section comments on the differences among some of the other influential Danish queens. The scant source material is briefly commented on, such as diplomas, coins, chronicles, and annals. A list of Danish queens beginning with Thyra, whose reign began in 918, up to Christine whose reign ended in 1513, is provided. The chapter gleans what it can from scant source material.

A guide to medieval Denmark.
See item no. 33.

Medieval Scandinavia: an encyclopaedia.
See item no. 652.

16th and 17th centuries

104 **Judicial behaviour in early modern Denmark.**
Jens Chr. V. Johansen. In: *Clashes of cultures: essays in honour of Niels Steensgaard.* Edited by Jens Christian V. Johansen, Erling Ladewig Petersen, Henrik Stevnsborg. Odense, Denmark: Odense University Press, 1992, p. 94-106.

Examines court records from local courts in Jutland, courts of appeal in Elsinore and on Falster, and the Supreme Court during the 1600s. The author examines the type and volume of cases tried and appealed, and speculates as to the reasons for the high number of cases. Significant factors include the accessibility of the courts to the general population during this period and the certainty of court action, such that even minor cases came before the court. The various categories of court cases and their corresponding totals for each court are provided in two appendices. This work is based

on data selected from three recently produced inventories of early modern judicial
records consisting of cases from 1569 to 1718.

105   **Denmark in the Thirty Years' War, 1618-1648: King Christian IV
       and the decline of the Oldenburg state.**
       Paul Douglas Lockhart.   Selinsgrove, Pennsylvania: Susquehanna
       University Press; London: Associated University Presses, 1996. 347p.
       maps. bibliog.

Denmark's role in the Thirty Years' War is often neglected in historical texts, and this
work gives the country its due as one of the great powers of post-Reformation Europe.
Moreover, the author takes the position that Christian IV's role in this conflict needs
to be examined in the light of the fact that he was not only a Scandinavian monarch
but also a Protestant German prince. His involvement went beyond a rivalry with
Sweden and territorial ambitions. Rather he was primarily concerned with protecting
his power and influence from interference by the Holy Roman Empire and preserving
the welfare of the Lutheran Church. This work is both an account of Denmark's
demise during this period from a great territorial power to a second-rate state, as well
as an investigation of the statesmanship of Christian IV who failed to achieve his goal
of an absolute monarchy. This book is carefully researched and well documented.

106   **Poor relief and health care in sixteenth century Denmark.**
       Thomas Riis.   In: *Health care and poor relief in Protestant Europe
       1500-1700.*   Edited by Ole Peter Grell, Andrew Cunningham.
       London; New York: Routledge, 1997, p. 129-46.

This book chapter examines the consequences of the Reformation for social welfare,
which saw the responsibility for poor relief and health care shift from the monasteries
and convents to the crown and the aristocracy. The author discusses how the poor
were defined by statute, and examines what the decline in religious charitable
resources meant for hospitals, physicians, apothecaries, and legislation regarding
hygienic measures. In the same book, E. Ladewig Petersen discusses the reorganization
of poor relief in Copenhagen in 1630 under the reign of Christian IV ('The wrath of
God: Christian IV and poor relief in the wake of Danish intervention in the Thirty
Years' War', p. 147-66). This initiative marked a centralization and professionalization of health care, and can be viewed as a very early precursor to the modern welfare
state.

107   **Should auld acquaintance be forgot . . . Scottish-Danish relations
       c. 1450-1707.**
       Thomas Riis.   Odense, Denmark: Odense University Press, 1988.
       2 vols. bibliog. (Odense University Studies in History and Social
       Sciences, vol. 114).

A work of social and economic history that examines Scottish emigration to Denmark,
particularly to the cities of Elsinore, Copenhagen, and Malmø. This study is based on
data from city archives, name registers, military records, and trade registers from these
Danish cities as well as from Scottish towns. In volume one, the opening chapter
provides as overview of Scottish-Danish foreign relations during this period.
Subsequent chapters present and discuss detailed information on the types of people
who emigrated from Scotland, such as merchants, military personnel, and refugees.

A final chapter looks more briefly at Danes in Scotland, who were primarily either courtiers to Danish royalty or students. This work presents a wealth of numerical data, but is admittedly lacking in an examination of the underlying reasons for emigration. Volume two comprises appendices, tables, and short biographies. These include population figures for the three cities, Scottish shipping figures to and from Baltic ports, biographies of persons living and working in Denmark, as well as Danes in Scotland classified by civilian or military status, the latter grouped by time period or by battle.

108   **Scotland's last royal wedding: the marriage of James VI and Anne of Denmark.**
David Stevenson.   Edinburgh: John Donald Publishers, 1997. 158p. bibliog.

Offers a lively account of the courtship, marriage, travels, and travails of James VI, son of Mary Queen of Scots, and his bride, Princess Anne, daughter of King Frederick II of Denmark. The reader learns about the many political, economic, and religious considerations that affected this royal union. There is also no shortage of intrigue and royal marital discord. The work contains a Danish account of the marriage. Translated by Peter Graves, it describes the negotiation of the union with the text of the demands of the Scottish envoys and the Danish response, provides a summary of the marriage treaty, and outlines the schedule of the civil ceremony which took place in Denmark. A religious ceremony was held later in Norway. This is an academic work, but the narrative style makes it very accessible to the general reader.

18th century

109   **Clash of cultures in a conglomerate state: Danes and Germans in 18th century Denmark.**
Ole Feldbæk.   In: *Clashes of cultures: essays in honour of Niels Steensgaard.*   Edited by Jens Christian V. Johansen, Erling Ladewig Petersen, Henrik Stevnsborg.   Odense, Denmark: Odense University Press, 1992, p. 80-93.

Offers a reinterpretation of some central aspects of 18th-century Denmark. The author observes that Danish national identity developed in the half century prior to 1798, the date considered to be the turning point in modern European nationalism. This work discusses the emergence of a bourgeois academic class in the 1740s reacting against a traditional agrarian noble society and against the rise of a German élite in Copenhagen. The culture clash began as an urban one where young Danish intellectuals proclaimed a love of the fatherland and the importance of preserving the Danish language. The author develops these ideas and also notes the significance of the dictatorship of German-born Johann Friedrich Struensee in 1770-72 as a key factor in the rise of anti-German sentiment. This work is significant for its claim of a critical attitude towards foreigners early on, as part of the development of Danish national identity.

110   Denmark and the Treaty of Kiel 1814.
Ole Feldbæk.   *Scandinavian Journal of History*, vol. 15, no. 4 (1990),
p. 259-68.
Discusses the long-term developments that led to the peace at Kiel, a treaty signed by
Denmark, Sweden, Britain, and Russia. Particular emphasis is on the 1772-1814
period, when the major theme is the struggle between Sweden and Denmark over
Norway, for its acquisition and retention respectively. The article examines the various
negotiating and military options available to each country at the time, and further
discusses these options in terms of political history and also in terms of foreign policy
considerations. The author offers commentary on Denmark's place in the Russian
alliance, Denmark's war with Britain and the battle of Copenhagen, the actions of
Gustaf III and Gustaf IV Adolf of Sweden, and of Frederik VI of Denmark. The
significance of the peace at Kiel for all the participants, particularly Denmark's
cession of Norway, is also discussed.

111   Political integration in the old regime: central power and local
society in the eighteenth-century Nordic states.
Harald Gustafsson, translated by Alan Crozier.   Lund, Sweden:
Studentlitteratur; Bromley, England: Chartwell Bratt, 1994. 195p.
bibliog.
A study of 18th-century political culture which compares the absolutism of Denmark-
Norway-Iceland with the representative government of Sweden-Finland. The work
describes the political and socio-economic structure of the Nordic societies; examines
the position and degree of influence in the decision-making process of various groups
– peasants, nobles and landowners, burghers, entrepreneurs, and officials; outlines the
channels of influence between the central authority and the local community – such as
the judicial and the administrative system – as well as informal and illegal channels
such as acts of disobedience and protest. Conclusions are drawn about the conditions
for political influence and the relationship between central power and local society.
The book is a final report from a cooperative Nordic research project and represents
the work of some thirty historians. The majority of the works cited in the bibliography
are not in English.

112   Carolina, queen of Denmark: a crown of shadows.
S. W. Jackman.   Lewes, England: The Book Guild Limited, 1987.
163p. bibliog.
A biographical study of this unfortunate queen, who like most princesses of her day in
the late 1700s, could be considered a pawn in international politics. Carolina Matilda,
youngest daughter of England's King George the Third, became queen of Denmark at
the age of fifteen when she was wed to Denmark's Christian VII. Although initially
well received by her new husband and by Danish royal society, she was ultimately to
fall from grace as she fell under the spell of court physician Johann Friedrich
Struensee, who ingratiated himself into the royal court for his own purposes. Carolina
becomes his puppet, a public uprising and a coup ensues, and execution and exiles
result. This tale is filled with romance and intrigue, and the book provides a lively and
detailed account. It could have benefited, however, from an explanatory preface to
provide orientation and historical context.

113 **The rise and fall of the Danish nobility, 1600-1800.**
Knud J. V. Jespersen. In: *The European nobilities in the seventeenth and eighteenth centuries. Volume two: northern, central and eastern Europe.* Edited by H. M. Scott. London; New York: Longman, 1995, p. 41-70.

Provides a systematic analysis of the structure of the Danish nobility and surveys its economic and political activities. The chapter turns on the establishment of the absolute monarchy in 1660 which represented a decisive break in the history of the nobility. The author examines the strength of pre-absolutist nobility, numerically small, but politically and economically powerful. This situation is compared with that of the nobility during the absolute monarchy, a time which saw not only a reduction in the number of nobles, but also the size of estates, and the reach of their political influence due to the crisis in the agrarian economy. This nobility was also split along economic, political, and class lines. The symbiosis between the monarchy and the nobility is discussed. The slow assimilation of the nobility into bourgeois society as a consequence of the end of ascription and the rise of a middle class is examined. Finally, there is a brief commentary on the state of present-day nobility. This chapter is one of the few English works on this topic. There is a guide to further reading for the book as a whole, but not for individual chapters.

114 **The Danish revolution, 1500-1800: an ecohistorical interpretation.**
Thorkild Kjærgaard, translated from the Danish by David Hohnen.
Cambridge, England: Cambridge University Press, 1994. 314p. bibliog.

A work of environmental history, this book examines the ecological, economic, socio-logical, and political changes primarily in 18th-century Denmark, an area which included Norway and northern Germany. The author discusses the shift from the use of wood as a raw material to the use of coal, clay and iron, and the impact of that shift on the changes in the landscape, disease patterns, and politics. The author documents the green biotechnical revolution that resulted in the rising influence of the farming class over the aristocracy, the emergence of a centralized bureaucratic government, and major changes in social life. The work also calls into question the significance of such developments as the agrarian reform legislation, usually considered decisive in the emergence of modern Denmark. The text is enhanced with numerous illustrations, maps, and diagrams.

19th century

115 **Denmark.**
Gerd Callesen. In: *The formation of labour movements 1870-1914: an international perspective, volume I.* Edited by Marcel Van Der Linden, Jürgen Rojahn. Leiden, the Netherlands; New York; Copenhagen; Cologne, Germany: E. J. Brill, 1990, p. 131-60.

This book chapter describes the origin and development of Danish workers' organizations in the late 19th and early 20th centuries. It describes the situation in agriculture and manufacturing; examines urban and rural or provincial developments; and looks at trade unions as both political organizations and class organizations. Other topics include the theory and ideology underlying the trade union movement, its international initiatives, and the unionization of working-class women. This chapter was meant as a survey of the existing literature as a first step towards international comparison in this area, and thus does not offer much original analysis. It is a concise statement of the facts.

116   **Educating middle class daughters: private girls schools in Copenhagen 1790-1820.**
Carol Gold.   Copenhagen: The Royal Library, Museum Tusculanum Press, 1996. 243p. bibliog. (Danish Humanist Texts and Studies, vol. 13).

Provides an account of the educational opportunities available to middle-class girls in the late 18th and early 19th centuries, and discusses how schooling played a part in the socialization of these girls. The book describes the social and economic conditions in Denmark at the time, the prescriptive literature on female behaviour, and the types of schools and the female teachers who ran them. But the study goes further and describes the functioning of the schools themselves, with an analysis of curricula, discipline and textbooks, that reveals the moral lessons and social expectations they contained. Middle-class girls in Copenhagen were often caught between the urban expectation that they become equal economic partners with their husbands and the provincial notions of the virtuous, passive woman. A case-study of one of the best known of the girls' schools is also provided. Where possible, the author extends her discussion to comparable conditions outside of Denmark. This clearly written book has interdisciplinary appeal and would be of interest to those studying history, sociology, and women's studies.

117   **Russia and Denmark 1856-1864: a chapter of Russian policy toward the Scandinavian countries.**
Emanuel Halicz, translated from the Polish by Roger A. Clarke. Copenhagen: C. A. Reitzels Publishing, 1990. 614p. bibliog.

Traces the attitude of Russia towards Scandinavia, in particular Denmark, after the Crimean War, from the Treaty of Paris in 1856 to the Treaty of Vienna in 1864. Russia's defeat in the Crimean War led to anti-Scandinavian attitudes and an abandonment of Denmark, previously her ally, in 1864. The position of Russia was of special importance for the history of Scandinavia, particularly for the course of the German-Danish conflict over the Schleswig-Holstein problem. Russia's siding with the German states is key to the understanding of political and military defeat of Denmark and the emergence of Prussia in the struggle for the unification of Germany. The problems faced by the Danish government and the differing attitudes towards Russia are also examined. This volume is a comprehensive and detailed work that is thoroughly researched and documented.

118 **Reform and revolution: the French Revolution and the case of Denmark.**
Henrik Horstbøll, Uffe Østergård. *Scandinavian Journal of History*, vol. 15, no. 3 (1990), p. 155-79.

Examines the rise and fall of Danish absolutism by way of a systematic comparison with the situation in France during the period of 1750-1850. The article aims to understand Denmark's reform process and the political climate created by this process. The example of the French Revolution did not produce a political movement against the absolute monarchy in Denmark, despite initially positive Danish attitudes towards the Revolution. A specific political ideology flourished under Danish absolutism among landowners, officials and intellectuals that advocated agrarian and many other types of reform. The absolutist regime supported agrarian reforms that conferred greater civic rights on the peasantry. These reforms, however, had the unintended consequence of eventually undermining absolutism. The authors conclude that while the end result of the process of social change during this period was the same for the two countries, political events took very different courses. This article is useful for its comparative aspect, as well as for the detail it provides on the reform process in Denmark.

119 **Industrial growth in Denmark, 1872-1913 – in relation to the debate on industrial break-through.**
Niels Buus Kristensen. *Scandinavian Economic History Review*, vol. 37, no. 1 (1989), p. 3-22.

Essentially a presentation and interpretation of new annual statistics for industrial growth at the turn of the 20th century. The author aims to revise previous calculations and to discover what the new calculations indicate about economic and societal structural changes. The figures presented constitute a revision of the work of Sv. Aa. Hansen. The procedures by which the new industrial value-added figures, estimates of the numbers of industrial workers, and price indexes for industrial growth were arrived at are described. The figures are then examined to determine a trend in average annual industrial real growth for four industrial census years in the given period. The author observes an industrial growth so gradual that use of the term 'breakthrough' can be credibly applied only to the lengthy period from about 1870 to about 1916.

120 **Romantic myths, student agitation and international politics: the Danish intellectuals and Slesvig-Holstein.**
Hans Kuhn. *Scandinavica*, vol. 27, no. 1 (1988), p. 5-19.

Offers a unique perspective on the ultimate loss of the German-speaking duchy, Slesvig(Schleswig)-Holstein, with a focus on student agitation during the 1840s and 1850s. The role that students and intellectuals played in influencing the course of political events is discussed against the backdrop of a spirit of nationalism, an outdated autocratic monarchy, and the transition to industrialization. Young intellectuals were able to have a powerful voice in an era of uncertainty where new economic and social interest groups had not yet taken hold. This intellectual climate also helped to distort public perceptions about Russian and English influences and Denmark's relationship with the Swedish-Norwegian government during this time of national crisis. Through its description of a specific event, this article provides significant commentary on aspects of the roots of Danish nationalism.

121 The Schleswig-Holstein revolt 1848-1850.
Johs. Nielsen, translated from the Danish by Marianne Henriksen.
Copenhagen: Tøjhusmuseet, 1993. 57p. maps.

Offers a detailed account of this civil war with international overtones during the reign of Frederik VII. The author focuses on the events immediately preceding the war, and describes the pre-war political debate, which was primarily the language dispute over German versus Danish and the national rights of Schleswig-Holstein. The roles of Germany who fought as an ally of Schleswig-Holstein, and Russia and Great Britain who intervened diplomatically, are also discussed. The author observes there was no winner in this war. Although the Danish monarchy remained intact, political tensions were not resolved. Both sides suffered significant military losses. The story is told with vivid descriptions of the battles and actions of the key players. The text is enhanced with numerous drawings, photos, and colour plates of thirteen paintings.

122 The Danes in Schleswig from the national awakening to 1933.
Lorenz Rerup. In: *The formation of national elites.* Edited by
A. Kappeler. Aldershot, England: Dartmouth Publishing; New York:
New York University Press, 1992, p. 225-53. maps. bibliog.
(Comparative Studies on Governments and Non-dominant Ethnic
Groups in Europe, 1850-1940, vol. VI).

Analyses the emergence of a Danish national movement in the duchy of Schleswig at the end of the 1830s. The chapter outlines the general conditions allowing the movement to take place in terms of economic factors, population factors, legal and administrative systems, and the implications of the various peace treaties of the period. It further profiles the activist leaders who took a decisive role in the Danish movement, and traces the élite and middle-class origins of the movement with the later inclusion of the farmers and the educated commoners. The primary focus of this case-study is the personalities of the national élites, i.e., élites in the sub-society of the non-dominant ethnic group, who took the lead in the patriotic movement. The discussion focuses on who these activists were, what their goals were, and how they went about their struggle. This work is significant in that it examines, in some detail, a special aspect of the history of the Danish border conflict.

123 National minorities in South Jutland/Schleswig.
Lorenz Rerup. In: *Ethnicity and nation building in the Nordic world.*
Edited by Sven Tägil. London: Hurst, 1995, p. 247-81. maps. bibliog.

Provides an account of the national tensions that have existed at the border area of South Jutland and Germany. The discussion begins with the first emergence of tension between opposing national identities in the 1830s, and covers the issue up to relations in 1955 with Germany's membership in NATO. The different factions and types of nationalism that developed throughout the period are described. Significant events in the conflicts between German North Schleswigans and Danish South Jutlanders, such as the Three Years' War (1848-50), the war of 1864, and the referendum of 1920 are also described. An important focus is the significance of language and culture for national identity, and the issue of the geographical distribution of language and its conflict with official policy. The chapter is a solid account of this complex issue in the history of the Danish '*helstat*' (the term for the monarchy, the duchies, as well as overseas colonial possessions).

124 **The Golden Age in Denmark: art and culture 1800-1850.**
Edited by Bente Scavenius, translated from the Danish by Barbara
Haveland.   Copenhagen: Gyldendal, 1994. 199p.

Denmark's Golden Age was characterized by an artistic and cultural awakening as
well as many social, political, and ideological changes that are considered to be the
foundation of modern Danish democracy and Danish national identity. This period is
associated primarily with the Copenhagen milieu and its influence on painting, literature,
music, and philosophy. This celebratory volume takes an interdisciplinary approach to
understanding this time and weaves together these areas in essays that cover art,
culture, economics, politics, the national character, and the many famous people who
were part of this intellectually and artistically prosperous time. The individual authors
represent areas such as art and art history, music, social science, drama, agriculture,
history, philology, and zoology. This is a visually beautiful volume printed on glossy
paper with an impressive collection of black-and-white and colour illustrations that
are fully captioned and indexed.

125 **Strolls in the Golden Age city of Copenhagen.**
Claus M. Smidt, Mette Winge, translated from the Danish by W. Glyn
Jones.   Copenhagen: Gyldendal, 1996. 209p. maps.

This work is actually both a history book and a tourism book. The book provides a
tour through the streets of Copenhagen, highlighting the people and places that played
a part in the city's history during the first half of the 19th century. The important
figures of the Golden Age include primarily artists – authors, painters, sculptors,
architects, actors and musicians – but some businessmen, scientists, journalists and
theologians also figured prominently. The book is organized by street addresses of
famous buildings, and profiles the structure as well as its famous inhabitants, with
factual information, anecdotes, and interesting trivia. The book aims to provide an
impression of the city as it was during this historical period. Detailed street maps of
the city are provided along with indexes of names and of street addresses. For a similar
work celebrating the history of Copenhagen in various essays, see: *Copenhagen –
gateway to Europe: an anthology* (Edited by John T. Lauridsen, Margit Mogensen.
Copenhagen: The Royal Library, The Danish National Archives, The Royal Danish
Arsenal Museum, 1996. 196p.).

The Second World War

126 **Seven years among prisoners of war.**
Chris Christiansen, translated from the Danish by Ida Egede Winther.
Athens, Ohio: Ohio University Press, 1994. 221p.

During the Second World War, the YMCA World Alliance called upon the Church of
Denmark to perform relief work in Great Britain, Belgium, Egypt, and the Allied
zones of Germany. The author, who was one of a few Danish citizens to carry out this
work, relates his experiences among both Allied and German prisoners of war in
Germany – work that continued even while Denmark was occupied by Germany, and
public opinion was against any type of aid. One section details the plight of 2,000

Danish police officers who were arrested and transported to German prison camps in 1944. Initially, their official status was that of convicts rather than POWs, a situation that was remedied through the efforts of the Danish Red Cross. This is an interesting book that recounts a little-known piece of history and bears witness to another example of Danish assistance during the war.

127   **Denmark and the German occupation: cooperation, negotiation or collaboration?**
Henrik Dethlefsen.   *Scandinavian Journal of History*, vol. 15, no. 3 (1990), p. 193-206.

Discusses the debate among historians on how to interpret Denmark's policy during 1940-43, the first phase of the German occupation. There has been a general aversion to the use of the word 'collaboration' among Danish historians who have viewed it in the negative. This author analyses the word in terms of the difference between sociological versus political collaboration, and also compares it to the term 'collaborationism' which has ideological implications. Denmark's policy is defined as one of political collaboration in that the political system continued to operate within the framework created by the Nazi presence. Further, this collaboration was not a function of powerlessness, but rather a demonstration of the political élite's ability to exercise power even under pressure conditions and attests to the fact that they were trying to preserve the greatest possible degree of independence. In addition to factual information about this period, this article offers insightful analysis in this controversial area.

128   **In the friendliest manner: German-Danish economic cooperation during the Nazi occupation of 1940-1945.**
Philip Giltner.   New York: Peter Lang Publishing, 1998. 258p. bibliog. (Studies in Modern European History, vol. 27).

Provides insight into Denmark's ethical position during the Nazi occupation through an in-depth analysis of the economic aspects of the Danish-German relationship and the economic basis for the decision to cooperate. The author observes that Denmark engaged in a bureaucratic cooperation with the Germans in order to lessen the worst effects of war. The goal was to maintain control of their own economy by maintaining control over German purchasing. The author also discusses Germany's view of the fragility of the Danish economy and Hitler's minimal strategic goal of 'occupied neutrality', a policy whose primary objective was the maintenance of social stability in Denmark. It is also observed that this policy remained intact throughout the occupation. Germany's consistency in its treatment of Denmark, as well as Danish cooperation, continued even after the 1943 withdrawal of the Danish Cabinet. The work is meticulously researched and economic data on German accounts and purchasing is presented.

129   **The rescue of the Danish Jews: moral courage under stress.**
Edited by Leo Goldberger.   New York; London: New York University Press, 1987. 222p. bibliog.

Approximately 7,800 Jews lived in Denmark in 1943 and around 7,200 were helped to safety in neutral Sweden. This book presents thoughtful reflections on the subject of the Danish rescue and aims to get past the myths and romantic embellishments that persist in the folklore of the Holocaust. Included here are analytical treatments of the subject by scholars in Scandinavian and Judaic studies and history, as well as personal narratives by prominent Danish Jews and resistance fighters. The articles and essays provide an examination of historical, political, and psychological factors in an attempt to explain why the Danes risked their lives. Although that question cannot be answered definitively, the work stands as a moving and fascinating tribute to this 'bright spot in the dark chronicles of the Holocaust'. Forty-five black-and-white photographs bring the subject to life.

130 **Sparks of resistance: the illegal press in German occupied Denmark April 1940-August 1943.**
Nathaniel Hong. Odense, Denmark: Odense University Press, 1996. 308p. bibliog. (Odense University Studies in History and Social Sciences, vol. 190).

Describes the scope and functioning of the illegal press that arose in Denmark during German occupation, and shows how it contributed to the subversion of the official policy of accommodation to Germany. This research traces the emergence of early, crude illegal communication strategies and borderline legal papers that laid the foundation for the outright illegal press with the criminalization of the Danish Communist Party in June 1941. The coverage by the illegal press of German intervention in Danish affairs and German exploitation of the Danish economy helped to expose and define the enemy, and to mobilize a grassroots opposition culture which developed into an active, organized resistance movement. This is an in-depth and meticulously researched study based on, among other source materials, extant editions of seventy-eight illegal newspapers publishing up to August 1943, and on the files of the Prosecutor for Special Affairs. The work makes a significant contribution to the literature on dissident presses as well as on the Danish Resistance movement.

131 **Foreign policy and rationality – the Danish capitulation of 9 April 1940. An outline of a plan of action.**
Hans Kirchhoff. *Scandinavian Journal of History*, vol. 16, no. 4 (1991), p. 237-68.

Provides a detailed discussion and analysis of the Danish government's actions regarding the Nazi occupation in an attempt to shed light on the debate over 'where the blame lies'. The underlying international factors behind the invasion are examined in the light of present-day knowledge. The government's perception of the risk of invasion, from both a long-term and short-term view, and the conclusions that were reached based on that perception, are examined. A detailed account of the important meeting between the government and the party chairmen on 8 April 1940 is provided. This account relies on a more thorough investigation of surviving source material from this meeting than previous accounts do. The author's main argument is that the government's action should be viewed as a rational response to the threat and the subsequent reality of invasion. The author aims for a more precise defence of this position. The concluding section discusses the relationship between public opinion and foreign policy, as the author observes that government's actions were mistaken in this respect.

132 **The Nordic destiny: the peculiar role of the German minority in North Schleswig in Hitler's plans and policies for Denmark.**
Vadis O. Lumans. *Scandinavian Journal of History*, vol. 15, no. 2, p. 109-23.
Analyses the relationship between the German minority in North Schleswig and the Third Reich. The author observes that Hitler aimed to foster cooperation between Denmark and North Schleswig, rather than pursue annexation of North Schleswig, in that the two would figure jointly in the new racial order. The work examines how the policy of cooperation was pursued during the occupation. The strained relations between Copenhagen and North Schleswig are examined. The nazification of the German minority in North Schleswig and revisionist demands for reuniting with Hitler's Germany are discussed. Danish reaction to North Schleswig at the end of the war is described.

133 **Danish rescue operation in perspective.**
Bent Melchior. In: *Rescue -43: xenophobia and exile.* Edited by John Strange, Ole Farver, Ove Nathan. Copenhagen: Munksgaard, 1993, p. 19-24.
The author of this commentary is the current Chief Rabbi of Denmark, whose relatives were saved during the 1943 rescue of the Danish Jews. This essay offers some personal observations has well as factual information on this event. The author praises the Danish citizens who quietly aided the Jews, the unconditional support of the clergymen of the Danish Church, and the active cooperation of Sweden in the rescue effort. Alternatively, the author comments on Denmark's restrictive refugee policy after the Nazi take-over of Germany.

134 **In Denmark it could not happen: the flight of the Jews to Sweden in 1943.**
Herbert Pundik, translated from the Danish by Anette Mester. Jerusalem, Israel; Hewlett, New York: Gefen Publishing, 1998. 176p. maps.
A moving and informative account of the flight of the Danish Jews to neutral Sweden. The author is a Danish Jew who fled Denmark at sixteen years old and grew up to become one of the country's leading journalists. This book weaves his story with those of others who fled, as well as the stories of the Danes who aided in the escape. This journalistic work provides factual accounts of events and of the actions of those in power. The text includes rare photographs and first-person accounts from the author's personal archives.

135 **The trial of collaborators in Denmark after the Second World War.**
Ditlev Tamm. In: *Crime and control in Scandinavia during the Second World War.* Edited by Hannu Takala, Henrik Tham. Oslo: Norwegian University Press, 1989, p. 136-54. (Scandinavian Studies in Criminology, vol. 10).
Examines the political conditions that led to the prosecution of collaborators in 1945. This author defines the concept of collaboration, and discusses Denmark's embrace of

collaboration as its official policy. The increased popularity of the resistance movement and the formation of the Freedom Council in 1943 are also discussed, along with the decision to draft legislation to prosecute collaborators. The position of the Danish Nazi parties in relation to collaboration is described. The outcomes of the trials themselves are only broadly outlined and some general statistics are reported. This is a somewhat general article that provides concise coverage of the topics.

20th century

136 Denmark during the First World War.
Bent Blüdnikow.   *Journal of Contemporary History*, vol. 24, no. 4 (October 1989), p. 683-703.

Examines the factors underlying Denmark's efforts to maintain neutrality during the First World War. The unique nature of this policy is also characterized in that it involved special consideration of German interests. The article focuses specifically on Denmark's involvement in matters concerning German and Austro-Hungarian POWs in Russia and the well-coordinated and carefully orchestrated efforts of the Danish Red Cross. It is observed that the Danish government was officially involved with all Red Cross activities abroad for the dual purpose of providing humanitarian aid and gaining political prestige that helped to ensure continued neutrality.

137 Socialist feminists and feminist socialists in Denmark 1920-1940.
Hilda Romer Christensen.   In: *Women and socialism, socialism and women: Europe between the two world wars.*   Edited by Hekmut Gruber, Pamela Graves.   New York; Oxford: Berghahn Books, 1998, p. 478-503.

Recounts the struggle for female autonomy in the Social Democratic Party and for general social reforms in the interwar years. The development of ties between Danish socialists and feminists is described in terms of the centrist shift within the Social Democrats, as well as the growth in urbanization, which disrupted traditional gender relations. A significant focus of the chapter is the tension within the party over women's interests and the creation of separate women's associations, as these signified party fragmentation. The creation and eventual party endorsement of the Women's Clubs' Network is examined. This era also saw the creation of the Working Women's Association. The struggles for married women's right to work and for reproductive freedom, and the resulting reforms are described. The divisions among women, such as middle-class housewives versus working-class wage-earners, and their implications for social reforms are also discussed. Conclusions are drawn regarding the lack of support for women's issues, and the barriers to women's organized reform in a welfare state with a strong labour movement.

138 **The struggle for the child's time – at all times. School and children's work in town and country in Denmark from 1900 to the 1960's.**
Ning de Coninck-Smith. In: *Industrious children: work and childhood in the Nordic countries 1850-1990.* Edited by Ning de Coninck-Smith, Bengt Sandin, Ellen Schrumpf. Odense, Denmark: Odense University Press, 1997, p. 129-59. bibliog.

This chapter reviews the legislation and regulation on children's paid work during the first half of the 20th century. It also describes the social and cultural factors underlying these laws, as well as the conflicts surrounding them. The analysis turns on two case-studies of child labour: milk delivery in the early part of the century, and work in the peat bogs during the Second World War. A significant conclusion of this analysis is that legislation and regulation actually had less of an effect on curbing child labour than did the extension of school hours. The shift from local regulation to national legislation is also examined. The author notes that this work is significant in that all previous research to date on child labour in Denmark is confined to the period prior to 1914. Nearly all the cited works are written in Danish.

139 **Interdependence versus integration: Denmark, Scandinavia and Western Europe 1945-1960.**
Edited by Thorsten B. Olesen. Odense, Denmark: Odense University Press, 1995. 246p. (Odense University Studies in History and Social Sciences, vol. 193).

Aims to refute the notion of Denmark as 'the reluctant European' or 'the foot-dragging Euro-sceptic'. This collection of revised and edited conference papers demonstrate that the country had a greater interest in certain aspects of European integration than is generally acknowledged, an interest that was greater than that of its Scandinavian neighbours. At the same time they show that some degree of reluctance regarding integration on the part of Denmark was really not very different from that of other Western European countries and can be accounted for by various factors. The papers in this volume that specifically address the Danish angle on this issue examine the Nordic orientation of Danish social democracy, the country's open-minded attitude towards integration given the development of the European Coal and Steel Community, and the politically powerful agriculture industry's interest in continental cooperation. The editor's introduction provides an insightful overview of Denmark's European dilemma during the early post-Second World War period.

140 **The historical perspective in Denmark: the treatment of refugees in the 1930's.**
Hans Uwe Petersen. In: *Rescue -43: xenophobia and exile.* Edited by John Strange, Ole Farver, Ove Nathan. Copenhagen: Munksgaard, 1993, p. 27-38.

Describes the adverse situation of the Hitler-refugees in Denmark. The author accounts for the country's restrictive refugee policies in terms of the country's foreign and domestic concerns at the time. Denmark's small size, its tradition of neutrality in international conflicts, and the unemployment and social inequalities of the 1930s provide some explanation for the attempts to avoid the influx of refugees and to strictly define the right of asylum. Relief work was the domain of refugee relief committees, rather than the Danish authorities. Hitler-refugees suffered further during the German occupation of Denmark with arrests, expulsions, and the closing down of the relief committees. While Denmark is deservedly commended for the rescue of the Danish Jews in 1943, this chapter is significant for its honesty regarding this 'dark chapter in Danish history'.

141 **'Lagging far behind all civilized nations': the debate over protective labor legislation for women in Denmark, 1899-1913.**
Anna-Birte Ravn. In: *Protecting women: labor legislation in Europe, the United States, and Australia, 1880-1920.* Edited by Ulla Wikander, Alice Kessler-Harris, Jane Lewis. Urbana, Illinois; Chicago: University of Illinois Press, 1995, p. 210-34.
Traces the development of protective legislation in the context of Danish party politics, parliamentary debates, and debates within women's organizations around the turn of the century, prior to Danish women's suffrage in 1915. The author sketches the main arguments for and against protective legislation, noting that the opponents of such legislation eventually won the battle against laws prohibiting night work for women. This debate's impact on the future of the Danish labour market is also assessed. The author observes that, with the exception of maternity leave, protective legislation was never enacted in Denmark, yet the country is characterized by a gender-segregated labour market even today. This situation is accounted for by both the nature of Danish industrial development and by the manner in which the difference/equality question was addressed during the fight against protective labour legislation.

142 **The politics of closed markets: Denmark, the Marshall Plan, and European integration, 1945-1963.**
Vibeke Sørensen. *The International History Review*, vol. 25, no. 1 (February 1993), p. 22-45.
An analysis of the significance of Marshall Aid for Denmark's post-war recovery. First, the general reluctance of the Scandinavian countries towards European integration is discussed in terms of both the structural differences between Scandinavia and the rest of Western Europe, and the impact of the 1930s economic crisis. Next, the implications of Marshall Aid for Denmark's austerity measures are examined, as well as Denmark's attitude towards Plan policies which emphasized the reconstruction of industry. Plan policies had to be balanced with the country's domestic conflict over economic planning and industrial transformation. Finally, the difference between the economies of Scandinavia and other European countries as they reintegrated into the world economy is addressed. This article presents detailed commentary on Denmark's domestic situation during the immediate post-war period, and also focuses on the interplay between domestic and international factors.

143 **Unemployment in Denmark in the 1930's.**
Niels-Henrik Topp. *Scandinavian Economic History Review*, vol. XLV, no. 2 (1997), p. 131-41.
This article critiques three existing measures of annual unemployment and presents two new estimates based on data from unemployment insurance funds and on official registration outside the funds, given that registration was voluntary. The author explains that this type of reassessment is significant in that these calculations can

affect conclusions regarding increases in unemployment in the early 1930s, evaluations of the effect of Danish economic policies on unemployment, and international comparisons. Although the focus of this work is on the calculation methods, it is clearly written and is also useful for its presentation of the annual data on unemployment during the 1930s.

Something rotten in the state of Denmark: eugenics and the ascent of the welfare state.

See item no. 255.

The survival of the Danish model: a historical sociological analysis of the Danish system of collective bargaining.

See item no. 416.

Biographies, Autobiographies and Memoirs

144   **A poet's bazaar: a journey to Greece, Turkey and up the Danube.**
Hans Christian Andersen, translated from the Danish and introduced by
Grace Thornton.   New York: Michael Kesend Publishing, 1988. 207p.
Andersen's travel memoirs, which he originally published in 1842, chronicle his long
journey from Denmark to Turkey and the Black Sea with a return trip up the Danube
to Vienna. Andersen made this nine-month trip by steamer, carriage, and railway.
Journal entries from 5 November 1840 to 12 July 1841 recount his adventures where
he attends Carnival in Rome, visits the Acropolis in Athens, and witnesses the
Dancing Dervishes in Turkey. This storyteller even relates some tales along the way
which later appeared in his *Collected Stories*. These are 'The Bronze Boar', 'A Rose
from Homer's Grave', and the Greek folk tale 'A Pact of Friendship'.

145   **The man whom women loved: the life of Bror Blixen.**
Ulf Aschan.   New York: St. Martin's Press, 1987. 237p.
The author of this biography is a godson of Bror Blixen and wrote the book as a
means of redressing the enormous attention bestowed upon his famous wife, Isak
Dinesen (Karen Blixen). The book chronicles Blixen's life from his early childhood to
his death in a car accident in 1946. It describes his relationship with Dinesen whom he
knew since childhood, their marriage of convenience and friendship, their African
adventure on the coffee farm, his professional hunting experiences, and the other
women in his life after Dinesen. This is a well-written, affectionate portrait that is
enhanced with many personal, black-and-white photographs.

146   **The pact: my friendship with Isak Dinesen.**
Thorkild Bjørnvig, translated from the Danish by Ingvar Schousboe,
William Jay Smith.   New York: St. Martin's Press, 1988. 169p.
Originally published: Baton Rouge, Louisiana: Louisiana State
University Press, 1983.
A personal memoir by one of Denmark's foremost poets that tells the story of his
intense four-year friendship with this famous writer, twice his age, who became his

mentor and muse. This work, which was originally published in Danish in 1974, was considered controversial at the time as the personal details revealed were viewed as a betrayal of confidence. The story is told through recollected conversations and letters, and is insightfully introduced by poet William Jay Smith, who was acquainted with both Bjørnvig and Dinesen. This book can be appreciated by readers both familiar and unfamiliar with Dinesen's life and work. It includes eight pages of black-and-white photographs.

147 Harmony and unity: the life of Niels Bohr.

Niels Blaedel, translated from the Danish by Geoffrey French. Madison, Wisconsin: Science Tech Publishers; Berlin; New York: Springer-Verlag, 1988. 323p. bibliog.

This book aims to bring together Bohr's scientific and personal life and to present this 'founder of quantum mechanics' to those outside of physics. Among the topics covered are Bohr's contribution to atomic theory and the role he played in this scientific revolution, his scientific and political international status, his so-called break with classical physics, and the life-long conflict between Einstein and Bohr. The work is based on material from the archives of the Bohr Institute of Physics as well as on personal letters from family members. Numerous private photographs are also included. The work includes a two-page chronology of Bohr's life and a complete list of his scientific publications.

148 Out of Isak Dinesen in Africa: the untold story.

Linda Donelson. Iowa City, Iowa: Coulsong List, 1995. 381p. bibliog.

This work claims to be the first book to provide a detailed analysis of the influences surrounding Dinesen's relationship with Denys Finch Hatton, and to clear up the myths surrounding her medical history. The author maintains that Dinesen's book, *Out of Africa*, was only a partial story and a romanticized account of her life on her family's coffee farm in Kenya. This biographical account is told in chronological order, covering each year of Dinesen's African adventure from 1913 to 1931. The book is well written and researched; the author herself lived for a time in Nairobi. It also includes a special appendix on Dinesen's medical history.

149 Niels Bohr's philosophical background.

David Favrholdt. Copenhagen: Munksgaard, 1992. 147p. (Royal Danish Academy of Science and Letters, Historical-Philosophical Monographs 63).

Aims to dispel certain myths about the various philosophical influences on Bohr's scientific ideas and argues that any attempts to trace Bohr's ideas back to a single philosopher or philosophers are mistaken. It is observed that the Danish philosopher and theologian Søren Kierkegaard, the American philosopher and psychologist William James, and the Danish philosopher Harald Høffding are usually credited as Bohr's main sources of inspiration. Each of these claims is refuted. The bulk of the book is devoted to the encounters between Bohr and Høffding – how close they were personally, how scientific their discussions were, and the similarities between their views. The author argues for an internalistic rather than an externalistic view of the history of science, and a more comprehensive view of Bohr's personal background. This work is thoroughly documented and includes excerpts from Bohr's private correspondence.

150 Junction City to Denmark: a boyhood journey.
Visti Favrholdt.   Junction City, Oregon: Danish American Heritage
Society, 1996. 216p.

The author's personal account of the move from his boyhood home of Junction City,
Oregon to the town of Haderslev, Denmark in 1933 at the age of thirteen. The family
moved when his father, a Danish pastor, decided to return to Denmark in search of
more secure employment. The account is based on the original letters the author wrote
to his best friend, where he movingly describes his difficulties: the language barrier,
the dark and cold climate, his problems in school, and the ridicule he was subjected to
at the hands of his peers. This is a unique book that describes the move from one
country to another as recorded by a teenage boy. It is also of historical significance in
that life in the Danish community in Junction City and life in Haderslev in the 1930s
and 1940s are vividly described.

151 Niels Bohr: his heritage and legacy.
Jane Faye.   Dordrecht, the Netherlands; Boston, Massachusetts;
London: Kluwer Academic Publishers, 1991. 263p. bibliog. (Science
and Philosophy).

Examines the influence of Danish philosopher Harald Høffding's notion of anti-realism
on Bohr's interpretation of quantum mechanics and conception of 'complementarity'.
The author provides evidence of frequent encounters between the two men over a
period of three decades to show that Høffding was Bohr's mentor. These intellectual
exchanges demonstrate a friendship, a teaching experience, and a similarity of ideas
which substantiate the claim that Høffding's influence on Bohr was direct, rather than
indirect as others have claimed. This work is a detailed account of the philosophy
underlying Bohr's scientific work and attests to the historical significance of
Høffding's ideas. It is well presented, thoroughly documented, and draws upon much
previously unpublished material. Some prior knowledge of subject matter is assumed.

152 Jacobsen of Carlsberg: brewer and philanthropist.
Kristof Glamann, translated from the Danish by Geoffrey French.
Copenhagen: Gyldendal, 284p. bibliog.

Tells the story of Jacob Christian Jacobsen (1811-87) founder of the Carlsberg
Brewery and the Carlsberg Foundation charitable trust. The author examines
Carlsberg's conceptual world and fundamental ideas in order to understand his entre-
preneurial success and his unprecedented patronage of science and the arts. Key to his
success was the fact that Carlsberg was an early proponent of research-based product
development, opening a research laboratory to study the basic processes of production.
The work also aims to shed light on Carlsberg's personality and character, and it
offers a candid, non-sensationalist view of Carlsberg's marriage and other family
relationships, especially his estrangement from his son Carl. This work is based
primarily on unpublished Jacobsen family papers and is enhanced with over thirty-five
illustrations. It is an intriguing and satisfying story. The bibliography consists almost
exclusively of Danish-language works.

153 **Biography of Danish literary impressionist Herman Bang
(1857-1912).**
Vivian Greene-Gantzberg.   Lewiston, New York: Edwin Mellen
Press, 1997. 230p. bibliog. (Scandinavian Studies, no. 2).
This work is the first study in English of the life and work of this Danish writer and
novelist who is considered one of the representatives of the 'Modern Breakthrough'.
This is a literary biography that discusses Bang's literary style and themes, and examines the connections between his life and work. The study draws upon previously
unpublished correspondence with authors, publishers, agents and translators, and
includes critical comments from the newspapers and journals of the day. Also
included is an excerpt in the original English of Klaus Mann's account of Bang's visit
to America.

154 **Otto Jespersen: facets of his life and work.**
Edited by Arne Juul, Hans F. Nielsen.   Amsterdam, Philadelphia:
John Benjamins Publishing, 1989. 154p. bibliog. (Studies in the
History of the Language Sciences, no. 52).
This volume is a collection of essays on the well-known Danish linguist and is meant
primarily for students and scholars of linguistics. In addition to biographical information,
the contributors discuss Jespersen's active professional life at Copenhagen University,
his advocacy for the teaching of English in Denmark, his contributions to Danish and
general phonetics, his thoughts on child language, and his place in the international
language movement with his work towards the creation of a universally accepted
auxiliary language. Jespersen is probably best known as a grammarian through the
publication of his major work *A Modern English Grammar* in seven volumes. One
chapter discusses Jespersen as a both a practising and a theoretical grammarian. This
volume also includes eight pages of black-and-white photographs.

155 **A linguist's life: an English translation of Otto Jespersen's
autobiography with notes, photos and a bibliography.**
Edited by Arne Juul, Hans F. Nielsen, Jørgen Erik Nielsen, translated
from the Danish by David Stoner.   Odense, Denmark: Odense
University Press, 1995. 380p. bibliog.
Otto Jespersen (1860-1943) is considered to be the best-known Danish linguist in the
English-speaking world. This autobiography describes his private life and his work.
That work includes not only Jespersen's scholarly work, but also his work in language
teaching. Jespersen challenged authority and the conservative tradition with his
campaigns for improved modern language teaching in schools, the study of phonetics,
spelling reform in Danish, and the creation of an international language. The editors
note that the autobiography is somewhat weak and uninteresting until Jespersen
discovers his interest in language and his life takes direction. Because the book was
originally written for a Danish audience in the 1930s, this translation is extensively
annotated. The bibliography includes over 800 works published during Jespersen's
lifetime. Twenty-five pages of black-and-white photographs are also included.

156 **Harald Westergaard: from young pioneer to established authority.**
Niels Kærgård, Thorkild Davidsen.   In: *European economists of the early 20th century, Volume I: studies of neglected thinkers of Belgium, France, The Netherlands and Scandinavia.*   Edited by Warren J. Samuels.   Cheltenham, England; Northampton, Massachusetts: Edward Elgar, 1998, p. 349-65.

A portrait of this leader in economic theory and statistics from the early 1880s to the late 1920s who is almost completely forgotten today. This essay provides a brief summary of Westergaard's career, his contributions to mathematical economics, his role in social reform as a leading layman in the Danish Church, and his influence on Danish economics and statistics. Westergaard's ideas became obsolete as he assigned a prominent position to the data itself and focused on the theory's applicability. This research strategy was at odds with the era's dominant thinking where *a priori* theoretical models and pure theory were becoming the focus. For a portrait of a more obscure figure in economics, whose ideas upon later analysis were deemed ahead of their time, see in the same volume as this Westergaard essay, 'The Danish economist Jens Warming: an odd genius' (p. 331-48) by Niels Kærgård, Peder Andersen, and Niels-Henrik Topp.

157 **Carl Nielsen.**
Jack Lawson.   London: Phaidon Press, 1997. 240p. bibliog.
(20th Century Composers).

This is the first full-length biography of Carl Nielsen (1865-1931) to be published in English. Nielsen rose from rural poverty to become Denmark's most influential composer. He is considered to be a master of the modern symphony and his symphonic works are noted for their 'progressive tonality', a musical innovation characterized by the use of two keys in one symphony. Nielsen was also recognized for his versatility as his works include operas, chamber and choral pieces, popular songs, and revitalized Danish folk songs. This volume takes the reader from Nielsen's childhood and membership in a military band as a teenager, through his becoming conductor of Copenhagen's Philharmonic, to his final and most creative years. It is well written and well researched, and includes a classified list of Nielsen's principal works and a select discography.

158 **Tania: a biography and memoir of Isak Dinesen.**
Parmenia Migel.   New York; St. Louis, Missouri; San Francisco; Toronto: McGraw Hill, 1987. 325p. bibliog.

This book was first published under the title *Titania* (New York: Random House, 1967; London: Michael Joseph, 1968. 325p.). The present edition offers a brief preface, where the author, who became Dinesen's confidant while they were together in Paris, explains that she wrote this biography at Tania's request. They worked together over many years of visits and interviews. Interviews were also conducted with Dinesen's family and associates. Migel feels this is an accurate account of Dinesen's life and work, not a dissection, but rather a 'lyrical interpretation in keeping with Tania's spirit and intent'. It is a balanced work and not overly burdened with Dinesen's well-known Africa experience. The text is enhanced with twenty-four pages of black-and-white photographs.

159 **Isak Dinesen: the life and imagination of a seducer.**
Olga Anastasia Pelensky.   Athens, Ohio: Ohio University Press, 1991.
218p.

This is a thorough account of the writer's life based on papers from both private and
library collections, and new interview sources in Africa, Denmark, and England. The
author examines Dinesen's life as an aristocrat who was born into a Victorian, Danish
family; an adventurer who ran a coffee plantation in Africa; and an author who
became a legend in her lifetime. The reader also learns of the themes shaping
Dinesen's life and work such as a tradition of adventure on her father's side, feminist
inclinations on her mother's side, and the Danish history of romance and masquerade,
and its traditions of the drama, theatre and pantomime. With new biographical
information, the author provides new interpretations of Dinesen's writings. The work
is documented with extensive chapter notes and includes sixteen black-and-white
photographs.

160 **Hans Christian Andersen: Danish writer and citizen of the world.**
Edited by Sven Hakon Rossel.   Amsterdam; Atlanta, Georgia:
Rodopi, 1994. 294p.

A biographical study that critically examines the best known of all Danish writers and
one of the greatest travellers of 19th-century literature. One aim of this volume is
to present a comprehensive picture of Andersen's personality and psychological
make-up. This happy storyteller and successful social climber who overcame extreme
poverty was also a disillusioned and conflict-ridden character. The five contributors
also pay attention to the older Andersen, an ageing artist fearful of losing his inspiration,
and fighting physical illness. Further, the work does not purport to analyse individual
texts in-depth. Rather, a coherent view of his achievements is presented in the context
of world literature. The contributors draw upon diaries, almanacs, autobiographies,
and letters. Much of this material has never before been seen in English. The
individual chapters contains explanatory notes and references, and it is the editor's intention that
each chapter can be read independently. The volume also includes a two-page
chronology.

161 **Niels Bohr: his life and work as seen by his friends and colleagues.**
Edited by S. Rozental.   Amsterdam; Oxford; New York; Tokyo:
North Holland Publishing. Reprinted, 1968; 1985. 355p.

A collective work that serves as a testimonial to the significance of Bohr's achievements in the area of atomic physics as well as his other activities in the Danish
community. Contributions include accounts of Bohr's early years; these are based on
letters, documents, and recollections of surviving witnesses. His scientific work is
discussed by other physicists, some of the details of which may be difficult for the lay
reader. There is a chapter, however, which describes his achievements in physics in
more popular language. Bohr's activities outside fundamental science, such as his
interest in Danish cultural life, are also discussed. Personal recollections include an
essay by his son. The text of Bohr's 'Open Letter to the United Nations', where he
calls for international cooperation and mutual openness for the progress of science, is
reprinted here. Many personal black-and-white photographs are included.

162   **August and Marie Krogh: lives in science.**
Bodil Schmidt-Nielsen.   New York; Oxford: Oxford University Press,
1995. 295p.

A loving and satisfying biography written by the daughter of these two medical researchers. The focus is on Danish physiologist August Krogh, who was recognized for his work in metabolism, exercise physiology, and animal physiology. Among his achievements, Krogh was awarded the Nobel Prize for medicine or physiology in 1920, and played a crucial role in beginning insulin production in Denmark, an area where the country remains a leader today. The book takes us from Krogh's early and school years, through his medical education and research, his marriage, his exile in Sweden during the Second World War, and finally, his last scientific work. The author is herself a physiologist and writes with this professional insight, in addition to her admiration and affection. Also included are a family tree, a chronology, a list of August Krogh's publications, and many personal photos.

163   **Hans Brenaa: Danish ballet master.**
Bent Schønberg, translated from the Danish by Joan Tate.   London:
Dance Books, 1990. 145p.

This work is both a biography of the distinguished dancer, teacher, and artistic director, as well as a recent history of the Royal Danish Ballet. The work is based on the author's own friendship with Hans Brenaa as well as on conversations with many others who knew him. It discusses Brenaa's life and career, how he became a member of the Royal Danish Ballet, and his fame as a Bournonville specialist, teaching and producing Bournonville ballets throughout Europe and the United States. The book includes numerous black-and-white photographs. Final sections provide a chronological survey of Brenaa's major roles in performances at the Royal Theatre, and an alphabetical list of performances in which Brenaa took part at the Royal Theatre.

164   **Hans Christian Andersen: the man and his work.**
Reginald Spink.   Copenhagen: Høst & Søn, 1981. 3rd ed. 64p.

A concise biography of Andersen with a focus on his childhood in Odense and youth in Copenhagen, and his relationship with the Collin family, one of a number of Andersen's outstanding patrons. The work also discusses some of Andersen's lesser-known accomplishments and adventures. The author is a noted translator of Andersen's works. The many illustrations include black-and-white photographs, drawings, and examples of Andersen's paper cuttings.

165   **Monica: heroine of the Danish resistance.**
Christine Sutherland.   London: Robin Clark, 1992. Originally
published, Edinburgh: Canongate, 1991. 242p.

A romantic and suspenseful biography of Monica de Wichfeld who was born and raised in Irish high society and married a Danish aristocrat. This brave woman joined the Danish resistance at the outbreak of the Second World War and was directly involved in underground activities from her lakeside estate. She was betrayed by one of her own, arrested, and sent to prison, where she displayed great courage, refusing to name her collaborators. Her sentence to death by firing squad sparked a national outcry and was commuted to life imprisonment. This inspiring biography was suggested by de Wichfeld's son who provided the author with personal documents and reminiscences. Eight pages of photographs are included.

166   **The lord of Uraniborg: a biography of Tycho Brahe.**
Victor Thoren.   Cambridge, England; New York; Melbourne:
Cambridge University Press, 1990. 523p.

A comprehensive biography of the 'father of modern astronomy' that aims to go
beyond previous works on Brahe. This work gives more prominence to Brahe's noble
lineage and its significance for his career. It also provides new analyses of Brahe's
scientific work which includes his solar theory, his development of what came to be
known as the Tychonic system, and his lunar theory. The author has tried to make this
book comprehensible to the lay reader, but warns that some of the technical parts
make for difficult reading. A glossary of technical terms is provided in an effort to
make the book accessible to anyone with an interest in astronomy or the history of
science in the late 16th century.

167   **The power of Aries: myth and reality in Karen Blixen's life.**
Anders Westonholz, translated from the Danish by Lise Kure-Jensen.
Baton Rouge, Louisiana; London: Louisiana State University Press,
1987. 127p.

This book was originally published in Danish in 1982 and the author is the grand-
nephew of Karen Blixen's uncle, Aage Westonholz, who provided the primary
financial backing for the family's coffee farm in Africa. Related here are Blixen's
experiences on the coffee farm, particularly details about the financial hardship. The
work also describes aspects of her personality reflected in her writings and her
relationships: her worship of the aristocracy she was born into and thus a snobbishness
she was famous for; her fascination with the puppet theatre and her penchant for view-
ing herself and others as 'puppets in the hands of destiny'; her religious sensibility,
although she subscribed to no formal religion. Previously unpublished letters between
Blixen and her uncle provided source material for this work. It is a very thoughtful,
informative, and well-written book.

Seven years among prisoners of war.
See item no. 126.

N. F. S. Grundtvig: an introduction to his life and work.
See item no. 214.

Encounters with Kierkegaard: a life as seen by his contemporaries.
See item no. 236.

Kierkegaard in Golden Age Denmark.
See item no. 237.

'With constant care . . .' A. P. Møller: shipowner 1876-1965.
See item no. 397.

Population

168 **Occupational impacts on mortality declines in the Nordic countries.**
Otto Andersen.   In: *Future demographic trends in Europe and North America*.   Edited by Wolfgang Lutz.   London; San Diego, California: Academic Press, 1991, p. 41-54.

Reports on a comparative study of differences in mortality for occupational groups in the five Nordic countries. The research is based on a dataset of all individuals aged twenty to sixty-four in 1971 who were followed for ten years. The article reports findings on overall mortality, mortality differences by gender, and differences by gender and occupational group. There is also data on occupational groups and causes of death. The study attempts an admittedly somewhat unrealistic estimation of the potential reduction in mortality if the mortality rates of high-risk groups was decreased to that of the lowest-risk groups (teachers), given the substantial differences that were found in mortality by occupational group. The conclusions of this study are not particularly informative, but the basic mortality data stands on its own.

169 **Europe's population in the 1990's.**
Edited by David Coleman.   Oxford: Oxford University Press, 1996. 346p.

A compilation of revised and updated papers from a 1993 conference sponsored by the British Society for Population Studies. These papers present international comparisons in demographic behaviour in an effort to provide indicators of a convergence of social behaviour in the 'new' Europe. Information on Denmark can be found throughout the book, in tables or text, on issues such as population and fertility projections, marriage and cohabitation rates, extra-marital birth rates, divorce rates, rates of single-parenting, attitudes toward gender roles, provision of family welfare benefits and maternity leave benefits, and public provision of child care. Given the European focus of the work, information is presented in a comparative framework. References follow each paper.

170   **Urban population in Denmark: patterns of location and change in a long-term perspective.**
Christian Wichmann Matthiessen.   In: *Innovation and urban population dynamics: a multi-level process.*   Edited by K. P. Strohmeier, Ch. W. Matthiessen.   Aldershot, England; Brookfield, Vermont: Avebury, 1992, p. 11-30.

Aims to describe and explain population trends for the period 1801-1986, based on census data. Overall patterns and dynamic periods are explained in terms of significant societal changes. Specific emphasis is given to urban growth patterns for the 1960-86 period, which is the most dynamic growth phase, and the process of suburbanization around the larger towns. A detailed mapping of specific chronological phases of this process is a primary aspect of this study. The correlation between urban size and urban growth, which the author observes as not statistically significant, is discussed. The relationship between urban growth and other growth factors such as the structure of employment is also discussed. Among the conclusions, is that recent urban growth can be attributed to the suburbanization process.

Nationalities and Minorities

171 The Viking Jews: a history of the Jews in Denmark.
Ib Nathan Bamberger.   New York: Soncino Press, 1990. 2nd ed. 162p.
bibliog.

Chronicles the history of the Danish Jews from their arrival in 1622, upon the invitation
of King Christian IV, to their return to Copenhagen at the end of the Second World
War. The author describes the Jews' earliest immigration and settlement in Danish
cities, outlines portraits of outstanding individual Danish Jews, and profiles the Jewish
community and its institutions. The work highlights the rapid assimilation of the Jews
into Denmark, and their progression to full political, social and economic equality.
The text of the Royal Decree of 1814, which granted full citizenship to the Jews, is
presented in its entirety. The final chapter deals with the German occupation and the
escape of the Danish Jews to safety in Sweden. The work includes some limited
census statistics and several black-and-white photographs of prominent Danish Jews.
A list of rabbis officiating in Copenhagen from 1687 to the present day is included in
an appendix.

**172 Minority education and ethnic survival: case study of a German
school in Denmark.**
Michael S. Byram.   Avon, England: Multilingual Matters Limited,
1986. 195p. bibliog.

The duchy of Schleswig became part of Denmark through a 1920 referendum creating
a sizeable German minority at the Danish-German border. This work provides some
insight into the life of this minority, with a focus on one school. Indeed, this group's
existence depends on its schools and the education and socialization of its children.
Through a qualitative study based on observations, interviews, discussions and written
documents, the author describes what being a member of the minority involves, and
describes the function of the school and how it is experienced by the pupils. What is
also interesting is the author's discussion of the transition period from school life to
society and working life, and its corresponding transition from the use of German to
Danish. This transition raises the issues of ethnic identity, and the connection between
language and culture.

173   **Christiania: the evolution of a commune.**
Adam Conroy.   Amsterdam: IISG Research Papers, 1995. 32p.
bibliog. (Available from International Institute of Social History,
Cruquiusweg 31, NL-1019 AT, Amsterdam).

Examines the 'Freetown' of Christiania, which is located within Copenhagen, as a
socio-political entity. The town's historical development since its inception in 1971 is
briefly traced. Its present structure – political, economic, social – is also described.
The bulk of the paper is devoted to a theoretical examination of the nature of
Christiania as an alternative way of life, a commune, a utopia, and as an urban village.
The author also examines the town's laws and norms, its control of conflict, and the
distribution of power. Christiania's relationship to the larger society and its future is
also discussed. This paper is published as a work in progress and is somewhat
superficial, yet it does provide factual information, as well as some insight into the
phenomenon of this unique and controversial 'social experiment'.

174   **Nordisk invandrar- och migrationsrapport.** (Report on Nordic
immigrants and migration.)
Curt Grundström.   Copenhagen: Nordic Statistical Secretariat, 1993.
117p. (Available from Nordic Statistical Secretariat, Sejrøgade 11,
DK-2100 Copenhagen Ø).

Presents national and adjusted statistics with accompanying text on aliens, immigration,
emigration, net immigration, naturalization, refugees, and asylum applicants. Statistics
are presented for various periods of time and for groups from various foreign
countries up to 1991. The entire text is presented in English and Swedish.

175   **Copenhagen on the housing battlefield: an analysis of the causes of
spatial segregation in a multi-ethnic metropolis and its effects on
the quality of teaching and the racist discourse.**
Jan Hjarnø.   Esbjerg, Denmark: South Jutland University Press, 1997.
145p. bibliog. (Danish Centre for Migration and Ethnic Studies,
Papers, migration, no. 23).

This publication is a study in urban development and international migration. It
examines the causes and consequences of the spatial segregation between Danes and
ethnic minorities since the late 1960s in Copenhagen, which currently has an ethnically
diverse population, and evidences ethnic inequalities in employment, education, and
housing. The topics covered include the urban development of Denmark generally, a
description of the country's immigration and refugee policies, the spatial development
of Copenhagen, Danish housing policy, and the settlement patterns of immigrants with
a focus on their areas of concentration. The author also examines the effect of spatial
segregation on education, observing that there is a negative effect on immigrant
children's chances of success. The housing and segregation issue is also examined in
terms of the generally negative attitudes of Danes towards foreigners. This paper is
significant as it represents a relatively new area of research in a country whose population
was very homogeneous until the 1960s.

176   **Gay and lesbian politics: assimilation or subversion: a Danish perspective.**
Karin Lützen.   *Journal of Homosexuality*, vol. 35, nos. 3/4 (1998), p. 233-43.

This article is essentially a commentary on the state of radical homosexual politics against the backdrop of the issue of registered partnerships. Denmark was the first country in the world to pass such legislation in 1989. This article is insightful in terms of its examination of the conservative aspects of what appears to be progressive legislation. The notion that the registered partnership reflects not so much the acceptance of homosexuality, but rather the declining significance of marriage as a necessary social institution in Denmark is put forth. The article also provides a brief look at the contemporary history of gay politics from the 1970s to the 1990s. The debates surrounding the issue of registered partnerships and some of the ideological splits within the homosexual community itself are also discussed. The author observes that the right of registered partnership stops short of parenthood and challenges gay rights organizations to address the issues surrounding this. This article also appeared in *Scandinavian homosexualities: essays on gay and lesbian studies*, edited by Jan Löfström (Binghamton, New York: The Haworth Press, 1998, p. 233-43).

177   **A short history of gay Denmark 1613-1989: the rise and possibly happy end of the Danish homosexual.**
Wilhelm von Rosen.   *Nordisk Sexologi*, no. 12 (1994), p. 125-36.

Offers a chronological account of gay history with an emphasis on events in the 20th century. Denmark's relatively late prohibition of sodomy, compared to other European countries, and the impetus for its subsequent decriminalization in 1933 in terms of the medical model of homosexuality are discussed. The social factors and the rationale behind the post-Second World War 'moral panic' are examined. The social changes in the 1960s and 1970s, and the rise of the gay liberation movement and more tolerant attitudes are described. The author also offers a detailed discussion of the 1989 registered partnership bill, describing the events leading up to the passing of the bill, the opponents' arguments, and the content of the legislation. Finally, there is brief commentary on why Denmark originated the registered partnership and what the future holds for same-sex relationships in Scandinavia in general. The article provides a very factual account and serves as a solid overview of this topic.

The rescue of the Danish Jews: moral courage under stress.
See item no. 129.

Overseas Populations

178　**A guide to the North American collections of the Danish Emigration Archives.**
　　　Nancy Ruth Bartlett.　Aalborg, Denmark: The Danish Emigration Archives, 1997. 369p.

This is the first printed guide to the personal papers and institutional records of the Danish Emigration Archives, which was founded in Aalborg, Denmark in 1930. The work provides an overview of the contents of the collections, and discusses their history as well as their research strengths. The guide's main purpose is to serve as an access tool to these original source materials relating to emigration to the United States and Canada. The guide contains 637 personal archives, the records of thirty-nine organizations, and an overview of the issues of eighty-two Danish-American newspapers and magazines available at the Archives. The personal archives include year of emigration; residence and occupation in Denmark and abroad; information on the size, scope, and content of the collection such as letters, clippings, and obituaries; and additional background information. There is also search field information for use of the 'Paradox' database (a summary description for each processed archival collection). English translations of important Danish archival terms are provided.

179　**Danish emigration to Canada.**
　　　Edited by Henning Bender, Birgit Flemming Larsen, translated from the Danish by Karen Veien.　Aalborg, Denmark: Danes Worldwide Archives, 1991. 210p.

Portrays the history of Denmark in Canada and Danish emigration up to the 20th century in various essays by both Danish and Canadian authors. Among the topics covered here are an archaeological expedition to Norse settlements from the year 1000 in Northern Canada; the adventures of later explorers and traders; the hardships of the settlers on the Canadian prairies in Alberta in the late 1800s; the role of Danish churches in maintaining ties with Denmark and in preserving the Danish language; the influence of the Danish language on Canadian English; the role of the folk high schools in preserving Danish heritage; and a comparison of Danish and Canadian farming techniques.

180 **Danish emigration to New Zealand.**
Edited by Henning Bender, Birgit Flemming Larsen, translated from
the Danish by Karen Veien.   Aalborg, Denmark: Danes Worldwide
Archives, 1990. 132p.

The aim of this volume is to shed light on Danish emigration in an eastward direction,
a topic that has been only sporadically covered. Various essays by primarily Danish
authors offer a statistical overview of emigration to New Zealand from 1871 to 1970;
letters home from three very different settlers, with accompanying commentary; a
profile of pioneering Danish dairy farmers and their agricultural technology; an
historical overview of Scandinavian-New Zealand contacts; an account of the role of
Danish churches; and an autobiographical account by a child of Danish immigrants.

181 **A Danish saga.**
Sanpete, Utah: Sanpete Historical Writing Committee and the Utah
Humanities Council, 1997. 118p.

A collection of thirty essays that pertain in some way to Denmark and the Danes of
Sanpete County, Utah. The writers are all current or former residents of the area. The
writings are based on actual people and events relating to the area's original Danish
settlers. The stories relate information from family records, historical registries,
interviews, and personal recollections. The book also includes several personal
photographs.

182 **Church divided: Lutheranism among the Danish immigrants.**
Thorvald Hansen.   Des Moines, Iowa: Grand View College, 1992.
161p. bibliog.

This book deals with the schism in the Danish Lutheran Church in America in 1894.
This divide reflected the differences between the theological concepts of N. F. S.
Grundtvig versus the pietism and rationalism of the Inner Mission. These two factions
existed in one mother Church in Denmark, but divided for a time in the United States.
The author explores the theological differences, the causes of the friction, the key
players involved, and the important meetings and conventions that took place. The
present day finds the two factions reunited, but the struggle represents a milestone in
the history of the Church among the immigrants. An opening chapter discusses the
'push and pull factors' that precipitated Danish emigration to the United States. Three
appendices provide a chart of Danish Lutheran Church groups in America, active
pastors in the Danish Lutheran Church in America from 1894, and the Church's
constitution and rules of procedure, adopted in 1893.

183 **Danish emigration to U. S. A.**
Edited by Birgit Flemming Larsen, Henning Bender, translated from
the Danish by Karen Veien.   Aalborg, Denmark: Danes Worldwide
Archives, 1992. 246p. bibliog.

In various essays, authors from both Denmark and the United States describe the many
different aspects of emigration and assimilation, and review the contributions of
Danes to American society over the last two centuries. The preservation of cultural
identity and heritage is described in essays about significant Danish-American writers,
the establishment of libraries, the founding of churches, and the use of religious
symbols as ethnic markers. Other topics include language assimilation and the

recollection of Danish; the hardships of Midwest settlement in the late 1800s; an account of the emigration experience of three clans; and an overview of current research and preservation efforts. There is also a thorough account of the Danish Immigration Museum in Iowa. This volume, includes an extensive bibliography of books, articles, and dissertations published after 1976 that treat the Danish-American experience.

184 **Blossoms of the prairie: the history of the Danish Lutheran churches in Nebraska.**
Jean M. Matteson, Edith M. Matteson. Lincoln, Nebraska: Blossoms of the Prairie, 1988. 247p. map. bibliog.

A comprehensive and detailed account that follows the chronological development of Danish Lutheran churches and mission sites in Nebraska from the1860s to the 1930s. The book is divided into two parts. Part one is a general history which discusses immigration and early church activity, the first pastors, the issue of Americanization and the switch to English usage, and other Danish organizations such as schools and social groups. Part two examines each congregation's history. The congregation's founding, pastors, and individual members are described, and interrelationships among the congregations are also examined. The book is extensively researched and includes numerous chapter notes and photographs. Biographical information on every pastor known to have served in Nebraska's Danish Lutheran churches from the time of their founding to the time they stopped using the Danish language is provided in an appendix.

185 **Out on the wind: Poles and Danes in Lincoln County, Minnesota, 1880-1905.**
John Radzilowski. Marshall, Minnesota: Crossings Press, 1992. 127p. maps. bibliog.

A study in ethnic history on the American prairie in southwest Minnesota. This work traces the two immigrant groups through their early settlement of the area, the economic crisis during the 1890s, and the following years of prosperity. Comparisons are drawn on various factors such as age and patterns of assimilation. Poles and Danes are also compared to the many other immigrant groups in the area at the time. The author devotes particular attention to the ways in which the Danes in Hope Township adjusted to the New World, and at the same time, succeeded in preserving their cultural heritage with the building of the Danebod Church and Folk School.

186 **Solvang: Denmark in the USA.**
Joanne Rife. Solvang, California: The Trykkeri Press, 1987. 3rd rev. ed. 49p.

A portrait of the Danish town of Solvang founded in 1911 in California's Santa Ynez Valley. This is a charming little book that provides a history of the founding of the town and a portrait of daily life. There are also descriptions of the significant buildings, organizations, cultural events and traditions, and the many hallmarks of the Danish heritage. A street map of the town and a chronology of important events in Solvang's first 75 years is also provided. The book contains numerous black-and-white and colour photographs.

187 **A new life: Danish emigration to North America as described by the emigrants themselves in letters 1842-1946.**
Niels Peter Stilling, Anne Lisbeth Olsen, translated from the Danish by Karen Veien. Aalborg, Denmark: Danes Worldwide Archives, 1994. 223p.

Tells the story of Danish emigration through passages from more than 1,000 letters sent to Denmark during a century of emigration. The passages and accompanying narrative text are organized in themes that include such topics as: the reasons for emigration, the journey across the Atlantic, first impressions of the New World, the struggle to become a farmer, family life and the experiences of women, and views on America. There is also a list of the letter-writers that includes the date of birth, birthplace, trade or background, year of emigration, and home and trade in the United States. Chapter notes refer the reader to select literature.

188 **Harmonien: an ethnohistorical sociolinguistic analysis of a Danish-American organization.**
Marianne Stølen. Odense, Denmark: Odense University Press, 1993. 159p. bibliog.

This work is the author's dissertation research published in book form. It traces the history of Harmonien, an organization for social and cultural exchange, which was founded in 1911 in Seattle, Washington. The basic issue examined here is how immigrants maintain their ethnic identity and at the same time adapt to the new culture. The emphasis is on the verbal manifestation of culture, i.e., language use. The study is essentially two investigations. A small-scale community study examines the changes over time of the community's identity, noting how it maintains its own cohesion and also adapts to the larger society. A micro-language study examines the Danish language usage of one individual as evidence of the preservation of Harmonien as an ethnic organization. The ethnographic nature of the research makes this work a rich information source on this example of Danish emigrants in America, which could be appreciated even by those readers without a background in sociolinguistics.

Language

Miscellaneous

189   Tense and mood in English: a comparison with Danish.
Niels Davidsen-Nielsen.   Berlin; New York: Mouton de Gruyter,
1990. 224p. bibliog. (Topics in English Linguistics, no. 1).
This is a professional book intended for advanced students, teachers, and professional
linguists. It compares time and modality expressions, realized grammatically, in
English with the corresponding categories in Danish. The focus on grammar omits
lexical time and modality expressions. Tense is interpreted as a broad category and
includes the perfect and future constructions. Mood is assumed to comprise morpho-
logically signalled constructions, such as the subjunctive and the imperative, as well
as syntactically signalled constructions, such as possibility and necessity. The book
aims both to give a detailed description of English and Danish usage, and to analyse
how tense and mood can be interpreted in the two languages. One of its main purposes
is to provide a descriptive basis for effective teaching material for advanced students.
Although the book assumes a knowledge of linguistics, advanced language learners
without this background might benefit from the examples given throughout the text.

190   More than loan-words: English influence on Danish.
Fritz Larsen.   *RASK*, vol. 1, no. 1 (1994), p. 21-46.
This article examines the implications of the persistent and massive influence of
English for the survival of the Danish language. The focus is on vocabulary and
semantic developments, in terms of 'covert influence', i.e., instances where there may
have been parallel, independent Danish development, such that the connection with
English cannot always be proved. The impact of English is demonstrated via some
seventy examples of the different ways that the presence of English manifests itself in
Danish. These examples include: loan words (the borrowing of an actual word),
semantic loans (the modification of the meaning of an existing Danish word), and loan
translations (the combining of existing Danish words in a new way). The author also
addresses the various perceptions and fears surrounding the alteration of the recipient

language in a situation of cultural dominance. The prejudice regarding bilingualism receives particular emphasis. The article helps to round out the debate over the future of the Danish language. On a lighter note, readers with a knowledge of Danish will find these examples interesting and fun to read.

191 **English and Danish contrasted: a guide for translators.**
Knud Sørensen.   Copenhagen: Munksgaard, 1991. 132p.

This book is meant as a guide for those who have to translate from Danish to English and vice versa. It is not a full contrastive grammar of the two languages. Rather, it discusses a number of areas where the two languages differ that experience has shown are problems for translators. The book was intended for Danish students of English, but of course can be used by those in the opposite situation. Since it is meant to be a practical book, it is not burdened by linguistic theory, although some linguistic terminology is used. Numerous examples are provided to illustrate the selected problem areas. The author emphasizes that the translator's task is to achieve linguistic and semantic equivalence; the result should be an idiomatic and cohesive translation, and not one that reads like a translation. Although this work is for translators who are assumed to possess a thorough knowledge of both languages, the information presented here can also benefit the intermediate language student.

Dictionaries

192 **Dansk-engelsk ordbog.** (Danish-English dictionary.)
Jens Axelsen.   Copenhagen: Gyldendal, 1995. 10th ed. 1,040p.
(Gyldendals Røde Ordbøger).

This is a hard-cover desk dictionary that contains 65,000 main entries. An irregular verb list is also included.

193 **Engelsk-dansk ordbog.** (English-Danish dictionary.)
Jens Axelsen.   Copenhagen: Gyldendal, 1997. 12th ed. 724p.
(Gyldendals Røde Ordbøger).

This is a hard-cover desk dictionary that contains 50,000 main entries and 25,000 expressions and phrases. An irregular verb list is also included.

194 **Engelsk-dansk/dansk-engelsk ordbog.** (English-Danish/Danish-English dictionary.)
Jens Axelsen.   Copenhagen: Gyldendal, 1998. 1,764p. (Gyldendals Røde Ordbøger).

This is the first paperback edition that combines the English-Danish and Danish-English dictionaries. The English-Danish part contains 50,000 main entries and 25,000 expressions. The Danish-English part contains 65,000 main entries. An irregular verb list is also included.

195 **Politikens visuelle ordbog: dansk engelsk tysk fransk.** (Politiken's visual dictionary: Danish English German French.)
Jean-Claude Corbeil, Ariane Archambault. Copenhagen: Politikens Publishers, 1992. 958p.

A conceptual, practical dictionary that is fully illustrated. The volume contains over 25,000 words in each language and over 3,500 illustrations. It is organized by topic so that words appear in their natural context, and so that the user can find a word without actually knowing it. The work covers all aspects of the physical surroundings of daily life in twenty-seven topical areas, examples of which include: plant and animal life, transport, communication, sport and leisure, and human anatomy. The words have been selected from texts written by experts in the given field.

196 **Juridisk ordbog: dansk-engelsk.** (Legal dictionary: Danish-English.)
Helle Pals Frandsen. Copenhagen: Gad, 1996. 207p.

This dictionary covers a variety of legal terminology in areas such as family and inheritance law, property, contract, and tort law, procedural law, public law, international law, and laws relating to the European Union.

197 **Juridisk ordbog: engelsk-dansk.** (Legal dictionary: English-Danish.)
Helle Pals Frandsen. Copenhagen: Gad, 1996. 2nd ed. 216p.

This dictionary covers numerous areas of legal terminology with special attention being paid to business law. Many examples of word usage in context are provided. It is based on both British and American English.

198 **Danish-English English-Danish dictionary.**
Revised by Marianne Holmen. New York: Hippocrene Books, 1990. 601p. (Hippocrene Practical Dictionary).

This is pocket-sized and good for the traveller. The definitions are basic and not extensive, but each entry provides more than enough to get by on. Entries also include compound words and idiomatic expressions where relevant.

199 **Engelsk-dansk ordbog.** (English-Danish dictionary.)
B. Kjærulff Nielsen. Copenhagen: Gyldendal, 1998. 6th ed. 1,824p. (Gyldendals Store Ordbøger).

This is a comprehensive English-Danish dictionary which contains 120,000 main entries and 50,000 expressions and phrases.

200 **Teknisk ordbog – dansk-engelsk.** (Technical dictionary – Danish-English.)
Edited by Thomas Nielsen. Copenhagen: L. & R. Fakta, 1997. 439p.

This paperback dictionary contains 30,000 main entries and also includes commonly used expressions. It emphasizes British English terminology, but it also offers American English terms. It covers many technical areas such as automobiles, planes, agriculture, computers, construction, chemistry, electronics, the environment, forestry, graphics, metals, photography, physics, statistics, telecommunications, television, and the media.

201 **Teknisk ordbog – engelsk-dansk.** (Technical dictionary – English-Danish.)
Edited by Thomas Nielsen. Copenhagen: L. & R. Fakta, 1997. 447p.
This paperback dictionary contains 30,000 main entries and also includes commonly used expressions. Its emphasis is on British English, but it also contains American English entries. It covers many technical areas such as automobiles, planes, agriculture, computers, construction, chemistry, electronics, the environment, forestry, graphics, metals, photography, physics, statistics, telecommunications, television, and the media.

202 **Dansk-engelsk industriordbog.** (Danish-English industrial dictionary.)
Jørgen Rohde. Copenhagen: Gyldendal, 1998. 1,222p.
This comprehensive Danish-English dictionary contains some 87,800 main entries in the most relevant technical and commercial topic areas. It also provides many examples of word usage in context.

203 **Engelsk-dansk idiomordbog.** (English-Danish dictionary of idioms.)
Linda B. Smith. Copenhagen: Paludan, 1995. 158p.
This handy dictionary contains idioms used in everyday language as well as expressions specific to finance, politics, and commerce. It is alphabetized by the most significant word in the English phrase, usually a noun. The English phrase or phrases are then presented in contextual examples followed by their Danish equivalents.

204 **Dansk-engelsk økonomisk ordbog.** (Danish-English economic dictionary.)
Annemette Lyng Svensson. Frederiksberg: Samfundslitteratur, 1996. 2nd ed. 424p.
This dictionary contains terminology related to accounting, finance, banking, insurance, and marketing. It includes the more common terminology as well as special economic terms.

205 **Engelsk-dansk økonomisk ordbog.** (English-Danish economic dictionary.)
Annemette Lyng Svensson. Frederiksberg: Samfundslitteratur, 1994. 3rd ed. 397p.
This dictionary contains terminology for accounting, finance, banking, insurance, and marketing. It is a bit short on examples of word usage in context.

206 **Dansk-engelsk handelsordbog 'for many reasons'.** (Danish-English business dictionary 'for many reasons'.)
Dorthe Unnerup-Madsen. Holstebro: Ventus, 1997. 6th ed. 707p.
This dictionary is aimed at translators, but its also useful for students and for those employed in the business community. It emphasizes word use in context and in practice. Each main entry contains numerous examples of the word in commonly used phrases and connections. It contains the most up-to-date and relevant business terminology. It is based on British English.

207 **Engelsk-dansk erhvervsfagligordbog 'for many reasons'.**
(Danish-English vocational dictionary 'for many reasons'.)
Dorthe Unnerup-Madsen.   Holstebro: Ventus, 1996. 686p.

This dictionary is aimed at both those employed in the business community as well as students in institutions of higher education. It covers many business-related areas such as trade and commerce, transport, marketing, advertising, information technology, politics, insurance, banking, and finance. It is also useful for legal and European Union terminology. Numerous contextual examples are provided.

208 **Dansk-engelsk ordbog.** (Danish-English dictionary.)
Hermann Vinterberg, C. A. Bodelsen.   Copenhagen: Gyldendal, 1998.
4th ed. 2,610p. (Gyldendals Store Ordbøger).

This is a comprehensive Danish-English dictionary. The preface did not specifically mention the number of entries, except to state that there have been 40,000 changes since the third edition, one half of which are additions. The work for this current edition began in 1990. The dictionary covers the Danish language since 1800, but the emphasis is on the language since 1950.

Courses and grammars

209 **Danish: a comprehensive grammar.**
Robin Allan, Philip Holmes, Tom Lundskær-Nielsen.   London; New York: Routledge, 1995. 628p. bibliog.

This is a substantial reference work on all aspects of Danish grammar. It is meant to serve as an aid to beginners, as well as the more advanced student, and to teachers. It is both general and comparative, concentrating on the areas which pose special problems for English speakers. The work aims at a balance between the accuracy of linguistic description on the one hand, and clarity and usability by non-linguists on the other. It is written for non-linguists, and many linguistic terms are defined. A comprehensive index facilitates rapid location of problem areas and details.

210 **Say it in Danish.**
Gerda M. Andersen.   New York: Dover Publications, 1958. 165p.

This is a pocket-sized, handy book for the traveller. It makes available, in simple form, most of the words and sentences you need to make yourself understood in everyday situations. The translations are idiomatic rather than literal, and the pronunciation is transcribed in a simple phonetic system. This is not a grammar book. Every phrase or sentence is complete in itself and can be used without a knowledge of grammar. The framework is also designed to help you form additional sentences with word substitution. The book contains over 1,440 practical entries. An extensive index helps you to locate the appropriate expression quickly.

Language. Courses and grammars

211 **Scandinavian Europe phrasebook.**
Ingibjörg Árnadóttir, Peter A. Crozier, Markus Lehtipuu, Doekes
Lulofs, Pär Sörme. Hawthorne, Australia; Oakland, California;
London; Paris: Lonely Planet Publications, 1997. 2nd ed. 349p.

A small pocket-sized phrasebook for Danish, Finnish, Icelandic, Norwegian, and
Swedish. The first section covers Danish, with a brief introduction to the language and
its pronunciation rules. That is followed by topical sections, examples of which
include 'greetings and civilities', 'emergencies', 'paperwork', 'accommodation', and
'shopping'. Each entry provides the English, the Danish, and a phonetic translation.
The book uses a simplified phonetic translation based on the International Phonetic
Alphabet. The editors caution, of course, that this can only approximate the exact
sounds of a language.

212 **Teach yourself Danish: a complete course for beginners.**
Bente Ellsworth. Chicago, Illinois: NTC Publishing Group, 1994.
281p. (Teach Yourself Books). (NTC Publishing Group, 4255 West
Toughy Avenue, Lincolnwood, Illinois 60646).

This course is written by a Dane who has been teaching Danish to native English
speakers since 1975 and is familiar with their particular problems. The course is
intended for absolute beginners and assumes no knowledge of any other foreign
language. The book aims to enable the learner to communicate in a wide range of
everyday situations. Each of the eighteen units contains dialogues, vocabulary,
comprehension questions, grammar notes, and exercises. The book comes with two
sound cassettes.

213 **Teach yourself Danish.**
H. A. Koefoed. New York: David McKay Company, 1989. 232p.
Originally published, Sevenoaks, England: Hodder & Stoughton, 1958.

This book is intended for language instruction at home, at your own pace, and
assumes no previous experience with Danish. The emphasis is on colloquial and
conversational Danish, and the texts incorporate the most common words and
expressions. The lessons are presented in an interesting context that also introduces
the student to aspects of Danish life and culture. In order to ensure an authentic
picture of the language and to show the different styles in use today, some texts are
borrowed from Danish literature. Each lesson has grammatical notes, oral and written
exercises, and corresponding answer keys. There are also separate sections on
grammar and pronunciation. An index of the 1,000 most common Danish words is
provided with references to their use in the texts.

76

Religion

Miscellaneous

214 **N. F. S. Grundtvig: an introduction to his life and work.**
A. M. Allchin. Aarhus, Denmark: Aarhus University Press; London:
Darton, Longman & Todd, 1997. 338p. bibliog.
This book offers an extended presentation of Grundtvig as a theologian. The book is
divided into three parts. Part one is biographical, but it is not meant to be complete or
balanced. Rather it provides a series of 'glimpses' into Grundtvig's life, focusing on a
few crucial, defining moments. Part two looks at five basic themes in Grundtvig's
writing, focusing primarily on the theological. It discusses Grundtvig's discovery of
the one Church of Christ and explains his vision of God and his embracement of the
doctrine of the Trinity. These theological views inform Grundtvig's view of social life
and human relationships. Part three presents doctrines of the Christian faith contained
in the many sermons and hymns written by Grundtvig for the Christian year. This
work is a significant contribution to the literature on Grundtvig in English. It contains
numerous quotations, most of which are translated here for the first time.

215 **A people and its church: the Lutheran Church in Denmark.**
Verner Bruhn, translated from the Danish by Michael Cain.
Copenhagen: The Church of Denmark Council on Inter-Church
Relations, 1994. 120p.
This book, which has been published specifically for a foreign readership, outlines the
development of the Church in Denmark from its inception up to the present day. The
book is divided into historical chapters. The missionary period discusses the Viking
age and the Danes' conversion to Christianity. The medieval period examines the
conflict and cooperation between the monarchy and the Church, and the Church's role
in education and culture. The Reformation and the Enlightenment describe a new
organization and a new liturgy, and the Church under the absolute monarchy. Modern
times of the 19th and the early 20th centuries examines the influence of the revivalists,

of Grundtvig, and of Kierkegaard, as well as the effects of industrialization and urbanization on Danish society, and the democratization of the Church. The questions confronting the Church today in terms of a changing of society are discussed. Concluding chapters describe the organization of the Church and its ecumenical activities.

216   **Communities of faith: sectarianism, identity, and social change on a Danish island.**
Andrew Buckser.   Providence, Rhode Island; Oxford: Berghahn Books, 1996. 264p. bibliog. (New Directions in Anthropology, vol. 5).

An ethnographic study that traces the rise of three religious groups on the small island of Mors from 1837 to 1990. Using interviews, participant observation and local archival material, the author aims to account for the why the Free Congregation, the Inner Mission, and the Apostolic Church arose when and where they did, why they declined after the Second World War, and why they still survive in modern society. The study examines the interaction between social change and religious awakening, and religion's role in creating identity and community for its members. The work involves a critique of secularization theory with its inherent assumption that science inevitably destroys religious institutions. The study also purports to be a redefinition of modern religion in terms of symbolic anthropology. This community-based research also provides a look into a little-studied culture on this interior island of western Jutland. This work is significant in terms of Denmark's reputation as a modern, progressive nation with an apparent lack of religion. It is an academic work that assumes some background knowledge, but it is quite accessible to the general reader.

217   **Freedom of religion in Denmark.**
Hanne Fledelius, Birgitte Ruul.   Copenhagen: The Danish Centre for Human Rights, 1992. 115p. bibliog.

This report is intended as a sort of handbook on the legal protection of religious freedom. The opening sections cover general aspects of international human rights law, define terminology such as 'religion' and 'tolerance', and describe the international organizations that guarantee human rights such as the United Nations and the Council of Europe. Other sections review Danish domestic legislation covering religious and related freedoms. The text of several articles of the constitution, as well as statutory law and special acts are included. The legal status of religious groups is described. There is extensive discussion on the extent to which Danish domestic law and practice conforms with international obligations in various situations where religious freedom is relevant. Among these are religion in the school, marriage laws, adoption laws, labour practices, objections to medical treatment, objections to military service, and treatment of prisoners. Procedures for the enforcement of human rights protections are outlined. Denmark's implementation of the European Convention on Human Rights is also discussed. This is a significant report given the fact that Denmark has become home to many migrant workers and refugees of various cultural backgrounds.

218 **Scandinavian values: religion and morality in the Nordic countries.**
Edited by Thorleif Pettersson, Ole Riis.   Uppsala, Sweden: Acta
Universitatis Upsaliensis, 1994. 212p. (Psychologia et Sociologia
Religionum, 10).

This volume comprises a series of research papers in the sociology of religion most of
which are based on survey data from the European Value Systems Study. The papers
represent the five Nordic countries (Norway, Iceland, Finland, Sweden, and Denmark)
and present and discuss findings for the individual nations and for the region as a
whole. Among the topics covered here are patterns of secularization as indicated by
commitment to religious institutions and the salience of religious beliefs; secularization's relationship with political attitudes, educational level, age, and gender; the
relationship between religious orientation and views on life and death such as suicide,
euthanasia, abortion, and killing in self-defence; gender differences in religious
values; and the relationship between national identity and degree of religiosity. The
opening chapter is actually a revised and extended version of a paper entitled
'Religious change in the five Scandinavian countries, 1930-1980' (*Comparative Social
Research*, vol. 10, 1987, p. 145-81) which compares religious conditions in the five
countries in terms of the official position of religion and its relationship to other social
institutions; the organizational development of the state churches; and the extent of
the people's participation in religious activities. It is an important foundation for the
rest of the volume.

Church divided: Lutheranism among the Danish immigrants.
See item no. 182.

**Blossoms of the prairie: the history of the Danish Lutheran churches in
Nebraska.**
See item no. 184.

Pre-Christian religion

219 **The Viking gods: pagan myths of Nordic peoples.**
Clive Barret.   Wellingborough, England: The Aquarian Press, 1989.
175p. bibliog.

This book is meant for a general audience. The introduction offers basic background
information on the origins of Viking mythology and the available sources of information. Subsequent chapters tell the tales of significant gods and goddesses. The book
contains nearly as many illustrations as it does text and reads like a storybook.

220 **The Penguin book of Norse myths: gods of the Vikings.**
Retold by Kevin Crossley-Holland.   London; New York: Penguin
Books, 1993. 276p. bibliog.

A collection of thirty-two myths with an extensive introduction. The opening sections
provide background on the Norse world, such as the nine worlds of the Norse cosmology;

a biographical survey of the Norse pantheon; and a survey of the primary literary sources including the work of Snorri Sturluson and Saxo Grammaticus. This scholarly work is also accessible to the general reader. It provides extensive endnotes, as well as a glossary of names and important terminology.

221 The lost beliefs of northern Europe.

Hilda Ellis Davidson.   London; New York: Routledge, 1993. 181p. bibliog.

This scholarly work is not meant to be an account of myths and beliefs themselves, but rather a consideration of the sources of information regarding pre-Christian religion in northern and western Europe. The work describes and evaluates the different types of evidence, pointing out the problems, as well as examining how our understanding of myths has been furthered. The sources discussed here include archaeological finds such as burial and ceremonial artefacts, memorial stones, and ornaments; accounts of mythical geography such as the sites of mythical battles and contests; and evidence of pre-Christian religious practices such as communal worship, and the cults of gods and goddesses. The final chapter considers various theoretical approaches to pre-Christian religion. Although much of the written source material on this topic is the Icelandic sagas, some of the archaeological evidence mentioned here is specific to Denmark.

222 Myths and symbols in pagan Europe: early Scandinavian and Celtic religions.

H. R. Ellis Davidson.   Manchester, England: Manchester University Press, 1988. 268p. bibliog.

A scholarly work that compares the religious beliefs of the Celts, Germans and Scandinavians, and attempts to account for a common origin of these beliefs extending to prehistory. The author looks for evidence of religious practices, and of the belief in a supernatural world, through an examination of archaeological evidence, and literature and folklore evidence, primarily from Iceland and Ireland. The author examines evidence of holy places and burial sites, rituals and sacrifice, battle rites such as the taking of heads, battle gods and goddesses, land spirits and ancestors, prophecy and dream interpretation, and myths and their interpretation. Some of the archaeological finds and pre-Christian art discoveries are located in Denmark. This is a well-researched work that is meant for both teachers and students of history and religion.

223 Scandinavian mythology.

H. R. Ellis Davidson.   London: Hamlyn Publishing Group, 1969. Rev. ed., 1982. Reprinted, 1988. 144p. bibliog.

A popular treatment of the stories of the gods that makes use of the source materials. The introduction discusses the sources of evidence and their significance. These include archaeology and art, the interpretation of Norse mythology in the works of Christian writers such as the Danish historian Saxo Grammaticus, and Icelandic poet and historian, Snorri Sturluson, and the poetic sources such as the Edda. The book includes numerous black-and-white and colour photographs of archaeological finds. The final chapter addresses the spread of Christianity and the intermingling of the storytelling of pagan and Christian religions. This book has also been published under the title *Viking & Norse mythology* (London: Chancellor Press, 1994. Reprinted, 1996. 144 p.).

224 An introduction to Viking mythology.
John Grant. London: Grange Books, 1990. 128p.
This is a basic book for a general audience. It presents a collection of creation myths, stories of individual gods, goddesses and heroes, and an account of the pre-Christian version of revelation. Chapter one is a dictionary of significant names and terminology in Viking mythology. Each entry provides a brief definition. The work includes many colour photographs and illustrations. A very short reading list is also provided.

225 Scandinavia.
Carolyne Larrington. In: *The feminist companion to mythology*.
Edited by Carolyne Larrington. London: Pandora Press, 1992,
p. 137-61. bibliog.
This book chapter is divided into five sections. The opening section is a description of the mythological world and the pantheon. Subsequent sections survey the various typologies of myths about women where goddesses are portrayed in various roles such as wives and mothers, the reluctant girl to be wooed, victims of abduction, brides, deviants accused of sexual misconduct, and warriors and heroines, as well as other females beings such as giantesses. Concluding sections comment on the state of Norse scholarship on women in myth, and the post-classical treatment of myth. The chapter is a solid reference source that provides a concise overview.

226 Norse myths.
R. I. Page. Austin, Texas: University of Texas Press, 1990. 80p. map.
(The Legendary Past Series).
A retelling of Norse legends about some of the more well-known gods and the mythical world. This work is of special interest in terms of its translations from major source materials. The introduction discusses these main sources such as the Edda and skaldic verses. There is a short section with suggestions for further reading.

227 Prolonged echoes: old Norse myths in medieval northern society. Volume I: the myths.
Margaret Clunies Ross. Odense, Denmark: Odense University Press,
1994. 325p. bibliog. (The Viking Collection. Studies in Northern
Civilization, vol. 7).
A study of old Norse myth in its Scandinavian cultural context. This work attempts to bring out broad-based cultural themes in the myths and what they mean for early Scandinavian thought. The author moves between discussions of the myths as a unified body of text and the meanings of individual texts. The work is not meant to be a standard description of the myths; it is a scholarly analysis and assumes some background knowledge. The classes and attributes of supernatural beings, their social world and social relations, and the concepts of creation, sacrifice and death are discussed. The author observes that Nordic mythology is always in a state of reinterpretation and takes into account medieval reformulations of old Norse myth. The book deals mainly with Icelandic myth sources and reinterpretations as these represent some of the richest evidence on this subject.

Cassell dictionary of Norse myth and legend.
See item no. 651.

Scandinavian mythology: an annotated bibliography.
See item no. 665.

Søren Kierkegaard

228 **Foundations of Kierkegaard's vision of community: religion, ethics and politics in Kierkegaard.**
Edited by George B. Connell, C. Stephen Evans.   Atlantic Highlands, New Jersey; London: Humanities Press, 1992. 245p.

A collection of essays by various scholars that aims to refute the view that Kierkegaard's category of the individual is an endorsement of 'asocial individualism', but rather is part of his vision of community. The book is divided into three parts. Part one addresses Kierkegaard's religious vision with three essays that examine the dialectic of God's transcendence and immanence. Part two looks at ethical thought, with three essays that examine the implications of Kierkegaard's characteristic dialectic for ethics and the relational self. Part three includes seven essays that document the reorientation of Kierkegaard's later writings toward the external, the objective, and the socio-political. These authors attempt to discern the implications of Kierkegaard's insights for modern-day social problems and political issues.

229 **Passionate reason: making sense of Kierkegaard's *Philosophical fragments*.**
C. Stephen Evans.   Bloomington, Indiana; Indianapolis: Indiana University Press, 1992. 205p.

A detailed examination of *Philosophical fragments* for the serious reader of Kierkegaard. This book treats this important pseudonymous work as a literary whole, scrutinizing its structure, purpose and order, as well as paying special attention to its irony. It also provides a contemporary reading of the work and places Kierkegaard's philosophy in the context of modern religious thought. The author finds the work to be relevant for the present day in terms of the meaning of (historical) Christianity for the here and now, and in terms of the place of (passionate) reason in the contemporary world.

230 **Kierkegaard.**
Patrick Gardiner.   Oxford; New York: Oxford University Press, 1988. Reprinted, 1996. 120p.

This is an introductory text on the life and thought of Søren Kierkegaard (1813-55) that is of admittedly limited scope. The author confines his discussion to Kierkegaard's distinctive positions on the status of ethics and religion, themes that most reflect the intellectual and cultural preoccupations of his time. This work examines the life and character of Kierkegaard to show how his views developed, and contrasts his positions to those of Kant, Hegel and Marx. Kierkegaard's emphasis on individual choice and its implications for existentialism is critically discussed. Finally, the author shows how Kierkegaard has influenced contemporary ethical theory and religious thought.

231   **Kierkegaard as religious thinker.**
David J. Gouwens.   Cambridge, England; New York; Melbourne,
Australia: Cambridge University Press, 1996. 248p. bibliog.

Approaches Kierkegaard as a religious thinker, which refers to the idea that 'his
thought is about religion and at the same time is religious' and provides the reader
with lessons in 'religious ways of thinking and living'. The author explains that this
view deviates from other approaches to Kierkegaard, which can be classified as
biographical, philosophical, deconstructionist, theological, or existentialist. Among
the topics discussed here are Kierkegaard's critique of Western philosophical and
theological reflection and his alternative subjective thinking approach to philosophy
and religion, i.e., psychological analysis combined with Christian concepts in a
religious understanding of the self. Kierkegaard's treatment of religion also includes
his notions of becoming religious, becoming and being Christian, and his understanding
of the relationship between Christ and the three Christian virtues: faith, hope, and
love. This work assumes some background knowledge but should be accessible to the
general reader.

232   **Kierkegaard, godly deceiver: the nature and meaning of his
pseudonymous writings.**
M. Holmes Hartshorne.   New York; Oxford: Columbia University
Press, 1990. 112p. bibliog.

The premise of this work is that Kierkegaard's own beliefs cannot be discovered in his
pseudonymous writings. This work focuses on Kierkegaard the ironist who was
profoundly influenced by Socrates. The author argues that Kierkegaard's parodies
have often been mistakenly taken as his own positions, and that although his use of
irony is commonly recognized, it is frequently ignored in interpretations of his works.
This work makes clear the ironic character of the pseudonymous writings and also
unveils their serious purpose. Indeed, Kierkegaard's subtlety may have obscured the
truth he wanted his readers to see. These pseudonymous writings are then compared to
two of his religious writings in order to contrast Kierkegaard's own position with that
of the pseudonyms.

233   **The philosophy of religion in Kierkegaard's writings.**
J. Thomas Heywood.   Lewiston, New York; Queenston, Ontario;
Lampeter, Wales: Edwin Mellen Press, 1994. 192p. bibliog. (Studies in
the History of Philosophy, vol. 30).

Discusses Kierkegaard's attempt to understand the nature of religious faith, i.e., to
what extent is faith knowledge. Through an examination of Kierkegaard's themes of
subjectivity and paradox, we see that faith requires uncertainty and can never be
completely objective. The paradox of faith is that it consists of both an inner certainty
and an objective lack of certainty. Faith is subjectivity and subjectivity is truth for the
individual. This work opens with an examination of the historical context of
Kierkegaard's philosophy with an emphasis on the anti-Hegelian aspects of his thinking. The question of the existence of God is also addressed in the light of the theme of
subjectivity. The final chapter is a six-point summary of Kierkegaard's significance
for the philosophy of religion. This is a scholarly work that assumes a knowledge of
philosophy.

234   **The point of view.**
Søren Kierkegaard, edited and translated by Howard V. Hong and
Edna H. Hong.   Princeton, New Jersey: Princeton University Press,
1998. 351p.

This work provides complete translations of *On my work as an author*, *The point of view for my work as an author*, and *Armed neutrality*. In addition to the main text, the translators provide an historical introduction regarding the original publication of these works and selected entries from Kierkegaard's journals and papers pertaining to the three works. Extensive notes are provided and the reader is also referred to general bibliographies of Kierkegaard studies.

235   *Works of love*: **some Christian deliberations in the form of discourses.**
Søren Kierkegaard, edited and translated by Howard V. Hong and
Edna H. Hong.   Princeton, New Jersey: Princeton University Press,
1996. 561p.

This is Kierkegaard's climactic consideration of erotic love and Christian (or religious-ethical) love, where, most significantly, love is viewed as a deed rather than a feeling. *Works of love* was originally published in 1847 in two parts, the 'First Series' and the 'Second Series'. In addition to the main text, the translators provide an historical introduction and selected entries from Kierkegaard's journals and papers pertaining to *Works of love*. Extensive notes are provided and the reader is also referred to general bibliographies of Kierkegaard studies.

236   **Encounters with Kierkegaard: a life as seen by his contemporaries.**
Edited by Bruce H. Kirmmse.   Princeton, New Jersey: Princeton
University Press, 1996. 358p. bibliog.

A collection of reputedly firsthand accounts in the form of letters, narratives and reports by those who knew Søren Kierkegaard. The collection serves as a sort of biography of this noted social and religious critic. Indeed, the first eight chapters are arranged to present his life in chronological order, covering his childhood and public school years, his university years, his engagement to Regina Schlegel, his formative years as a young writer, and his later years of controversy. Another chapter offers five portraits by his contemporaries. Two appendices provide the text of an 1849 public address by his brother, Peter Christian, and the Kierkegaard family tree. Detailed commentary is provided by the editor in extensive endnotes to each chapter. The bibliography offers works that are primarily in Danish. Since Søren Kierkegaard left neither memoirs nor an autobiography, this collection is a significant commentary on his life.

237   **Kierkegaard in Golden Age Denmark.**
Bruce H. Kirmmse.   Bloomington, Indianapolis: Indiana Univeristy
Press, 1990. 558p. bibliog.

Provides analysis and interpretation of Kierkegaard's writings against the backdrop of the social and political times in which he lived. The first part takes the reader through the agrarian reforms and the rise of the peasantry in the countryside juxtaposed with the Golden Age conservative politics and religion of the urban high culture in Copenhagen. A second part analyses this important writer's reflections on society, religion and politics, which tell us much about Danish society as it moved from an absolute monarchy to a constitutional and popular government. This is a comprehensive work that serves as not only a review of Kierkegaard's life and literary career, but also as an important information source on the country's social, religious, and political history. It is well researched and clearly written.

238 **Selves in discord and resolve: Kierkegaard's moral-religious psychology from *Either/or* to *Sickness unto death*.**
Edward Mooney. New York; London: Routledge, 1996. 140p. bibliog.

Considers Kierkegaard's attempts to explore issues of the self in works that, for example, trace the story of Job (*Eighteen upbuilding discourses*; *Repetition*) or the story of Abraham (*Fear and trembling*). Further, through *Either/or*, the author examines Kierkegaard's view of the role of choice in the development of moral personality, and in *Sickness unto death*, we see that Kierkegaard presents the self as a complex set of relationships. The author examines Kierkegaard's use of rational critique, poetic and literary portraits, and philosophical excursions to explore the self in motion, its identity and its aspirations. The author argues that Kierkegaard does not espouse a single theory of the self, but rather offers a moral-religious psychology for examining issues of the self. This is an academic book that is appropriate for both the scholar and for the student who is embarking on a study of this subject for the first time.

239 **A re-appraisal of Kierkegaard.**
Howard A. Slaaté. Lanham, Maryland; New York; London: University Press of America, 1995. 157p. bibliog.

Discusses Kierkegaard as a religious philosopher, focusing on his holistic interpretation of human existence. This Kierkegaard saw rationalistic philosophies as limited and stilted ways of thinking that failed to do justice to the total self. Rather, reason, intuition and emotions work together to give the self a complete picture of reality. Further, Kierkegaard embraced a faith perspective, a Christ-focused faith, and saw the need for a higher type of ethics. This volume examines Kierkegaard's philosophical perspective with discussions of the meaning of existence as it pertains to the individual self; the problem of pure reason given that human existence is irrational and transrational; and the basis of ethics, in terms of individualism and existentialism. Kierkegaard's religious impact is also discussed. This clearly written book assumes a knowledge of philosophy and theology, as well as a familiarity with Kierkegaard.

240 **Kierkegaard.**
Peter Vardy. London: Fount Paperbacks, 1996. 101p. (Fount Christian Thinkers).

This is an introductory text that aims to bring Kierkegaard's thoughts and intentions to the average reader in an accessible non-academic style. The author discusses how Kierkegaard deals with the related issues of faith and truth; explains Kierkegaard's three stages of life (the aesthetic, the ethical, and the religious); and discusses Kierkegaard's consideration of the God-relationship and his radical understanding of Christian love. In a different vein, the book also aims to help readers think through the meaning and purpose of their lives, and to reintroduce traditional Christianity and the notion of eternal truth to the modern world. The opening chapter is a brief biographical sketch. Suggestions for further reading are also provided.

241 **Kierkegaard.**
Julia Watkin.   London: Geoffrey Chapman, 1997. 120p. bibliog.
(Outstanding Christian Thinkers).
Discusses Kierkegaard as a Christian thinker who believed in the God of traditional
Christianity. However, as the author explains, this is sometimes difficult to see given
his often attack-like presentation of Christianity. This work first looks at
Kierkegaard's personal and cultural background, and his assumptions about the
Christian universe. It then goes on to explore his development as a writer, examining
the tensions in his authorship over Christianity on the one hand as 'godly enjoyment
of the world', and on the other hand as 'total self denial'. The book aims to present
Kierkegaard in a new light and to serve as an introduction to new readers. It also
deliberately avoids the traditional 'three stage' approach (the aesthetic, ethical, and
religious) to examining the movement of Kierkegaard's thought and writing. The
chapter on authorship provides a helpful chart that lists Kierkegaard's pseudonymous
works, works under his own name, and journals and papers.

242 **Kierkegaard and modern continental philosophy: an introduction.**
Michael Weston.   London; New York: Routledge, 1994. 200p.
Argues that Kierkegaard's pseudonymous writings, which are characterized by a
comic and ironic tone, represent his attempt to break away from traditional forms of
philosophy. The author applies Kierkegaard's 'ethical critique of philosophy' to the
metaphysical tradition of Hegel and Plato, as well as to the post-metaphysical thought
of Nietzsche, Heidegger, and Derrida. A fundamental difference between Kierkegaard
and these other thinkers is his emphasis on the first-person position from which any
individual, including the philosopher, must speak, i.e., the thinker is an individual
whose questioning about life must have the character of self-questioning carried out in
the first person, which precludes the essential philosophical exercise of a purely
intellectual inquiry. This is an academic work which assumes some knowledge of
philosophy.

**Søren Kierkegaard and his critics: an international bibliography of
criticism.**
See item no. 664.

Society

Social services, health and welfare

243 **The Nordic lights: new initiatives in health care systems.**
Edited by Anita Alban, Terkel Christiansen.   Odense, Denmark:
Odense University Press, 1995. 362p.

This book is a collection of concise articles by various scholars, several of which relate specifically to the Danish health care system. The historical roots of health care legislation, the role of the general practitioner as the gatekeeper of the system, the official goals of the health care system, and its organization, administration and financing are described. There is also a discussion of recent trends in the provision of health care such as the focus on patients' rights, the free choice of hospital, and maximum guaranteed waiting times for surgery. These new initiatives are evaluated in terms of quality of service, respect for the individual, equal access to services, and efficient use of resources. There is a special focus on the county of Funen's innovations in management, budget, and planning. Of particular importance here is the influence of local government on the delivery of public hospital services and the resulting increase in efficiency. Finally, the primary care sector is discussed from the perspective of both the patient and the provider, with an emphasis on the payment system and financing.

244 **The welfare state versus the social market economy – comparison and evaluation of housing policies in Denmark and West Germany with special importance attached to social housing and rent control.**
Hans Skifter Andersen, Asger Munk.   *Scandinavian Housing &*
Planning Research, vol. 11, no. 1 (February 1994), p. 1-25.

Compares the housing policies of Denmark and Germany as a means for examining general hypotheses regarding the influence of political ideology and economic conditions on housing policy and the housing market. The influence of Denmark's welfare state and Germany's social market economy on social housing, rent control and owner-occupied housing are examined. This comparative piece offers a good overview of Denmark's housing policy, as well as an examination of the societal conditions regarding housing, and the objectives and the effects of the country's housing policy. Various topics such as housing subsidies, general performance of the housing market, regulation of the private rental market, types of social housing, and tenant participation and influence are discussed. The authors conclude that economic conditions appear to have a greater influence on housing consumption and housing policy, and further, that Denmark has pursued a more egalitarian housing policy than Germany.

245 **Children's culture in Denmark.**
Bente Buchhave, Birgit Wanting. *Scandinavian Public Library Quarterly*, vol. 26, no. 3 (1993), p. 20-25.

A discussion of the country's official cultural policy on children, which came to be known as 'A good childhood in Denmark', and which was due to the efforts of a 1987 committee of representatives from fifteen different ministries. This umbrella policy has resulted in the implementation of various local projects under the name of 'Children as fellow citizens' and has resulted in specific policy regarding children built into Denmark's library act and the act on general education. This article provides background on the rationale for this policy and some brief commentary on local efforts.

246 **Retirement: a time of transition. Denmark.**
Bente Holmgaard. Dublin: European Foundation for the Improvement of Living and Working Conditions, 1985. 151p.

Part of a report on the 'impact of retirement on the living conditions of retired workers'. The research was conducted in three EU member states: Belgium, Denmark, and Ireland. This report for Denmark provides various research findings based on both national statistics and survey results for a random, national sample of pensioners aged 60-72. There is information on types of pension arrangements, pensioners' reasons for retirement and their attitudes towards retirement, and issues related to pensioners' living conditions such as health, finances, social contacts and use of social services. The report is primarily descriptive. A final section provides an overview of Danish policy regarding pensions and the elderly.

247 **Social policy in Denmark.**
Ministry of Social Affairs. Copenhagen: Ministry of Social Affairs, 1995. 2nd ed. 31p. (Available from Danish Ministry of Social Affairs, Slotsholmsgade 6, DK-1216 Copenhagen K).

Provides a brief overview of the structure and services of the social welfare model. The organization and financing of social services is described. The types of care for the various groups in society are outlined. These include: child and family policies such as day care, health care, and maternity leave; retraining and rehabilitation for the unemployed; care of the elderly; services for the disabled; and care for the least privileged groups and the socially excluded. The various types of transfer payments such as unemployment benefits, housing benefits, and retirement pay are also outlined.

248 **Children and young people in Denmark: growing up in the 1990's.**
Ministry of Social Affairs, The Inter-Ministerial Committee on
Children.   Copenhagen: Ministry of Social Affairs, The Inter-
Ministerial Committee on Children, 1992. 94p.

A status report that provides an overview of children's situation and a basis for new
initiatives. The Inter-Ministerial Committee on Children, which comprises fifteen
different ministries, aims 'to create harmony and continuity in policies affecting
children' and to 'improve the conditions in which children grow up and live'. The
Committee is unique not only in Denmark but also internationally. The report is
divided into twenty-two short sections that cover such issues as family patterns, daycare provision, education, leisure and cultural opportunities, electronic media, diet,
housing conditions, crime, substance use, and children with special needs. This report
is a revealing portrait of Denmark as a pro-child society that has increased its
awareness of childhood in the last decades of the 20th century.

249 **Hovels to high rise: state housing in Europe since 1850.**
Anne Power.   London; New York: Routledge, 1993. 434p. bibliog.

This work traces the development of urban housing patterns and state sponsorship of
social housing up to the present day in five countries: France, Germany, Denmark,
Britain, and Ireland. A major theme of the book is the role of government in helping to
provide housing, particularly to marginal groups. Information for the book was
gathered by the author in visits to each country between 1987 and 1991. The sixty-
seven-page section on Denmark begins with a brief introduction to the political and
social development of the country and continues with an in-depth look at the development of social housing, the organization of social housing and tenants' democracy,
and the incidence of private house building for both owner occupation and private
renting. There is a special focus on how 'mass' housing estates arose after the Second
World War and after the waves of immigration beginning in the 1960s, and the
government rescue of these housing areas. The author provides a comprehensive
introduction that clearly outlines the work's major issues and themes.

250 **Families with young children: the situation in Denmark.**
Jacob Vedel-Petersen, translated from the Danish by Birte Nielsen.
In: *Social work and the European Community: the social policy and
practice contexts.*   Edited by Malcolm Hill.   London: Jessica
Kingsley Publishers, 1991, p. 129-41.

Describes the principal features of family policy and recent trends in social work with
families. The primary sources of social support are described. These include annual
cash payments, social service and school-sponsored daycare options (seven types are
mentioned), maternity and paternity leave, child support payment requirements from
absentee parents, housing support, and health and dental benefits. The social and
financial situation of families is evaluated and limited data is presented. Families with
special needs, such as those experiencing alcohol and drug abuse, violence and
frequent partner changes, are also addressed, as are the new trends in assistance to
these families. The article is primarily a descriptive work that is admittedly somewhat
superficial in it coverage, but informative nonetheless.

Social conditions and problems

251 Denmark: AIDS and the political 'pink triangle'.

Erik Albæk. In: *AIDS in the industrialized democracies: passions, politics and policies.* Edited by David L. Kirp, Ronald Bayer. New Brunswick, New Jersey: Rutgers University Press, 1992, p. 281-316.

A discussion of Denmark's discovery of and reaction to AIDS. The author describes and analyses how the disease was conceptualized and how public policy was determined. These developments are presented against the backdrop of the Nordic context of egalitarianism, secularization, and moral permissiveness. The author observes, for example, that the country was the first to pass national legislation recognizing same-sex registered partnerships; that matters concerning religion, morality and sexuality have no significance in the public sphere; that cultural communities are not geographically segregated. The political conflict over AIDS became a struggle over scarce resources and was not a reflection of homophobic attitudes. The bulk of this chapter examines the combined efforts of the medical and gay communities in the fight against stigmatizing health measures and attempts at 'de-homosexualizing' AIDS, and strategies for securing funding for research and education. The media attention devoted to AIDS is also discussed. The chapter is extremely well written and is insightful both in terms of the AIDS issue and the nature of Danish society.

252 Towards a new welfare model: the EC Poverty III programme in the Danish context.

John Andersen, Jørgen Elm Larsen. Copenhagen: Forlaget Sociologi, 1993. 141p. bibliog.

Poverty III is the umbrella title of an EC initiative to combat social exclusion and to foster the integration of marginalized groups. An overall description of the principles of Poverty III is given. Labour market exclusion in Denmark and mainstream strategies to combat unemployment are described, and a critique of these strategies is provided. A portrait of poverty is offered in terms of absolute and relative poverty, and their extent, characteristics and causes are discussed. The existing research on poverty is examined, and profiles of typical recipients of social assistance are provided. New initiatives in labour market policy, reforms of unemployment insurance schemes, and experimental social programmes are examined. One chapter outlines the objectives, strategies and challenges of two local social projects: the BIK project in Aalborg, and the SAMIKO project in and around Copenhagen.

253 Suicide in Denmark, 1922-1991: the choice of method.

U. Bille-Brahe, G. Jessen. *Acta Psychiatrica Scandinavica*, vol. 90 (1994), p. 91-96.

Describes the choice of suicide method for a seventy-year period using data on all registered suicides. The authors use a simple five-category comparison since the method-of-death statistics varied over the years. The categories are poisoning, hanging, drowning, shooting, and other methods. Frequencies of method are reported over time, and differences by age and sex are also noted. It is observed that an early preference for hanging gave way to poisoning as the most frequent choice. Later years have seen a rise in more violent methods. It is also noted that Denmark reports more cases of self-poisoning than other Scandinavian countries. In-depth analysis is beyond the scope of this article, but there is cursory mention of societal factors that might be related to choice of method.

254 Breast cancer in Denmark: incidence, risk factors, and characteristics of survival.
Marianne Ewertz. Copenhagen: Marianne Ewertz, 1993. 91p.

A review based on a compilation of papers that together represent the author's research to fulfil the requirements for the doctorate of medicine. The review and the individual papers, which have been previously published in medical journals, are presented in this single volume. This is scientific research on breast cancer epidemiology which examines a variety of hormonal and reproductive factors, dietary factors, lifestyle factors such as alcohol use and smoking, and social factors such as socioeconomic status, urban versus rural residence, and occupation type. The research is based on data from the Danish Cancer Registry for the period 1942 to 1982, national morbidity statistics, and a population-based case-control and follow-up study. The incidence of breast cancer in men is also examined. This is clearly written research that is not overly burdened by medical jargon.

255 Something rotten in the state of Denmark: eugenics and the ascent of the welfare state.
Bent Sigurd Hansen. In: *Eugenics and the welfare state: sterilization policy in Denmark, Sweden, Norway, and Finland.* Edited by Gunnar Broberg, Nils Roll-Hansen. East Lansing, Michigan: Michigan State University Press, 1996, p. 9-76.

Denmark was the first European state to introduce national legislation concerning eugenic sterilization in 1929. This work is primarily an historical account of the eugenics movement during the 20th century. The background for the eugenics movement is set with an account of the popularity of biological determinism and physical anthropology in Denmark, given the worship of the Nordic physical and mental type. The institutionalization of the mentally retarded and the mentally ill is also described. Leading figures in the eugenics movement including scientists, politicians and philanthropists, are profiled. The social measures and legislation that resulted from their efforts are described in a history of the sterilization law. Finally, the opposition to eugenics is discussed. The work stops short of any present-day discussion of eugenics, stating that the topic has fallen out of the public consciousness since the 1970s with the advent of free sterilization, legalized abortion, and chemical alternatives to sterilization.

256 Child protection in Denmark.
Margit Harder. In: *Protecting children in Europe: towards a new millennium.* Edited by Margit Harder, Kenneth Pringle. Aalborg, Denmark: Aalborg University Press, 1997, p. 9-34. bibliog.

Provides an overview of the situation of at-risk children in Denmark that should be of value to students, teachers and practitioners in social work. Included in this chapter is historical background on the country's recognition of child abuse and neglect, and its early and recent child protection laws, particularly the development of social reforms since the 1960s. The current status of children is described, with statistics on children generally and on children in need of special support, and an account of existing legislation concerning families and children. The types of interventions, their results, and perspectives for the future are then discussed. The author notes that the trend toward de-institutionalization has prompted the use of more extensive assistance within families and the use of smaller, private institutions. Child protection efforts are stymied by the difficulty in identifying at-risk children as well as a lack of resources and spaces. Future recommendations include better co-ordination of the various social service sectors, better education of staff, increased involvement of schools, and more placement and counselling options.

257 **Domestic violence and child contact arrangements in England and Denmark.**
Marianne Hester, Lorraine Radford.   Bristol, England: The Policy Press, 1996. 58p. bibliog.

Reports the findings from qualitative interviews with both women who have been in violent relationships, and the professionals who work in the area of family violence. The interviews address the women's experiences of living with violent men, the impact on their children, and the negotiations and arrangements concerning child contact with fathers after the couple separates. Among the major findings is the fact that contact often does not work in the best interests of the child since abuse of the mother continues after separation. In Denmark, however, women are less likely to be pressured into problematic contact arrangements, and both mother and child have access to greater formal support. This is a significant report in that it addresses an issue in family violence that has received little attention. Although this report focuses primarily on England, there is a section that reports the findings from Denmark separately and in relation to the English findings. Descriptions of legislation on children, parental authority and contact, and on domestic violence for both countries are included in appendices.

258 **Copenhagen: a war on socially marginal people.**
Jørgen Jepsen.   In: *European drug policies and enforcement.*   Edited by Nicholas Dorn, Jørgen Jepsen, Ernesto Savona.   Basingstoke, England: Macmillan Press; New York: St. Martin's Press, 1996, p. 9-32.

Examines the war on drugs in two areas of Copenhagen: Vesterbro, a working-class neighbourhood, and the 'Free City of Christiania' an old barracks area taken over by hippies and political activists in 1971. The chapter provides the details of specific police operations and their results, which were largely unsuccessful, and offers a critique. Background on each neighbourhood is also provided, as well as a brief overview of drug use and drug enforcement in Denmark. The chapter is also informative for the insight it provides into Christiania, which has been the subject of controversy since its inception.

259 **Did the crisis hurt the Danes?**
Eggert Petersen.   In: *Did the crisis really hurt?: effects of the 1980-1982 economic recession on satisfaction, mental health and mortality.*   Edited by Ruut Veenhoven.   Rotterdam, the Netherlands: University of Rotterdam Press, 1989, p. 64-93.

Examines the findings from three existing Danish studies of the effects of the 1980s economic recession. The three studies examined objective living conditions during the

1976-86 period; life conditions, lifestyle, and attitudes regarding the recession in 1982; and political-psychological development and life changes during the period 1982-86. For the periods studied, the author generally observes that except for a slight decline in real income, Danes saw an improvement in objective living conditions such as housing. Further, their lifestyle remained unchanged or improved, with the exception of more attention being paid to energy consumption. Socially underprivileged groups were hardest hit by the recession in that they did not thrive socially and personally, and experienced more stress. These findings are discussed in terms of active and passive coping strategies. The work assumes some knowledge of quantitative research methods, but is still accessible to the general reader.

260 **Alcohol, drugs and other social problems in Denmark.**
Ove Rasmussen. In: *Social problems around the Baltic Sea.* Edited by Jussi Simpura, Christopher Tigerstedt. Helsinki: Nordic Council for Alcohol and Drug Research, 1992, p. 133-47. (NAD Publication, no. 21).

Presents data comparing perceptions of the seriousness of social problems with the reality of their prevalence, and examines how these statistics have varied over time. Data on perceptions of the seriousness of unemployment, foreign debt, environmental problems, immigration, narcotics abuse, and alcohol abuse is presented for 1990 and for the period 1980 to 1987. Data on actual unemployment, alcohol consumption, and deaths from narcotics use is presented for the 1960-90 period. Prevalence data on criminal offences, divorces, suicides and traffic casualties is also presented for the period 1960 to 1990. This article is brief and the text is somewhat superficial, but the book's editors note that the contributors were under strict time schedules.

261 **Alcohol and drugs in the workplace: attitudes, policies and programmes in Denmark.**
Knud-Erik Sabroe. Aarhus, Denmark: Institute for Psychology, Aarhus University, 1994. 91p.

This work is a country report for the International Labour Office in collaboration with the Commission of the European Communities. With combined survey data and interviews in ten organizations and seven businesses, the report covers such topics as the nature and extent of substance abuse problems, worker–employer relations, the availability of assistance in terms of policies and programmes, testing and screening, and the costs of the substance abuse problem as well as the responses to the problem. The results are framed in terms of majority views on the various issues. The author notes that the report is exploratory and limited by the unrepresentativeness of the sample. It is still informative, however, and it is well written and organized. The data is clearly presented in numerous figures and tables. The report includes a brief section of country-wide facts on alcohol and drug misuse.

262 **Criminal law and penal sanctions.**
Knut Sveri. In: *Criminal violence in Scandinavia: selected topics.* Edited by Annika Snare. Oslo: Norwegian University Press, 1990, p. 11-28. (Scandinavian Studies in Criminology, vol. 11).

A concise article that outlines the similarities and differences between the criminal justice systems in Denmark, Finland, Norway, and Sweden as regards crimes of violence such as intentional homicide and assault. The author discusses the definitions of various violent crimes and their corresponding punishments as stated in each country's criminal code; the level of violent crime as measured by both official police statistics and victim surveys; the role of the prosecutor in the investigation and charging of violent crime; and the types of punishments meted out to offenders. It is observed that although the four countries evidence some similarities in their criminal codes, differences emerge when the operation of the criminal justice systems is examined. Despite some differences in administration, all four countries do exhibit a humanitarian approach to criminal policy.

263 **Juvenile contracting in Denmark: paternalism revisited.**
Jørn Vestergaard. In: *Youth, crime and justice.* Edited by Annika Snare. Oslo: Norwegian University Press, 1991, p. 73-97. (Scandinavian Studies in Criminology, vol. 12).

Discusses a recent innovation in the punishment of juvenile crime known as juvenile contracts. In the Danish criminal justice system, where the age of responsibility is fifteen, the term 'juvenile' does not really exist, although the social welfare system may intervene when the offender is under eighteen years of age. The juvenile contract option is used for petty offenders, aged fifteen to seventeen, who have committed property crime, vandalism, or joyriding. These offenders contract to engage in some type of employment, educational pursuit, or extra-curricular activity, which can effectively erase their official record. This author analyses the pros and cons of this criminal justice policy, examining both its ethical and practical problems. The rebirth of the treatment model is discussed. Parallels with the community service option are drawn.

Corrections in two social welfare democracies: Denmark and Sweden.
See item no. 324.

A comparison of punishment systems in Denmark and the United States.
See item no. 331.

The welfare state

264 **Poverty and welfare in Denmark.**
P. Abrahamson. *Scandinavian Journal of Social Welfare*, vol. 1 (1992), p. 20-27.

Discusses a variety of topics relative to the problem of poverty, as well as its existence as a critique of the welfare state. It is observed that Denmark was virtually silent on the issue of poverty until the mid-1980s when the issue could no longer be ignored. The scant research on poverty is discussed along with various approaches to the definition and quantification of poverty. The myth of the universalist welfare state is discussed, where social policy is often dependent on a labour market affiliation. It is noted that Denmark's welfare system operates in reality as an achievement-performance model of social policy servicing two different groups: those connected to the labour market versus the society's more marginalized groups such as the long-term unemployed. The cultural and sociological consequences of this dual welfare model are discussed. The future of welfare is foreseen as a sort of 'welfare pluralism', with private and voluntary organizations playing an increasingly important role in social insurance. The advantages and disadvantages of privatization, decentralization and de-bureaucratization are commented on. This article is noteworthy for its critical stance regarding the success of the welfare state.

265 **The Nordic welfare state under pressure: the Danish experience.**
Bent Rold Andersen. *Policy and Politics*, vol. 21, no. 2 (1993),
p. 109-20.
Argues that the specific features of the Danish welfare state make it less fiscally vulnerable to problems posed by European integration than other countries. The uniqueness of the Nordic welfare model is described and explained in terms of how it differs from the Continental welfare model. It is observed that Denmark remains the most purely Scandinavian model in terms of the size of its public sector, which is financed by general taxation. Further, this universalist system delivers services efficiently, with relatively low public expenditure. It is argued that the perceived burdens of a large public sector and a high tax rate need not be viewed as impediments to economic harmonization, and that value clashes, i.e., Nordic solidarity and equality versus the Continental emphasis on individual freedom and market incentives may pose bigger problems. The author notes that a greater challenge to the legitimacy of the Danish welfare state is the expectation of more and better-quality services, given the increased participation of women in the labour force.

266 **The Scandinavian welfare model in crisis? achievements and problems of the Danish welfare state in an age of unemployment and low growth.**
Jørgen Goul Andersen. *Scandinavian Political Studies*, vol. 20, no. 1 (1997), p. 1-31.
An essentially positive account of the viability of the Scandinavian welfare model in changing economic times, with the Danish welfare state as the example. The article outlines the basic characteristics and principles of the Danish model that contribute to social and gender equality, while dispelling some common myths; describes the achievements of the 1980s and the 1990s in standards of care, material well-being, and the maintaining of equality; and discusses some of the fundamental problems that threaten the welfare state such as budgetary pressures, ageing populations, and work incentive problems. The author observes that the Danish example of the welfare state is 'still alive and in good shape' and has managed to avoid inequality in the face of mass unemployment. This is an informative and well-written article that provides a solid overview of this topic.

Society. The welfare state

267 **Sources of welfare state support in Denmark: self-interest or way of life?**
Jørgen Goul Andersen. In: *Welfare trends in the Scandinavian countries.* Edited by Erik Jørgen Hansen, Stein Ringen, Hannu Uusitalo, Robert Erikson. Armonk, New York; London: M. E. Sharpe, 1993, p. 25-48.

Provides an empirical analysis based primarily on 1985 Danish survey data. This article examines whether differences in attitudes toward the welfare state are based on economic self-interest or on other 'way of life' factors. Hypotheses and their theoretical underpinnings are stated throughout the analysis. Attitudes regarding specific types of welfare state programmes or regarding levels of public spending are compared on self-interest factors such as having a public sector versus private sector occupation, being a state-dependent versus a private sector wage earner, and being a user versus a non-user of a public service. Attitudes are also compared on 'way of life' factors such as social class as measured by type of wage earner in various occupations or being self-employed, family structure as measured by the employment patterns of husbands and wives, and gender. Differences by age and educational level are also examined. The article assumes some knowledge of social science quantitative research methods, but the general reader can easily overlook the methodological references.

268 **Reorganizing the Danish welfare state 1982-93: a decade of conservative rule.**
Kim Viborg Andersen, Carsten Greve, Jacob Torfing. *Scandinavian Studies*, vol. 68, no. 2 (Spring 1996), p. 161-87.

This article analyses the ideological and substantive changes fostered by three consecutive conservative coalitions during the aftermath of the economic recession and the oil crisis of the 1970s. Conservative reorganization policies – economic, social, and public – are examined for their underlying intentions, and their effect on macro-economic problems as well as on citizens' living conditions. Efforts at privatization are discussed. International parallels are also drawn. The authors conclude that the changes on the whole did not constitute a 'neo-liberal' counter-revolution in that the coalitions were minority governments, interest groups were resistant to major change, and the institutions of the universalist welfare state were too strongly rooted. In an epilogue, the authors comment briefly on the situation facing the majority government that came to power in 1993 and on the future of the welfare state.

269 **The Scandinavian origins of the social interpretation of the welfare state.**
Peter Baldwin. *Comparative Studies in Society and History. An International Quarterly*, vol. 31, no. 1 (January 1989), p. 3-24.

Argues against the social interpretation of the welfare state, i.e., that welfare reforms represented a victory for the working class and the Left in the post-war era. Using Denmark and Sweden as examples, this work examines the origins of Scandinavian social policy's unique features – its universalist coverage of all citizens and its tax-based financing (versus premiums). For Denmark, this analysis focuses on the demands of agrarian society in the late 19th century as they faced the shift from grain farming to the more labour-intensive animal and dairy farming. It is observed that social insurance was formed at the turn of the century as the result of narrow interest disputes between the rural middle class on the one hand and bureaucrats and urban

96

élites on the other. It is only later that universality and tax financing become progressive ideas embraced by socialist groups. This focus differs from other analyses of welfare state origins that emphasize the land reforms, the cooperative movement, and the influence of popular education.

270 **The welfare society in transition: problems and prospects of the welfare model.**
Edited by William Cave, Per Himmelstrup. Copenhagen: The Danish Cultural Institute, 1994. 232p.

A compilation of remarks from a 1994 conference sponsored by the Danish Ministry of Foreign Affairs. The participants included Denmark, the United States, as well as Eastern and Central Europe and Africa, with Denmark representing the Scandinavian case of the welfare society. Of the book's seventeen contributions, five are exclusively devoted to Denmark while three others discuss Scandinavia in general. The conference was convened to enrich the debate over the welfare society in the light of current issues such as increased migration which threatens ethnic peace and the welfare society's commitment to equality, and American experimentation with privatization of public services – an idea which is gaining popularity in the Nordic countries. The volume contains papers on the philosophical and historical roots of the welfare model, the erosion of the system, and ethical and moral considerations. The overall perspective of the work is that, despite its problems, the welfare model is not on the verge of collapse. Rather, it is dynamic and can adapt to change. Further, while Denmark's version of this model is rooted in its particular history, certain elements can be applied in other parts of the world.

271 **Modern welfare states: policies and politics in social democratic Scandinavia.**
Eric S. Einhorn, John Logue. New York; London: Praeger, 1989. 340p. bibliog.

An analytical book on the welfare model in Denmark, Norway and Sweden. The opening chapter provides background, and examines the successes and limitations of the welfare model. Subsequent chapters address the structure of Scandinavian democracy, its political institutions, parties, voters, and interest groups; the welfare state's key policy areas such as social services and transfer payments, domestic politics and international relations, economic policy and the market economy; and industrial relations and centralized bargaining. Concluding chapters discuss moral and economic criticisms, and offer a future perspective. Throughout the book there is an emphasis on the historical and political aspects of the welfare model. The political dominance of the social democratic parties since the Great Depression is noted, as well as the powerful role of economic interest groups in governmental decision-making. Three appendices provide information on election results, parliamentary seat distributions, and governing parties and coalitions for the three countries since 1918.

272 **The Scandinavian model: welfare states and welfare research.**
Edited by Robert Erikson, Erik Jørgen Hansen, Stein Ringen, Hannu Uusitalo. Armonk, New York; London: M. E. Sharpe, 1987. 251p. bibliog.

This book both describes and evaluates the Scandinavian welfare state in topical chapters by various scholars from Denmark, Sweden, Norway, and Finland. Its point of departure is that a single Scandinavian welfare model does exist, although it is manifested in slightly different forms in each country. Part one provides background, examining the development of Scandinavian society and the shift from agrarian societies to modern industrial welfare states. The underlying ideology of the welfare state, changes in the political and economic structure, and the development of its social policies (social security, labour market, housing) are examined. Part two looks at some of the problems that continue to plague welfare societies such as inequality and poverty. Two chapters here are based on Danish research, examining inequality and the redistribution of income. Part three characterizes a Scandinavian model of welfare research and provides examples. Most of the chapters are thorough and detailed, and the information is clearly presented.

273 Contemporary Danish society: Danish democracy and social welfare.

Bjarne Hastrup.   Copenhagen: Academic Press, 1995. 270p.

Examines various facets of the welfare state such as welfare policies, democracy, economy and trade, unionization of the population, Danish national identity and mentality, and the country's place on the world stage. The work is descriptive, yet takes a critical stance in its overriding theme that there are problems with the Danish welfare model and it will have to be modified to ensure its survival. The work emphasizes how the Danish model differs from those in the rest of Europe, such that the book is not a detailed picture of all aspects of Danish society. The author describes the Danish model in terms of two important threads: the high standard of living with a relatively even distribution of incomes compared to other Western countries, and the country's strong international economic model. This is a factual, yet highly readable book. It would also be a good choice for the reader looking for one general book about Danish society.

274 Three Danish authors examine the welfare state: Finn Søeberg, Leif Panduro, and Anders Bodelsen.

Frank Hugus.   *Scandinavian Studies*, vol. 62, no. 2 (1990), p. 189-213.

This article examines the social criticism contained in the literary works of three Danish authors writing after the Second World War. The article's author first observes that, despite their relatively high standard of living, Danes frequently express discontent over the bureaucratic excesses of the welfare state as well as the various other social problems that have come into existence such as rising violence and crime, the isolation of individuals, and problems of drug and alcohol abuse. Further, social scientists have noted that increased standards lead to increased expectations, which in turn lead to frustration and alienation when these expectations are not met. In their novels and short stories, the three authors echoed these observations and went on to offer solutions to the problems of the welfare state. Their optimistic works expressed faith in the decency and pragmatism of mankind and faith in the Danes' sense of community, and offered grass-roots notions for salvaging the welfare state. This article is a literary analysis, but it also provides significant commentary on Danish society.

275 **Welfare administration in Denmark.**
Edited by Tim Knudsen. Copenhagen: Ministry of Finance,
Department of Management and Personnel, 1991. 391p.

This work contains a broad spectrum of articles by various scholars, which are written
for readers unfamiliar with Danish history and institutions. The topics include: the
basic principles of Danish central administration; a profile of the public sector and its
problems; popular attitudes towards the welfare state; the administration of labour
market policy; the interplay between social policy and labour market policy given the
country's prolonged mass unemployment; the contributions of private institutions in
social, health, educational and cultural affairs; child welfare policies; and the historical development of the health care system, and the present-day policy of care of the
elderly and disabled at home. The opening article compares the Danish and Swedish
state cultures, discusses the evolution of the modern welfare state and the principle of
'consensual democracy'.

276 **Denmark: a troubled welfare state.**
Kenneth E. Miller. Boulder, Colorado; Oxford: Westview Press,
1991. 224p. bibliog. (Westview Profiles/Nations of Contemporary
Europe).

The author introduces the reader to the nation, its people and its history. The emphasis
of the work is on the country's government, politics and economy in the post-Second
World War era, a period where the welfare state has undergone significant changes,
yet has endured. Rather than being entirely critical, the work is also descriptive and
provides an overview of Danish culture and society. This book is a solid introduction
to Denmark as an example of the 'Scandinavian Model' and a chronicle of the country
as a modern welfare state in the 20th century.

277 **Local welfare systems in Denmark in a period of political
reconstruction: a Scandinavian perspective.**
Søren Villadsen. In: *Comparative welfare systems: the Scandinavian
model in a period of change.* Edited by Bent Greve. London:
Macmillan Press; New York: St. Martin's Press, 1996, p. 133-64.
bibliog.

Discusses the impact of the 1982-93 political reconstruction on the local government-
based welfare model and on local democracy. This eleven-year period was marked by
changing bourgeois coalitions led by the same Conservative prime minister. The
period was wedged between social democratic coalitions, the preceding period being
marked by fiscal instability. The consequences of this political reconstruction include
an impact on welfare policies, such as: local government spending on social services
and the development of new strategies of decentralization. Key features of current
local government are its democratic structure, its relative autonomy, and its administrative division into communes (municipalities) and larger counties. The chapter
examines the development of the local government system in terms of the welfare
state model and the 'mixed democracy model' with particular emphasis on the Danish
version. Differences between Denmark and the other Nordic countries are noted.

Women and the welfare state in the Nordic countries.
See item no. 279.

The gendered Scandinavian welfare states: the interplay between women's roles as mothers, workers and citizens in Denmark.
See item no. 286.

Women and the welfare: between private and public dependence. A comparative approach to care work in Denmark and Britain.
See item no. 287.

Marginalization, citizenship and the economy: the capacities of the universalist welfare state in Denmark.
See item no. 405.

The welfare state and taxation in Denmark.
See item no. 411.

Women and Gender Issues

278 **Gender, managers, and organizations.**
Yvonne Due Billing, Mats Alvesson. Berlin; New York: Walter de Gruyter, 1994. 260p. bibliog.
A study of the social and organizational processes that usually prevent, but sometimes facilitate, the recruitment and functioning of women in management positions. The researchers note a 'modest presence' of women in the position of middle-level manager. The book first provides a comprehensive and critical analysis of the existing empirical and theoretical literature, and then reports results from three case-studies of Scandinavian organizations: Denmark's National Board of Social Welfare, Scandinavian Airlines, and the Danish Ministry of Foreign Affairs. The three organizations are examined separately and comparatively on dimensions such as the nature of work, sex ratios, educational level and qualification structures, history, social climate, the division of labour, and barriers to women. The final part of the book attempts to develop a more general theoretical understanding of the area in an attempt to account for the 'gendered nature of management'. The work is noteworthy for its theoretical contributions, its examination of the functioning of these organizations, and for the information it provides on the position of women in Danish society.

279 **Women and the welfare state in the Nordic countries.**
Elina Haavio-Mannila, Kaisa Kauppinen. In: *Women's work and women's lives: the continuing struggle worldwide.* Edited by Hilde Kahne, Janet Z. Giele. Boulder, Colorado; Oxford: Westview Press, 1992, p. 224-47. bibliog.
Reports on the features of Nordic society that impact women for the five Nordic countries (Denmark, Finland, Iceland, Norway, and Sweden). General demographic, economic, and other background factors are presented. Specific focus is then given to indicators of social equality between men and women, milestones to equal opportunity, the growth of the public sector and the provision of public daycare, and the effort to strengthen the role of the father with maternity-parental leave that can be divided between the two parents. In terms of working lives, information on employment rates,

101

sex segregation of the labour market, and gender differences in salaries and wages, and in unpaid household work is presented. There is also a general discussion of the welfare state and women's economic equality. The authors conclude that, despite the advances for women in Nordic countries, sexual equality in the welfare state is both 'myth and reality'.

280　**Women in Denmark.**
　　　Edited by Hanne-Vibeke Holst, translated from the Danish by W. Glyn
　　　Jones.　Copenhagen: Ministry of Foreign Affairs, Department of
　　　Information, 1995. 39p.

This is a glossy stylized publication which comprises a series of profiles and portraits of issues relative to the contemporary woman. The articles profile such topics as a childcare institution; a portrait of a feminist Danish man; a woman in politics; a career woman who returned to working in the home following the introduction of the Parental Leave Act in 1994; a Generation X woman, i.e., a child of two working parents and a product of Danish childcare institutions; a Greenlandic woman. There are also articles on the gender income gap and the illusion of equal pay, and on lifestyle issues such as alcohol use and smoking. This is an informative publication that identifies some significant issues for today's woman, but its style is popular and somewhat superficial. It is, however, not pretending to be anything else.

281　**Women's employment and part-time work in Denmark.**
　　　Søren Leth-Sørensen, Götz Rohwer.　In: *Between equalization and
　　　marginalization: women working part-time in Europe and the United
　　　States of America.*　Edited by Hans-Peter Blossfeld, Catherine Hakim.
　　　Oxford; New York: Oxford University Press, 1997, p. 247-71. bibliog.

Describes and analyses female labour market participation for the period 1980-89 based on a national longitudinal dataset created from public registers. The researchers identify four states of labour market participation: full-time, part-time, unemployed, and out of the labour force. Various rates of labour force participation are presented in terms of age and birth cohort. The relationship between family lifecycle factors such as consensual unions, marriages and children is explored. Educational and vocational training, and public or private sector employment are also taken into account. The analysis also attempts to identify how these factors relate to labour market transitions, such as the transition from full-time to part-time employment or from part-time work to unemployment. Implications, conclusions and future developments are discussed. Although this study makes use of quantitative methods, the information is clearly presented for the general reader.

282　**Sexual rights of young women in Denmark and Sweden.**
　　　Katarina Lindahl, Maritta Viktorsson, Nell Rassmussen.　Hellerup,
　　　Denmark: The Danish Family Planning Association; Stockholm: The
　　　Swedish Association for Sex Education, RFSU, 1995. 24p. (Available
　　　from The Danish Family Planning Association, Aurehøjvej 2, DK-2900
　　　Hellerup).

This publication presents the Scandinavian viewpoint regarding the position of women in society, and outlines the milestones regarding sexuality, and sexual and reproductive rights. The key to the Scandinavian view is that sexual and reproductive rights are viewed as important to society in general, and are part of an overall social, economic, and human rights perspective. The historical and political background of women's rights is briefly described. The various rights and protections are discussed, such as compulsory sex education in schools, the availability of safe and affordable contraceptives, confidential counselling, abortion, health care, sexual preference, protection from sexual harassment, and legal rights regarding rape. The relevant legislation is referred to throughout the discussion. The work makes clear the positive social and legal situation for women in Danish and Swedish society.

283 **Equality in Denmark: the Danish national report to the fourth world conference on women 1995.**
Ministry of Foreign Affairs. Copenhagen: Ministry of Foreign Affairs, 1994. 88p. (Available from Ministry of Foreign Affairs, Asiatisk Plads 2, DK-1448 Copenhagen K).
Reports on the situation of women in Denmark, since the third conference in 1985. The opening chapter looks at global trends affecting women's progress. In separate chapters, the report covers employment, health and family life, education, and selected issues such as women in the military, women's participation in foreign affairs, and violence against women. A chapter on Danish aid efforts regarding women in developing countries is also included. Each chapter outlines the relevant initiatives or legislation, offers some appraisal of effectiveness, points out problems and obstacles, and offers a future perspective. Limited statistics are presented. Four appendices provide comments from non-governmental organizations. The report is brief and concise.

284 **Women in Denmark in the 1980's.**
Ministry of Foreign Affairs. Copenhagen: Ministry of Foreign Affairs, 1985. 63p.
Describes in words and black-and-white photographs the steps taken towards equality between the sexes during the United Nations Decade for Women, 1975-85. The situation of women is examined in various arenas such as family life, school, the labour market, politics, and the health care system. Women's contributions to media and the arts, their experiences in violent relationships, and their involvement in various grassroots movements are also discussed. This work is a short overview, yet it provides a great deal of information for the period covered, and it is clearly written. Descriptive statistics and accounts of the relevant legislation for the topic at hand are provided throughout the text. The book testifies to the high visibility of women in Denmark.

285 **Soap, pin-up and burlesque: commercialization and femininity in Danish television.**
Vibeke Pedersen. *NORA*, vol. 2, no. 1 (1993), p. 74-89.
Examines the performances of three of the new young Danish female television hosts in relation to the breaking up of monopoly, commercialization, and deregulation of television. The breakthrough of these new female hosts was a novelty of the 1991-92 television season which evidenced an increase in the number of programmes hosted or co-hosted by women. This article considers the meaning and significance of these new female hosts and observes that they are important for deregulated television which relies significantly on visual images. The new female hosts offer visual appeal as

sexual objects and as a personification of emotion and extravagance. The author makes use of feminist theory's investigation of the connection between gender and visual representation, and draws comparisons to the Hollywood cinema's iconography of women, in order to examine television and women in terms of the post-modern condition. This scholarly piece is also accessible to the more general reader.

286 **The gendered Scandinavian welfare states: the interplay between women's roles as mothers, workers and citizens in Denmark.**
Birte Siim. In: *Women and social policies in Europe: work, family and the state.* Edited by Jane Lewis. Aldershot, England: Edward Elgar Publishing, 1993, p. 25-48.

This book chapter examines the situation of women in the welfare state, past and present, and 'the reality of male domination' that has characterized gender relations. The author discusses the current feminist discourse on the gendered welfare state; the historical development of the welfare state since 1960; the changes in women's daily lives as mothers, workers, and as citizens; and changes in the perceptions of equality. There is information on Denmark's social and family policies, women's political participation, women's integration into the labour market and the gendered division of labour, and changes in women's reproductive behaviour. The chapter is good for its comparative dimension, discussing Denmark in relation to the other Scandinavian countries. There is a complete bibliography at the end of the book, rather than for the individual chapters.

287 **Women and the welfare: between private and public dependence. A comparative approach to care work in Denmark and Britain.**
Birte Siim. In: *Gender and caring: work and welfare in Britain and Scandinavia.* Edited by Clare Ungerson. London; New York: Harvester Wheatsheaf, 1990, p. 80-109. bibliog.

A comparative analysis that offers a gender perspective on the modern welfare state and care work, examining its implications for the position of women in society. The author observes, in the case of Denmark, that the state has taken increasing responsibility for the care of children, the sick, the elderly, and the disabled. This situation has resulted in women's personal economic independence, but at the same time, a new form of oppression in terms of their dependency on the state as workers, consumers, and clients. This is contrasted with the social policies of Britain, where the state has taken less of a role in care. These policies assume women's economic dependency on their husbands and perpetuate the sexual division of work in society. The article also examines the women's political power in both countries and feminist strategies towards the welfare state. This article is insightful and informative for both the gender perspective and basic information on Danish welfare state social policy.

288 **A gender gap that vanished: tolerance and liberalism.**
Lise Togeby. In: *Women in Nordic politics: closing the gap.* Edited by Lauri Karvonen, Per Selle. Aldershot, England; Brookfield, Vermont: Dartmouth, 1995, p. 313-41. bibliog.

Examines the increasing levels of Danish women's political tolerance since the 1970s, such that by 1990 differences between men's and women's tolerance no longer exist. The concept of tolerance is defined and the prevailing theories that have been used to explain women's formerly weaker political integration are discussed. The author finds these theories – the structural, situational, and socialization explanations – not wholly satisfactory in accounting for the gender difference of the 1970s and suggests that female culture theory should be the point of departure for understanding this difference. The increase in women's political tolerance is then examined in the light of an increase in women's social resources such as education, labour market participation, and political involvement. These developments are more generally attributed to the breakdown of a specific women's culture with the social movements of the 1970s, including the women's movement, making for a more democratic and less authoritarian society. An earlier version of this paper was published in *Scandinavian Political Studies*, vol. 17, no. 1 (1994), p. 47-68.

289   **Political implications of increasing numbers of women in the labour force.**
Lise Togeby.   *Comparative Political Studies*, vol. 27, no. 2 (1994), p. 211-40.
This article examines the implications of women's labour market participation for party choice, political attitudes, and general political participation. Specifically, five hypotheses are tested: that women's political participation will increase and reach the level of men's; that women will become more feminist, demanding more gender equality; that women will move to the left on political issues; that women and men will have equal political dominance in the family; that marriage, family and home-making issues will influence men and women similarly. Findings are reported and conclusions are drawn. The research is based primarily on survey data from Danish election studies conducted since 1971. An introductory section discusses changes in women's life situation over past decades, and presents various data on gender differences in labour market participation, part-time employment, and time used on unpaid housework. The research generally finds that women have become more integrated into the political system.

Women in the Viking Age.
See item no. 88.

Socialist feminists and feminist socialists in Denmark 1920-1940.
See item no. 137.

Women and men in the Nordic countries: facts and figures 1994.
See item no. 433.

The state of women's history in Denmark.
See item no. 470.

31 women artists from 31 Danish art museums.
See item no. 531.

Discipline and emancipation through sport: the pioneers in women's sport in Denmark.
See item no. 586.

Space and gender at the Faroe Islands.
See item no. 679.

Politics

290 Denmark: environmental conflict and the 'greening' of the labour movement.
Jørgen Goul Andersen. *Scandinavian Political Studies*, vol. 13, no. 2 (1990), p. 185-218.

Considers the lack of an influential Green Party in one of the most environmentally conscious nations in the world. The article contains a brief history of environmental mobilization, the issues that occupied the movement, and the response of the party system to environmental issues. Using data from various surveys up to 1989, subsequent sections provide a systematic examination of the development of environmental attitudes among Danish voters; a description of the social composition of members and activists in the environmental movement; an examination of the social variations in environmental issues in terms of age, gender, and class; and a look at the relationships of these factors to various models of environmentalism, such as the 'new middle class' model or the 'post-materialist value' model. The political consequences of environmentalism in terms of cleavages in the party system are discussed in some detail. A final section comments on the unsuccessfulness to date of the Danish Green Party and provides a social profile of its membership in terms of age, gender, class, and previous party affiliation.

291 Denmark: the decline of the membership party?
Lars Bille. In: *How parties organize: change and adaptation in party organizations in Western democracies*. Edited by Richard S. Katz, Peter Mair. London; Thousand Oaks, California: Sage Publications, 1994, p. 134-57. bibliog.

Discusses the declining ability of the eight major political parties to maintain their position as the prime organizing political force in Danish society. The author briefly accounts for the Danish conception of party organization based on the constitution, the structure of government, and the electoral laws, and describes the nature of the membership party. The decline in individual membership and in the number of local branches in discussed. The importance of affiliated membership is also noted. Changes in the pattern of representation in the leading bodies of the parties (the national conference, the party congress, and the national executive) is discussed in terms of the marginalization of individual membership. The financial importance of party members is addressed. The actual role of the parliamentary party in party leadership is also discussed in terms of the formal separation of the parliamentary party and the membership party. The author observes that parties are becoming less a part of society, and more a part of the state, given their influence on decision-making in the public sector.

292 **Denmark.**
Ole Borre. In: *Electoral change: reponses to evolving social and attitudinal structures in Western countries.* Edited by Mark N. Franklin, Thomas T. Mackie, Henry Valen. Cambridge, England: Cambridge University Press, 1992, p. 145-66.

Provides an empirical analysis of the electoral support for the broad classifications of socialist and bourgeois parties, given that each side has managed to maintain roughly half of the vote throughout major socio-demographic shifts since 1960. The research is based on voter surveys from 1971 and 1987, and examines the effects of variables such as social class, church attendance, home ownership, left–right attitudes, public versus private employment, and birth cohort membership (before 1930, between 1930 and 1945, and after 1945) on voting behaviour. The author observes that long-term trends in party support are not evident, and that the voter base across socialist and bourgeois parties has changed over time. It is specifically noted that voting is no longer class-based. This chapter is not overly burdened with quantitative analysis and is clearly presented for the general reader.

293 **Voting and political attitudes in Denmark: a study of the 1994 election.**
Ole Borre, Jørgen Goul Andersen. Aarhus, Denmark: Aarhus University Press, 1997. 352p. bibliog.

With survey data from 2,000 voters in the 1994 election along with data from previous surveys, this work examines the relationship of political attitudes to voting choice in the 1994 election, as well as during the previous two decades. The character and development of the Danish electorate is described and hypotheses are tested regarding voting behaviour. Among the topics examined are: the origin and history of the Danish party system, the various voting models, performance ratings of the various governments and their leaders, the social bases of party support, generational and gender differences in voting, attitudes towards various policies and towards the welfare state, attitudes towards European cooperation and towards immigration. This book offers a systematic presentation of Danish political attitudes and voting behaviour, a topic which was previously dealt with primarily in journal articles. It is thorough and well presented. The work is useful for comparative studies with other advanced industrialized democracies in that many of the hypotheses examined here were developed in other countries, particularly the United States.

294 Adapting Danish interests to European integration.

Henning Bregnsbo, Niels Christian Sidenius. *Scandinavian Political Studies*, vol. 16, no. 1 (1993) p. 73-91.

Based on questionnaire data and selected interviews, this article examines how government and private business have had to adapt to the new political environment presented by the European Community (EC). The authors observe that Denmark's tradition of political decision-making can be characterized as liberal-corporatist, where public policy tends to be the outcome of institutionalized cooperation between organized interests and government. The new political environment of the EC, however, is a less corporatist and more pluralist one. The article describes the functioning of the Common Market Committee in Denmark's parliament and how its powers have expanded since its inception in 1973. The behaviour of the various sector ministries is also discussed, as well as the lobbying strategies of organized interests in manufacturing and agriculture. The authors conclude that national corporatism remains strong, coupled with an awareness of the more pluralistic international system.

295 Crisis politics in Denmark, 1974-1987.

Erik Damgaard.   In: *The politics of economic crisis: lessons from Western Europe.*   Edited by E. Damgaard, P. Gerlich, J. J. Richardson.   Aldershot, England; Brookfield, Vermont: Avebury, 1989, p. 70-88.

This informative piece discusses the government's reaction to the oil crisis of the early 1970s, in the light of Denmark's 1973 electoral upheaval, which resulted in extreme party fragmentation. Other economic problems at the time included an increase in unemployment and inflation, as well as an increase in the balance-of-payments deficit. The author analyses the differing perceptions of these problems and their solutions within the fragmented party system. Of particular significance during this period is the influence of the Liberal–Conservative minority coalition government which came to power in 1982. This coalition called for a decrease in public expenditure, an increase in the total level of taxation, and a modernization of the public sector. The success of these policies is evaluated.

296 Who governs? parties and politics in Denmark.

Erik Damgaard, Palle Svensson.   *European Journal of Political Research*, vol. 17, no. 6 (November 1989), p. 731-45.

Aims to illustrate how minority governments survive and operate, using as an example the period 1982-88 when the Danish government was a Liberal–Conservative minority coalition. Key factors in this minority government's ability to stay in power were its ability to compromise, to accept defeat, and to obtain support from at least one opposition party. The article further examines the link between party and policy in a minority government with a look at patterns of inter-party cooperation with respect to the passing of various bills. The authors find unique patterns of majority formation that depend greatly on the given issue or policy. The most significant finding is that sometimes the normal roles of governments and oppositions are in fact reversed, a finding that does not fit existing theories of government formation. This article is significant for its demonstration of the flexibility of Danish parliamentary government.

297 **Reading the cards on the table: Danish politics in the era of European integration.**
Leslie C. Eliason. *Scandinavian Studies*, vol. 64, no. 4 (Fall 1992), p. 544-81.

Examines Danish politics under Conservative-led governments that came to power in 1982, highlighting the interplay between domestic reforms and European Community participation. The Danish case is presented in a larger European context, with an emphasis on economic issues. The article specifically looks at the government's solutions to fiscal problems that had been building up since the oil crisis of the early 1970s, such as unemployment, inflation, budget and trade deficits, and an over-expanded public sector. These solutions include reforming the budgeting and accountability system, deregulation of the public sector, privatization of some public responsibilities, and modernization of the public sector. Each of these is described in terms of its content and the accompanying political background. Some evaluation of each measure is also offered. The final sections look at the implications of the Danish experience for other Scandinavian countries, and for the welfare model in general.

298 **Denmark.**
Kevin Featherstone. In: *Socialist parties and European integration: a comparative history.* Kevin Featherstone. Manchester, England: Manchester University Press, 1988, p. 76-106.

This book chapter is a case-study of the Danish Social Democratic Party's response to the issue of European integration. In broader terms this issue is framed as the non-communist Left's response to supranational integration, a notion that is driven by and represents concerns of the Centre and Right. The chapter begins with a brief history of the origins of the Social Democratic Party, its ideology, and its long experience in coalition government. The party's record on European matters is discussed in detail and is characterized by an overriding concern for domestic issues, an emphasis on free trade and economic cooperation, and an overall resistance to supranationality. The party's performance in various negotiations, agreements and referendums is charted up to the Single European Act which was drawn up at the Luxembourg Summit in 1985.

299 **Solidarity or egoism? The economics of sociotropic and egocentric influences on political behavior: Denmark in international and theoretical perspective.**
Douglas Hibbs. Aarhus, Denmark: Aarhus University Press, 1993. 72p. biblog. (Voters in Scandinavia, no. 1).

This monograph is essentially an evaluation and critique of existing Danish research on voting behaviour and opinion. This body of research attempts to determine the relative importance of sociotropic and egocentric motivations for voter behaviour and opinion. The sociotropic and egocentric motivations can be more simply defined as voting according to the public interest versus self-interest. The first chapter provides background on the sociotropic–egocentric debate. Chapter two reviews recent research in Denmark on the importance of these motivations for voting intentions and government competency ratings. The third chapter examines the pure theory of electoral choice and applies it to the sociotropic–egocentric question. Several chapters evaluate some of the methodological issues in econometric research such as measurement and specification error, and apply these insights to the conclusions that have been drawn in the Danish as well as other Scandinavian research. One chapter reviews the American research that has utilized pooled time-series of cross-sections to disentangle the sociotropic and egocentric effects. This is a very methodologically oriented work and is more suited to readers with an understanding of factor analysis and regression.

300 **Friends and rivals: coalition politics in Denmark, 1901-1995.**
Kenneth E. Miller. Lanham, Maryland; New York; London: University Press of America, Inc., 1996. 285p. bibliog.

Describes and analyses how Danish governments have been formed in elections during the 20th century. Since 1909 no single political party has had a majority of parliamentary seats and every government has had to rest on some sort of alliance. The resulting coalitions, however, have often been something other than what would be predicted by theory. The author examines the short-term crises and long-term historical factors that have made formal winning coalitions relatively infrequent and minority coalitions more the norm. The situation will most likely persist, with factors such as issue-voting and a decline in party identification characterizing Danish elections. This work, which is detailed and well researched, is clearly written and suitable for both the scholar and the general reader.

301 **Danes and their politicians: a summary of the findings of a research project on political credibility in Denmark.**
Gunnar Viby Mogensen, translated from the Danish by Susanne Marslew, Thomas L. Jakobsen, Tim Caudrey. Aarhus, Denmark: Aarhus University Press, 1993. 85p. (Voters in Scandinavia, no. 2).

Examines the relationship between the Danish electorate and their representatives in Parliament based on a survey of 2,000 Danes and on in-depth interviews with 23 voters and with politicians representing all the parties in parliament. Using various data sources, the study also includes an historical analysis of the changing roots of Danish politics, primarily since the Second World War, and an account of the influence of television on voters' opinions. The researchers find that political distrust is more likely among the socially disadvantaged and the politically alienated or unrepresented; Danes remain fixed in their belief in democracy and social values, although their relationship with their politicians has become unstable; and television has contributed to the decreased level of trust in politicians through its choice of topics and journalistic bias. The analysis also highlights the issues of European cooperation and immigration policies. Included in this work are three polemical papers on the topic of public distrust by former Danish political figures.

302 **Reactive voting in Danish general elections, 1971-1979.**
Peter Nannestad. Aarhus, Denmark: Aarhus University Press, 1989. 207p. bibliog.

Uses survey data to test a theory of reactive voting in the five Danish elections of the 1970s. This decade was a time of great electoral volatility, evidenced particularly by the parliamentary upheaval of the 1973 election, where support for the five established parties was drastically reduced. In a reactive situation, voting is seen as an informed, rational choice reflecting factual knowledge and the voter's belief system. Voters have a clear understanding of the parties' positions in the system and knowledge of the parties' parliamentary behaviour. Voter perceptions are only marginally affected by party preference, party identification, or social class. In this analysis the reactive situation is viewed in comparison to the social-psychological, the structural, or the issue-voting models of voting behaviour, where voting is primarily determined by emotional party identification, social class, or short-term factors, respectively. This is an academic work based on quantitative data analysis, but it contains a wealth of information that is accessible to the general reader.

303 **The birth, life, and death of small parties in Danish politics.**
Mogens N. Pedersen.   In: *Small parties in Western Europe: comparative and national perspectives.*   Edited by Ferdinand Müller-Rommel, Geoffrey Pridham.   London; Newbury Park, California: Sage, 1991, p. 95-114. (Sage Modern Politics Series, vol. 27).

Describes and analyses the role of small parties in a developmental perspective, where the author applies his 'lifespan model' which views parties as 'mortal organizations'. It is observed that small parties that come and go are a permanent fixture of Danish politics, which has been characterized by minority coalitions throughout the 20th century. Using the lifespan model, certain phases and the conditions for reaching them are defined: a party's declaration or emergence, its legal authorization, and its parliamentary representation and relevance. Also discussed are the duties of the small party in parliament, its systemic position, its role in the political arena, and its disintegration. Throughout the chapter, the discussion moves between the general theory and specific examples from the Danish system. Readers should note that the references for this chapter are at the end of the entire book.

304 **The Danish 'working multiparty system': breakdown or adaptation?**
Mogens N. Pedersen.   In: *Party systems in Denmark, Austria, Switzerland, The Netherlands, and Belgium.*   Edited by Hans Daalder.   London: Frances Pinter Publishers, 1987, p. 1-60.

Discusses changes in the party system during the early 1970s especially in the light of the electoral upheaval of 1973. Although the fact that five incumbent parties were defeated and five new parties were formed was a dramatic quantitative change, the author argues that the party system itself did not experience a full-blown breakdown. Further, the decline in class-based party organization was not very different from the changes experienced by other European systems at the time. This work is very informative and contains much discussion on the character and performance of the 'new' and the 'old' parties and an assessment of the party system in general.

305 **The defeat of all parties: the Danish *Folketing* election, 1973.**
Mogens N. Pedersen.   In: *When parties fail.*   Edited by Kay Lawson, Peter H. Merkl.   Princeton, New Jersey: Princeton University Press, 1988, p. 257-81.

Provides a clearly written and insightful analysis of what has been referred to as a 'landslide election' and one of the most volatile electoral situations in Western Europe since the Second World War. All five incumbent parties lost and five new parties, three of which were brand new, entered the system. It is frequently noted that party alignment had previously been linked to social class, but the 1973 election evidenced a weakening of class–party bonds and a more issue-oriented party alignment. The author develops a broader framework to explain this upheaval, citing long-term social-structural and political factors, short-term factors related to party strategies and policies, short-term triggers, and facilitating structural conditions. Previous analyses are critiqued and a final section places the election in a larger, comparative perspective.

306 **Social mobility in Denmark.**
Gunnar Sehested-Larsen.   In: *Social mobility and political attitudes: comparative perspectives.*   Edited by Frederick C. Turner.   New Brunswick, New Jersey; London: Transaction Publishers, 1992, p. 79-101.

A work of social science research that examines the relationship between social mobility and political attitudes such as left-wing/right-wing sympathies, and a range of other attitudes and expectations. Among these are voting behaviour, views on communism, views on industrial democracy, views on the reduction of income differences, views on Danish membership in NATO, predicted personal future, and satisfaction with personal financial situation. Social mobility is conceptualized as upward or downward mobility compared to parents' status, and is measured by a classification of occupational prestige. Empirical findings are presented based on data from a 1980 national survey. Theoretical and methodological issues are considered, but actual discussion of the findings is rather limited. The work assumes some knowledge of quantitative research methods, particularly measurement issues.

307 **The nature of declining party membership in Denmark: causes and consequences.**
Lise Togeby.   *Scandinavian Political Studies*, vol. 15, no. 1 (1992), p. 1-19. bibliog.

Using election survey data from 1971, 1979 and 1987, this article describes the nature of declining party membership by examining changes in formal party membership versus changes in other forms of political participation such as trade union membership and attendance at meetings, participation in a grassroots organization, consumption of political news, and voting behaviour. Social equality in these forms of political participation is also examined through looking at differences by educational level, occupation type, and gender. The findings are discussed in terms of existing theory on political participation. The author observes that declining party membership can be attributed to economic and socio-demographic causes, and has consequences for the socializing and mobilizing functions of parties, as well as for their democratic legitimacy. The findings are interesting in terms of their implications for political inequality in a society that strives for egalitarianism.

A gender gap that vanished: tolerance and liberalism.
See item no. 288.

Political implications of increasing numbers of women in the labour force.
See item no. 289.

Denmark: experiments in parliamentary government.
See item no. 309.

Government

National

308 The *Folketing* and Denmark's 'European policy': the case of an 'authorising assembly'.
David Arter.   In: *National parliaments and the European Union*.
Edited by Philip Norton.   London: Frank Cass & Company, 1996,
p. 110-23.
Examines how the *Folketing* (the Danish Parliament) has adapted to the challenges posed by European integration, and what variables shape the institutional changes that have taken place. Specifically, the chapter describes the emergence, formalization and reorganization of the Market Relations Committee (renamed the European Affairs Committee in 1994), which coordinates the *Folketing's* handling of European Union matters. The committee's authority and formal relationship with the *Folketing* is described, as well as its power and control in the wider context of the party policies and legislative culture of the *Folketing*. This work assumes some understanding of Danish government and party politics.

309 **Denmark: experiments in parliamentary government.**
Erik Damgaard.   In: *Parliamentary change in the Nordic countries*.
Edited by Erik Damgaard.   Oslo: Scandinavian University Press,
1992, p. 19-49.
Examines various developments in the Danish parliamentary government. This chapter describes the norms of government formation, discusses the parliamentary basis of governments before and after the landslide election of 1973, closely looks at the developments of the 1980s, and attempts to place the current Danish system into a theoretical perspective. The author notes that the fragmentation of the traditional party system since 1973 has resulted in a sequence of weak minority governments, yet an active parliament characterized by inter-party competition. Although this parliament is very representative and has assumed increased importance, its capacity to handle

serious economic problems has been reduced. Short-term thinking and temporary solutions often result. A balance between adaptability and representativeness on the one hand, and long-term thinking and accountability on the other is called for.

310 **Parliamentary questions and control in Denmark.**
Erik Damgaard.   In: *Parliamentary control in the Nordic countries: forms of questioning and behavioural trends.*   Edited by Matti Wiberg.   Helsinki: The Finnish Political Science Association, 1994, p. 44-76. bibliog.

Examines the special procedures for questioning ministers on the floor of Parliament. These include questions, interpellations, and committee questions. The work broadly outlines the development of the rules governing questioning activity, and analyses the frequency of use of these various instruments over time. The author observes an over-all increase in legislative activity in the 1970s following the party fragmentation in the 1973 election, and more recently, a stabilization. The work also aims to explain both the developments of the rules, as well as the development in legislative activity with reference to both internal parliamentary factors and to external factors such as political and social developments. Questioning activity is also examined in terms of the specific political parties and their distance from governmental power, i.e., whether they are governing or opposition parties. This work looks at some specific issues in Danish parliamentary control, but at the same time provides general information about the functioning of the Danish government and insight into party competition strategy.

311 **Denmark.**
John Fitzmaurice.   In: *Parliaments and parties: the European Parliament in the political life of Europe.*   Edited by Roger Morgan, Clare Tame.   Basingstoke, England: Macmillan; New York: St. Martin's Press, 1996, p. 236-58. bibliog.

Provides a detailed account of the functional relationship between the European Parliament (EP) and the *Folketing* (the Danish Parliament) set against the backdrop of Denmark's reluctant membership in the European Union (EU) and its defensive stance toward EU matters. The cooperative model of Danish parliamentary government and the informal nature of Danish politics is noted. The nature, purpose, and function of Denmark's Market Relations Committee (MRC), in terms of its safeguarding of Danish interests in EU policy matters, are described. The influence of the Danish political parties in the EP is discussed, with a focus on the activities of the Social Democrats, the *Venstre* party, and the Socialist People's Party. General Danish attitudes toward the EU are summarized. Decision-making procedures in the MRC, and the relationship among *Folketing* members, MRC members, and the Danish EP members are discussed. The author notes only a minimal influence of EP resolutions in Denmark, but foresees better relations as part of a practical response on the part of Denmark.

312 **Standing orders of the *Folketing*.**
The *Folketing*, revised translation by Birgite Wern.   Copenhagen: The *Folketing*, 1994. 67p.

This work is the English translation of the text of the 'Standing Orders of the *Folketing*' (the Danish Parliament) as of 17 December 1953, with the latest amendments added on 22 April 1994. Among the topics addressed are procedures for elections, committees, drafting and adopting of bills, amendments, constitutional bills, independent proposals and resolutions, petitions, debates, votes, appointments, and leave of absence. An appendix outlines allotted speaking times for various Parliament members during different events.

313 The Danish ombudsman.
Edited by Hans Gammeltoft-Hansen, Flemming Axmark.
Copenhagen: DJØF Publishing, 1995. 242p.

An idea that originated in Sweden, the office of the ombudsman was created in Denmark in 1955, the first of its kind in a modern welfare state. Denmark's ombudsman has inspired similar offices worldwide, and this book was published to meet the international need for information on this 'gift from Scandinavia to the world'. The work provides factual information on the principles, operation and jurisdiction of the ombudsman; case assessment and processing; the history and development of the institution; its position and relationship to other parts of government; and its human rights philosophy. A summary of each of fifteen significant cases in Denmark is provided, and the texts of the Danish Ombudsman Act and the Ombudsman Directives are reproduced in appendices. The book is an excellent information source, broad as well as thorough.

314 Committees as actors or arenas: putting questions to the Danish standing committees.
Henrik Jensen. In: *Parliamentary control in the Nordic countries: forms of questioning and behavioural trends.* Edited by Matti Wiberg. Helsinki: The Finnish Political Science Association, 1994, p. 77-102. bibliog.

Attempts to draw a more accurate picture of the standing committees (versus *ad hoc* committees) of the Danish Parliament as 'arenas' for political parties and their representatives, instead of looking at them as 'unified actors', an approach the author finds to be a common misrepresentation and one that ignores the partisan dimension of the committee members. In developing this 'arena' metaphor of the standing committees, which were introduced in 1972, the author describes the ways in which questions are put to committees. The description takes the form of a structural aspect, a procedural aspect, and an individual aspect. Included in this description is a model for how questioning behaviour is structured by the committees, an outline of the procedures for putting questions to the committees, and an examination of the characteristics of the questioners and their motives. The discussions are based on data from the 1991-92 period. In the concluding summary, the author acknowledges some of the problems associated with the 'arena' metaphor. This article is a theoretical effort, but it also contains some basic information on the instruments used for parliamentary questioning.

315 **Prior parliamentary consent to Danish EU policies.**
Jørgen Albæk Jensen. In: *National parliaments as cornerstones of European integration.* Edited by Eivind Smith. London; The Hague; Boston, Massachusetts: Kluwer Law International, 1996, p. 39-48. (European Monographs, no. 11).

Examines how Denmark has adapted its existing political institutions to major changes in policy-making, given that the Danish constitution contained no provision to guarantee formal influence of the *Folketing* (the Danish Parliament) on European Union policies affecting Denmark. This chapter specifically discusses the operation of the mandate procedure of the European Affairs Committee and how it provides a flexible solution to balance the actions of the government and of the *Folketing*. The political, practical, and legal implications of the committee are discussed in the light of the principle of 'negative parliamentarism'. This work assumes some familiarity with the operation of the Danish government.

316 **Denmark: the referendum as minority protection.**
Palle Svensson. In: *The referendum experience in Europe.* Edited by Michael Gallagher, Pier Vincenzo Uleri. Basingstoke, England: Macmillan; New York: St. Martins's Press, 1996, p. 33-51. bibliog.

Examines the referendum in terms of the representative character of the Danish political system. The constitutional background and the various types of referendums are reviewed, where the evolution of these types is viewed as a movement away from the principle of the sovereignty of the people and direct democracy towards minority protection and representative democracy. The history of referendums held in Denmark during the 1916-95 period is reviewed, and a table of voter turnout and voting results is included. The historical discussion is framed by issue: constitutional amendments, voting age, and European Community (EU) participation. Electoral behaviour at significant EC referendums is described, the political impact of the referendum – which the author views as limited – is commented on, and the future of the referendum is discussed as it has been a subject of recent debate. The author notes that support for more use of referendums is greatest among the politically powerless.

Local and regional

317 **The Danish case: rational or political change?**
Erik Albæk. In: *Towards the self-regulating municipality: free communes and administrative modernization in Scandinavia.* Edited by Harald Baldersheim, Krister Ståhlberg. Aldershot, England; Brookfield, Vermont: Dartmouth Publishing, 1994, p. 41-68. bibliog.

Provides an account of Denmark's free commune 'experiment', an idea which was adopted from Sweden. Free communes are municipalities which receive special dispensation from national legislation and regulations governing local affairs. The idea is discussed as an extension of both the Local Government Reform enacted in 1970, and of the public sector modernization programme of the 1982 Conservative-led government. The passing of the Free Commune Act, its aims, and its basic principles are described. The implementation of the experiment in 1992, in terms of the number and types of project proposals and the approval process, is discussed. The issue of evaluation receives special attention in that there was no official plan, and evaluation was left to the local councils themselves. The implications of the lack of evaluation are examined, such as the political motivation of the experiments, and legislative issues involved in using the experience gained. The bibliography contains primarily Danish-language works.

318 **International handbook of local and regional government: a comparative analysis of advanced democracies.**
Alan Norton. Aldershot, England; Brookfield, Vermont: Edward Elgar, 1994. 559p. bibliog.

A comparative review of nine countries: France, Italy, Germany, Sweden, Denmark, Britain, the United States, Canada, and Japan. Each country is reviewed in a separate chapter, on various dimensions, some of which include: the status of local government, concepts and values, inter-authority relations and organizations, inter-governmental relations, local government services and their implementation, local finance, electoral representation, and the internal organization of local authorities. Among the topics covered in the chapter on Denmark are the values of self-government, unitary administration, representativeness, and the concept of community. The municipalities' relationships with the counties and with national government are described. An outline of various government services is presented, which delineates the responsibilities of each level (local, regional, national). Local taxation (local, property) and financial transfers are described. The coverage of these topics is rather brief, as the work is intended to allow for national comparisons.

319 **Decentralization and local government: a Danish-Polish comparative study in political systems.**
Edited by Jerzy Regulski, Susanne Georg, Henrik Toft Jensen, Barrie Needham. New Brunswick, New Jersey; Oxford: Transaction Publishers, 1988. 271p.

A comparative work that offers a great deal of factual information about Danish local government. The information about each country is readily accessible in separate chapter sections. Opening chapters provide general information on the distinction between the private and public sector, and public sector activities. The national political system is described in terms of its basic structure and operation. Regarding local government, the legal basis for its formal institutions and for public participation in decision-making are discussed. The economic and historical development of local government is described. The ways in which local governments represent the interests of local societies is addressed in a discussion of the controls exercised over local government by the central administration, and the relationship between local councils and the electorate. Specific local issues such as finance, local government's influence on industrial development and on the labour market, the administration of the social welfare system, land-use planning, and infrastructure are described, and some case-studies are presented. Finally, the implications of the observed decentralization process in the two countries for theory development are addressed.

320 **Centralized economic control in a decentralized welfare state: Danish central-local government relations 1970-1986.**
Jens Tonboe. In: *State restucturing and local power: a comparative perspective.* Edited by Chris Pickvance, Edmond Preteceille.
London; New York: Pinter Publishers, 1991, p. 18-47. bibliog.
Examines the relationship between central and local politics and the public economy since the local government reforms of 1970, which saw a decentralization of the welfare state, and more autonomous local governments. The author describes the 'municipalization' of Denmark in terms of the expansion of local government in the period 1970 to 1980, the spending cuts and central regulation of local government from 1980 to 1986, the increasing local political activity of the unions, and the implications for households and local politics of increased female participation in the labour force. Throughout the examination of these issues, the author observes the interplay between centralized and decentralized control. The concluding section offers some sociological perspectives.

Local economic development in Denmark.
See item no. 366.

Denmark and other Scandinavian countries: equalization and grants.
See item no. 380.

Municipalities and counties in Denmark: tasks and finance.
See item no. 383.

The Legal System

321 **Nordic studies in information technology and law.**
Edited by Peter Blume. Deventer, the Netherlands; Boston,
Massachusetts: Kluwer Law and Taxation Publishers, 1991. 225p.
bibliog. (Computer/Law Series, no. 7).
Examines various legal issues and problem areas in connection with computerized
legal information in Denmark, Sweden, Norway, and Finland. The field is referred to
in the Nordic countries as 'legal informatics'. The book contains both specific topical
articles by researchers in the four countries, as well as more general comparative
information across the four countries. Regarding Denmark, there are concise, detailed
accounts of data protection legislation, legal information services, and legal informatics in legal education. This book aims to make Nordic research accessible to the
international community. It contains a rather extensive bibliography of works on
Scandinavian legal informatics published in English, German and French.

322 **Danish law in a European perspective.**
Edited by Børge Dahl, Torben Melchior, Lars Adam Rehof, Ditlev
Tamm. Copenhagen: Gad Jura Publishers, 1996. 543p.
Describes Danish law, with a particular focus on what would be of interest to an international audience. The book is divided into numerous chapters, each of which is
devoted to an individual area of law such as inheritance, property, torts, contracts,
family law, criminal law, environmental law, finance, tax, and labour. There are also
chapters on general topics such as Danish legal heritage, the constitution, the judiciary,
the social system, and legal studies. Each chapter emphasizes elements in the given
area which reflect a particularly Danish solution to a universal legal issue. The book is
not meant to be an exhaustive analysis of Danish law, yet it is far more than a general
introduction and treats particular features in some depth. Included in appendices are a
table of Danish statutes (the statute title is in English and the explanatory note is in
Danish); a table of Danish cases; and a table of European Court of Justice cases.

323 **Corporations and partnerships in Denmark.**
Mogens Ebeling, Bernhard Gomard.   Deventer, the Netherlands;
Boston, Massachusetts: Kluwer Law and Taxation Publishers, 1993.
250p.

A comprehensive legal reference on the law of limited and private companies and limited and 'sleeping' partnerships. The book is divided into three major sections. Part one provides general background on Denmark from a business point of view along with historical background on the legislation regarding companies and partnerships. The various types of companies and partnerships and their structures are defined. Part two covers companies and includes such topics as formation; rights, rules and regulations regarding shareholders, management duties and powers; employee participation and the role of employee representatives; liquidation; mergers and takeovers; and taxation. Part three covers the legal status of the various types of partnerships.

324 **Corrections in two social welfare democracies: Denmark and Sweden.**
Finn Hornum.   *Prison Journal*, vol. 68 (1988), p. 63-82.

Provides an examination of the key elements of the correctional systems of Denmark and Sweden in an effort to enlighten American correctional policy. A primary purpose is to review the developments in Scandinavian correctional policy within their social and cultural contexts. The opening sections of the article describe the political, economic and social aspects of Danish and Swedish society, and their general philosophies of the causes and the control of crime. The administration of the Danish and Swedish criminal justice systems and their criminal codes are also described. The correctional systems are described in detail in terms of management and staffing, the types of institutions, inmates' rights and prison living conditions, education and work programmes, treatment programmes, the importance of probation and parole, and the effectiveness of the system. The conclusion regarding lessons for American corrections is quite brief, the main point being that it is not impossible to apply Scandinavian models to American criminal justice.

325 **Danish business law.**
Bent Iversen, Jørgen Nørgaard, Morten Wegener, Niels Ørgaard,
translated from the Danish by Hanne Grøn.   Copenhagen: DJØF
Publishing, 1998. 557p.

This book is an English translation of a Danish-language text which was published in 1997. The work is divided into eight major sections. The introduction includes an overview of the legal system and a survey of the court system. It also describes the types of legal rules, and national and international sources of law. Other sections cover compensation in tort law and insurance; contract law; sale of goods and supply of services; financing and security of credit; business and the workforce; international choice of law; and environmental regulation. This is a broad and comprehensive text on all aspects of business law. It covers not only areas of purely Danish law, but also those areas that reflect international cooperation such as laws relating to the European Union or laws which have resulted from international conventions. The preface briefly orients the reader to some basic characteristics of Danish business law.

326 **Denmark.**
Per Jacobsen. In: *Temporary work and labour law of the European Union and member states.* Edited by R. Blanpain. Deventer, the Netherlands; Boston, Massachusetts: Kluwer Law and Taxation Publishers, 1993, p. 77-90.

Provides a concise survey of the state of labour law relating to temporary workers, the primary feature of the Danish system being the very limited regulation in this area since a lifting of restrictions in 1990. The chapter surveys the legal framework surrounding the temporary work option, examines the limited role of trade unions and collective bargaining agreements, and discusses the limited role of government. The work also discusses the operation of temporary work firms, the use of temporary employees, and working conditions, health and welfare. This area of law is considered significant in the light of the increase in part-time employment in the European Union since the early 1980s, and the need for flexibility in the face of international competition.

327 **Criminal law in Denmark.**
Lars Bo Langsted, Vagn Greve, Peter Garde. Copenhagen: DJØF Publishing, 1998. 221p. bibliog.

A comprehensive text that is an ideal reference for all aspects of the criminal justice system. The first part of the book is introductory and provides an overview of the system and the historical background of the criminal code. The chapters in the second part of the book include the general principles of the substantive criminal law, the scope of criminal statutes, the general principles of criminal liability, grounds for justification and excuse, the rules for incomplete or partially perpetrated offences, and the classification of criminal offences. The chapter on the sanctioning system delineates the types of punishments and the principles of sentencing. The chapter on criminal procedure covers the investigation, pre-trial, and trial stages. The final section deals with the structure and functioning of the prison system with a discussion of prisoners' rights and conditions for early release. The authors present complex legal material in a reasonably clear fashion, and provide context and background for the factual information.

328 **Prisons in Denmark.**
Ministry of Justice Department of Prisons and Probation. Copenhagen: Ministry of Justice Department of Prisons and Probation, 1990. 85p.

Provides an overview of the prison system, with descriptions of its organizational structure and capacity, along with individual profiles of each of ten open prisons and six closed prisons. The work describes the general functioning of prisons in terms of prisoners' work, education, leisure activities, health, leave, visits, and disciplinary actions. The general philosophy of imprisonment is also discussed, a key principle being the 'principle of normalization' whereby prison life is meant to approximate as much as possible to a normal existence. Restrictions are used to prevent escape, and the system operates with a general treatment philosophy. The criteria for placement in a closed versus an open institution are also discussed. The information presented here is general and somewhat brief; the individual prison profiles comprise the entire second half of the work.

329 **Equality in law between men and women in the European Community, Denmark.**
Ruth Nielsen.   The Hague; Boston, Massachusetts; London: Martinus Nijhoff Publishers; Luxembourg: Office for Official Publications of the European Communities, 1995. 152p. bibliog. (Equality in Law Between men and Women in the European Community).

Part of an encyclopaedia compiled by a European Community (EC) network of experts on the implementation of EC equality directives. The work is presented in two sections. Section one is a commentary on Danish labour law with an overview of the law and its sources, definitions of basic concepts with relevant conditions and examples, and explanations of pertinent legislation. Section one is written in such a way as to allow for comparisons among the member states. Section two contains legislative texts currently in force in Danish law which implement the principles laid down in EC equality directives. Pertinent cases are summarized. This is a reference work on equality in the working environment that would be of interest to those in the legal profession, government, and academia. The bibliography contains sources that are primarily written in Danish.

330 **Responsibility – a key word in the Danish prison system.**
William Rentzmann.   In: *Negotiating responsibility in the criminal justice system.*   Edited by Jack Kamerman.   Carbondale, Illinois: Southern Illinois University Press, 1998, p. 94-109.

Discusses the concept of responsibility in light of the structural changes in the Danish Correctional Service over the preceding ten years, where decentralization has resulted in a delegation of power to municipalities, local management, and on down to individual correctional staff. The concept of responsibility is examined in terms of both staff and inmates. Staff members often have responsibility for the actual treatment of two or three inmates. Inmates have responsibility for the administration of their daily lives and must take responsibility for their crime. Responsibility is discussed as part and parcel of the correctional service's principle of normalization, i.e., the normalizing of prison conditions, as much as possible, to the outside community. The chapter also touches on open prisons, extended leave schemes, and conditional sentences, as they relate to responsibility. The author is the general director of the Danish Prison and Probation Service. Excerpts from the Danish Prison and Probation Service's 1994 mission statement 'Program of Principles for Prison and Probation Work in Denmark' are included in an appendix.

331 **A comparison of punishment systems in Denmark and the United States.**
William L. Selke.   *International Journal of Comparative Applied Criminal Justice*, vol. 15, no. 2 (Fall 1991), p. 227-42.

Examines Danish correctional policy in terms of the social and political values it reflects regarding the causes of crime and the ability of the criminal justice system to control crime. Scandinavian and American attitudes towards these issues are compared. The nature and extent of crime and punishment in Denmark and the state of Indiana are compared, using crime and sentencing data from the mid-1980s. The study also incorporates interviews with various staff members from five major prisons in Denmark, which house serious offenders, and with personnel from the Department of Prisons. From information gathered in the interviews, Danish prisons are described somewhat generally in terms of their physical structure, philosophies and goals, the role of prison guards, management practices, and programmes and special services for inmates. Brief comments are given on the evaluation of the effectiveness of imprisonment. The author encourages consideration of the Danish model by other societies, despite the special nature of Danish society. Although the empirical data is somewhat dated, the ideas expressed in this article remain timely.

332 **Agrarian land law in Denmark.**
   Helge Wulff. In: *Agrarian land law in the Western world.* Edited by Margaret Russo Grossman, Wim Brussard. Wallingford, England: CAB International, 1992, p. 35-50.
Provides a description of various aspects of agrarian land law. The section on legislation reviews the acts and laws related to planning, farm structures, forestry, nature conservation, and environmental protection. Conflict resolution options and judge-made law are also described. A section on government policy describes its aims, and its central and local administration. A final section comments on how well agrarian land law functions in terms of planning, controlling urban sprawl, determining farm structures, protecting forests and wetlands, and combating water pollution. The chapter is an overview, and coverage of the topics is rather brief. It should be considered a starting point. The reference list cites exclusively Danish-language works.

Freedom of religion in Denmark.
See item no. 217.

Employment protection under strain. (Sweden, Denmark, The Netherlands).
See item no. 424.

Foreign Relations

Foreign and security policy

333 Danish and European security: summary.
Copenhagen: Danish Commission on Security and Disarmament, 1995.
40p.
This work is the English summary of a 300-page Danish-language report, a comprehensive analysis and evaluation of Danish security in the new European context of the post-Cold War era. This work outlines the patterns, conflicts and challenges of the international and European situation, and describes the various existing security organizations. It discusses the 'Europeanization' of Danish foreign and security policy that has occurred, where the emphasis is on the European Union and its political as well as its economic significance. Denmark has also become involved in the Baltic region on a larger scale and has increased its use of military means in efforts such as peacekeeping in Yugoslavia and military cooperation with the Baltic States and Poland. The democratization of Denmark's foreign policy is also discussed in that there is greater involvement on the part of the Parliament and an increased use of referendums in the area of foreign policy. This concise, clear summary is very informative and provides an excellent overview.

334 Adaptation and activism: the foreign policy of Denmark 1967-1993.
Edited by Carsten Due-Nielsen, Nikolaj Petersen.   Copenhagen:
DJØF Publishing, 1995. 304p. bibliog.
Analyses the major aspects of Danish foreign policy – security, economy, integration, and foreign aid – in a compilation of papers by foreign policy experts. The chapters can be read separately and references follow each chapter. The editors' introduction successfully summarizes and ties the papers together. The papers cover such topics as Denmark's alliance policies through détente, the New Cold War, and the post-Cold War phase; the politics of Danish defence; the country's relationship with the Soviet

Union and Central and Eastern Europe; the European Union and Denmark's economic policies; development policy; and foreign policy choices for the 21st century. Each chapter stresses the interplay between international and domestic factors, and shows Denmark's evolution from a passive to a more active stance in foreign relations. This work is appropriate for both scholars and general readers.

335 **The other side of international development policy: the non-aid economic relations with developing countries of Canada, Denmark, the Netherlands, Norway, and Sweden.**
Edited by Gerald K. Helleiner.   Toronto; Buffalo, New York; London: University of Toronto Press, 1990. 187p.

This work argues that a complete assessment of a country's overall contribution to the developing world requires an assessment of that country's trade policies as well as its aid relations. The work presents data on the changing pattern of the trade and investment relations with Third World countries for three Scandinavian countries, the Netherlands, and Canada. Chapter three is devoted to Denmark and describes the evolution of policies in the 1970s and 1980s in the light of that era's worldwide economic downturn and Denmark's joining the European Community in 1973, the result being a shift from liberal to more protectionist policies. The editor's opening chapter is a thorough overview which succeeds in putting the issue in perspective across the five countries.

336 **Denmark: security policy and foreign policy – a new activism.**
Bertel Heurlin.   In: *Security problems in the new Europe: six essays on European, German, Baltic, Nordic, and Danish security.*   Bertel Heurlin.   Copenhagen: Political Studies Press, 1995, p. 96-117. bibliog.

Examines the strengths and weaknesses of Denmark's position in the post-Cold War era with a look at the impact of the 'internationalization' and the 'Europeanization' of national foreign and security policy. These two important developments – the results of the end of the Cold War and the emergence of the European Union – signal crucial changes and choices for Denmark. The structural and process-level implications of these developments are discussed, as the country adapts to its new responsibilities as a producer, rather than a consumer, of security. Explanations for Denmark's attitudes and policies are discussed in terms of the country's need to integrate into the international system while simultaneously surviving as an independent unit. Five different foreign policy efforts are examined in terms of how this balance is maintained. This work assumes some familiarity with the issues and terminology of international relations.

337 **Danish foreign policy yearbook.**
Edited by Bertel Heurlin, Hans Mouritzen.   Copenhagen: Danish Institute of International Affairs, 1997- . annual. bibliog.

Presents articles on various topics related to Danish foreign policy within a regional and an international context. The opening essay reviews the international situation for the previous year. Subsequent scholarly articles in the two current editions have discussed such topics as Danish security interests in the Baltic Sea; the balance of international and domestic concerns; recent considerations in foreign aid, international assistance and disaster relief; and the fluctuations in Danish foreign policy during the 20th century. Recent foreign policy statistics and the results of relevant public opinion polls on foreign policy are also presented, as well as the texts of selected documents characteristic of Danish foreign policy.

338 **Danish neutrality: a study in the foreign policy of a small state.**
Carsten Holbraad.   Oxford: Clarendon Press, 1991. 190p.

Describes and analyses Danish foreign policy for the period 1720-1990 in times of crisis and war among greater powers. The author explains that the country's foreign policy has been characterized by a long tradition of neutrality in international conflict. Denmark's neutrality has rarely been motivated by moral concerns, but rather has frequently been based on economic and international political concerns. Each chapter outlines the events for a particular period of time and identifies the attitudes under-lying what the author sees as an historical succession of different versions of neutrality. The bulk of the work focuses on the latter part of the 20th century and Denmark's role in NATO and the European Community. Indeed the country's neutralist tendencies in NATO have shown signs of change with the revolutions in Eastern Europe and the fall of the Berlin Wall. Denmark's current foreign policy is seen as emerging with a new commitment to alliance solidarity and European integration.

339 **National security and Danish defence policy.**
Fini Høyer-Olsen, Nikolaj Petersen.   In: *Bulgaria and Denmark and the new Europe.*   Edited by Georgi Karasimeonov, Mette Skak.
Sofia: St. Kliment Ohridsky University Press, 1994, p. 96-109.

Discusses the significance for Denmark of the new crisis management focus in NATO strategy following the end of the Cold War. The author observes that Denmark is vulnerable to being drawn into conflicts in the North Atlantic and in North and Central Europe, and that the security of other member states is affected by the preservation of Danish sovereignty. The country's security responsibilities in terms of its technological, social and economic developments are discussed. It is noted that Denmark has not been a leader in military technology, and that its consensus-style domestic policy-making was more suitable to pre-Cold War security concerns. Recommendations are made regarding increases in military budget allocations and adaptations in policy-making. The country's contributions to European security, such as its increased participation in UN operations and its efforts to work within the NATO framework, are also discussed.

340 **Small states and security regimes: the international politics of nuclear non-proliferation in Nordic Europe and the South Pacific.**
John Scott Masker.   Lanham, Maryland; London: University Press of America, 1995. 162p. bibliog.

This book generally attempts to shed light on the role of small states, in the shadow of the great powers, in nuclear non-proliferation arrangements. Chapter four deals with the Nordic case, analysing Denmark's and Norway's reluctant membership in NATO and the various nuclear weapons debates. The chapter specifically addresses why Denmark and Norway rejected the Finnish proposal of a Nordic regional nuclear-free zone, examining the links between domestic, regional, and global factors that shaped Danish and Norwegian policy. There is also emphasis on the countries' sensitivity to the American reaction to their activities and relations with the Soviet Union.

341 **Denmark and the CSCE.**
Peter Michael Nielsen. In: *Bulgaria and Denmark and the new Europe.* Edited by Georgi Karasimeonov, Mette Skak. Sofia: St. Kliment Ohridsky University Press, 1994, p. 125-42.

Discusses Denmark's interests in the Conference on Security and Cooperation in Europe (CSCE), a series of meetings beginning in 1966, now on its way to becoming an international organization. The changing rationale for the CSCE since the end of the Cold War from an emphasis on détente to an expansion of conflict prevention and conflict resolution efforts is discussed. The author observes that Denmark has always had a keen interest, given its exposed position during the Cold War, and would like to see the current efforts of the CSCE further expanded, as well as a stronger focus in the area of human rights as it relates to the rights of national minorities to self-determination. The effectiveness and the limitations of the CSCE are discussed, as well as its future in terms of what type of organization it should become, and what role it would play in relation to NATO. All these issues are examined in terms of how they accord with Danish interests. The author speculates on whether Denmark will continue to retain its high profile in the CSCE.

342 **Danish policies toward the Baltic States.**
Ole Nørgaard. In: *The Baltic States in international politics.* Edited by Nikolaj Petersen. Copenhagen: DJØF Publishing, 1993, p. 155-74. bibliog.

Analyses Danish policy towards Estonia, Latvia and Lithuania, before and after independence, noting the interplay among foreign policy, security policy, and economic aid. It is observed that Denmark has been a relatively strong supporter of the Baltic States, and has had to reconcile its interests concerning Russia, its own domestic politics, respect for the national rights of the Baltic peoples, and human rights concerns for immigrants. In a somewhat general manner, the author discusses the Danish support effort in terms of its assumptions about the transition to a pluralist democracy and a market economy. Support is further appraised in terms of the scope of the various programmes, their implementation, and their coupling to overall foreign policy goals. The author grapples with the basic question of how much Denmark should try to influence developments inside the Baltic States and offers general recommendations for the long term.

343 **The debate on European security in Denmark.**
Ole Karup Pedersen. In: *European polyphony: perspectives beyond East-West confrontation.* Edited by Ole Weaver, Pierre Lemaitre, Elzbieta Tromer. London: Macmillan Press, 1989, p. 269-82.

Discusses the non-military tradition in Danish foreign policy in the context of the country's history and its core values. The debate over security has been a democratic one with participation by political parties, the government, diplomats, the military establishment, independent research institutions, and journalists and political scientists. It has been characterized by widespread doubts over the extent to which military means promote Danish security. Further, Danish governments have traditionally stressed the 'political' aspect of NATO, and have seen its main function to be the demilitarization of Europe. Denmark favours all efforts to promote European security through demilitarization, and would like to see its pacifist core values take root, particularly in Eastern Europe.

344 **Adapting to change: Danish security policy after the Cold War.**
Nikolaj Petersen. In: *European security 2000*. Edited by Birthe
Hansen. Copenhagen: Political Studies Press, 1995, p. 99-116.
bibliog.

Analyses the Danish reaction to changes in the external security environment and the
development of new security policies. A general shift towards an activist security
stance is noted in terms of NATO, the Western European Union (WEU) and the
Conference on Security and Cooperation in Europe (CSCE). Regarding NATO,
Denmark's role as producer rather than a consumer of security is discussed. The
implications of the European Union defence exemption for the EU and the WEU are
discussed, as is the lower priority Denmark currently gives to the CSCE. More
specifically, Danish participation in UN peacekeeping missions, support for the
integration of the Baltic States into Western Europe, and the restructuring of defence
forces for participation in international security initiatives are described. Throughout
the article analysis is attempted as to the reasons for the policy shift in terms of the
characteristics of internationalization, militarization, and Europeanization.

345 **For the sake of peace: the Danish UN effort here and now.**
Per Amnitzbøl Rasmussen. Copenhagen: The Information and
Welfare Services of the Danish Armed Forces, 1993. 50p. map.

A testimonial to Denmark's commitment to the United Nations peacekeeping mission.
This work is a survey in words and pictures of Danish peace operations in various
countries in Eastern Europe, the Middle East, and the former Soviet Union. The text
offers information on the dates and locations of Danish engagements, mission resolutions and titles, number of personnel, and further details about the operations. The
numerous colour photographs, some a full page, depict the everyday life and working
conditions of the Danish UN soldiers. A two-page chart provides information on
Danish UN operations from 1948 to 1993.

346 **Collective Western European resort to armed force: lessons from
Danish, Italian and British experiences in the Gulf and former
Yugoslavia.**
Kristian Schmidt. Copenhagen: DJØF Publishing, 1994. 82p. bibliog.

This work addresses the issue of whether a common foreign and security policy for
Europe is likely and desirable. The author assesses opinions, perceptions, and attitudes
towards the use of armed force through interviews with ministry officials, diplomats,
members of parliament, and members of research units. The three countries were
chosen to reflect the diversity of European Community membership. The test cases of
the Gulf War and the conflict in the former Yugoslavia represent instances of
collective armed intervention outside the NATO area which generated much debate.
The information is presented in four themes relative to the use of armed force: domestic
foundations of national policies, international relations, military planning, and the
implementation of national policies. The author attempts to assess the degree of
convergence on all these elements and the implications for European security policy.

347 **Danish aid: old bottles.**
Knud Erik Svendsen.   In: *Western middle powers and global poverty: the determinants of the aid policies of Denmark, the Netherlands, Norway and Sweden.*   Edited by Olav Stokke.   Uppsala, Sweden: The Scandinavian Institute of African Studies, 1989, p. 91-115. bibliog.

Discusses Denmark's aid policies in terms of the country's ideology and predominant basic values and political norms. Specifically the author examines the formation of aid policies as part of the political process, noting the debates and disputes over the purpose of Danish aid. The basic features of aid policies are described, such as the official purpose of aid and the ways in which aid is channelled to recipient nations. Other issues include the volume of aid, multilateral versus bilateral aid, and the choice of recipient countries. Much of the discussion is framed in terms of the attempts that have been made to change Danish aid since the mid-1970s that actually resulted in little change, and the country's own means of evaluating its aid policies. Statistics are presented up to 1985.

348 **Denmark: social development and international development cooperation.**
Knud Erik Svendsen.   In: *Welfare, development, and security: three Danish essays.*   Ministry of Foreign Affairs.   Copenhagen: Ministry of Foreign Affairs, 1995, p. 35-58.

Examines Denmark's formulation and implementation of development aid policy against the backdrop of its own social history and social development. The work discusses the major features of Denmark's social history and development and its participation in international development cooperation from the 1950s to the 1990s. The various influences on that participation are also examined. Danish strategy has not been to introduce social arrangements similar to those of its own history, but rather to introduce individual country strategies based on partnerships with the recipients. There has been a tradition of the transfer of resources to alleviate poverty, with a recent emphasis on the linkage between economic growth and social development. The author notes that the magnitude of social problems in developing countries poses a significant challenge for the future of Denmark's partnerships with aid recipients.

European integration

349 **When no means yes: Danish visions of a different Europe.**
Edited by Hanne Norup Carlsen, Ross Jackson, Niels L. Meyer.
London: Adamantine Press, 1993. 150p.

An anthology of essays by various scholars and professionals who provide background and reasons for the 1992 'no' vote on the Maastricht Treaty. Some of the contributors also present alternative visions of what Europe could become. The book is divided into various broad themes including culture and democracy, economics and sustainable development, and national security. Specific essays examine the 'no' vote in terms of its legal import, its significance for labour, and its significance for women. Other essays offer perspectives in terms of social welfare philosophy, Nordic history, the Danish view on European economic growth and free trade, and on environmental protection. The book reveals much about the cultural background of the Danes, given that the contributors frame their analyses in a cultural or historical perspective. The book as a whole can be viewed as a lively discussion.

350 **The Danish no to Maastricht.**
Niels Finn Christiansen. *New Left Review*, no. 195 (September/ October 1992), p. 97-101.
Explores the mixture of motives that lay behind the Danish rejection of Maastricht in 1992. (The 'no' victory was won by a very narrow margin and the referendum in the following year resulted in a 'yes'.) This author shows that the 'no' campaigners represented an alliance of extremely diverse interests and came from a broad spectrum of the Danish population with differing political viewpoints. Generally they were motivated by a concern for preserving the country's sovereignty and the Danish model of democracy. They comprised organized cross-party opposition to the European Community, a smaller more loosely organized group of neo-nationalists, middle- and working-class strata fearing the elimination of the welfare state, and trades unionists concerned over the internationalization of the collective agreements that underlie the Danish labour market. This article offers a concise and coherent presentation.

351 **Looking to Europe: the EC policies of the British Labour Party and the Danish Social Democrats.**
Jens Henrik Haahr.   Aarhus, Denmark: Aarhus University Press, 1993. 340p. bibliog.
Compares the policies regarding the European Community (EC) of two nationally important social democratic parties, from the 1960s until the present day. The positions of both these parties have undergone significant changes. The work examines how and why the policies of the two parties developed, and frames the analysis in theoretical propositions regarding the behaviour of political parties and the dynamics of regional integration. Chapters eight and nine focus specifically on Denmark, with an analysis of the EC policies before and after the Single European Act and the 1986 referendum, and during the negotiations leading up to Maastricht. The development of the party's ultimate endorsement of Denmark's participation in the European Monetary Union is demonstrated. The work assumes some background in political science for the theoretical discussions, but the factual information is clearly presented for the general reader.

352 **The Nordic states and European unity.**
Christine Ingebritsen.   Ithaca, New York; London: Cornell University Press, 1998. 219p.
The aim of this book is to account for the relatively swift changes in Nordic foreign and security policies since the Single European Act in 1985, given their status as small, trading nations, traditionally sceptical toward political integration. It is observed that the Nordic countries must reconcile national politics with supranational policy, or more specifically, the interests of powerful trade unions with business-led European Union (EU) policy. The book's emphasis is on the political power of 'leading sectors' (Danish farmers and the agricultural export industry, for example) in

EU-related policy choices. The leading sector approach is applied to the Nordic countries in general with specific references to individual situations, as each country is affected somewhat differently by EU accession. The information in this book is based on interviews with trade union representatives, government ministries, parliamentary committees, industry leaders, special-interest groups, and the military.

353 **European integration and Denmark's participation.**
Edited by Morten Kelstrup.   Copenhagen: Copenhagen Political Studies Press, 1992. 383p.

Aims to contribute to the theoretical debate within political science and international relations in three areas: the overall European process; the development and character of the European Community; and the special aspects of the integration policy of a small state. Four out of twelve chapters deal specifically with Denmark. The issues addressed include: the relationship of political-administrative institutions to the country's culture and the significance of state culture for Danish integration policy; the significance of Danish attitudes towards sovereignty for Danish integration policy since 1945; the position of the Danish political parties towards European integration; and finally the cleavages in public attitudes towards integration following the 1992 referendum on the Maastricht agreement. The book's intended audience is the international research community and university students. The editor's thorough introduction notes that the book deliberately grapples with difficult theoretical issues.

354 **Denmark and the European political union.**
Finn Laursen.   In: *The intergovernmental conference on political union: institutional reforms, new policies and the international identity of the European Community.*   Edited by Finn Laursen, Sophie Vanhoonacker.   Dordrecht, the Netherlands: Martinus Nijhoff Publishers, 1992, p. 63-78.

Discusses the development of Denmark's position on European integration up to the period just prior to the 1992 referendum on Maastricht. The focus is on the second of two Intergovernmental Conferences leading up to Maastricht, the first dealing with economic and monetary union, the second with political union. This chapter provides details on the positions of the major parties, particularly the Social Democrats. It is also very informative in terms of the detailed discussion it provides on the content of the Danish Memorandum of 1990 and on the Danish contributions to the content of the various draft treaties. The chapter features the problems and tensions within the Danish political system as the country moved cautiously towards its pro-integration stance.

355 **Denmark and EC membership evaluated.**
Edited by Lise Lyck.   London: Pinter Publishers; New York: St. Martin's Press, 1992. 253p. (EC Membership Evaluated Series).

Part of a series which examines the costs and benefits of European Community (EC) membership for the state as a whole and within the areas of economic policy, foreign relations, the political and legal system, and social, educational and cultural policies. In this volume on Denmark, nineteen contributors from the fields of business, economics, political science, and social and cultural studies report information and give their perspective, in an academic work that is written so as to be accessible to a general audience. Although increased economic integration is seen as more positive than negative by most Danes, they fear a loss of national and cultural identity. Denmark has striven to maintain a high degree of sovereignty, yet it has incorporated most EC directives into law. This Danish ambivalence regarding EC membership is taken into consideration in many of these chapters. An editor's postscript provides an account of the 1992 referendum on ratification of the Maastricht Agreement. (Denmark voted 'no' in 1992, but voted 'yes' in the following year, after the publication of this work.)

356 **Denmark and European integration.**
Thomas Pedersen.   In: *Bulgaria and Denmark and the new Europe.*
Edited by Georgi Karasimeonov, Mette Skak.   Sofia, Bulgaria:
St. Kliment Ohridsky University Press, 1994, p. 58-80.

This article looks in depth at several important issues such as the costs and benefits to Denmark, particularly concerning defence policy, of supranational European Community (EC) institutions; Denmark's relationship to Germany in terms of the struggles among Europe's great powers over control of the EC's development; and the implications for other countries of the Danish 'opt-out' clauses in the Edinburgh Agreement. The author also speculates on the development and significance of an informal Nordic bloc within the EC as other Nordic countries prepare for membership. The opening section describes the overall trends in Danish EC policy, noting the actions of the Social Democratic party. This article is particularly good for the level of detail and insight it provides on these issues concerning Denmark in the wider European context.

357 **Denmark and the European Union.**
Thomas Pedersen.   In: *The European Union and the Nordic countries.*
Edited by Lee Miles.   London; New York: Routledge, 1996,
p. 81-100.

This chapter provides an interpretation of Denmark's attitude towards European integration that differs from most discussions of this topic. The author observes that recent policy choices actually represent a departure from the country's traditional reservations towards integration. It is noted that official Danish European Union (EU) policy underwent a fundamental change at the close of the 1980s and showed a commitment towards membership in a supranational community. The change can be seen in the endorsement of the Treaty on European Union in 1991 and the Edinburgh Agreement of 1992. The chapter provides a good overview of the historical evolution of Danish EU policy, and then examines the causes for the recent policy redirection. Interestingly, the four opt-out clauses which Denmark negotiated at the Edinburgh Summit (these relate to citizenship, defence policy, and currency union) are interpreted as having limited significance. The chapter offers theoretical analysis applying Hermann's theory of foreign policy change which is then supplemented with classical integration theory. There is a bibliography for the entire book, but not for individual chapters.

358 **Denmark and the European Union 1985-1996: a two-level analysis.**
Nikolaj Petersen.   *Cooperation and Conflict*, vol. 31, no. 2 (June 1996),
p. 185-210.

Describes and explains the significant changes in Danish European Community (EC) policies in the course of a decade. This article is significant for its focus on the balance that was struck between the domestic and the international agenda, as the country moved from a 'foot-dragging posture' to more active support to 'yes' and 'no' flip-flopping on the Maastricht referendums. The author provides a theoretical analysis using change theory and the 'two-level games' perspective to explain policy shifts based on the need to balance external and domestic environments. Throughout this analysis the more general reader can benefit from the wealth of factual information on the important milestones in Denmark's EC membership. The author describes Denmark's participation in the various Inter-Governmental conferences and the country's many concessions, retractions, and defensive positions. The article is very clearly written and well organized.

359 **In the strategic triangle: Denmark and the European Union.**
Nikolaj Petersen. In: *European integration and disintegration: East and West.* Edited by Robert Bideleux, Richard Taylor. London; New York: Routledge, 1996, p. 93-110.

Examines Danish European Community (EC) policies in terms of 'the strategic triangle' – politicians, public opinion, and other EC member states – where all three corners must be in balance. The author argues that the balance is often difficult in that domestic factors have a major impact on Danish European policy. The work describes how policy is formulated in the light of domestic factors. It goes on to discuss Denmark's relations with the EC, since joining in 1973 up to the present day, and highlights the significant legislation and initiatives. The implications for Denmark of the 1991 Maastricht Treaty and of the Edinburgh Summit the following year are also discussed. This chapter is significant for its use of 'the strategic triangle' model and for its focus on the centrality of domestic politics for Danish European policy. A final section examines the theoretical implications of this approach for the study of European integration as a whole.

360 **The Danes said *no* to the Maastricht treaty: the Danish EC referendum of June 1992.**
Karen Siune. *Scandinavian Political Studies*, vol. 16, no. 1 (1993), p. 93-103.

Examines the Danish 'no' to Maastricht with an analysis of the voting patterns by age, gender, political party, and the reasons for a 'no' vote. It is reported that the most important reason for an anti-EC position was the fear of the loss of sovereignty, rather than any fear associated with economic issues. A significant aspect of this analysis is discussion of the role and the impact of the media in the referendum campaign. The author concludes that the 'no' vote was not simply a protest vote against party politicians who had come to accept the European Community (EC), but rather it was an informed 'no' against the parts of the Maastricht Treaty that gave more and more political power to the EC.

361 **The Danish yes to Maastricht and Edinburgh: the EC referendum of May 1993.**
Palle Svensson. *Scandinavian Political Studies*, vol. 17, no. 1 (1994), p. 69-82.

Provides an analysis of the results of the May 1993 referendum and draws comparisons with the Danish 'no' in June 1992. Voting trends are examined in terms of age, gender, employment categories, reported interest in politics, and party membership. With only a seven per cent net change, the author finds that Danish voters did not really act very differently. The article also discusses the background of the May referendum and the campaign leading up to it. General comments on this 'experiment in direct democracy' are also offered.

362 **Danish public opinion and the European Community.**
Torben Worre. *Scandinavian Journal of History*, vol. 20, no. 3 (1995), p. 209-27.

This article examines the nature and development of Danish public opinion on European integration over a forty-year period and analyses the reasons it has come to play a decisive role in policymaking. The sources of opposition to the European Community, such as the fear of foreign competition and loss of sovereignty, are discussed, and the results of the four referendums (1972, 1986, 1992 and 1993) on integration are interpreted. Attitudes regarding the EC have been unstable, but long-term trends show distinct phases of consensus and opposition. Attitudes have also been independent of party preference. The issue of European integration has evolved from a question of 'in versus out' to one of 'more versus less integration'. This article is clearly written, and provides an excellent overview of this topic for both the scholar and the general reader.

363 **Denmark at the crossroads: the Danish referendum of 28 February 1986 on the EC reform package.**
Torben Worre. *Journal of Common Market Studies*, vol. 26, no. 4 (June 1988), p. 361-88.

Provides a detailed account of the situation where fifty-six per cent of Danish voters approved the reforms that became known as the Single European Act, the first systematic revision of the Treaty of Rome. The article is based on survey data from 999 voters that was collected in the weeks immediately following the referendum. The article contains an overview of the history of public opinion regarding the European Community (EC); a discussion of Denmark's EC policy in terms of the various political parties; an examination of the constitutional conditions surrounding the referendum; and an outline of the campaign arguments for approval or rejection of the reform package. Finally, voter opinion on these arguments, how these opinions developed, the final motives for the voters' choices are examined. This article is useful not only for its look at voter opinion, but also for the detailed examination of this experience with the use of a referendum.

Denmark in international affairs: publications in languages other than Danish 1965-1995.
See item no. 663.

Economy

364 **European Community: economic structure and analysis.**
London; New York: The Economist Intelligence Unit, 1989. 2 vols.
maps. (EIU Regional Reference Series).
A special report that provides background and perspective on European Community
issues such as agricultural, economic, and environmental policy, as well as individual
country studies on member nations. These chapters are overviews and report very
general information. Volume one of this two-volume set contains the chapter on
Denmark, and reports on such issues as the country's economy (the main economic
sectors being agriculture, fishing, and forestry), politics, government, international
relations, and foreign trade. This work is a concise reference for economic information
and data up to 1987.

365 **The productivity mystery: industrial development in Denmark in
the eighties.**
Allan Næs Gjerding, Björn Johnson, Lars Kallehauge, Bengt-Åke
Lundvall, Poul Thøis Madsen.   Copenhagen: DJØF Publishing, 1992.
131p. bibliog.
Analyses the unexpected decline in Denmark's productivity growth rate, particularly
in the manufacturing sector during the 1983-86 period, a time when the business cycle
pointed towards growth, exhibiting an increase in production, investment, and
employment. The authors observe that traditional economic explanations fall short,
and they turn to a compound examination of global economic changes, the specific
structural and cyclical problems affecting the Danish economy, and the behaviour of
individual firms. Individual firms' investments in new technology and in manpower
planning are examined in an effort to determine whether the investments are
sufficiently technologically advanced and whether they are labour-demanding or
labour-saving, a key factor in unravelling 'the productivity mystery'. Cautious policy
recommendations are offered. The study is based on public statistics, interviews, and
surveys. The work is an English translation of a Danish summary report.

366 **Local economic development in Denmark.**
Edited by Sven Illeris.   Copenhagen: Local Governments' Research
Institute, 1988. 100p. bibliog.

Presents a series of research papers which have examined regional efforts to promote
economic development. The lead paper acquaints the reader with local trends,
chronicles the development of regional imbalances in agriculture, urbanization,
manufacturing and population growth, and describes the relative autonomy of local
governments. Other papers address such issues as promoting growth in local firms
versus selling local businesses to non-local industries; taking into account regional,
cultural differences in new firm creation; promoting economic development in isolated
areas and medium-sized towns; and the role of services and information technology in
local economies.

367 **The Danish economy in the twentieth century.**
Hans Christian Johansen.   London; Sydney: Crooms Helm, 1987.
221p. (Crooms Helm Series on the Contemporary Economic History of
Europe).

A general work which surveys Denmark's economic developments, problems, and
attempted solutions against the general economic and political trends from 1920 to
1980. The book is descriptive in nature and its presentation is primarily chronological,
taking the reader through the post-First World War era, the Danish experience of the
Depression, the Second World War and the German occupation, the post-Second
World War reconstruction, and the economic downturn of the 1970s. The text is
supplemented with forty-five tables. The work provides an adequate overview.

368 **Time and consumption: time use and consumption in Denmark in
recent decades.**
Edited by Gunnar Viby Mogensen.   Copenhagen: Danmarks Statistik,
1990. 440p.

The main purpose of this research work is to establish a connection between time use
and the consumption of goods and services, taking into account recent social and
economic changes in Denmark. The research presented in this book aims to go beyond
explanations of consumption patterns that focus on changes in personal disposable
income, the relative prices of goods and services, and demographics. The study
identifies patterns of time use since the 1960s in order to explain changes in consumption
patterns and, ultimately, changes in the patterns of production. The research is based
on existing statistics, survey data of a large sample of adult Danes, and qualitative
interviews. The study is broadly conceived and examines factors such as the determinants of time use trends in and outside the work force, time use and untaxed (black)
activities, as well as issues such as preferences for selected activities and work sharing
at home. Innovative and more precise operational definitions of work and leisure time
have been developed for this study. This work is clearly written and is accessible to a
wide readership.

369   **The shadow economy in Denmark 1994: measurement and results.**
Gunnar Viby Mogensen, Hans Kurt Kvist, Eszter Körmendi, Søren
Pedersen.   Copenhagen: The Rockwool Foundation Research Unit,
1995. 118p. bibliog.

The 'shadow economy', or the non-declared part of the market economy, has come
under increasing focus in Denmark. This research attempts to determine the scale and
nature of these 'black' activities using survey data from large representative samples
of adult Danes. Surveys of this nature have been carried out every two years in
Denmark, beginning in 1980 up to the present day, with a very high response rate. The
main findings of these surveys are summarized here, including the type and extent of
black activities, regional variations, and variations by age, gender, and occupation.
The report also defines the terms used in the research, and includes an evaluation of
the methodological problems in the surveys such as interviewer effects, question
formulation, and changes in the approach and sequence of the questions over time.
This report represents a significant effort in estimating the size of Denmark's shadow
economy and aims to allow for international comparisons with other industrialized
countries.

370   **Danish design or British disease?: Danish economic crisis policy**
1974-1979 in comparative perspective.
Peter Nannestad.   Aarhus, Denmark: Aarhus University Press, 1991.
285p. bibliog. (*Acta Jutlandica LXVII*, 2; Social Science Series 20).

The underlying thesis of this work is that politics is central to economic performance;
the work's focus is on the policy choices of government and trade unions during a
period of high unemployment and inflation. Denmark's performance is compared to
that of Austria, Germany, Sweden and the United Kingdom in that these countries
were most different from Denmark in terms of economic outcomes – Denmark seen as
the worst here – but most similar in terms of their social democratic governments. The
work emphasizes a Keynesian economic perspective and assumes a knowledge of
economics and research methods. The general reader would need to feel comfortable
with such terminology.

371   **Benelux and Denmark: economic unions, decolonization, and the**
perils of openness.
Larry Neal, Daniel Barbezat.   In: *The economics of the European*
Union and the economies of Europe.   Edited by Larry Neal, Daniel
Barbezat.   New York; Oxford: Oxford University Press, 1998, p. 274-95.

Discusses the similarities and differences in the economic situations of Belgium,
Luxembourg, the Netherlands, and Denmark. These countries are examined together
since they are all small constitutional monarchies, who are dependent on foreign trade,
and who trade heavily with Germany. Included in the information on Denmark are
macroeconomic indicators for the 1960-97 period such as GDP growth rates, inflation,
and unemployment. The authors also discuss the expansion of the private service and
the public sectors in Denmark during the 1960s; the change in exchange rate policy in
the light of the 1970s oil price shocks; efforts to curb government spending in the
1980s; and the positive view, coupled with reluctance, towards European Union
initiatives regarding foreign and security policy, and economic and monetary union.
The chapter provides a solid overview of recent significant economic policy as well as
insight into the implications for further European integration.

372 **OECD economic surveys: Denmark.**
Organization for Economic Cooperation and Development.   Paris:
OECD Publications, 1962- . annual.

An annual review of the country's economy that examines macroeconomic indicators
in general and reviews the progress of specific policies. Recent special topics have
included the educational system and workforce competency; the OECD Jobs Strategy,
and housing market policies. Appendices provide many basic country statistics that
allow for international comparisons. Numerous tables, graphs, and figures are included
throughout the text.

373 **The institutional history of the Danish polity: from a market and
mixed economy to a negotiated economy.**
Ove K. Pedersen.   In: *Institutional change: theory and empirical
findings.*   Edited by Sven-Erik Sjöstrand.   Armonk, New York;
London: M. E. Sharpe, Inc., 1993, p. 277-99. bibliog.

This chapter provides an analysis of Denmark's mix of institutional structures and
how they developed. The author explains that the country's institutions reflect a blend
of a market, a mixed and a negotiated economy, where market power and state authority
come together in the public, semi-public, and private spheres. The development of the
institutions of wage formation and of the organization of the welfare state is discussed
in an overall look at the country's institutional history in connection with the labour
market. The establishment of specific new institutions and clusters of institutions that
have resulted from the shift from demand- to supply-side economic policymaking is
also examined. The author shows that a system for generalized political cooperation
has developed in Denmark, and that the system can be seen as a prerequisite for a
negotiated economy. The chapter assumes some theoretical background in the social
and economic sciences.

374 **The economic development of Denmark and Norway since 1870.**
Edited by Karl Gunnar Persson.   Aldershot, England; Brookfield,
Vermont: Edward Elgar Publishing, 1993. 654p. bibliog. (The
Economic Development of Modern Europe since 1870).

A comprehensive volume consisting of previously published book chapters and
periodical articles. The works included chronicle the countries' industrialization,
economic and technological development, and growth in foreign trade. There are also
sections on wages, unions, the labour market, and the role of the public sector.
Particular mention is made of the Norwegian whaling and electronics industries,
Danish shipping, and Danish banking and fiscal policy. The articles themselves deal
with Denmark and Norway separately. The editor's introduction attempts with only
limited success to present the volume as a coherent whole, and to discuss Norway and
Denmark in their Scandinavian context. This book is primarily intended for the
scholar, but the general reader can choose from among the chapters.

375 **Growth policies in a Nordic perspective.**
Pentti Vartia, Rolf Jensen, Gunnar Eliasson, Arne Selvik.   Odense,
Denmark: Odense University Press, 1987. 367p.

A joint comparative economic analysis conducted by four research institutes in
Denmark, Finland, Norway and Sweden. The work examines the Nordic countries'

potential in the global market place; how industrial policies can contribute to economic growth; and whether or not Nordic potential is best realized as a unit or as separate economies. Chapter three reports on Denmark with a review of economic policies, export performance, labour market developments and employment trends, investment patterns and medium-term growth prospects. Denmark's economic recovery after 1982 is examined in an international and historical perspective. The report, which was published in 1987, provides economic estimates up to 1990. A statistical appendix provides various economic data on each of the four countries for the 1950-85 period.

The Danish economy: a quarterly bulletin.
See item no. 619.

Finance

376 Disinflationary stabilization policy – Denmark in the 1980s.
Torben M. Andersen. In: *Exchange rate policies in the Nordic countries.* Edited by Johnny Akerholm, Alberto Giovannini. London: Centre for Economic Policy Research, 1994, p. 100-32. bibliog.

Analyses the changes that resulted from the monetary policy shift in 1982 and the economic developments since that time. A shift in government from a social democratic minority coalition to a liberal-conservative minority one brought a disinflationary policy based on a fixed exchange rate and a tight fiscal policy. The details of that policy initiative and subsequent others are laid out. The theoretical aspects of the stabilization policy, its credibility for interest rates and wages, and its effects are examined. Policy lessons from the Danish experience are explored. Two discussion commentaries by other scholars are attached to the chapter. For a related examination of Danish monetary policy in the decade following the 1982 change of government that focuses on the effect on interest rates with a more much mathematical presentation, see Peter Erling Nielsen's chapter in this same book (p. 59-99), entitled 'Monetary policy in Denmark in the last 10 years'.

377 Denmark.
Merete Christensen, Jens O. Elling.   London; New York: Routledge, 1993. 222p. bibliog. (European Financial Reporting).

A comprehensive overview of Denmark's financial reporting policies and practices in the light of the recent European Community (EC) directives that aim towards more harmonized accounting practices among member nations. The volume describes the various types of business entities; the development of the capital market; the taxation of corporations; accounting and auditing regulations; accounting policies and practices; the form and content of published financial statements; and the form and content of financial reporting by banks and insurance companies. The work is detailed, with fifty-two tables, five figures, and eighteen computational and reporting examples. Three appendices provide illustrative financial statements; compare financial reporting between Denmark and the United States, and between Denmark and the International Accounting Standards; and provide the text of significant EC directives and Danish legislation. This volume is a valuable reference source.

378   **Doing business in Denmark.**
Copenhagen: Price Waterhouse, 1995. 227p.
An information guide that does not aim to be exhaustive, but rather to answer important, broad questions. The book opens with a country profile with hints for the business visitor. Specific topics include: the business environment such as government policy, public/private sector cooperation, labour/management relations, the implications of European Union membership; foreign investment and trade opportunities, incentives, and restrictions; business entities and business regulations; banking and finance; exporting to Denmark; labour relations and social security; auditing and accounting practices; the tax system and administration, the corporate tax system, taxation of foreign corporations, shareholders, partnerships; and value added tax. An introduction to Price Waterhouse worldwide and in Denmark is also provided.

379   **Denmark: from external to internal adjustment.**
Torben Iversen, Niels Thygesen.   In: *Joining Europe's monetary club: the challenge for smaller member states.*   Edited by Erik Jones, Jeffry Frieden, Francisco Torres.   New York: St. Martin's Press, 1998, p. 61-81.
Examines Danish exchange rate policies and their implications for domestic economic and political concerns. Danish exchange rate policies up until the 1980s and their close links to German monetary policies are analysed. The adoption of the hard currency policy since 1982 with the coming to power of a centre-right government is discussed. The policy shift is also examined in terms of public and private sector alignments and realignments. The Danish opt-out from the common European currency is also addressed. Throughout the article, various economic theories are brought to bear on the Danish situation. The country's political-economic institutions are also a significant focus.

380   **Denmark and other Scandinavian countries: equalization and grants.**
Jørgen R. Lotz.   In: *Financing decentralized expenditures: an international comparison of grants.*   Edited by Ehtisham Ahmad. Cheltenham, England; Brookfield, Vermont: Edward Elgar, 1997, p. 184-209.
Examines financial relations between central and local governments primarily in Denmark, but also in Sweden and Norway. The chapter briefly describes the structure of local governments and the local assignment of expenditure functions. The administration of various types of local taxes and other revenue sources (property, personal income, revenue sharing, commercial revenue, borrowing) is also described. Several issues regarding grants are examined, such as local taxation rights as a financial safety-valve, vertical fiscal balance, types of grants (specific, general, capital), and budgeting for grants. The rationale for equalization and the aims of legislation are examined. Two types of equalization models are described: the 'Robin-Hood model' and the grant model. There are examples of how expenditure needs and tax bases per

capita are provided. A final section comments on cooperation between local and central government. The coverage of these topics is brief. The article is useful for an overview of the basic aspects of local financing and equalization.

381 **The Nordic countries and the internal market of the EEC.**
Edited by Lise Lyck.   Copenhagen: Copenhagen School of Economics and Business Administration Press, 1990. 235p.

A revised and condensed selection of papers from the 1989 workshop. These papers discuss the implications of the European Community (EC) Internal Market for the Scandinavian welfare states. The Internal Market, whose central elements include the elimination of border controls, tax and excise duty harmonization, and abolition of subsidies that favour domestic producers, is of particular concern to the Nordic countries who rely heavily on their trade with other EC countries. Of the seventeen chapters, three deal exclusively with Denmark, discussing the effect of tax harmonization on the welfare state; the adverse consequences for Denmark if duty-free sales are abolished before tax harmonization is achieved; and the overall impact of financial integration for Danish banking in the 1990s. Another chapter uses Denmark as a point of departure for examining the issues facing the Nordic welfare states in general.

382 **Denmark: economic development in the eighties and the strategy for the nineties.**
Ministry of Finance.   Copenhagen: Ministry of Finance, 1991. 30p.

A concise and informative publication that is essentially an advertisement aimed at potential foreign investors. The publication describes the successful strategies of the 1980s which lowered inflation, improved the balance of payments, increased production, and helped Denmark adapt to the international marketplace. Nineteen charts and graphs help to report the country's public and private savings and investment strategies, its production strategies, and its fiscal growth. A final section outlines the goals for the nineties. The authors would like foreign investors to take note of Denmark's central position in Europe and to see the country as a 'bridge to the big European Market'.

383 **Municipalities and counties in Denmark: tasks and finance.**
Ministry of the Interior.   Copenhagen: Ministry of the Interior, 1996. 64p.

Provides a general overview of the organization and structure of local government which comprises 14 counties and 275 municipalities. The publication focuses on the division of tasks, finances, and the efforts at equalization of economic resources. Local income sources, taxes bases, and expenditure needs are described, with budget information for 1996. The division of tasks at the local versus the state level is compared. The relative size of local authorities in an international context is briefly discussed. Key economic figures for the country are presented for 1994. The text is supplemented with fourteen figures and seven tables.

384   **The accounting profession in Denmark.**
Edited by Steven F. Moliterno.   New York: American Institute of
Certified Public Accountants, 1994. 79p. (Professional Accounting in
Foreign Countries Series).
Offers a concise presentation of all aspects of accounting in Denmark. Regarding the
profession itself, entry and licensing requirements, professional standards and ethics,
and   membership   requirements   for   professional   organizations   are   described.
Descriptions of statutory auditing requirements are given, as well as a summary of
significant auditing standards and a comparison of these with American standards.
Accounting principles and practices, and the form and content of financial statements
are also described, and are compared to American standards. The checklists for the
American comparisons are detailed in appendices. In terms of the business environment, the forms of business organizations, requirements for public sale and listing of
securities on the stock exchange are described, and definitions of types of taxes are
given. Lists of outstanding auditing and accounting pronouncements, and translated
illustrative financial statements are provided in appendices. The editor notes that this
work is not meant to be a comprehensive review of the accounting profession, but
rather is intended to highlight differences from accounting in the United States.

385   **Tax policy in the Nordic countries.**
Edited by Peter Birch Sørensen.   Basingstoke, England; London:
Macmillan, 1998. 234p.
A collection of five papers by various Nordic scholars and tax economists. The papers
relate to applied and policy-oriented studies of recent tax policies given the tax
reforms of the early 1990s. The topics include the theoretical and practical arguments
for and against the Nordic dual income taxation system, a system which is considered
unconventional. The implications of this system for the special problems of small
businesses are discussed. Corporate income taxation is also covered. Pressures on
Nordic fiscal systems in the light of European integration and mobile tax bases are
discussed. A future perspective is also offered in terms of adjustments, reforms, and
emerging tax debates. The papers deal with the Nordic countries generally as well as
specifically, and there is information on Denmark throughout the book in both the text
and the tables. The work is not overly technical. References follow each paper.

386   **Financial services in transition: an examination of market and
regulatory forces in Denmark and the UK.**
Jon Sundbo.   In: *Financial institutions and social transformations:
international studies of a sector.*   Edited by David Knights, Tony
Tinker.   Basingstoke, England: Macmillan; New York: St. Martin's
Press, 1997, p. 117-34. bibliog.
Examines strategic developments in personal and retail financial firms including
general and life insurance companies, retail banks, and credit card companies. The
chapter is based primarily on empirical data from two Danish studies, and is supplemented with European and British data. The point of departure is the competitive
environment in financial services given economic deregulation. An opening section
reviews the stagnating market conditions in Denmark during the economic recession
of the 1980s. Subsequent sections examine the response of financial firms such as
standardization of services, cross-industry mergers, self-service distribution systems,
and market segmentation. Consumer responses are also examined and a shift from

passive to active consumer behaviour is noted. Regulatory frameworks are also described such as Denmark's consumer ombudsman. The focus of the chapter is the benefit to consumers of a more market-oriented environment.

387   Denmark and European integration.

Niels Thygesen.   In: *The challenge of globalization and institution building: lessons from small European states.*   Edited by Randall W. Kindley, David F. Good.   Boulder, Colorado; Oxford: Westview Press, 1997, p. 87-105.

Discusses the purely financial ramifications of Denmark's participation in the EMS (European Monetary System) and the EMU (European Monetary Union). The article specifically addresses the apparent paradox that the country's willingness to take part in European joint currency arrangements turned to reluctance to proceed to full EMU participation. Developments in monetary integration since the 1970s are reviewed from a Danish perspective. Denmark's rationale for EMS participation and its reorientation in exchange rate policies and capital controls is examined. The national compromise and exemptions for Denmark in the Maastricht Treaty are also outlined. The connection between international currency policies and domestic concerns is a major focus of the discussion.

Science, Technology
and Industry

388   **The struggle over North Sea oil and gas: government strategies in
      Denmark, Britain and Norway.**
      Svein. S. Andersen.   Oslo: Scandinavian University Press; Oxford:
      Oxford University Press, 1993. 204p. bibliog.
The premise of this work is that natural resource management reflects a country's
national idiosyncrasies. The author examines the problems faced by the three
countries in the development of petroleum policies and activities over a thirty-year
period. Taking a comparative approach, the work accounts for differing government
ambitions with a cross-national examination of policy paradigms and traditions of
resource extraction. Where Denmark's economic policy has been traditionally liberal
and characterized by market-based solutions, Norway's has been more interventionist,
and has more readily relied on government-based strategies. Britain has fluctuated
between the two extremes. The book is particularly valuable for its account of the shift
in the Danish government's laissez-faire model in the 1960s and 1970s to a more
ambitious role in offshore activities in the 1980s.

389   **Cooperation in Denmark.**
      Claus Bjørn.   Copenhagen: The Federation of Danish Cooperatives,
      1988. 47p.
Describes the history of the cooperative movement and outlines how the system operates today. This particular method of pooling resources is characterized by member
ownership and democratic control. The movement began in the middle of the 19th
century as a pragmatic economic solution to the social problems created by early
industrialization and the emergence of the modern working class. The first cooperatives
were a consumers' retail society, a dairy, and a bakery. Today cooperative societies,
and societies with a structure resembling cooperatives, are extensively used in many
sectors of the country's economy, by both producers and consumers, to meet their
mutual needs. They have been strongest in the agricultural sector. This work is an
overview and is meant to be an introduction to this topic for an international audience.
It is written in an easy-to-read style and includes illustrations. Limited descriptive
statistics are provided for 1986-87.

390 **Social dynamics of the IT field: the case of Denmark.**
Finn Borum, Andrew Lloyd Friedman, Mette Mønsted, Jesper
Strandgaard, Marianne Risberg.   Berlin; New York: Walter de
Gruyter, 1992. 328p. bibliog. (de Gruyter Studies in Organization,
no. 39).

A collection of articles which analyse the information technology (IT) field from the
various perspectives of these five authors. The overriding perspective is on the nature
of organizations and cultures that characterize the IT field and the actors within these
organizations. The case of Denmark allows for a national analysis with such unique
features as the welfare state's utilization of centralized information systems, the
country's high level of unionization, and the apprenticeship mode of training, which is
prevalent in its IT field. The work represents three years of research based on both
qualitative and quantitative data gathered from significant Danish IT firms, small and
medium-sized enterprises, and trade unions. This is a clearly written academic work
that is also accessible to the general reader who is comfortable with the terminology of
organizational theory. It contains a wealth of information on Danish IT firms.

391 **Technological innovation and organizational change: Danish
patterns of knowledge, networks and culture.**
Edited by Finn Borum, Peer Hull Kristensen.   Copenhagen:
Copenhagen Business School Institute of Organization and Industrial
Sociology, 1989. 289p. bibliog. (New Social Science Monographs).

This collection of essays provides a multifaceted examination of the causes of technological innovation and organizational transformation in general, and it specifically
looks at the country's information technology (IT) field, and the wind-power, plastics
and dairy industries. The various authors show that in Denmark technological innovation has often been based on learning and doing, rather than on science. Informal
learning in interaction with competing firms, with suppliers of raw materials and
equipment, and with customers who place their own unique technical demands on
products generates new technical knowledge. This has been particularly true in
Denmark where industry is characterized by many small and medium-sized firms
operating in social networks. Further, Denmark's IT field operates with a well-devel-
oped worker subculture, where skilled workers are relatively autonomous in relation
to management, and shape technology according to the context in which it is to be
applied. The clear writing style makes this a very accessible academic work.

392 **Dairy products from Denmark.**
Aarhus, Denmark: Danish Dairy Board, 1994. 59p.

An industry handbook with information and illustrations to give the reader an impression of the wide range and high quality of Danish dairy products. There is extensive
information on milk, butter, and many different types of cheese. Cultured milk
products, which are quite popular in Denmark, are mentioned only briefly. Processes
such as production, quality control, and treatment are detailed. Specific product
information is provided such as fat content and nutritional value, as well as various
industry specifications. This book is an industry publication aimed at importers,
wholesalers, and retailers, but it would also be of interest to the health-conscious
consumer.

393　Danish dairy & food industry – worldwide.

Odense, Denmark: Danish Dairy & Food Industry – Worldwide.
1976- . bi-annual.

An industry periodical sponsored by the Danish Dairy Managers Association and the Danish Dairy Engineers Association. This publication deals with all aspects of the food industry such as production instrumentation and technology, quality control, and food processing. Recent issues have also included environmental protection, energy management, and packaging.

394　Danish farmers and their cooperatives.

Copenhagen: The Federation of Danish Cooperatives and The
Agricultural Council, 1993. 35p. (Available from The Federation of
Danish Cooperatives, Vester Farimagsgade 3, DK-1606
Copenhagen V).

Written in simple English, this publication is aimed at potential foreign partners, particularly the farmers in the new democracies of Eastern Europe. The work describes the basic aspects of the business relationships of Danish farmers and how they are organized into cooperative societies that own commercial cooperative dairies, slaughterhouses, and farming supply companies. Introductory information is given on the history and tradition of these farmer-owned and farmer-governed societies. In simple text and clear tables, the basic principles of cooperatives are outlined, key terms are defined, by-laws and management and decision-making processes are described. Background information is also given on the relevant Danish and international organizations. Oddly, the work does not provide any contact information for any of these organizations.

395　Denmark: horse sense manufacturing.

Frank Gersten, Jens O. Riis.　In: *International manufacturing
strategies: context, content and change.*　Edited by Per Lindberg,
Christopher A. Voss, Kathryn L. Blackmon.　Boston, Massachusetts;
Dordrecht, the Netherlands, 1998, p. 88-101. bibliog.

Provides a picture of Danish manufacturing based on survey data and other socio-economic data. The authors briefly outline the structure of the various sectors of trade and industry. They also comment on the socio-cultural dimensions of industry such as individualism, power distribution, and gender relations. A major focus of the chapter is a summary of the results of the Danish part of the 1993 IMSS (International Manufacturing Strategy Survey) study which surveyed eighteen major Danish manufacturers in metal products and machinery on such issues as company goals, market share, and the number of products and their revenue percentages. From the IMSS data, the authors create a typical portrait of 'horse sense manufacturing' and outline its principles of success such as close customer contact, the balance of conflicting goals, and cooperation between unions and employers. The chapter also reports other economic data on trade balance, organizational management, manufacturing and technology indicators, and market and cost indicators.

396 **Food technology in a modern food system: the case of Denmark.**
Otto Ditlev Hansen, Erik Juul Jørgensen. Hørsholm, Denmark: The
Institute for Food Studies and Agroindustrial Development, 1993. 70p.

The aim of this publication is to give a brief overview of the various Danish food technology sectors including food processing; food and beverage packaging machinery,
equipment, utilities, and materials; and food additives and ingredients. There is a brief
discussion of the historical development of the industry, as well as its more recent
growth in terms of both size and structure. Further, the report illustrates the importance of the food technology industry to the country's total economy, and highlights
Denmark's global significance in this industry, particularly as a leader in the development of advanced technologies. There is also a section on innovations for the coming
decades and a profile of research and development efforts. This is a professional
report, that assumes some familiarity with industry terminology. The reader can also
see an earlier report by the same authors, *Food technology in Denmark* (Hørsholm,
Denmark: The Institute for Food Studies and Agroindustrial Development, 1990.
57p.), for a somewhat less technical discussion.

397 **'With constant care . . .' A. P. Møller: shipowner 1876-1965.**
Ove Hornby. Copenhagen: J. H. Schultz, 1988. 325p.

This work is part biography, but its concentration on Møller's business achievements
makes it more an account of the Maersk shipping companies, the largest shipping
conglomerate in Denmark, and one that is recognized worldwide. The book is divided
into historical periods which include the turn of the century to 1920, the years between
the First and Second World Wars, the Second World War and the German occupation,
and the post-war period to 1965. Based on company archives and personal interviews,
the author provides lively accounts of the shipping industry as a whole and the
favourable financial conditions around the turn of the century; the difficulties between
the two World Wars and Møller's survival of the Depression in the 1930s; the loss of
ships and seamen's lives during the Second World War; and post-war rebuilding and
expansion. The economic situation in the period to 1965 is described, along with the
management and organization of the companies and Møller's interest in charitable
foundations. Appendices include fleet and shipyard lists and financial figures for the
1904 to 1965 period.

398 **State-of-the-art information technologies in Danish libraries.**
Gitte Larsen. Copenhagen: National Library Authority, 1996. 102p.

This report is part of a wider Nordic study on the use of information technology (IT)
in Nordic libraries prepared for the European Commission. Based on survey questionnaires and telephone interviews with both public libraries and research libraries, the
study attempts to describe the extent of information technology in Danish libraries.
This report concentrates on new IT initiatives after 1991 with an emphasis on the most
recent initiatives. All types of electronic databases and IT-based user services in all
types of libraries are described. Local library systems, national co-ordination systems,
and international networks are also discussed. Included in appendices are both an
English and a Danish version of the questionnaire, and a list of all Danish research
libraries selected for the study.

399 **Shipbuilding policy in a global competitive environment: the international competitiveness of the Danish shipbuilding industry.**
Ministry of Business and Industry. Copenhagen: Ministry of Business and Industry, 1996. 147p.

This work discusses the Danish shipbuilding industry in the context of its major competitors in Europe and Asia, along with analyses of Denmark's present and future competitiveness. It is shown that Danish shipyards have been a relative stronghold primarily due to their high average man-hour productivity, and this report sees them remaining fully competitive on a level global playing field. Prediction models for the shipbuilding market show that the demand for new tonnage will increase along with a parallel growth in shipbuilding capacity in a number of new market economies. This surplus capacity underlines the need for the establishment of normal competitive conditions. The report argues for the need for a fair international policy of free and equal competition in an industry that has been characterized by unfair competition because of state aid, dumping, and protectionism. This work is a comprehensive economic report that is clearly presented for the general reader.

400 **Technological and organizational change: implications for labour demand, enterprise performance and industrial policy.**
Ministry of Business and Industry. Copenhagen: Ministry of Business and Industry, 1996. 137p. bibliog.

An analysis conducted as part of the OECD 1994 project 'Technology, Productivity and Job Creation', this report includes various discussions and analyses that address the structural and economic changes in industry brought on by the information and communication technologies (ICT) revolution. The topics include: unemployment and marginalization in the labour market; capital-intensive (versus labour-intensive) economic growth; the adaptation of manufacturing enterprises to a knowledge-based economy; and implications of ICT and organizational change for productivity, innovation, employment, and skill requirements. The report notes the increased economic growth brought about by ICT as well as the social and economic costs, and challenges to the education system. The final chapter outlines policy implications of the analyses and provides an overview of Denmark's industrial strategy and recent policy measures.

401 **Science, technology and innovation policies: Denmark.**
Organization for Economic Cooperation and Development. Paris: OECD Publications, 1995. 187p.

Part of the OECD series of Science, Technology and Innovation (STI) Policy Reviews of individual member countries. The purpose of this review is to evaluate the Danish STI system so that research and development (R&D) can be strengthened, and its results can benefit industry and society. The review evaluates the various institutions that play a role in R&D: ministries, universities, government research institutes, and the business sector. The work is organized in two major sections: a background report on Denmark's relevant STI features and policies based on interviews with decision-makers at all levels of the STI system, and the OECD examiners' assessment of the major problems. Among the examiners' general recommendations are the need for a national R&D strategy, more strategic government support of research that can lead to wealth creation, and increased government effort to stimulate the creation and growth of small firms. Thirty-one tables and eleven figures are included.

402　**Technology policy in Denmark.**
Edited by Jørgen Lindgaard Pedersen.　Copenhagen: Institute of
Organization and Industrial Sociology, Copenhagen School of
Business, 1989. 249p. (New Social Science Monographs).

In a collection of seven essays, Danish social scientists examine the interaction of
technology and society, based on the notion that technology assessment should be a
precondition of technology policy. The opening essay describes the development of
Danish technology policy from 1970 to 1987, and summarizes its various objectives
and instruments. Other topics covered include Denmark's political options regarding
technology policy in relation to other larger Western European countries; the impact
of the Danish patent system on industrial innovation in the pharmaceutical and foodstuffs industries; and government initiatives in the information technology and the
biotechnology industries. A final section examines the need to involve users of
technology in the policy debate with two case-studies: one of the health sector, and
another of the sugar beet and shipbuilding industry in one local region. The book is
explicitly aimed at a readership of politicians, administrators, and researchers.

403　**Biotechnology in Denmark.**
Jørgen Lindgaard Pedersen, Inger-Marie Wiegman.　Lyngby,
Denmark: Institute of Social Sciences, Technical University of
Denmark, 1987. 44p.

Describes the biotechnology field from a technology assessment perspective, which
identifies the social participants in the field along with their goals, means, and
resources. Implicit in this perspective is an interest-group model where technical
development is viewed as a consequence of the different strategies of different interest
groups – industry, science, politics, and the public. In three separate chapters, the
authors examine biotechnology in the pharmaceutical, foodstuffs, and chemical
industries. Also included is a chapter on the environmental risks posed by – and the
public opposition towards – genetic engineering. A concluding chapter discusses the
distribution of resources in the biotechnology field as a whole. This work does not
deal with human genetics and deals only to a limited degree with the ethical and moral
aspects of biotechnology. The work is concise and the information is clearly
presented.

404　**EDI in the public sector: the Danish Info-Society 2000 Plan and the
democratic route to informate the public sector.**
Mogens Kühn Pedersen.　In: *EDI and data networking in the public
sector.*　Edited by Kim Viborg Andersen.　Boston, Massachusetts;
Dordrecht, the Netherlands: Kluwer Academic Publishers, 1998,
p. 275-302.

Considers a societal issue of EDI (electronic data interchange), the information technology that allows for the exchange of information across different computer systems.
The author addresses whether it is possible to have a democratic way of implementing
EDI in the public sector, given EDI's potential to divide citizens and to change the
nature of governing. A particular focus of the chapter is the government's role in
implementing EDI, and the author examines both the content and progress of the
country's Info-Society initiative, as well as the plan's 'hidden premises' about the
information society that reveal its inherent 'contradictions and hazards'. These
premises are then applied specifically to the EDI case in order to explain EDI's

contribution to the information infrastructure in terms of both its operational impact and its impact on the legitimacy of the public sector. This chapter can be appreciated by those without a technical knowledge of information technology. The work is aimed primarily at professionals and students in computer science, business, and public administration.

Technology in Denmark.
See item no. 69.

Denmark Review/Business News from Denmark.
See item no. 621.

Export directory of Denmark.
See item no. 657.

ISO 9000 Denmark: a register of quality certified companies in Denmark.
See item no. 658.

Kompass-Denmark: register of Danish industry and commerce.
See item no. 659.

Employment

405 Marginalization, citizenship and the economy: the capacities of the universalist welfare state in Denmark.
Jørgen Goul Andersen.   In: *The rationality of the welfare state.*
Edited by Erik Oddvar Eriksen, Jørn Loftager.   Oslo; Stockholm;
Copenhagen; Oxford; Boston, Massachusetts: Scandinavian University
Press, 1996, p. 155-202.

This chapter discusses features of the welfare state that address unemployment, and assesses the effects of the welfare system with data from two 1994 nation-wide surveys. The work is a case-study of Denmark as a universalist ideal-type welfare state and as a citizen income system that has survived economic and social crises since the late 1970s. The features of the country's unemployment benefit system that provides public transfer income for almost all unemployed adults are also discussed in some detail. The author discusses the effects of unemployment on social citizenship such as labour market and social marginalization, and political participation and polarization. The survey data is brought to bear on these issues. It is observed that Denmark has managed to alleviate citizenship problems, balancing the expenses of unemployment with the maintenance of social integration. There is a bibliography for the book as a whole. This is a well-organized and clearly written chapter, that is very informative about the workings of the welfare state employment benefits.

406 Demand and capacity constraints on Danish unemployment.
Torben Andersen, Per B. Overgaard.   In: *Europe's unemployment problem.*   Edited by Jacques H. Drèze, Charles R. Bean.   Cambridge,
Massachusetts; London: The MIT Press, 1990, p. 156-201.

This chapter represents the Danish contribution in a ten-country effort to understand Europe's high unemployment problem since the 1970s. The chapter examines causal factors underlying the rise and the persistence of unemployment through an estimation of a macroeconomic model for the Danish economy for the period 1952 to 1984. This is an academic work based on econometric modelling techniques. The general reader can avoid the equations and still benefit from the text. Opening sections provide some general economic background and discuss the trends in unemployment and the causal factors.

407 Unemployment in Denmark.
Peter Jensen. In: *The Nordic labour markets in the 1990's, part 1*.
Edited by Eskil Wadensjö. Amsterdam: Elsevier, 1996, p. 19-64.
Provides an empirical description of high, persistent unemployment, which has been a feature of the Danish economy since the oil price increases of the early 1970s. The chapter reviews the historical development of the unemployment rate; examines differences in the distribution of unemployment by gender, age and occupation, as well as briefly looking at regional, seasonal, and citizenship variations; and examines the dynamic aspects of unemployment such as 'inflow' and duration figures, long-term unemployment, and temporary layoffs. Labour market policies are also described in terms of passive measures such as unemployment benefits and early retirement, and active measures such as training programmes. These empirical descriptions are presented in an effort to understand the underlying causes of high and persistent unemployment, and the author offers some analysis. An appendix explains the definitions used in the Danish unemployment statistics.

408 Denmark.
Jørn Loftager, Per Kongshøj Madsen. In: *The new politics of unemployment: radical policy initiatives in Western Europe*. Edited by Hugh Compston. London; New York: Routledge, 1997, p. 123-45. bibliog.
Describes and analyses two unconventional measures to combat long-term unemployment: paid leave arrangements, where employed persons are made to take leave for education, child care, or a sabbatical, while the vacancy is filled with a previously unemployed person; and citizens' income schemes where an individual receives an unconditional state-guaranteed benefit that is not means tested, of an amount fit to meet basic needs. The chapter first presents background on the unemployment situation for the period 1970-95, discussing various policies and outlining the 1994 labour market reform package. Regarding the paid leave arrangement, the issues addressed include the political background for its adoption and implementation; its economic, social, and political implications for the individual, the labour market, the public sector, and society as a whole; barriers to its extension; and its long-term prospects. Regarding citizens' income proposals, the political origins, the economic and employment aspects, and the main arguments in the debate are discussed. The authors also address how realistic an option citizens' income is, given the widespread élite opposition. The chapter is quite thorough and clear in its presentation.

409 Work incentives in the Danish welfare state: new empirical evidence.
Edited by Gunnar Viby Mogensen. Aarhus, Denmark: Aarhus University Press, 1995. 274p. bibliog.
Among the welfare states in Northern Europe, Denmark has some of the most generous levels of benefits and has had a permanently high level of unemployment since the early 1980s. Responding to a lack of scientific research in this area, this work examines the possible disincentive effects of high taxes and transfer payments on the country's labour supply in a study carried out between 1993 and 1995. Data

sources include a labour force survey conducted by the Danish Central Bureau of Statistics, interviews by the present volume's research group, and statistics from Danish administrative records. Various statistical analyses examine such issues as levels of labour market participation, the wage situation for various occupational groups, disposable income comparisons for employed versus unemployed persons, the effect of a hypothetical tax cut on work behaviour and attitudes, and work behaviour related to undeclared (black) labour and do-it-yourself activities. Gender differences are noted throughout the analysis. This book has a wide appeal beyond labour market research and would also be of interest to those in economics, government, and sociology.

410 **The public employment service in Denmark, Finland and Italy.**
Organization for Economic Cooperation and Development.   Paris: OECD Publications, 1996. 217p. bibliog.

A comprehensive and detailed report on the operation of the Public Employment Service (PES) and the administration of benefits, training, and job creation measures. The report is based on country visits during the second half of 1994. For each country there is background information on the labour market such as industrial relations, wages, turnover, unemployment, and labour market and social policies. Simultaneous country information is provided on the structure and management of the PES; the matching of job-seekers with vacancies, trends in placement, and indicators of performance in penetrating the labour market; the provision of income replacement benefits in the form of unemployment insurance and social assistance; and employment and training programmes. The report is essentially descriptive and the information is presented in a primarily comparative format. The concluding chapter provides a concise summary of the similarities and differences among the three countries. The history of each country's main unemployment benefits, and information on partial unemployment benefits in Denmark and Finland, are provided in appendices.

411 **The welfare state and taxation in Denmark.**
Peder J. Pedersen. In: *Welfare and work incentives: a North European perspective.*   Edited by A. B. Atkinson, Gunnar Viby Mogensen.   Oxford: Clarendon Press, 1993, p. 241-88.

This book chapter considers the major changes in the level and structure of taxes and benefits since the early 1960s, and the impact of such a transformation on work incentives. The tax structure of Denmark emphasizes personal income tax over labour market contributions, and has a comparatively high value added tax. Further, the benefit structure is characterized by a 'universality' principle, where eligibility is not dependent upon labour market experience or contributions. Pedersen examines the country's recent economic background and trends in the labour market, and describes the main characteristics of the tax and benefit system, emphasizing the personal income tax, and such features as unemployment insurance, subsidized day care, rent support, education benefits, and early retirement. The work also reports existing research findings on the disincentive effects of the tax and benefit system on the decision to enter the labour force, the transition between employment and unemployment, participation in do-it-yourself activities, and the choice of early retirement. This is an informative piece, that also provides a good overview of the operation of the welfare state. References are provided for the entire book, and not for individual chapters.

Women's employment and part-time work in Denmark.
See item no. 281.

Labour market studies – Denmark.
See item no. 417.

Labour Relations and Trade Unions

412 **Development and crisis of the Scandinavian model of labour relations in Denmark.**
Bruno Amoroso. In: *European industrial relations: the challenge of flexibility.* Edited by Guido Baglioni, Colin Crouch. London; Newbury Park, California; New Delhi, India: Sage Publications, 1990, p. 71-96.

Examines industrial relations against the backdrop of the economic difficulties in the 1970s and the 1980s, such as rising unemployment and changes in the employment structure, and in light of the austerity measures taken by the centre-right government in the 1980s. The political and organizational problems in the Danish Federation of Trade Unions (Landsorganisation i Danmark or LO) are discussed. The trade unions saw an overall strengthening in terms of membership, but a weakening in terms of their influence on the collective bargaining process. The situation of the Confederation of Danish Employers (Dansk Arbejdsgiverforening or DA) is reviewed. The industrial relations system is analysed with a discussion of the relations between the government and LO, and relations between LO and DA. The collective bargaining process itself is examined in terms of its forms, content, and conflicts. Finally, the future of the system of unions and industrial relations is commented on. This is a comprehensive and detailed chapter for the period under study.

413 **Wage formation in Denmark.**
Torben Andersen, Ole Risager. In: *Wage formation and macroeconomic policy in the Nordic countries.* Edited by Lars Calmfors. Odense, Denmark: Odense University Press, 1990, p. 137-87. bibliog.

This paper attempts to study the determination of wages in the light of the collective bargaining process between trade unions and employer federations that characterizes the Danish labour market. The authors provide a brief overview of the problems in the Danish economy, outline the wage bargaining institutions, and proceed with an analysis of the determination of wages and employment in the manufacturing sector.

They also examine the effectiveness of restrictive incomes policies and their influence on wage restraint. A final section outlines policy implications. This is a scholarly work and assumes a knowledge of statistics and econometric modelling, and of union behaviour and wage bargaining theory. The statistical analyses in this chapter are based on economic data up to 1988. The final pages of the chapter include comments by other scholars.

414   **The Nordic labour relations model: labour law and trade unions in the Nordic countries – today and tomorrow.**
Niklas Bruun, Boel Flodgren, Marit Halvorsen, Håkan Hydén, Ruth Nielsen.   Aldershot, England; Brookfield, Vermont: Dartmouth Publishing, 1992. 272p. bibliog.

The main focus of this work is the role of the trade union movement in the development of labour law. The book deals with the special characteristics of the Nordic model in Denmark, Finland, Norway, and Sweden. These four countries have somewhat different economic and political models, yet are characterized by uniform regulation of the labour market. The opening chapter examines the organizational background and structure of the trade union movement as it relates to labour law. Subsequent chapters discuss collective agreements and their regulation; the collective and individual aspects of employment protection; the trade unions' traditionally less prominent role in the regulation of the working environment; and sex discrimination. The final chapter examines the future of the trade union movement in the light of increasing internationalization. Each chapter compares and contrasts the four countries, and unique features, such as Denmark's European Union membership, are discussed. The book includes a list of the relevant labour organizations in each country with an English translation of the organization's name.

415   **Labour market consensus: the main pillar of the Danish model.**
Jesper Due, Jørgen Steen Madsen, Carsten Strøby Jensen, translated from the Danish by Seán Martin.   Copenhagen: Ministry of Labour, 1993. 32p.

This short publication is a good starting point for background on the country's collective bargaining process. The structure and framework of the system, where legislation is the exception and not the rule, is described. The main results of the 'September Compromise' of 1899, which are still in force today, are outlined. The mechanisms for dealing with breaches of collective agreements, and for industrial arbitration are described. The concept of 'centralized decentralization' is also discussed. Data on trade union membership is provided. The text is concise and clear, and much of the information is presented in clear charts.

416   **The survival of the Danish model: a historical sociological analysis of the Danish system of collective bargaining.**
Jesper Due, Jørgen Steen Madsen, Carsten Strøby Jensen, Lars Kjerulf Petersen, translated from the Danish by Seán Martin.   Copenhagen: DJØF Publishing, 1994. 264p. bibliog.

An overall analysis of the system of labour market organization and collective bargaining since its formation at the end of the 19th century up to the present day. The authors examine the socio-cultural factors that have helped to shape Danish industrial relations, which are characterized by both a decentralized organizational structure and a centralized collective bargaining structure. Particular focus is placed on the relations between the two dominant organizations in the private sector labour market for employers and workers which are, respectively, DA (Dansk Arbejdsgiverforening), i.e., the Confederation of Danish Employers, and LO (Landsorganisation i Danmark), i.e., the Danish Federation of Trade Unions. The historical analysis provides a backdrop for discussing recent developments and challenges, such as the crisis faced by the labour market at the end of the 1970s and subsequent revitalizations of the collective bargaining system. Future perspectives for 'the Danish Model' are also discussed. A list of abbreviations comprises over fifty organizations involved in the collective bargaining system with both the Danish name and the official English designations used by these groups.

417 **Labour market studies – Denmark.**
Jens Henrik Haahr, Helle Ørsted, Hans Henrik Hansen, Peter Jensen.
Luxembourg: Office for Official Publications of the European
Communities, 1996. 196p. bibliog.
This report analyses the functioning of the Danish labour market. Separate chapters address the following topics: the unemployment situation and its causes 1980-95, and the impact of macroeconomic policies; the historical development and present administrative structure of labour market policies; the organization and regulation of the industrial relations and wage negotiation system; labour market legislation; the tax and benefit system and the education and training system in relation to the labour market; state intervention in business and employment; and the national debate over strategies for limiting unemployment. Assessments are discussed at the end of each chapter. Various statistics on population and labour force developments, the structure of the work force, and wage and salary trends are presented in three appendices. An executive summary is also provided.

418 **Wage determination and sex segregation in employment in Denmark.**
Rita Knudsen, Lisbeth Pedersen.   Manchester, England: Manchester
School of Management, University of Manchester, 1993. 133p. bibliog.
This report was produced for the European Commission's network 'Women At The Labour Market'. Taking into account the fact that unlike other European Community countries, wages and working conditions in Denmark's labour market are determined by collective agreements, a significant portion of the report describes the organizations and system of wage determination in the private and public sectors. The degree of organization in chosen branches of industry is also discussed. Characteristics of wage determination are closely examined for three branches: the textile and clothing industry, the telecommunications industry, and the banking industry. A final section discusses the policies and activities around the issue of equal pay and the future outlook. The report is descriptive and the authors note that it is limited by the fact that an explanation of gender differences in wages is beyond its scope. The report could have benefited from a clearer presentation of the issues.

419   **The labour market reform in Denmark: background and perspectives.**
Jens Lind.   In: *Transformation of the Nordic labour relations in the European context.*   Edited by Timo Kauppinen, Virpi Köykkä.
Helsinki: The Finnish Labour Relations Association, 1994, p. 175-99.
bibliog.

Examines a labour market reform that took effect in 1994, when Denmark's unemployment rate had reached twelve per cent. The reform, which is a political effort to strengthen the labour market and to reduce unemployment, is observed to be an elaboration of already existing measures. The author outlines the reform's most significant features – a new system of financing unemployment benefits, a revised administrative structure, a reorganization of measures to activate the unemployed, and an expanded system of leave opportunities. The pros and cons of these features as well as the possible consequences are discussed. The reform is also examined in terms of the notion of structural unemployment, the social integration aspect of unemployment policy, and the influence of the European Union on labour market policy.

420   **Industrial relations and the environment: Denmark.**
Borge Lorentzen, Kim Christiansen, Michael Sogaard Jorgensen.
In: *Industrial relations and the environment: ten countries under the microscope. Volume I.*   Edited by Andrea Oates, Denis Gregory.
Luxembourg: Office for Official Publications of the European Communities; Dublin: European Foundation for the Improvement of Living and Working Conditions, 1993, p. 87-167. bibliog.

This European Union report introduces and analyses the policies, legislation, and regulations from Danish employers and trade unions, that pertain to the internal working environment and to the external environment. The focus of this report is significant in that these groups had previously been at odds with the environmental movement, and supported unlimited industrial growth instead. The report examines collective bargaining relations between employers and employees regarding decisions in internal and external environmental strategy; describes independent initiatives on the part of both trade unions and employers, discussing the parties' motivations and the status of the policies; and looks at current conflicts in the industrial relations arena regarding environmental concerns and economic growth. The bibliography contains primarily Danish-language works and the list of pertinent legislation does not provide English translations.

421   **Trade union democracy and individualization: the cases of Denmark and Sweden.**
Morten Madsen.   *Industrial Relations Journal*, vol. 27, no. 2
(June 1996), p. 115-28.

Examines union members' relationship to their union in the light of the fact that there has been a spread of individualist values, particularly among younger employees. The opening section discusses the theoretical framework for looking at collectivist versus individualist orientations and union democracy. The empirical findings are based on 1992 employee survey data from the Federation of Trade Unions in both countries. (In Denmark, this is the Landsorganisation i Danmark or LO.) The author examines the relationship between collectivist-individualist orientations and union meeting participation, the representativeness of the unions, and opinions regarding union legitimacy. The challenges facing unions in terms of effective representation of members' interests are discussed.

422   **Denmark: return to decentralization.**
   Steen Scheuer.   In: *Industrial relations in the new Europe.*   Edited
   by Anthony Ferner, Richard Hyman.   Oxford; Cambridge,
   Massachusetts: Basil Blackwell, 1992, p. 143-97. bibliog.

Aims to characterize the trend toward decentralized collective bargaining and to address whether it should be considered a crisis for the Danish Federation of Trade Unions or LO (Landsorganisation i Danmark), the country's major trade union confederation, or merely a return to old patterns that existed before the strong centralization in the 1960s and 1970s. The work describes the nature of the Danish economy and the labour market; describes the origins of the Danish model of industrial relations; and outlines the key system dynamics and features of the union structure. The impact of the 1970s economic crises on industrial relations, the policy changes of the 1980s during a period of conservative-liberal government, and the trend towards decentralization are also discussed. There is a particular emphasis on the role of unemployment insurance funds in explaining the persistence of high union density, albeit outside LO. The work concludes with remarks on the significance of the current trends for the future of Danish industrial relations. Various data on union membership is presented up to 1990.

423   **The future of the Nordic model of labour relations.**
   Bernt Schiller.   In: *The future of the Nordic model of labour relations:
   three reports on internationalization and industrial relations.*   Edited
   by Bernt Schiller, Knut Venneslan, Hans Ågotnes, Niklas Bruun, Ruth
   Nielsen, Dennis Töllborg.   Copenhagen: Nordic Council of Ministers,
   1993, p. 9-91. bibliog.

This report discusses the Nordic model generally. It examines the effect of the European Community (EC) on labour relations in the light of the deregulation of markets and the transfer of labour relations from the national to the supranational level. The opening chapter outlines the central features of the distinct Nordic labour relations model. It is observed that internationalization challenges Nordic collective bargaining, and subsequent chapters address what the effect of internationalization on Nordic industrial relations will be, and to what extent EC regulations might dominate over the regulations of individual nation-states. In order to illuminate this discussion, some background on the development of the EC regulations is presented. The prospects for European collective bargaining as well as the prospects for a Nordic response are described. The report also looks at how the situation affects the character of Nordic transnational companies, trade unions, and employers. A final chapter offers future recommendations.

424 **Employment protection under strain. (Sweden, Denmark, The Netherlands).**
Taco van Peijpe. The Hague; London; Boston, Massachusetts: Kluwer Law International, 1998. 177p. bibliog. (Bulletin of Comparative Labour Relations Law 33).

A study in comparative labour law that looks at the differences in employment protection in three countries with similar economic, social and political structures that are also experiencing shifts in power from labour to capital. These countries are also characterized by different labour relations traditions that allow for points of comparison, i.e., Denmark's reliance on collective bargaining, Sweden's emphasis on legislation, and The Netherlands' corporatist tradition and low unionization rate. The introduction comprises a concise survey of industrial relations in each country. This is followed by a general discussion on employment protection, which also brings in the employment protection systems of the United States, Japan and Germany for comparison. Recent developments in employment protection in Denmark, Sweden and the Netherlands are then compared and assessed with particular attention paid to the influence of the European Union, economic internationalization, high unemployment, and the declining influence of social democracy.

Statistics

425 Health statistics in the Nordic countries.
Copenhagen: Nordic Medico Statistical Committee. annual.

Recent issues of this work have included statistics relating to population and fertility; consumption patterns in food groups, alcohol and tobacco; medical treatment, morbidity and accidents; mortality and causes of death; and health care expenditures. There is also individual country information on the organization and administration of health services. Numerous appendices define terminology and codes. Special topics, which vary from year to year, have included the occurrence and survival rates of low birth-weight babies; incidence, trends, risk factors, and geographical and social differences in cardiovascular diseases; differences in life expectancy rates by sex, age and lifestyle. Parallel text is presented in Danish and English.

426 Kriminalstatistik. (Criminal statistics.)
Copenhagen: Danish National Bureau of Statistics. annual.

Recent editions present tables on offences, convictions and punishments. Examples of these include reported and cleared criminal offences by type of offence, sex and age of offender, area of residence, and location of the crime. Conviction information is also reported by type of offence, sex, age, and residence of the offender, type of punishment, and length of imprisonment. Sentences imposing a fine are presented by type of offence and age and sex of offender. There is also limited information on traffic offences and offences against 'special legislation' (e.g., Firearms Act, Aliens Act, Tax Control Act). English translations of all table titles are provided and there is an appendix with English translations of column and row headings for all tables.

427 Levevilkår i Danmark statistisk oversigt. (Living conditions in Denmark: compendium of statistics.)
Copenhagen: Danish National Bureau of Statistics and the National Institute for Social Research, 1976- . irregular.

This work has been published every four or five years since 1976. It presents statistics in the following areas: population; family; health; education; work; economy; housing;

leisure; political activity; personal safety; conditions for children and young people, and for the elderly. English translations are provided for the preface, the list of contents and table titles, as well as row and column headings, and survey questions, where applicable.

428 **Major city regions of Scandinavia: facts and figures.**
Helsinki: City of Helsinki Information Management Centre, 1992.
112p.

This is the first companion publication to the database NORDSTAT that provides basic background and statistical information on sixteen cities in a format that allows for comparison. The four major Danish cities represented are Copenhagen, Aalborg, Odense, and Aarhus. For each city there is varying information on topics such as population, housing, education, jobs and employment, infrastructure, and culture. The compilation of these statistics is a cooperative effort among the regions, and topics are included based on their significance for a given urban area. The book includes information for obtaining the statistical tables in the NORDSTAT database, which is updated annually and expanded periodically.

429 **Nordisk statistisk årbog.** (Nordic Statistical Yearbook.)
Copenhagen: Nordic Council of Ministers, 1963- . annual.

Presents comparable statistics on life in Denmark, Finland, Iceland, Norway, Sweden, Greenland, the Faroe Islands and Åland, aimed at highlighting the similarities and differences. Statistics are provided in the following categories: population, health, housing, leisure, education, income and social protection, election, the labour market, price indexes, GDP, national accounts, public spending, agriculture, manufacturing, building, energy and water, and tourism. The most recent editions include areas such as environmental protection, research and development, and information and communications technology. The preface, introduction and user guide, table of contents, table titles, and explanatory text are presented in English. The previous English title of this work was *Yearbook of Nordic Statistics*.

430 **Politiets årsberetning.** (Annual report of the police.)
Copenhagen: Commissioner of the Police Information Service, 1968- .
annual. (Available from Commissioner of the Police Information
Service, Anker Heegaards Gade 5, DK-1780 Copenhagen V).

Recent editions present tables on arrests, imprisonments, violations of the penal code, and traffic violations for the country's fifty-four police districts. Information for Greenland and the Faroe Islands is given separately. Penal code violations are presented with crimes reported, cases cleared, and gender and age breakdowns. English translations are given for the table headings and an extensive Danish-English word list is provided. The volume also includes various narrative reports on police activities in Danish. A brief English summary is provided.

431 **Statistical bulletin: selected statistics of the Faroe Islands.**
Torshavn: Statistical Bureau of the Faroe Islands, 1993- . annual.
(Available from Statistics Faroe Islands, P. O. Box 2068, FR-165
Argir).

This concise bulletin consists only of tables with no accompanying text. All the tables,
however, are presented in English. Statistics are provided in the following areas:
population, imports and exports, GDP by industry branches, national accounts, wages
by industry, the fishing industry, unemployment, and banking.

432 **Statistisk årbog.** (Statistical Yearbook.)
Copenhagen: Danish National Bureau of Statistics. annual.

A comprehensive reference book with information on the social and economic
conditions in Denmark and summary information on Greenland and the Faroe Islands.
The work includes statistics in the following areas: area, climate, and environment;
population; housing; national elections; education; culture; social security; justice; the
labour market; income and consumption; agriculture; fishing; manufacturing;
construction; transport; tourism; internal and external trade; public finance, and
national accounts. English translations are provided for the preface, the explanation of
symbols, table titles as well as row and column headings, the alphabetical subject
index, and various classification codes and indexes. Similar information can be found
in *Statistisk tiåroversigt* (Statistical Ten-Year Review) and *Statistisk månedsoversigt*
(Monthly Review of Statistics), both of which are also published by the Danish
National Bureau of Statistics.

433 **Women and men in the Nordic countries: facts and figures 1994.**
Copenhagen: Nordic Council of Ministers, 1994. 96p.

Presents tables, diagrams and accompanying descriptive text relating to the similarities
and differences in the lives of men and women in the five Nordic countries: Sweden,
Norway, Denmark, Finland and Iceland. (Due to a lack of statistics the Faroe Islands,
Greenland and Åland have been omitted.) The work was compiled as part of a cooperative effort to promote gender equality in the Nordic region and not only provides
information on men's and women's employment, income and education, but also aims
to shed light on previously statistically neglected areas such as the sharing of paid and
unpaid work, time use, lifestyle and health issues, and women in politics. The tables
and diagrams are well presented and the text is clearly written.

Nordisk invandrar- och migrationsrapport. (Report on Nordic immigrants
and migration.)
See item no. 174.

Environment

Planning

434 **Safety of cyclists in urban areas: Danish experiences.**
Lene Herrstedt. Copenhagen: Danish Road Directorate, 1994. 119p.
(Traffic Safety and Environment, Report 10).
The bicycle is a major form of transport in Denmark, and cycle traffic is one of the greatest problems of road safety. This work reports the results of a three-year study and summarizes efforts in five areas: recessed stop lines; new designs at four-way intersections; new road markings at T-intersections; cycle lanes in urban areas; and bus stop designs. The report outlines the general accident situation, describes the analytical methods which include accident investigations and video recordings of behaviour patterns, evaluates the various strategies, and offers recommendations for improvement as well as for future research. This is a technical report for those with a special interest in transport safety and town planning.

435 **Space and welfare: the EC and the eclipse of the Scandinavian model.**
Ib Jørgensen, Jens Tonboe. In: *Scandinavia in a new Europe.*
Edited by Thomas P. Boje, Sven E. Olsson Hort. Oslo: Scandinavian University Press, 1993, p. 365-403. bibliog.
This chapter examines the effect of European integration on Scandinavian society, particularly the regional policy aspect of the Scandinavian welfare model. Specific attention is given to Danish welfare policy since the early 1980s, the country's regional differences in resources and social policy, and planning policy related to Copenhagen's regional development as a means of securing Denmark's high international ranking. The authors note that the increasing internationalization of the economy risks benefiting only those regions which are already economically strong. This is a scholarly piece with a focus on the development of sociological theory, but it is of value for its substantive information on Denmark.

165

436   **Ecological urban renewal in Copenhagen: a European model.**
      Helene Hjort Knudsen.   Copenhagen: Agency of Environmental
      Protection, City of Copenhagen, 1993. 91p. (Available from Agency of
      Environmental Protection, City of Copenhagen, Flaesketorvet 68,
      DK-1711 Copenhagen).

The final report on the European Community project 'Planning Model for the
Ecological Renewal of Old City Areas'. This thorough and detailed report covers all
aspects of the urban renewal plan for minimizing the consumption of resources and
environmental damage in Copenhagen's Vesterbro district. The legal, financial, and
political conditions for ecological renewal are described, as well as the development
of the plan, the planning process in terms of cooperation between citizens and local
government, and the implementation of demonstration projects. Specific future efforts
in the areas of heating, electrical savings, water savings, sewage treatment, waste
management, traffic, and the greening of the district are outlined. A final section
examines similar efforts in four other European cities. The report concludes that the
Copenhagen model can be used in a European context with modifications. The report
is well organized, clearly written, and visually well presented.

437   **Urban planning in Denmark.**
      Bo Larsson, Ole Thomassen.   In: *Planning and urban growth in the
      Nordic countries.*   Edited by Thomas Hall.   London; New York;
      Melbourne; Madras, India: E. & F. N. Spon, 1991, p. 6-59. bibliog.

A survey of the development of urban planning design and legislation in the country's
four major cities and in other important medium-sized towns. The work examines
chronologically the shift from pre-industrial to modern planning in the light of
political, economic, and societal changes; government-sponsored social housing after
the First World War; industrial housing after the Second World War; the effects on
planning of rapid urban growth after the 1960s followed by stagnation in the 1970s;
planning reforms of the 1970s; the present-day national planning system; and issues
for the future. A short annotated bibliography is provided, and, although the annotations are in English, cited works may be in Danish only, or may offer only an English
summary. The text is enhanced with numerous illustrations and planning diagrams.

438   **Guide to Danish landscape architecture 1000-1996.**
      Annemarie Lund, translated from the Danish by Martha Gaber
      Abrahamsen.   Copenhagen: The Danish Architectural Press, 1997.
      295p. maps. bibliog.

A comprehensive guide and reference work that includes both historical and contemporary examples of landscape architecture such as crafted gardens, landscape
parks, cemeteries, grounds of buildings, playgrounds, and plazas. The work provides a
detailed chronological presentation of 200 projects including plans, photographs, and
descriptions. An additional 300 other gardens are listed, each with a brief annotation.
The opening chapter is an introduction to the history of landscape architecture. Site
addresses are provided so that this book also functions as an excursion guide. The
bibliography cites only Danish-language works.

439   **The ecological city: Denmark.**
Ministry of Environment and Energy, Ministry of Housing and
Building.   Copenhagen: Ministry of Environment and Energy,
Ministry of Housing and Building, 1995. 83p.

This work is the national report for the OECD project on the 'Ecological City'. It
describes various projects and initiatives aimed at making cities ecologically sustainable. The report profiles five municipalities that are major regional centres in Denmark,
describing nine initiatives that demonstrate how well-functioning municipalities
improve the urban environment. A key factor in Danish efforts is that environmental
protection must be integrated into all decisions. The projects profiled include examples
of urban renewal and restructuring, waste management, and integrated urban districts,
as well as ways of making rural communities viable. A national overview describes
various action plans in the areas of transport, spatial planning, pollution control, and
energy conservation. The report also highlights the general public's involvement in
the various efforts, and cooperation between different political and administrative
levels.

440   **The bicycle in Denmark: present use and future potential.**
Ministry of Transport.   Copenhagen: Ministry of Transport, 1993.
61p.

A concise and informative overview that describes the role of this everyday mode of
transport used regularly by one-third of the adult population. The work includes a
brief discussion of the Danish tradition of bicycling; data on bicycle traffic habits,
theft, and accidents; a description of the infrastructure for bicycles that includes such
topics as the national cycle route network and bicycle facilities on public transport.
The reader should note this discussion does not include maps or any detailed route
information. There is also a description of planning, research, legislation and
education regarding bicycle traffic. A final section looks at current and future
initiatives to promote and safeguard bicycle use.

441   **Spatial planning in Denmark.**
Niels Østergård.   Copenhagen: Ministry of Environment and Energy
Spatial Planning Department, 1994. 24p.

A summary publication that outlines the key features of the 1992 Planning Act and
describes how spatial planning is carried out in practice at the national, regional, and
local levels. Denmark experienced significant urban development between 1945 and
the mid-1980s, and the country emphasized a growth-oriented planning philosophy.
Current efforts have shifted the emphasis to preserving and improving the environment. This publication describes recent examples of urban renewal and maintenance of
natural landscapes. There is also information on rural zone administration, appeals procedures, and overall land management. This publication is targeted to authorities and
planners. It is a concise, detailed, and informative overview.

Environmental protection

442 **Governance by green taxes: making pollution pay.**
Mikael Skou Andersen. Manchester, England; New York: Manchester University Press, 1994. 247p. bibliog.

This work is a comparative study of water pollution control policies in Denmark, France, Germany, and the Netherlands, that analyses the role of green taxes in practice. The author compares the differences in policy design and effectiveness for the four countries, and observes that only Denmark has treated industry leniently, failing to use green levies and opting instead to invest in public sewage works. In the chapter on Denmark, policy choices and their effectiveness are examined in the light of the country's general consensus-seeking policymaking style that reflects interest-group preferences. The various roles played by government, private industry, and the public sector in the implementation of water pollution policies are discussed. The book is recommended for students and specialists in environmental studies, political studies and economics, as well as for administrators. It is also clearly written for the general reader who may want to skip over the theoretical discussions.

443 **Denmark.**
Peter Munk Christiansen. In: *Governing the environment: politics, policy, and organization in the Nordic countries.* Edited by Peter Munk Christiansen. Copenhagen: Nordic Council of Ministers; Stockholm: The Nordic Council, 1996, p. 29-102. bibliog.

Describes the content of current environmental policy in Denmark; the organization and administration of environmental policy at the parliamentary, cabinet, and regional and local levels; and the characteristics of policy-making processes. The historical development of environmental policy, the role of special interest organizations – given the cooperative style of Danish policy-making, the handling of complaints and appeals, and environmental research and development are also discussed. Two case examples are provided: pollution control in the manufacturing and transport sectors, and the protection of nature and natural resources via land-use regulation. Attempts are made to draw conclusions about the country's political capacity to deal with new environmental policy problems. As part of a larger work, this chapter is written to allow comparison in the Nordic countries, and to foster theoretical development in terms of the 'conditions for capacity national policy-making'.

444 **Denmark: energy efficiency, water purification, and policy instruments.**
Anders Christian Hansen. In: *Environmental transition in the Nordic and Baltic countries.* Edited by Hans Aage. Cheltenham, England; Northampton, Massachusetts: Edward Elgar, 1998, p. 94-108. bibliog.

Examines energy consumption, energy policy, domestic resources, and environmental policies. These topics are discussed in terms of developments since the oil price shocks of the 1970s. Energy consumption is discussed generally, and it is noted that Denmark ranks above the average for Western Europe. Special mention is made of transport. The major objectives of energy policy are outlined. Domestic resources such as energy, fish stocks, forests and agriculture are reviewed. The characteristics of Danish environmental regulations are described, and their effect on emissions to air, emissions to the aquatic environment, soil pollution, and solid waste. Emphasis is given to the fiscal aspects of energy and environmental policies. The chapter is a concise overview.

445 Afforestation experience in the Nordic countries.
Finn Helles, Michael Linddal.   Copenhagen: Nordic Council of Ministers, 1996. 159p. (NORD 1996:15).

A five-country report meant to serve as an inspiration to other countries facing afforestation challenges. Introductory chapters provide a general discussion of afforestation, its potential objectives and its various impacts. Forestry conditions in each of the five Nordic countries are also outlined. Individual chapters present assessments of each country's afforestation experience, discussing both successes and failures. Chapter three is devoted to Denmark, and describes various periods of afforestation from 1789 to the present day in terms of both state and private efforts. Political and socioeconomic factors are discussed and afforestation efforts are evaluated in general. The concluding chapter outlines lessons learned for achieving cost-efficient, sustainable, and flexible new forests in terms of the objectives, means, and implementation of afforestation.

446 The making of the new environmental consciousness: a comparative study of the environmental movements in Sweden, Denmark and the Netherlands.
Andrew Jamison, Ron Eyerman, Jacqueline Cramer, Jeppe Læssøe. Edinburgh: Edinburgh University Press, 1990. 216p. bibliog.

Chapter three of this book chronicles the rise of the new environmentalism in Denmark against the backdrop of the country's various governments and economic developments. The industrial production and technological innovation of the 1960s was accompanied by a lack of concern for environmental problems. The 1970s, however, gave rise to a new political culture and a 'many-headed grassroots movement' characterized by participatory action. The professionalization of the environmental movement in the 1980s by groups such as Greenpeace meant a more passive involvement on the part of ordinary people, leading these authors to question whether the new environmentalism can still be considered a social movement. The work relates the emergence of environmentalism to current theories of social movements and social change. Some theoretical knowledge is assumed, although an opening chapter defines the major concepts and issues.

447 Environmental administration in Denmark.
Mogens Moe.   Copenhagen: Ministry of Environment and Energy, Danish Environmental Protection Agency, 1995. 209p. bibliog.

Provides an overview of the way environmental problems are dealt with in Denmark. The opening chapters describe the environmental problems facing the country, and give basic information on European Community (EC) requirements for environmental legislation and on Denmark's relationship with the EC. The country's decision-making process with its marked decentralization of authority to the counties and municipalities is also addressed. Chapters discussing legislative measures are divided by the various sources of pollution such as industry, agriculture, consumers, and special facilities and services. Economic measures such as service charges and environmental levy systems are discussed. A final chapter looks at law enforcement and examines criminal penalties and the role of the judicial system. The author also analyses the impact and effect of the various measures. This book is aimed at readers with some familiarity with the administrative, political, and legal aspects of environmental issues. The text is enhanced by over sixty illustrations. Most of the referenced source material is in Danish.

448   **Energy policies of IEA countries: Denmark 1998 review.**
      Organization for Economic Cooperation and Development,
      International Energy Agency.   Paris: OECD Publications, 1998. 128p.

A comprehensive review of all aspects of Danish energy policy. The work describes the structure and organization of the energy sector in terms of both governmental and regulating agencies. It also describes energy consumption and supply by sector and by fuel. The report looks at energy efficiency and taxation regarding carbon dioxide, sulphur dioxide, and nitrogen oxides emissions. Initiatives regarding individual energy sources which include electricity, heat, gas, oil, coal, and renewables (wind, biomass) are reviewed. A specific aim of the report is to examine environmental policies and performance measures, as well as the reconciling of environmental and market liberalization issues. Government involvement in the country's energy achievements and its role in a liberalized market are also considered. Critiques and recommendations are offered throughout the report.

449   **Biological diversity in Denmark: status and strategy.**
      Edited by Christian Prip, Peter Wind, Henrik Jørgensen.
      Copenhagen: Ministry of Environment and Energy, 1996. 196p.
      bibliog.

Denmark has been one of the world's greatest offenders in the destruction of virgin forest land in the last half of the 20th century. It has also implemented some of the world's most extensive nature conservation legislation. This work reports on the country's fulfilment of Article 6 of the 1992 Convention on Biodiversity. The report describes the various ecosystems – seas, coasts, countryside, forests, urban areas; describes various species and genetic diversity; discusses the methods for acquiring scientific knowledge; and profiles Denmark's cooperation in international efforts. Each chapter includes a current status section, reports on the conservation efforts to date, and makes recommendations for the future. This report is written for a broad readership. There is a great deal of factual information that is deliberately not referenced, and popular titles of legislative acts are used. It is an overview, but it is also sufficiently detailed and includes many special features and inserts. Greenland and the Faroe Islands are not covered in this report. The bibliography consists primarily of Danish-language reports.

Industrial relations and the environment: Denmark.
See item no. 420.

Architecture

450 Women in Danish architecture.
Edited by Helle Bay, Lisbeth Pepke, Dorte Rathje, Nina Tøgern, Jette Wagner, translated by Gerda Hvidberg Henriksen. Copenhagen: The Danish Architectural Press, 1991. 82p.

Aims to introduce outstanding female architects to Denmark and to the international community. The editors explain that they have consciously excluded men from this volume, and have sought to introduce women involved in research, design, and town planning. The work of forty-two architects is featured here, and each was free to arrange her own contribution. They have generally presented their work or work-in-progress with photographs, sketches, and technical diagrams and plans, all of which are accompanied by explanatory text. The architectural examples include a church, a school, an exhibition hall, a traffic terminal, a teaching centre for the handicapped, various types of housing, and building restoration. Parallel text is presented in Danish and English.

451 Sketches and measurings: Danish architects in Greece 1818-1862.
Margit Bendtsen, translated from the Danish by Séan Martin. Aarhus, Denmark: Aarhus University Press, 1993. 383p. bibliog.

Many Danish buildings reveal architectural characteristics demonstrated in Athens. This is due to the efforts of eight Danish architects and one Danish painter who visited Greece to study the antique monuments. Prompted by Enlightenment philosophy and a political trend towards democracy, their specific aim was to gather accurate information for the incorporation of Classical features in Danish buildings. They succeeded in this endeavour and in turn exerted their own influence on architecture in Athens. This volume is a catalogue of 162 sketches, measurings, and paintings which are part of the collection of the Library of the Royal Danish Academy of Fine Art. They depict examples of Greek, Byzantine, and Turkish architecture. The illustrations are in colour. No descriptive text is provided in the catalogue. The author's introduction provides background information on each of the architects and on the various monuments and sites included in this work.

452 Contemporary Danish housing.
Edited by Kim Dirckinck-Holmfeld, translated from the Danish by Peter Avondoglio. Copenhagen: The Danish Architectural Press, 1992. 108p.

This book is a general survey of housing development in the 1980s as seen by various architects. A key observation of this work is that while housing development generally stagnated in the 1980s, much experimentation also took place. The main part of the book profiles dominant forms of housing types. These include multi-storey, tower blocks, dense/low-rise, and ecologically oriented. The best examples of these housing types throughout the country are reviewed. The development of housing plans during this period is evaluated, as well as technical developments over the past half-century and their effects on architectural designs. Current architectural trends in housing are also discussed. The work contains numerous diagrams and colour photographs. The work is presented in parallel English and Danish text. There is also a summary in German.

453   **Copenhagen spaces.**
Edited by Kim Dirckinck-Holmfeld, Susanne Møldrup, Marianne
Amundsen.   Copenhagen: The Danish Architectural Press, 1996.
176p. map.

Celebrates the city with a portrait of its new complexes, squares, parks, and preservation initiatives. These architectural efforts are presented in four parts: the harbour, the
city centre, the bridge area, and the new Ørestad area. Each site is presented with
beautiful colour photographs, diagrams, and descriptive text. There are a total of
forty-five sites and they are keyed on a city map. The work is presented in parallel
Danish, English, and German text.

454   **Architecture in the Scandinavian countries.**
Marian C. Donnelly.   Cambridge, Massachusetts; London: The MIT
Press, 1992. 401p. map. bibliog.

This work is an historical survey of architecture in eighteen Scandinavian cities. The
book is divided into historical periods and architectural styles: prehistoric, the Middle
Ages, the Renaissance, Baroque and Rococo, Neoclassicism, vernacular, eclectic and
early modern, and architecture since the First World War. For Denmark, the cities of
Odense, Ribe and Copenhagen are covered. Many different types of buildings are
included, such as churches, palaces, government buildings, and homes. The text
provides background information and detailed descriptions of special features.
Construction dates and the names of the architects are provided for each building. The
text is enhanced with numerous black-and-white photographs and diagrams. While the
book is comprehensive, the author points out that it is not meant to be exhaustive, but
rather aims for a balanced presentation of the accomplishments of the five
Scandinavian nations.

455   **Urban architecture and identity – a Danish approach.**
Steen Holmgren, Ole Svensson.   *Scandinavian Housing & Planning
Research*, vol. 11, no. 3 (August 1994), p. 129-44.

Presents the general content of the Danish Building Research Institute's project on the
preservation of urban architecture, which has been ongoing since 1988. The project's
primary aim was to produce a working method that would result in guidelines for new
construction and alteration. These guidelines would also have to take into account
inevitable urban development and change. The authors explain that the urban areas of
interest were those areas that were not necessarily of historic value, but rather
possessed an identity based on their everyday architecture. These urban areas had
managed to escape development and 'retained a wholeness and coherence' that gave
them a certain invaluable quality. This article first discusses some general theoretical
works on urban architecture, then goes on to examine Denmark's regulation of urban
architecture providing specific information on the general method of analysis, and
guidelines and legislation regarding preservation.

456   **Cohousing: a contemporary approach to housing ourselves.**
Kathryn McCamant, Charles Durrett, Ellen Hertzmann.   Berkeley,
California: Ten Speed Press, 1994. 2nd rev. ed. 288p. bibliog.

Cohousing was pioneered in Denmark and is a prime example of the Danes' appreciation
of the social impact of the physical environment. This living arrangement combines

the autonomy of private dwellings with community living, entailing a sharing of common living spaces, such as kitchen and dining area, laundry, children's playrooms, workshops, and guest rooms. In three parts, this book introduces the concept of cohousing, profiles eight Danish communities which illustrate the diversity of cohousing, and discusses the mechanics of developing such a community with specific design considerations and suggestions. The book is primarily based on fieldwork conducted in 1984 and 1985 in Denmark, the Netherlands, and Sweden. General characteristics of cohousing are discussed such as group decision-making, resident management, and the intentional neighbourhood aspect. The second revised edition includes a fourth part which documents the experiences of six pioneering North American colonising communities. The text is enhanced with numerous photographs and diagrams.

457 **Dwelling, at home – in community – on earth: the significance of tradition in contemporary housing.**
Jorn Orum-Nielsen, in collaboration with Mike Pease. Copenhagen: The Danish Architectural Press, 1996. 261p. bibliog.

The premise of this book is that a thorough understanding of traditional Danish buildings and towns can provide a basis for building new communities, as well as remaking the old. The work is a tribute to the Danish ability to create community by emphasizing the fit between the physical environment and the social life. The book is a history of community and housing design – a history which is built upon the *længe*, Denmark's traditional housing style. The development, construction, and adaptability of the *længe* are chronicled, and its influence on the organization of towns is highlighted. This profile covers prehistory to the modern day, including the successes and failures of the 20th century. There are descriptions of the row housing of the 1920s and 1930s, various examples of large-scale planned housing, and cohousing projects. Specific examples of housing are reviewed in detail. Many photographs and diagrams are provided, along with a map of site locations.

458 **Guide to Danish architecture I, 1000-1960.**
Jørgen Sestoft, Jørgen Hegner Christiansen, translated from the Danish by Peter Avondoglio. Copenhagen: The Danish Architectural Press, 1991. 271p.

Part one of this work is a brief historical survey of Danish architecture from prehistoric times up to industrialism's influence on the building industry. This overview discusses periods, styles, and outside influences. The main body of the book, part two, is the guide, which is arranged chronologically, but also deals with works thematically. Selected unique works are discussed independently. The guide covers cathedrals, churches, monasteries, castles, palaces, town and gentry houses, theatres, museums, and government buildings. Each work is presented with black-and-white photographs, sketches, and plans. The book includes approximately 850 illustrations, a complete index of places, and a fold-out map. This book would also be of interest to historians and art historians.

459 **Arne Jacobsen: works and projects.**
Felix Solaguren-Beascoa de Corral. Barcelona, Spain: Gustavo Gilli, 1991. 2nd ed. 222p.

This book is a catalogue of Jacobsen's architectural works. The introduction provides brief background information, and discusses Jacobsen's transition from Nordic

Classicism to Modernism. The works, which include private houses, housing developments, schools, factories, sports installations, public buildings, and town halls, are presented with black-and-white photographs and diagrams, all of which are captioned. A chronological list of projects from 1921 to 1976, a list of awards received, and limited examples of Jacobsen's furniture designs, are provided in appendices. The book is presented in parallel Spanish and English text. It received the American Institute of Architects' Award in 1990 for excellence in international architectural book publishing.

460   **The aesthetics of Danish bridges.**
       Kyo Takenouchi.   Copenhagen: The Royal Danish Academy of Fine
       Arts, School of Architecture, 1995. 79p. bibliog.

Describes the structural design of Danish bridges, both large and small, from an aesthetic point of view. The major bridges from the 1930s to the present time are included, along with the projects scheduled to be finished soon after this work's publication. This includes the Great Belt Link Project which links eastern and western Denmark, as well as the Øresund Link Project which will comprise part of the road and railway network linking Scandinavia to the European continent. The book also provides examples of Danish civil engineers' contributions abroad. In addition to the aesthetics of the structural design, the author, a non-Dane who has studied bridge construction worldwide, also comments on the harmony between the bridge and its surrounding landscape, and emphasizes the importance of cooperation between architects and engineers. Numerous pictures and drawings enhance the text.

Education

Miscellaneous

461 **New information technology in education – Denmark.**
Lise Dalgaard, Vagn Larsen. Luxembourg: Office for Official
Publications of the European Communities, 1992. 131p.

A report on the use of new information technology (NIT) in primary and lower secondary schools, and in general upper secondary education. The introduction outlines the structure, the administrative organization, financing, curriculum, and educational policies of the relevant school systems. Subsequent chapters describe various NIT initiatives, their integration into the curriculum, evaluations of these initiatives, and teacher training. The ways in which NIT and education impact each other is discussed. Special attention is given to the gender issue with a look at girls and computer studies. Final chapters discuss future developments. This report is detailed and aims to be comprehensive. It is straight reporting without much elaboration or context.

462 **Educational indicators in the Nordic countries: describing educational status and student flows.**
Copenhagen: Nordic Statistical Secretariat, 1991. 57p.

This work is a general survey of the Nordic educational systems that examines structure and performance. The particulars of each system are described in separate chapters for Denmark, Finland, Norway, and Sweden. In other chapters, statistics are presented on transfer and completion rates for the various levels of education. The report is presented entirely in English.

463 **Report to OECD. Danish youth education: problems and achievements.**
Ministry of Education. Copenhagen: Ministry of Education, 1994. 143p.

Provides a comprehensive examination of the developments and reforms in the educational system since the last OECD review in 1977-79. The report includes an introduction to the country and a description of the educational system and its historical background. The report's emphasis is on vocational-oriented education, upper secondary education, and alternative types of youth education. Detailed information is provided on organizational structure, curricula, examinations, funding, teacher qualifications, and internationalization. The problem of drop-out is also examined, along with the corresponding action plans and initiatives to combat the problem. This thorough and informative report presents statistics up to 1992, and includes eighteen tables and twelve figures.

464 **Denmark: a study of the educational system of Denmark and guide to the academic placement of students in the educational institutions of the United States.**
Valerie A. Woolston, Karlene Dickey. Washington, DC: PIER World Educational Series, 1995. 147p.

This is a reference work for the professional educator or admissions officer, but it would be of interest to anyone who wanted to understand the Danish educational system. The research is extremely thorough and the report is of very high quality. This full country report describes the structure and content of the entire system from pre-school to university. At the time of its publication, it is the first American work in twenty years for the American admissions community on the Danish educational system. There are separate chapters on the health sciences and teacher training. There is also a formal set of placement recommendations and guidelines for admissions officers. Sample documents are provided as well as a glossary of Danish terms.

Primary education

465 **School life in Denmark.**
Knud Holch Andersen, translated from the Danish by Peter A. Rohling. Vejle, Denmark: Kroghs Publishers, 1994. 119p. bibliog.

Offers a portrait of everyday school life and a concrete description of the different sides of education. The book's emphasis is the *folkeskole* (the public school) education which requires nine years. The book's point of departure is an authentic public school situation, which is profiled in words and photographs in terms of its structure and subjects, the participation on the part of both pupils and teachers, and the education of the teachers themselves. The book also provides historical information on Danish education in general, and information on the various other educational opportunities available to young people and adults. This book is helpful in understanding the Danish attitude towards education as a lifelong pursuit that prepares the individual for participation in democracy and in working life, as well as how the educational system's historical roots are preserved and continue to be developed in the present day.

466　**The Danish *friskole*: a segment of the Grundtvigian-Kold school tradition.**
Edited by Thorstein Balle, Margaretha Balle-Petersen.　Faaborg, Denmark: The Danish Friskole Association, 1995. 32p. (Available from The Friskole Office, Prices Havevej 11, DK-5600 Faaborg).

Describes the *friskole*, which is an independent primary or secondary school. Independent private schools are an important aspect of the Danish system. They are free of control by public authorities, and they also receive economic grants from the state. This publication describes the historical foundation of the *friskole* in the grass-roots movements of the middle 1800s, and the influence of N. F. S. Grundtvig's and Christen Mikkelsen Kold's views on mankind and education. The fundamental principles such as the rights of parents as the highest authorities with regard to upbringing and education, and the rights of the minority to be protected from the majority are discussed. In that the *friskole* is a private school, the principles of ideological freedom, economic freedom, freedom of employment, and student freedom are discussed, as well as the governing of the school and the guiding principles of the curriculum. Brief profiles of three *friskoler* are included. A list of useful addresses is provided.

467　**Education in Denmark: aspects of the work of the *folkeskole*.**
Her Majesty's Inspectorate.　London: Her Majesty's Stationery Office, 1989. 27p.

A useful and informative guide to understanding the Danish public school system which educates young people aged seven to sixteen. Based on a seven-day visit to Denmark covering ten schools, this brief publication provides description and commentary rather than evaluation. There is information on the administration and organization of the *folkeskole*; policies and practices regarding the curriculum and assessment of students' progress; and the role of support agencies, teachers, parents, and pupils in decision-making. Appendices describe such areas as the subjects taught, the aim of each subject, and the guidelines for teaching history.

468　**The Danish *folkeskole*: visions and consequences.**
Bent Brandt Jensen, Mogens Nielsen, Erik Stenstrup.　Copenhagen: The Danish Council for Educational Development, 1992. 257p.

A synthesis of twenty-five evaluation reports that resulted from a 1987 parliamentary resolution establishing a research and development programme for the *folkeskole* (the public school). An introductory chapter provides historical background on the *folkeskole* and its philosophy. The main part of the book presents the results, recommendations, and conclusions of the evaluation reports in terms of the resolution's seven-point programme. These points embrace the following ideas: the school as a local cultural centre; an integrated approach to education (versus a subject-based approach); the extended function of the class tutor; new forms of cooperation inside and outside the school; new models of organization and administration; the use of colleges of education as educational centres; and greater economic freedom for individual schools. Discussions aim for a broad context with references to English and American literature. Brief summaries of the individual evaluation reports and the text

177

of the parliamentary resolution are provided in appendices. References follow the individual chapters.

Secondary and higher education

469 **Contemporary sociology in Denmark.**
Heine Andersen, Britt-Mari Belgvad, Mogens Belgvad.   In:
International handbook of contemporary developments in sociology.
Edited by Raj P. Mohan, Arthur S. Wilke.   London: Mansell
Publishing, 1994, p. 64-85. bibliog.

A general survey of the state of sociological research and education. The introduction examines the beginnings of sociology, its institutionalization, and its development. Subsequent sections look at some of the prominent intellectuals and their work, sociology's establishment in universities, and the establishment of government-sponsored research. Other sections review the major methodological and theoretical trends, and discuss some of the significant intellectual debates. The discipline's various subfields such as welfare and living conditions, the labour market, political sociology, medical sociology, and criminology are also described. A final section discusses the sociology of law. The authors observe that Denmark has lagged behind other Scandinavian countries in accepting sociology as an independent science, but that the future holds more promise. This is a concise but thorough review that references some of the discipline's most important publications.

470 **The state of women's history in Denmark.**
Nanna Damsholt.   In: *Writing women's history: international perspectives.*   Edited by Karen Offen, Ruth Roach Pierson, Jane Rendall.   Basingstoke, England; London: Macmillan, 1991, p. 231-38.

This chapter surveys the 'state of the art' of women's history as an academic discipline in Denmark. Among the topics covered are the status of women's history in the university in the light of recent changes in the educational system at the upper-secondary level. The predominant themes in the field which include the period from 1850 to the present day, the Middle Ages, religious and ethical questions, and biographies are described. The prevailing methods and theories are also discussed, such as patriarchy and deconstructionism. Current problems such as the writing of women's history into general history, and integrating the discipline into the academic mainstream are also noted. Finally, organizational issues such as the paucity of permanent academic positions and the need to rely on private research funding are mentioned. This is a brief chapter and somewhat superficial.

471 **Technology and new institutions: a comparison of strategic choices and technology studies in the United States, Denmark and Sweden.**
Lars Fuglsang.   Copenhagen: Academic Press, 1993. 226p. bibliog.

The main purpose of this book is to examine technology as a social institution. Among the issues this work examines are the various national efforts in relation to technology assessment and technology studies. It also aims to understand how technology studies relates to the wider cultural perspective. In the Danish context, the author observes that technology assessment is related more to the political culture than to the educational culture, and further that this political culture is based on a tradition of self-organization and public debate. In that vein, technology assessment in Denmark is strongly influenced by key interest groups and is institutionalized in loose networks rather than being institutionalized in the academic culture. The prospects for developing technology studies in Danish institutions compared to its development in Swedish and American institutions are also examined. The book is recommended for students and specialists in science and technology studies and in the sociology of technology.

472   **Higher education in Denmark: a guide for foreign students and institutions of higher education.**
Copenhagen: The Secretariat of the Danish Rectors' Conference, 1994. 95p.

A handy reference that provides basic information on institutions of higher education and very complete information on how to contact them. The volume contains a brief summary of pre-university education and the overall structure of the Danish system of higher education. There is also general admissions information for foreign students at all levels including qualifying exams, recognition of foreign degrees, language requirements, and practical tips. Programme descriptions, addresses and phone numbers are provided for each of the twenty universities and fourteen colleges that are part of the Danish system. This is a very clear and informative guide which allows readers to judge where they fit into the system. It is a good starting point for researching the educational possibilities in Denmark.

473   **Secondary education in Denmark.**
Steffen Jensen.   Strasbourg, France: Council of Europe Press, 1995. 65p. (Guide to Secondary Education in Europe).

Presents the major elements of secondary education structures and policies. This work provides a detailed description of the country's educational system and the various types of secondary education – general, higher preparatory, commercial, technical, and vocational. It also discusses the transition from upper secondary education to higher education, and the necessary qualifications. There is information on policy-making and the responsibilities of government, the administration and organization of the educational system, and the financing of the educational system. The various curricula, the grading scale, the forms of examinations, and other methods for the evaluation and assessment of students are also described. A short section discusses the European dimension and the internationalization of Danish secondary education. Selected statistical data is presented in an appendix. This work is concise and informative and is part of a series that is presented to allow for international comparisons.

474   **Vocational education and training in Denmark.**
Søren P. Nielsen.   Berlin: CEDEFOP-European Centre for the Development of Vocational Training, 1995. 115p. bibliog.

A comprehensive and detailed monograph on all aspects of vocational education. The report contains information on the history of vocational training, the current structure and content of the system for young people and for adults, and the administration and financing of the system. Specific topics include: admissions policies; syllabuses and examinations;

on-the-job training; types of training such as commercial, clerical, and agricultural; combating youth unemployment; and continuing education schemes. The statutory basis for many of the system's features is noted throughout. The report is primarily descriptive and is enhanced with numerous tables and figures. It aims for a format that can allow comparison with other European Union member states, and the information is presented very clearly. A short concluding section comments on problems and perspectives. Appendices provide definitions of key terms and a list of relevant institutions and organizations.

The folk high schools and adult education

475 **Danish social movements in a time of global destabilization: essays on the heritage of Reventlow and Grundtvig, the *efterskole* and the postmodern.**
Steven M. Borish. Vejle, Denmark: Nornesalen and Kroghs Publishers, 1996. 421p.

The author examines the Danish path to modernization with an in-depth look at the origin and development of the Danish *folkelig* movements (people's progressive, social movements) which include: the *efterskole* (continuation schools for adolescents), the Danish Land Reforms, rifle associations, local meeting-houses, and the agricultural cooperatives. The work also examines the wider issue of the state of these social movements in the light of post-modern cultural change and global destabilization. It is an insightful commentary on the survival of the modern welfare state in a country where the civil society outside the state and the market-place has always played an important role. The work is a collection of essays by the author and each can be read in isolation. They are nearly equally divided between theoretical and descriptive chapters, providing plenty of material for both the scholar as well as the general reader.

476 **The land of the living: the Danish folk high schools and Denmark's non-violent path to modernization.**
Steven M. Borish. Nevada City, California: Blue Dolphin, 1991. 488p. bibliog.

An unusual and fascinating book that combines anthropology and historical analysis to examine Danish culture and national character, past and present. The point of departure of the work is the critical role of education in any society undergoing modernization. A unique aspect of Danish educational history that has endured for 150 years is the Danish folk high school. This secondary institution is open to all adults, is entirely non-competitive, is outside the mainstream educational system, and, to a great degree, is state-supported yet free from state control. The author examines the historical circumstances surrounding its emergence, as well as its present-day functioning and what that tells us about contemporary Denmark. The book also stands as a tribute to 19th-century poet and philosopher N. F. S. Grundtvig, who provided the impetus for the folk high school movement. This is a highly readable and thoroughly enjoyable ethnography.

477 **Schools for life.**
Edited by Henning Eichberg. Copenhagen: The Association of
Danish Folk High Schools, 1992. 117p.

A collection of articles that demonstrate the influence of the Danish folk high school
concept around the world. The contributors represent Africa, Ghana, India, Australia,
Great Britain, Hungary, the United States, and Denmark. The articles relate both
concrete experiences in folk education as well as philosophical reflections on the
general meaning of the concept. The collection demonstrates the intercultural
differences regarding the form the education takes and the principles it embraces. Folk
high schools go by many names such as residential colleges, popular academies,
liberal adult education, and non-formal education. Some schools reflect a concern for
democracy, others spirituality, still others nationalism or anti-colonialism. These
articles also attest to the common underlying principle in folk education which is its
radical anti-mainstream element. The editor's preface discusses the challenge in
translating the term 'folk education' linguistically and culturally.

478 **A Grundtvig anthology: selections from the writings of N. F. S.
Grundtvig (1783-1872).**
Edited by Niels Lyhne Jensen, translated by Niels Lynhe Jensen,
Edward Broadbridge. Cambridge, England: James Clarke &
Company, 1984. 195p.

Aims to acquaint the foreign student with Nikolaj Frederik Severin Grundtvig through
his own words. This volume contains translations of some of Grundtvig's historical,
theological, educational, devotional, and poetical writings. In addition to sermons and
poems, included here are 'Universal Historical Learning', which is part I of the introduction to Norse mythology; 'The School for Life', which is part I of Grundtvig's
main essay on education; selections from 'Within Living Memory', a series of lectures
which became part of Grundtvig's handbook on world history; and selections from
'Elementary Christian Teachings'. An editor's introduction describes how the events
in Grundtvig's life influenced his thoughts and writing. Enough nuance is provided to
give the reader an impression of this extraordinary man's personality. A two-page
chronology of his life is also included. Each chapter opens with an explanation and
perspective by leading scholars of Grundtvig's work.

479 **N. F. S. Grundtvig: selected educational writings.**
Compiled by Max Lawson. Helsingor, Denmark: The International
People's College and the Association of Folk High Schools in
Denmark, 1991. 110p.

Nikolaj Frederik Severin Grundtvig has been referred to as 'the father of Western
adult education'. His notion of the folk high school, a shared residential learning
community, has received international attention over the years. This work presents
seven of Grundtvig's most notable essays related to education. These essays had
appeared elsewhere and had been translated by others. This compiler brings them
together here with limited interpretation and discussion. An introductory chapter
provides a brief profile of Grundtvig's life and the major tenets of his educational
philosophy. Among these are the emphasis on fellowship; oral communication; and
knowledge as a matter of living interaction and mutual education between teachers
and students ('the living word') which leads to enlightenment about life, Grundtvig's
basic educational aim.

480 **The folk high school 1970-1990: development and conditions.**
Edited by Ebbe Lundgaard.   Copenhagen: The Association of Folk
High Schools in Denmark, 1991. 91p.

This book is a survey of the situation of the folk high school that was prepared as a
basis for new legislation. It opens with a brief introductory chapter on the folk high
school's history. This is followed by a discussion of the folk high school's development
since 1970 in terms of education for the 'leisure time society'. The similarities and
differences between the various types of residential schools are examined. There is a
look at state and local student financial support. There is also a discussion of the special
place of the folk high school and the Grundtvigian tradition of the 'enlightenment of
the people', within the new educational developments and increasing options for adult
education. Finally, the adaptability of the folk high school is examined, and its future
in the information society. This part also examines the demographic changes in the
student population. Tables report the increase and decrease in folk high schools for
each year as well as the annual numbers of students. The report is a solid overview of
the folk high school and other forms of adult education in modern Danish society.

481 **In search of the culture of Denmark.**
Shigeyoshi Matsumae, translated by Maurice Jenkins.   Tokyo: Tokai
University Press, 1991. 108p.

A personal account of this Japanese author's one-month stay in Denmark during a
study tour of Europe in 1933. The author believed that the foundation of a country can
be found in its history, its system of education, its spiritual ethos and its religion, and
that Denmark offered a unique look at these aspects of culture, particularly in its folk
high schools. In addition to stops in four major cities, visits to eight folk high schools
are described in some detail with reference to their physical characteristics, their
educational practices and daily life, and the principal inhabitants. Through this
author's eyes the culture of Denmark could be found in its rural villages; the folk high
schools at the time offered an education that was rooted in the history and religion of
Denmark; and the very foundation of the country rested on a 'patriotism based on
faith'. Concluding sections relate how the author went on to found Tokai University,
which was based on the ideals of the folk high schools, as well as the Tokai University
European Centre outside Copenhagen.

482 **Adult education in Denmark and the concept of** *folkeoplysning*.
Ministry of Education, Department of Adult Education.   Copenhagen:
Danish Research and Development Centre for Adult Education, 1993.
44p. bibliog. (Available from Danish Research and Development
Centre for Adult Education, Tordenskjoldsgade 27, DK-1055
Copenhagen K).

Discusses various aspects of adult education, an area which has received significant
attention from the Danish government as a solution to social problems. An historical
overview of the country's long tradition of adult education and the influence of
N. F. S. Grundtvig is provided. This discussion includes the cultural definition of
folkeoplysning, which loosely refers to general adult education and enlightenment.
The concept receives significant elaboration here. The link between *folkeoplysning*
and democracy is also discussed. The report describes the current elements of adult
education and the many types of programmes that fall under this umbrella term. The
need for adult education in terms of life satisfaction and survival in the labour market

receives significant attention. Appendices provide excerpts from relevant legislation, a diagram of the educational system, and a list of addresses of relevant institutions.

483   **Adult education and everyday life.**
Henning Salling Olesen, translated from the Danish by Margaret Malone.   Roskilde, Denmark: Adult Education Research Group, Roskilde University, 1989. Reprinted, 1996. 189p. bibliog.

This work, which is only a partial presentation of a work that was originally published in Danish in 1985, is a theoretical and political discussion on adult learning. An introduction provides an overview, but not a concrete historical description, of the tradition of adult education beginning with the folk high schools up to recent theory and practice. Adult learning is discussed in terms of popular enlightenment, 'education for life', the demands of the labour market, and the renewal of the welfare state. The work further examines the many facets of the notion 'experience', a key concept in the book, in that 'experiencing our own reality is a central problem in adult life today'. A concrete example of the teaching and learning experiences of brewery workers is presented in some detail. Models for analysing, planning and structuring teaching and learning processes are also presented, but this section is not specifically related to the Danish experience in this translated version. The bibliography contains works that are primarily written in Danish. The book is aimed at educators and educationally oriented readers in trade unions or socially conscious groups.

Literature

Criticism and trends

484 **Isak Dinesen and the engendering of narrative.**
Susan Hardy Aiken. Chicago, Illinois; London: University of
Chicago Press, 1990. 323p. (Women in Culture and Society).

This author notes that narrative is one site in the public discourse from where women
have been able to speak, albeit within a masculine symbolic order and in a male-
oriented language. This work examines Dinesen's creation of narrative within a larger
cultural context, focusing on the intricacies of gender, sexuality, and representation in
Dinesen's writings. It attempts to show the relevance of contemporary theories of
sexual difference and signification for reading Dinesen, in that her writings themselves
blur the boundaries between fiction and theory. Dinesen's work demonstrates the
inseparability of gender and the engendering of narrative, and stands as an enquiry
itself into how sexual difference informs the ways in which 'we tell ourselves as
stories'. This book is not an exhaustive coverage of Dinesen's writings, but rather
emphasizes a few important texts, i.e., the great narratives written early in her career.
This is a scholarly work that assumes background knowledge and may not be of
interest to the general reader.

485 **Heritage and prophecy: Grundtvig and the English-speaking
world.**
Edited by A. M. Allchin, D. Jasper, J. H. Schjørring, K. Stevenson.
Aarhus, Denmark: Aarhus University Press, 1993. 330p.

This book focuses on the theme of N. F. S. Grundtvig's relation to England and the
parallels between this noted Danish poet, philosopher and theologian and his
European contemporaries. Grundtvig's four visits to England in the mid-1800s are
discussed, along with his lifelong interest in England's literature and history. The
broad body of Grundtvig's work and interests is examined in various categories:
European romanticism, hymn-writing, theological studies, his national and political

involvement, and his international influence on education. This work is a collection of papers by various scholars who attempt to understand both Grundtvig's influence on 19th-century Europe as well as his relevance to the present day. It is a significant work in that it extends the reach of this great literary figure, who remains somewhat unknown outside Denmark.

486 **Danish literature: a short critical survey.**
Poul Borum. Copenhagen: The Danish Institute, 1979. 140p. bibliog.
This survey is divided into historical periods. The first chapter briefly discusses literature from the Middle Ages, the Renaissance, the Reformation, the Baroque period, the 18th century, and the modern period of the early 20th century. The emphasis, however, is on the more contemporary literature from the 1940s through to the 1970s, and the author attempts to place Danish writers in an international context. The book is written in an easy style and is meant for a general audience. The bibliography comprises Danish works in English translation.

487 **Quests for a promised land: the works of Martin Andersen Nexø.**
Faith Ingwersen, Niels Ingwersen. Westport, Connecticut; London: Greenwood Press, 1984. 156p. bibliog.
Aims to provide a brief, critical introduction to the works of Nexø, who is probably best known for his epic novel *Pelle the Conqueror*. The opening chapter provides background on Nexø's life and times, and the concluding chapter attempts to assess Nexø's position in world literature. In addition to *Pelle*, the authors summarize and analyse *Ditte, Humanity's Child* and *Morten the Red* in detail. Other early works, later narrative fiction, and memoirs are also examined. The authors observe the Marxist ideology in Nexø's work, as well as his optimism for the future of the working class. The selective bibliography includes all Nexø's works translated into English at the time, as well as many secondary sources.

488 **Idyll and abyss: essays on Danish literature and theatre.**
Aage Jørgensen. Aarhus, Denmark: Centre for Undervisning og Kulturformidling; Seattle, Washington: Mermaid Press, 1992. 107p.
In these seven 'occasional pieces' the author comments on the 'new' Danish literary criticism of the 1970s and 1980s; the influence of the Youth Rebellion of 1968 on Danish theatre as exemplified by the cooperative, democratic theatre group, Solvognen; the themes of sexuality and passion underlying Danish Golden Age literature; Per Olov Enquist's play *Fra regnormenes liv*; Hans Egede Schack's novel *Phantasterne*; Adam Oehlenschläger and Homeric poetry; and the life and work of Peder Hegelund. These essays have been published previously in professional journals and conference proceedings, and have been revised for inclusion in this volume.

489 **Isak Dinesen: critical views.**
Edited by Olga Anastasia Pelensky. Athens, Ohio: Ohio University Press, 1993. 243p. bibliog.
This volume is a collection of twenty-six essays intended for students, scholars, and readers of Isak Dinesen. Among the contributors are scholars, writers, critics and reviewers whose words reflect the range of ideas, often contradictory, surrounding Dinesen's work. These reprinted essays appeared originally in a variety of books and

journals from 1952 through to 1992. This collection is the first of its kind published in English.

490 Tove Ditlevsen and the aesthetics of madness.
Antje C. Petersen. *Scandinavian Studies*, vol. 64, no. 2 (Spring 1992), p. 243-62.

Investigates the interplay between autobiography, madness and suicide in Ditlevsen's autobiographical fiction and memoirs. The article cites many examples of real-life occurrences in fictional works, and examples of the subject matter of mental illness, madness, and suicide. A preoccupation with these topics is noted. Ditlevsen's work is also placed in the larger genre of women's writing with madness as a literary motif, and parallels are drawn with Sylvia Plath's *The Bell Jar*. This is an informative as well as an analytical article that can serve as a partial introduction to the work of this well-known Danish author.

491 A history of Danish literature.
Edited by Sven H. Rossel. Lincoln, Nebraska; London: University of Nebraska Press, 1992. 709p. bibliog. (A History of Scandinavian Literatures, vol. 1).

Discusses Danish and Faroese literature from their beginnings to the 1990s. Works are viewed comparatively in an international context. Social and cultural history is also brought into the discussion. The volume is divided into historical periods and literary genres such as antiquity and the Middle Ages, the Reformation, the Enlightenment, Romanticism and Realism, the modern breakthrough, the two World Wars, and the post-Second World War period. The contributors apply diverse methods of literary criticism. Some use a sociological method; others come from the standpoint of intellectual history; some examine the development of a genre; and others analyse the ideological changes within a genre. As an innovation over past treatments of Danish literature, special sections on women's and children's literature are included. The book is meant for students, scholars, and for a general readership. The selective bibliography is organized chapter by chapter and focuses on works, primarily in English, that provide further bibliographical references.

492 Ludvig Holberg: a European writer. A study in influence and reception.
Edited by Sven H. Rossel. Amsterdam, Atlanta: Rodopi, 1994. 237p.

The aim of this collection of essays by Holberg scholars is to present this 'father of Norwegian and Danish belles lettres' as the international figure he was. The focus is on his impact on foreign literature and his place in the European tradition. Holberg is considered one of the foremost playwrights of the classical comedy, but also worked in other genres such as the satirical poem and the fable. The essays interpret his work in terms of the various influences on him such as Greek and Roman antiquity, German-speaking Europe, the Romance world – particularly French culture and literature – and the Anglo-American world. The book reflects Holberg's cosmopolitan life and makes clear that he wrote for an international audience. Each chapter is meant to be read independently and includes its own bibliography. The work also provides a two-page chronology.

493   **The witch and the goddess in the stories of Isak Dinesen: a feminist reading.**
Susan Stambaugh.   Ann Arbor, Michigan; London: UMI Research Press, 1988. 139p. bibliog.

Concern about the position of women was a central subject of Dinesen's fiction. This book presents a survey of Dinesen's work from a woman's perspective, examining her descriptions of the restrictions faced by 19th-century women and their resentment towards these restrictions, her presentations of patriarchy and the ways in which women undermined it, and her examinations of misogyny. Dinesen's female wisdom figures included whorelike characters, witches, and goddesses. The author argues, however, that Dinesen's attitude towards feminism was more complex than an apparent glorification of women and women's wisdom, and she attempts to explicate what Dinesen intended to say. Her critical stance draws upon biography and the history of literature, particularly 19th-century British literature in which Dinesen appears to have been firmly grounded. The book takes a theme, rather than a chronological approach, to Dinesen's body of work.

494   **Isak Dinesen Karen Blixen.**
Edited by Bodil Wamberg.   Copenhagen: Spektrum, 1992. 64p.

A compilation of three essays that were originally written and published in 1985 in honour of Karen Blixen's centenary. Contained here are 'On Being Oneself' by Marianne Juhl; 'Who Am I' by Thorkild Bjørnvig; and 'The Empty Space Between Art and Church' by Aage Henriksen. Bjørnvig and Henriksen were both close friends of Blixen and interpret her work accordingly. Juhl, a student of Blixen, discusses the letters from Africa with reference to the personal and external factors that played a part in Karen Blixen's development both as a writer and as a liberated and confident woman. Newcomers to Blixen will find this little volume to be a solid introduction to the life and work of this famous and significant writer.

495   **Isak Dinesen and narrativity: reassessments for the 1990s.**
Edited by Gurli A. Woods.   Ottawa, Ontario: Carleton University Press, 1994. 240p. bibliog.

A compilation of fourteen essays by Dinesen scholars from North America and Europe. This volume brings together Dinesen criticism from a feminist perspective and criticism that deals with her work in the light of recent developments in modern literary theory. The essays are grouped into three sections: the first analyses gender issues in connection with the feminist aspects of Dinesen's writing; the second finds similarities between Dinesen's work and that of the French Symbolist Movement and the British Victorian poets; the third approaches Dinesen's work from various critical stances such as rhetoric and deconstruction. The editor provides a thorough and illuminating introduction.

Dictionary of Scandinavian literature.
See item no. 655.

A checklist of Danish literature after 1945: based on the holdings of the Memorial Library of the University of Wisconsin-Madison.
See item no. 668.

Translations

496 New Danish plays.
Edited by Hans Christian Andersen.   Norwich, England: Norvik
Press, 1996. 263p.

This is the first publication in English of plays by four of the best-known living
Danish dramatists. The plays are *Fair Kirsten* by Kai Nissen, a radio play, translated
by Julian Garner; and three stage plays: *Leonora* by Sven Holm, translated by Hans
Christian Andersen; *Morning and Evening* by Astrid Saalbach, translated by Marlene
S. Madsen; and *Odysseus from Vraa* by Jess Ørnsbo, translated by Hugh Matthews.
These four playwrights belong to the post-modern age of the Danish theatre that had
its beginnings in the 1960s. The editor's introduction provides a brief history of the
Danish theatre and discusses the significance of these authors and their works.

497 Katinka. (Ved vejen.)
Herman Bang, translated from the Danish by Tiina Nunnally.   Seattle,
Washington: Fjord Press, 1990. 174p.

A classic ill-fated love story about the depressing existence of a young woman in a
small railway town. The story demonstrates Bang's concern with societal oppression
of the individual.

498 Georg Brandes: selected letters.
Georg Brandes, edited and translated from the Danish by W. Glyn
Jones.   Norwich, England: Norvik Press, 1990. 275p.

Danish critic Georg Brandes (1842-1927) is considered to be one of the great
European letter writers whose correspondence extended over sixty years. He had a
wide circle of international friends and acquaintances, was sought after as a lecturer,
and writers deluged him with their works for review. Brandes was a brilliant child and
an intellectually arrogant and complex young man. His sense of justice often led him
to take the side of the oppressed, but at the same time, he held an unsympathetic view
of those he considered culturally inferior. His letters show a development from
left-wing and collectivist sympathies to an individualism tainted with a distrust of
democracy. The letters included in this volume are those written to cultural personalities,
rather than to family. They were selected to show glimpses of his correspondence over
the years in order to demonstrate the evolution of his personality and interests.

499 Double Danish: contemporary short stories from Denmark.
Selected and translated from the Danish by Per K. Brask.   Dunvegan,
Ontario: Cormorant Books, 1991. 120p.

An anthology of ten short stories by ten well-known Danish writers. The collection is
built around the theme of 'the life of the mind' in a modern European urban domestic
environment. The stories are meant to convey the craziness of modern daily life, the
bizarre, and the surreal. The authors are also dramatists and their stories contain
elements of psychodrama and theatricality. The authors represented here are Benny
Andersen, Jytte Borberg, Bo Green Jensen, Ulla Ryum, Niels Hav, Astrid Saalbach,
Claes Johansen, Hanne Marie Svendsen, Svend Åge Madsen, and Dorrit Willumsen.

500 **A fighting pig's too tough to eat.** (En gris som været oppe at slås kan man ikke stege.)
Suzanne Brøgger, translated from the Danish by Marina Allemano.
Norwich, England: Norvik Press, 1997. 282p.

This anthology makes available fourteen of the author's personal essays written between 1976 and 1995, in addition to the short 1979 autobiographical novel that is the title of this volume. These essays reflect on a variety of topics that include cosmic energy, female power, the author's Jewish heritage, her traumatic childhood, and the power of fire. Brøgger has been described as unconventional in her lifestyle and writing; in that respect she has been compared to her countrywoman Karen Blixen. Her early writings are considered polemical and her later work visionary. The translator's introduction comments on Brøgger's subject matter, influences, and style.

501 **Tove Ditlevsen: 'Complete freedom' and other stories.**
Selected and translated from the Danish by Jack Brondum.
Willimantic, Connecticut: Curbstone Press, 1982. 87p.

A collection of short stories by this widely read and sometimes contoversial author. Here Ditlevsen explores such themes as anti-semitism in 'The Oranges', father–son relationships in 'The Dagger', and greed in 'A Good Deal'.

502 **Early spring.** (Tidligt forår.)
Tove Ditlevsen, translated from the Danish by Tiina Nunnally.
Seattle, Washington: The Seal Press, 1985. 227p.

The memoirs of one of Denmark's best-loved and most read authors. This book describes her first eighteen years growing up in a working-class neighbourhood in Copenhagen during the 1930s, where she always dreamt of becoming a writer to escape her surroundings. Ditlevsen's writing has been described as lyrical, witty, and romantic.

503 **No man's land: an anthology of modern Danish women's literature.**
Edited by Annegret Heitmann, translated from the Danish by Anne Born, Else Gress, Susanna Nied, Christine Badcock, Paula Hostrup Jessen, James McFarlane. Norwich, England: Norvik Press, 1987.
211p. bibliog.

A collection of prose and poetry by ten 20th-century Danish women writers: Karen Blixen, Elsa Gress, Inger Christensen, Suzanne Brøgger, Kirsten Thorup, Dorrit Willumsen, Dea Trier Mørch, Juliane Preisler, Pia Tafdrup, and Merete Torp. This anthology confronts the issue of female life-style or consciousness outside the boundaries of male experience. Each of these writers brings her own perspective. The editor's introduction is thorough and enlightening as it compares and contrasts their contributions around the theme of female identity.

504 **Borderliners.** (De måske egnede.)
Peter Høeg, translated from the Danish by Barbara Haveland.
London: Harvill Press, 1995. 277p.

A novel with psychological tension set in Copenhagen in the 1970s. Peter, the narrator, has grown up in institutions and now has a chance at a normal life when he is accepted to an élite private school. He and his new-found friends, outsiders like himself, discover the school is using them in an experiment in controlling children. This is a compelling and disturbing story that directs sharp criticism towards the regimented Danish educational policies of the period.

505 **The history of Danish dreams.** (Forestilling om det tyvenden århundrede.)
Peter Høeg, translated from the Danish by Barbara Haveland.
New York: Farrar, Straus and Giroux, 1995. 356p.

Høeg's first novel is a social satire that blurs fantasy and reality, past and present. The dark tale is a multi-generational saga dealing with Danish social classes over the last century.

506 **Smilla's sense of snow.** (Frøken Smilla's fornemmelse for sne.)
Peter Høeg, translated from the Danish by Tiina Nunnally.   New York: Dell Publishing, 1994. 499p. Originally published, New York: Farrar, Straus and Giroux, 1993.

The best-selling novel by one of Denmark's most popular contemporary and internationally recognized writers. The story's heroine, Smilla, suspects that there is more to the death of a six-year-old boy who fell from an apartment roof in Copenhagen. A native Greenlander and a physicist, Smilla becomes involved in an investigation of a cover-up that takes her on an expedition to the Arctic ice-cap. This is a highly original novel, and a suspenseful and satisfying mystery. This novel is also available by another translator with the title *Miss Smilla's feeling for snow* (translated from the Danish by F. David. London: Harvill Press, 1993. 410p.).

507 **Moral reflections & epistles.** (Moralske tanker.)
Ludvig Holberg, translated from the Danish by P. M. Mitchell.
Norwich, England: Norvik Press, 1991. 197p.

Norwegian-born Ludvig Holberg (1684-1754) settled in Copenhagen to pursue his academic career. He is well known as a writer of comedies and sometimes referred to as 'the Danish Molière'. He was also, however, an historian, critic, and an articulate scholar. This volume is a collection of some of his reflective essays that comprise the 'Moral Reflections'. They are of a serious and philosophical nature and provide insight into the ethical and moral questions that concerned 18th-century intellectuals. Among the essays included here are 'On Studies', 'About Writers', 'On Virtue', 'On Friends and Enemies', 'On the Peasantry', 'On Decorum', and 'On Reform'.

508   **Seventeen Danish poets: a bilingual anthology of contemporary Danish poetry.**
Edited by Niels Ingwersen.   Lincoln, Nebraska: The Windflower Press, 1981. 164p.

A collection of sixty-five poems published between 1948 and 1980, with an emphasis on those published after 1970. This era is known as the Modernistic tradition, and the poems included here provide varying examples of the genre. The poets represented here are Ole Wivel, Erik Knudsen, Lise Sørensen, Thorkild Bjørnvig, Jørgen Gustava Brandt, Per Højholt, Klaus Rifberg, Benny Andersen, Charlotte Strandgaard, Henrik Nordbrandt, Kristen Bjørnkjær, Marianne Larsen, Murat Alpar, Vita Andersen, Simon Grabowski, Hanne Marie Jensen, and Iris Garnov. The editor's preface provides only brief commentary. Each poem is presented in its entirety in Danish and in English.

509   **Barbara.**
Jørgen-Frantz Jacobsen, translated from the Danish by George Johnston.   Norwich, England: Norvik Press, 1993. 258p.

This novel is considered to be a much-loved 20th-century classic in Danish-Faroese literature. It is a passionate story set in the Faroe Islands in the 1750s, reflecting their dramatic beauty and the starkness of life there. The main character has been described as 'an amoral Cleopatra' and one of the most complex female characters in modern Scandinavian literature.

510   **New Danish fiction.**
Edited by Thomas E. Kennedy, Frank Hugus.   *The Review of Contemporary Fiction*, vol. 15, no. 1 (Spring 1995), 198p.

This entire issue features recent work by fourteen contemporary Danish writers who represent a wide range of styles. The writers included are Suzanne Brøgger, Peter Høeg, Vita Andersen, Jens Christian Grøndahl, Knud Holst, Kirsten Thorup, Bo Green Jensen, Ib Michael, Peer Sibast, Ulla Ryum, Klaus Linggaard, Vibeke Grønfeldt, Dorrit Willumsen, and Sven Holm. These pieces were originally published in Danish from 1975 to 1990, and appear in this issue by various translators. Brief background information on each author is provided.

511   **Days with Diam.** (Dage med Diam.)
Svend Åge Madsen, translated from the Danish by W. Glyn Jones. Norwich, England: Norvik Press, 1994. 246p.

A unique and intriguing novel by one of Denmark's most important experimental novelists. This author is concerned with the unstable or illusory nature of reality. This novel has been described as a 'mathematical puzzle', that teases the reader on a journey through shifting identities and solutions.

512   **Harmless tales.** (Ufarlige historier.)
Villy Sørensen, translated from the Danish by Paula Hostrup Jessen. Norwich, England: Norvik Press, 1991. 137p.

A collection of short stories by one of Denmark's most highly-rated contemporary writers of fiction and the recipient of numerous awards. These are fantastic tales that relate to ethical and moral issues without preaching. They contain bizarre episodes that often take unexpected turns. The editor gives a thorough and insightful introduction with background on the author, as well as discussion of the plots, characters, themes, symbolism, and humour contained in these tales.

513 **Spring tide.** (Springflod.)
Pia Tafdrup, translated from the Danish by Anne Born.   London;
Boston, Massachusetts: Forest Books, 1989. 83p.

A book of poetry about desire and about women's passion. Tafdrup writes what she calls 'the syntax of desire' whereby she attempts not merely to write about desire, but to demonstrate it. She also has tried to write about 'the not yet thought, but sensed'. The title 'spring tide' denotes the highest tide at the new and full moon. Throughout the book, this cycle of nature is linked with the female cycle and the cycle of desire. Tafdrup's poetry has been described as intelligent, sensual and modern, and accessible without being simplistic.

Danish children's literature.
See item no. 618.

Danish literary magazine.
See item no. 620.

Literature from Denmark published in English between 1980 and 1991.
See item no. 661.

The Arts

Visual arts

514   **From the Golden Age to the present day: two centuries of art and
craft in Denmark.**
Edited by Finn Andersen, Ian O'Riordan.   Edinburgh: City of
Edinburgh Museums and Galleries, and the Danish Cultural Institute,
1995. 126p.

This volume commemorates the exhibition at the 1995 International Festival in
Edinburgh. The exhibition, which was held at the City Art Centre, presented contemporary Danish art and craft with works illustrating the romanticism of the 19th
century's Golden Age, the Skagen painters of the turn of the century, and the
modernists, surrealists and expressionists of the 20th century. The decorative arts are
also represented here in ceramic, glass, silver, and textiles. Special sections provide
brief biographies of artists and craftspersons. The volume is beautifully illustrated
with colour photographs and each work is numbered and catalogued.

515   **Carl-Henning Pedersen. Else Alfelt.**
Edited by Marianne Barbusse, translated from the Danish by Vivien
Andersen, Martha G. Abrahamsen.   Herning, Denmark: The
Carl-Henning Pedersen and Else Alfelt Museum, 1993. 207p.

A catalogue of the works of 20th-century abstract artists Carl-Henning Pedersen, and
those of his late wife, Else Alfelt. The book is also a profile of the lives of these two
artists, who were patrons of the arts and very active in Denmark's contemporary art
scene. A series of essays by various contributors examine the artists' background,
their style and influences, and their impact on the art world. There is also much background information on the modern art scene, and the founding of various museums in
Denmark in the 20th century. The catalogue is primarily devoted to Pedersen, but it
presents numerous colour photographs of paintings by both artists. Brief outline

biographies of the two artists are also provided, as well as a list of the museums that have exhibited their works.

516 **Danish sculpture around 1900.**
Ernest Jones Bencard, Flemming Friborg, translated from the Danish by James Manley. Copenhagen: Ny Carlsberg Glyptotek, 1995. 239p. bibliog.

This volume is a catalogue of 135 works, produced from 1860 to 1920 by twenty-six Danish sculptors. The authors explain that these works represent a period of Danish sculpture for which there has been little interest or appreciation. The period came along in the shadow of Neo-classicism and has been condemned as trifling by Modernists. Not much literature exists on these artists and their works, and the aim of this volume is to reassess the works and to show how the artists reflect the artistic taste of their age. Each sculpture is presented with a black-and-white photograph and descriptive text. The authors' introduction places the works in their historical and artistic context. The bibliography consists of works that are exclusively in Danish.

517 **The amazing paper cuttings of Hans Christian Andersen.**
Beth Wagner Brust. New York: Ticknor & Fields, 1994. 80p. bibliog.

This is the story of Andersen the artist, rather than the writer. Andersen often made paper cuttings while telling a fairy tale and then gave them to the children in his audience. The paper cutting helped keep the children engrossed not only in the story, but also in how the cutting itself would turn out. These whimsical works of art – swans, clowns, angels, and the like – numbered into the hundreds, possibly thousands. This is a unique book and includes twenty-nine pages of illustrations of the cuttings, which can now be found primarily in museum collections. Although this book is recommended for young readers, it can be appreciated by readers of all ages.

518 **The Spirit of Copenhagen.**
Ruth Eaton. Copenhagen: Danish Design Centre, 1996. 71p.

A book commemorating an exhibition of the same name in celebration of Copenhagen's designation as the European Capital of Culture 1996. This work represents the vision of four photographers and one architect, who aimed to capture the city's urban spirit, and to portray the relationship between the physical and social environments. The book comprises approximately 200 black-and-white photographs that pay homage to the architecture, the arts, intimate urban spaces, the social fabric, water and nature in the city, and even the prevalence of the bicycle. This work is a fascinating city portrait with parallel text in Danish and English.

519 **Scandinavian modernism: painting in Denmark, Finland, Iceland, Norway and Sweden 1910-1920.**
Edited by Carl Tomas Edam, Nils-Göran Hökby, Birgitta Schreiber.
New York: Rizzoli International Publications, 1989. 262p.

The catalogue from a joint exhibition of Scandinavian art. The text consists of an essay on Modernism for each country as well as a shorter background essay for each artist. The Danish artists featured in this catalogue are Harald Giersing, Karl Isakson, Jens Adolf Jerichau, Vilhelm Lundstrøm, Jais Nielsen, Olaf Rude, William Scharf, Sigurd Swane, and Edvard Weie. The paintings, which are contributed from ten different Danish museums, are featured as full-page colour plates. Each work is designated with both its Danish and English name, and each is briefly described.

520   **P. S. Krøyers fotografier.** (P. S. Krøyer's photographs.)
      Elisabeth Fabritius, Marianne Saabye, translated from the Danish by David Hohnen.   Copenhagen: The Hirschsprung Collection, 1990. 188p. bibliog.

Features the photographs of one of the most famous of the Skagen painters. Krøyer's photographs were mainly taken during the 1890s in Skagen. They constitute a separate part of his artistry and were not taken merely as an aid to his painting. They are personal photos of his home, the interior decor reflective of the Aesthetic Movement and the Arts and Crafts Movement, and of his intimate circle. The book presents some 140 photographs (of the 250 that have been preserved), and the text provides background information on Krøyer's artistic and personal life in Skagen, along with insight into the circumstances behind the photographs. The text is presented in both Danish and English. The bibliography includes primarily Danish works.

521   **Peter Brandes: Notre Dame des fleurs.**
      Orfeo Isak.   Edinburgh: Talbot Rice Gallery, 1992. 134p. bibliog.

Peter Brandes is considered one of Denmark's leading contemporary artists in painting, printwork, ceramics, and photography. This volume presents a partial offering of his recent works included at the 1992 exhibition at Edinburgh's Talbot Rice Gallery. Fifty plates depict works in acrylic on canvas. Six other pages are black-and-white full-page reproductions of a then work-in-progress in stained glass windows. The text of a 1992 interview with Brandes is also included. Aside from the interview, no other text is provided, i.e., there is no descriptive text accompanying these untitled works. The bibliography includes books, catalogues, and graphic art portfolios.

522   **Richard Mortensen: painting 1929-1993.**
      Edited by Anders Kold, Kirsten Strømstad, translated from the Danish by David Hohnen.   Copenhagen: Royal Museum of Fine Art; Aarhus, Denmark: Aarhus Museum of Art, 1994. 194p.

The exhibition catalogue for one of the most gifted of 20th-century Danish abstract painters, known for his use of colour. The book includes essays on Mortensen's background, style technique, studies, and teaching. The eighty-four works featured represent the various periods in the artist's development, such as the erotic mysteries and botanical abstracts of his 1930s surrealistic period, the violent Expressionism in his post-war works, and the preoccupation with the threshold and window motifs in his later years. The biographical information is fairly extensive for this type of book.

523   **Heavenly light: the University of Copenhagen in Our Lady's Square.**
      Photographed by Jens Lindhe, written by Henrik Sten Møller, translated from the Danish by David Hohnen.   Copenhagen: Rhodos, 1993. 129p.

A beautiful collection of photographs of the area in and around the University of Copenhagen which includes the Latin Quarter and Our Lady's Square. The text offers architectural and historical commentary that only those well acquainted with the area could provide. The content of the photos ranges from stately buildings, the oldest of which dates to the 15th century, through graffiti-scrawled walls, to the intimate close-up of a stairway or window. The work is a tribute to a lovely and intriguing urban area. A numbered map provides a walking tour of the area.

524 The Golden Age of Danish painting.
Catalogue by Kaspar Monrad, essays by Philip Connisbee, Bjarne Jørnaes, Kaspar Monrad, Hans Vammen. New York: Hudson Hills Press, 1993. 237p.

Presents the exhibition catalogue for the first American exhibitions of Danish art of the romantic period held at the Los Angeles County Museum of Art and New York's Metropolitan Museum of Art during 1994. The works of seventeen Golden Age painters are represented here. For each artist a biographical sketch is provided and a detailed description of their exhibited works. The directors' foreword expresses regret that some works of national importance had to remain in Denmark. The opening essays discuss the Copenhagen School of painting, Danish society during the Golden Age of the early 19th century, and various features of this artistic period. This volume is beautifully illustrated with 105 colour photographs, many of which are full-page illustrations. An earlier similar exhibition at London's National Gallery is commemorated in Monrad's *Danish painting: the Golden Age* (London: The National Gallery, 1984. 272p.).

525 Per Kirkeby: the art of building.
Lars Morell, translated from the Danish by Mette Mouritsen, Lone Mouritsen, Greg Pilley, Peter Ballantine, photographed by Jens Lindhe. Skodsborg, Denmark: Aristo, 1996. 350p.

A somewhat unstructured portrait of this internationally known contemporary abstract painter, graphic artist, and sculptor. The book includes three essays that deal with Kirkeby's drawings, paintings, brick sculptures, and his use of light and space. The bulk of the book comprises an impressive photo series interspersed with interview excerpts. Kirkeby is first and foremost a painter, but his large-scale monumental brick sculptures can be found all over Europe. For a catalogue of some 190 of these sculptures, see *Per Kirkeby: brick sculpture and architecture: catalogue raisonné* (Edited by Herbert Abrell, Lars Morell, Rudolf Sagmeister. Köln, Germany: Walther König, 1997. 279p.).

526 The house of wisdom.
Otto Norn, Søren Skovgaard Jensen, translated from the Danish by Jean Olsen. Copenhagen: Christian Ejlers Publishers, 1990. 155p.

Provides an interpretation of the artistry of the golden altar found in Sahl Church in Western Jutland. The authors discuss the religious and philosophical significance of this monument, which dates back to about 1200. This is a detailed analysis of this work of art including the arch and its crowning relief, the crucifix and retable, and the two towers. The many images and inscriptions contained in the Sahl altar are interpreted in terms of traditional Christian doctrine and classical philosophy, but are also examined in the light of contemporary Christian thought. The work is enhanced with thirty-two black-and-white, close-up photographs by Gérard Franceschi. These exquisite photographs are presented as full-page plates. The entire text is presented in both English and Danish.

527 **Christen Købke 1810-1848.**
Edited by Hans Edvard Nørregård-Nielsen, Kaspar Monrad, translated from the Danish by W. Glyn Jones. Copenhagen: Royal Museum of Fine Art, 1996. 397p.

The catalogue from a 1996 exhibition of the work of this Golden Age painter known for his quiet landscapes and intimate portraits. The book includes essays on various topics such as Købke's methods and style, his international reach, analyses of specific paintings, and biographical information on his education, debut, and foreign travels. Some 240 works are displayed here, many as full-page colour plates. There is also a list of the whole of Købke's works, beyond the exhibition paintings.

528 **The Golden Age of Danish art: drawings from the Royal Museum of Fine Art.**
Hans Edvard Nørregård-Nielsen, translated from the Danish by David Hohnen. Alexandria, Virginia: Art Services International, 1995. 255p. bibliog.

Features drawings in pen, pencil, ink, and chalk by eleven Golden Age painters. The artists featured here are Jens Juel, Nicolai Abildgaard, Christoffer Wilhelm Eckersberg, Wilhelm Bendz, Wilhelm Marstrand, Martinus Rørbye, Christen Købke, Johan Thomas Lundbye, Peter Christian Skovgaard, Dankvart Dreyer, and Bertel Thorvaldsen. An extensive illustrated essay on the period profiles the historical and cultural situation in Copenhagen, as well as mentioning the individual artists. In separate sections, each artist also receives a one-page profile and a commentary is provided on each work that is featured. A total of seventy drawings are included, many as full-page colour plates.

529 **Figurfald.** (Figurefall.)
Edited by Karsten Ohrt, Lene Burkard. Odense, Denmark: Brandts Textile Factory Hall of Art, 1992. 64p.

This book commemorates the exhibition 'Figurefall' held at Brandts Textile Factory Hall of Art in 1992. The exhibition and the book deal with the coming together of Bertel Thorvaldsen, one of the greatest sculptors of the 19th century, with five of Denmark's most exciting contemporary young sculptors. These artists presented their work along with four of Thorvaldsen's works that were recast in plaster, making them 'new' for this exhibition. The book contains colour photographs of all the works included in the exhibition, with accompanying descriptive and analytical text by art historian Mikkel Bogh. An additional commentary on trends in sculpture and architecture from the Neo-classical to Deconstruction is provided by literary historian Henrik Oxvig. Brief biographies of all the artists are also included. The entire text is presented in both Danish and English.

530 **Leda's transformation from paper to fresco: Arne Haugen**
Sørensen's sketches for the decoration of *Folketeatret* in 1991.
Marianne Saabye, translated from the Danish by David Hohnen.
Køge, Denmark: The Køge Museum of Art and The Køge Sketch
Collection with Brandts Textile Factory Hall of Art, The Southern
Jutland Museum of Art, and The Randers Museum of Art, 1991. 93p.
bibliog.

Traces the artist's creative process that culminated in his decorations for the side walls
of the entrance way, a niche in the entrance way, and the ceiling in the foyer of
Folketeatret (The People's Theatre) in Copenhagen. The author follows the process
from the reinterpretation of the Leda motifs for their new space to the technicalities of
fresco painting. The work includes thirty-eight pages of colour photographs of the
artist's preliminary work depicting this Spartan queen in water-colours, tiles, acrylic,
glass and fresco, as well as the final works for the theatre. In addition to biographical
information on the artist, a selected bibliography is provided but these works are in
Danish.

531 **31 women artists from 31 Danish art museums.**
Marianne Sørensen, translated from the Danish by Jane Rowley.
Copenhagen: Ministry of Culture, 1995. 68p.

A tribute to the works of women artists past and present. The book's introduction
discusses the position of women in Denmark's art scene, and emphasizes the historical
neglect of women in art education, art literature, and other art venues. The author sees
this work as one way of redressing this gender imbalance. The book is primarily an art
guide. A single artist is selected to represent each museum. Each profile provides brief
information on the artist and the period she painted in, and gives a description of the
painting that is featured. All paintings are shown as full-page colour photographs and
each museum is designated on a numbered map.

532 **Vilhelm Hammershøi and Danish art at the turn of the century.**
Poul Vad, translated from the Danish by Kenneth Tindall.   New
Haven, Connecticut; London: Yale University Press, 1992. 462p.
bibliog.

This comprehensive volume is the first full-scale treatment of the life and work of
Vilhelm Hammershøi (1864-1916), a leading Danish painter of his generation. The
artist's significance is discussed in the context of both Danish art and the European art
scene. The author, an art historian and novelist, provides detailed readings of
significant and characteristic works from each phase of Hammershøi's career which
includes the interiors, the figure compositions, architectural pictures, and landscapes.
The artist's relationships with the art critics, patrons, dealers, and writers of his day
are also discussed. Included in this volume are the texts of two interviews with
Hammershøi from Danish magazines and a five-page chronology of his life. A
complete numbered catalogue of the 262 illustrations is also provided. For a more
recent treatment of Hammershøi, see *Vilhelm Hammershøi 1864-1916: Danish painter
of solitude and light* by Mikael Wivel (Copenhagen: Ordrupgaard; New York: Harry
N. Abrams, 1998. 191p.).

533 **The painters of Skagen.**
Knud Voss, translated from the Danish by Peter Shield. Tølløse,
Denmark: Stok-Art, 1990. Reprinted, 1994. 260p. bibliog.
This volume showcases the beauty of the art of Skagen and tells the story of the area.
Skagen is both the town and the peninsula at the tip of the North Jutland peninsula,
and it is known for its unique light. Its artists produced their work during the mid-
1800s, and in the early 1900s, a time when the Danish provinces and the landscape
became a source of pictorial subjects. The work of these painters is characterized by a
tradition of depicting people and contrasts in the conditions of daily life. Although
landscapes are also a part of the Skagen art, it is the human condition that is its focus.
The major works of eighteen artists are shown here in colour photographs. Among
these are Vilhelm Melbye, Julius Exner, Holger Drachmann, Carl Locher, Karl
Madsen, Michael Ancher, Anna Ancher, Viggo Johansen, P. S. Krøyer, Christian
Krohg, and Oscar Björk. Descriptive text provides biographical and anecdotal information about each artist and commentary on their paintings. A final chapter describes
the establishment of the Skagen Museum, where the majority of these paintings have
their home.

Music and dance

534 **The music of Per Nørgård: fourteen interpretative essays.**
Edited by Anders Beyer. Aldershot, England: Scolar Press, 1996.
304p.
A compilation of insightful and perceptive analyses of the music of this visionary
composer whose works include operas, ballets, choral works and chamber music.
Among the contributors are composers, musicians, music critics, writers, and academicians. The composer himself provides an autobiographical piece that focuses on the
early influences in his life and also includes a chronology. A selected list of Nørgård's
works is provided and a sampler CD accompanies the book. For a brief discussion of
Nørgård's background, career, and the influences on music, see 'Per Nørgård: the role
of the artist in a model welfare state' by Jean Christensen (In: *Nordic experiences.*
Edited by Berit Brown. Westport, Connecticut; London: Greenwood Press, 1997,
p. 13-23).

535 **Nielsen: symphony no. 5.**
David Fanning. Cambridge, England: Cambridge University Press,
1997. 127p. bibliog.
Considered to be Denmark's greatest composer, Carl Nielsen produced his Fifth
Symphony in 1921-22. This author sets the Fifth in its symphonic historical context,
and offers both a straightforward commentary on the music and a thorough re-
examination of Nielsen's handling of harmony and tonality. This analysis aims for a
distinctive view of Nielsen's work, one that is more rounded and detailed than what
has been hitherto available. In a close reading of the music, the author tries to focus on
Nielsen's musical personality and the manner in which his complex musical structures
reflect his ethical stance and his psychological growth. The discussion is partially

based on existing commentaries of Nielsen's work, including some by the composer himself, which appear here for the first time in English. A final chapter includes a summary of the symphony's composition history, the different editions, early performances, and all twenty-six recordings to date.

536 **Experiencing music: a composer's notes.**
Vagn Holmboe, translated by Paul Rapoport. London: Toccata Press, 1991. 142p. bibliog. (Musicians on Music, no. 5).

Presents personal essays by Danish composer, music researcher, critic, and teacher, Vagn Holmboe. Most of the book is the translation of 'Music – the Inexplicable', which was first published in Danish in 1981. In this essay Holmboe tackles such issues as where musical ideas come from; the role of performers in interpretation of music; what listeners do when they listen to music; and the composers' working methods and their own awareness of them. The translator-editor, a musicologist who has also studied linguistics, provides an insightful introduction that includes biographical information on Holmboe, discusses his articles on music and his ethnomusicological reports, and looks at his musical compositions which include symphonies, string quartets, chamber works, and piano and organ solos. Holmboe's reputation is well established in Scandinavia, and this book opens his achievements to the English-speaking world.

537 **The Bournonville ballets: a photographic record 1844-1933.**
Compiled and annotated by Knud Arne Jürgensen. London: Dance Books, 1987. 179p. bibliog.

A salute to the work of 19th-century Danish choreographer August Bournonville who directed ballet at the Royal Theatre in Copenhagen from 1830 to 1877. This volume offers 478 photographs that comprise twenty-four ballets, five divertissements, and four operas. All photos are captioned with text drawn either from the original libretti or Bournonville's memoirs and production notes. An introductory essay sets the work in its historical context. Music, scenery, and costume credits as well as performance information are provided for each ballet. Also included are a complete list of pictures with accompanying photographic information, and indexes of performers, composers, and writers. The book stands as an historical record of not only theatrical tradition, costume and stage design, but also ballet photography itself.

538 **Music in Denmark.**
Edited by Knud Ketting, translated from the Danish by Michael Chestnutt. Copenhagen: The Danish Cultural Institute, 1987. 111p. bibliog.

This work surveys the country's music scene with a current overview; a description of art music's historical development; essays on the different types of music such as folk, operetta and revue, jazz, and rock; and a discussion of the state of musical education. Public subsidies receive particular mention in terms of the types and distribution, and it is noted that although musical life is supported by the state, it is not directed by it. The book includes a list of Danish musical organizations and institutions, as well as a map showing towns with symphony orchestras and with music conservatories, and the locations of art music and rhythmic festivals. The text is enhanced with numerous black-and-white and colour photographs.

539   **The Nielsen companion.**
Edited by Nina Miller.   London; Boston, Massachusetts: Faber &
Faber, 1994. 666p. bibliog.

A comprehensive collection of essays by leading Carl Nielsen scholars that surveys
his achievements and analyses the roots of his revolutionary style. The work is divided
into two main parts. Part one offers aesthetic, cultural, and historical perspectives on
Nielsen's unique style. The bulk of the volume, however, consists of part two, which
examines the orchestral, solo, chamber, and vocal music. The editor explains that this
is not an exhaustive treatment of all the genres Nielsen composed in; rather, it is an
in-depth analysis of seminal works. Further, throughout part two, she provides seven
'Interludes' that address diverse topics related to Nielsen's techniques, style and
procedures. Included in an appendix are twenty-seven letters written by Nielsen to
friends, family, and colleagues. The editor's detailed prelude is a helpful overview of
the volume, and her introduction discusses the scope of Nielsen research to date, his
musical influence, and his position in Danish music.

540   **Music in Copenhagen: studies in the musical life of Copenhagen in
the 19th and 20th centuries.**
Music Department, University of Copenhagen, translated by James
Manley.   Copenhagen: C. A. Reitzels Publishers, 1996. 299p.

This work is actually a special English issue of the University of Copenhagen's music
department's yearbook, *Musik & Forskning* (Music & Research). It is a series of
studies by individual researchers brought together to shed light on Copenhagen as a
musical city and to compare it to other European musical cities. Among the articles
are historical pieces which examine Golden Age composers of the symphony and the
opera; other articles look at dance, contemporary music, and jazz. There is also a
study of Copenhagen's reception of Beethoven and the influences the composer and
the city had on each other. The work as a whole shows that while the musical life of
Copenhagen was open to external influences, the city itself provided conditions,
comparable to other European cultural centres, that allowed its musical life to flourish.

Hans Brenaa: Danish ballet master.
See item no. 163.

Nordic Sounds.
See item no. 623.

**The compositions of Vagn Holmboe: a catalogue of works and
recordings with indexes of persons and titles.**
See item no. 653.

Musical Denmark Yearbook 93-94.
See item no. 660.

**Twentieth century Danish music: an annotated bibliography and
research directory.**
See item no. 666.

Carl Nielsen: a guide to research.
See item no. 667.

Theatre and film

541 Speaking the language of desire: the films of Carl Dreyer.
Raymond Carney. Cambridge, England; New York: Cambridge University Press, 1989. 363p.

This work aims to 'rehabilitate' the work of Carl Dreyer for a new generation and to open it up for the common viewer. The author observes that this film-maker's work has remained too unknown and neglected, and contrasts Dreyer's methods to those of more familiar film-makers, in an effort to make it more accessible. The first part of the book offers a theoretical approach to understanding Dreyer's general style. The second part of the book concentrates on Dreyer's final three sound films: *Day of Wrath* (1943), *Ordet* (1955), and *Gertrud* (1964), each of which are discussed in detail in individual chapters. A filmography of these three films is included, along with a brief reading list and a list of available videos of Dreyer's films.

542 The actor's way.
Erik Exe Christoffersen, translated by Richard Fowler. London; New York: Routledge, 1993. 224p. bibliog.

Discusses over twenty-five years of dramaturgy at the Odin Theatre in Holstebro, Denmark under the direction of Eugenio Barba. The Odin Theatre was originally established in Norway by Barba in 1964, and moved to Holstebro the following year at the invitation of the local government. It is one of the few remaining theatre groups of those established in the 1960s, when the conception of theatre was changing to one that attempts to create a social relation between the actor and the spectators. The life of the Odin Theatre, which still retains its core group of original members, is discussed through interviews with four actors who talk about their experiences in terms of their craft, training and technique, as well as their motivation and the personal and social meaning of their work. The account is presented in four chronological sections based on various phases in the theatre's development. A list of the Odin Theatre's productions from 1965 to 1992 is provided in an appendix.

543 Scandinavian cinema: a survey of films and film-makers in Denmark, Finland, Iceland, Norway and Sweden.
Peter Cowie. London: Tantivy Press, 1992. 288p. bibliog.

A full-length study of film that discusses all the major films, the film industry, cultural trends, and underlying themes. The book includes a chronology of cinematic, political and cultural events in all the Nordic countries for the period 1896 to 1991; a general survey of the industry and its key figures for each country; a filmography with a selected list of significant films for each country for the period 1910 to 1991; a special section on the films of Carl Theodore Dreyer; a dictionary of directors by country; and an index of films. The book is extensively illustrated with some 300 black-and-white photographs. This is a one-of-a-kind reference work for film buffs and newcomers alike.

544 **Ludvig Holberg: the playwright and his age up to 1730.**
Jens Hougaard, translated from the Danish by Jean and Tom
Lundskær-Nielsen.   Odense, Denmark: Odense University Press,
1993. 140p.

Presents Holberg's plays in a broad Danish and European context and offers some
very detailed analyses of Holberg's work. The various influences present in the plays
are discussed. Holberg's scholarly work at the University of Copenhagen and his
evolution into a poet and satirist during Danish literature's neo-classical period is
described. The Italian and French background in his work is also examined. His
'comedies of character' are analysed, noting his use of humour and satire to attack the
main character's persistence in an act of ludicrousness. Also examined is Holberg's
relationship to feudal drama and his treatment of the subject of culture conflict. The
common threads throughout his work are noted. A select list of Holberg in English is
provided and a list of Holberg's comedies is included in an appendix.

545 **Carl Th. Dreyer.**
Edited by Jytte Jensen.   New York: The Museum of Modern Art,
1988. 95p. bibliog.

Carl Th. Dreyer (1889-1968) is considered one of the masters of the cinema and made
fourteen feature films between 1818 and 1964. This book commemorates the Carl Th.
Dreyer film exhibition at New York's Museum of Modern Art. The work presents a
filmography of the fourteen films, four essays on Dreyer's life and work, and the text
of Dreyer's screenplay to the film *Medea*, in English translation. The four essays
provide biographical information, and examine such topics as Dreyer's depiction of
women in his films – particularly women's suffering; his exploration of the spiritual
and the metaphysical; and his special ability as a director for translating the written
word into image. The book contains many black-and-white still photographs from
Dreyer's films.

546 **A history of Scandinavian theatre.**
Frederick J. Marker, Lise-Lone Marker.   Cambridge, England:
Cambridge University Press, 1996. 384p. bibliog.

Provides a survey of the history and development of theatre in Denmark, Sweden, and
Norway, examining the major styles and trends in historical periods from the Middle
Ages to the present day. The emphasis in this book is on the art of the theatre, and not
on sociological or political factors. The book is divided into two parts. Part one
examines the Middle Ages to the 19th-century Golden Age; 18th-century Danish
playwright Ludvig Holberg receives attention here. Part two covers modern and post-
modern theatre; the Danish Royal Theatre and stage director William Bloch are noted
here. The book is intended for the general reader with no knowledge of the
Scandinavian languages. It is extensively documented and includes numerous black-
and-white illustrations. The bibliography is divided by country and includes many
non-English sources.

547 **The Danish cinema before Dreyer.**
Ron Mottram. Metuchen, New Jersey; London: The Scarecrow Press,
1988. 310p. bibliog.
This work provides a description and critique of the Danish cinema during the years
immediately preceding the First World War, and an examination of the prominent
position it occupied in the international market. The work covers three historical
periods: 1896 to 1909, a period dominated by non-fiction films, but which also saw the
development of fiction films; 1910 to 1914, the period known as the 'golden age' of
Danish cinema; and 1915 to 1917, a time of both artistic and economic decline. The
author analyses surviving films and the individuals who made them, and also
examines the distribution, exhibition, and critical reception of Danish films in the
United States. The author notes that the history of Danish cinema is largely the history
of the production company, Nordisk Films Kompagni, which dominated Danish film
production in the period under study. A filmography which supplies basic credit
information and plot synopses of selected films made from 1903 to 1917 is provided in
an appendix.

548 **Breaking the waves.**
Lars von Trier, translated from the Danish by Jonathan Sydenham.
Copenhagen: Per Kofod Publishers, 1996. 159p.
This is the manuscript to the film *Breaking the waves*, written and directed by Danish
film-maker Lars von Trier, and awarded the jury's Grand Prize at the 1996 Cannes
Film Festival. The film was shot in English on locations in Denmark and Scotland.
The story is set in the early 1970s in a small religious community on the north coast of
Scotland. It is the story of the naïve and innocent Bess who falls in love with Jan, an
oil-rig worker and a man of the world. An accident leaves Jan bedridden and he
convinces Bess she must prove her love for him by carrying on with her life. This is a
story about human emotions, sacrifice, and doing 'good'. In addition to the film manuscript, the book includes a preface by Swedish film writer and director, Stig Björkman,
and a director's note by von Trier. Film credits and biographical notes on the actors
are also provided.

549 **Denmark.**
Astrid Söderbergh Widding. In: *Nordic national cinemas.* Edited
by Tytti Soila, Astrid Söderbergh Widding, Gunnar Iversen. London;
New York: Routledge, 1998, p. 7-30.
Provides a chronological account of Danish film from the first public screening in
1896 up to the present day. The chapter examines Denmark's silent film years and its
early 'golden age', the subsequent period of decline, the transition to sound, the film
revival following the Second World War, the influence of the 1960s youth culture, and
the breakthrough of the modern film. The important films, the major directors and the
significant genre in each period are discussed. A theme throughout the discussion is
the state regulation, influence, and subsidy of the film industry. This chapter is a concise overview of the topic. Eight black-and-white still photographs from significant
Danish films representative of the various genres are included.

Applied arts and design

550 Living design in Denmark: Danish designers in the nineties.
Edited by Kjeld Ammundsen, translated from the Danish by Martek, photographs by Søren Nielsen.   Copenhagen: Living Design in Denmark Organizing Committee, 1995. 104p.

This book features the work of eighteen designers, both the up-and-coming and the more established, whose work was exhibited in 1995 at 'living design' exhibitions in Barcelona and Madrid. The book describes each designer's work as well as the design process. These are objects that serve everyday needs, but they are characterized by an innovative use of materials and unique production processes. The objects include kitchen items of porcelain, ceramic, wood and rubber; cutlery; furniture of wood, steel and glass; clothing of natural fibres and ecological textiles; jewellery and other accessories; and logos and signs. The book aims to show the human being behind the product, and to show the link between Danish design and nature. The objects are featured in black-and-white photographs.

551 Georg Jensen: a tradition of splendid silver.
Janet Drucker.   Atglen, Pennsylvania: Schiffer Publishing, 1997. 318p. bibliog.

This book is a biography of this internationally acclaimed silversmith, a survey of his accomplishments, an account of the Georg Jensen Company, and a catalogue of his many creations which include jewellery, hollowware, and flatware. It is printed on glossy paper and beautifully illustrated in colour and black-and-white photographs. A partial list of museum collections with Georg Jensen silver, a list of selected artists of the Georg Jensen silversmithy, and an explanation of the markings that have been used by the company are provided in an appendix. A two-page chronology of Jensen's life is also provided.

552 Light years ahead: the story of the PH lamp.
Edited by Tina Jørstian, Poul Erik Munk Nielsen, translated from the Danish by Tam McTurk.   Copenhagen: Louis Poulsen & Company, 1994. 304p.

This book describes Poul Henningsen's role in the evolution of electric lighting, and features the creation of the classic three-shade PH lamp, which was the result of years of attempts to 'shade and control electric lighting'. The lamp represents both a break-through in modern lighting, and one of the first examples of the phenomenon of Danish design. Various contributors discuss Henningsen's all-around artistic activity and his theoretical insights. The work also follows the lamp's design chronologically, and discusses how it solves the problem of lighting through glare-free, multi-shade, diffuse lighting. The lamp's commercial success is also discussed. The text is enhanced with numerous photographs and diagrams.

553 **Erik Magnussen.**
Henrik Sten Møller, translated from the Danish by Kennedy English
Language Service. Copenhagen: Rhodos, 1990. 107p.

Profiles the creations of this well-known Danish ceramist and designer, whose work is
characterized by simple beauty as well as functionality, and has been displayed in
museums throughout the world. Among the 'beautiful everyday goods' presented here
in text and in black-and-white and colour photographs are Magnussen's variations on
the teapot in stoneware and pewter; dinnerware in synthetics (such as melamine),
porcelain, and glass; kitchenware, where a lid becomes a bowl, and a saucer allows
liquid to run away from the bottom of the cup; the stainless steel thermos pot, cutlery,
and the nutcracker designed for Stelton; synthetic cutlery and kitchenware designed
for Rosti; chairs of steel tubing that can stack and hang; and functional, comfortable
office chairs that avoid looking like machines. Parallel text is presented in Danish and
English.

554 **Danish chairs.**
Noritsugu Oda, Takako Murakami, translated from the Japanese by
Patricia Yamada. Kyoto, Japan: Korinsha Press, 1996; San Francisco:
Chronicle Books, 1999. 224p. bibliog.

Celebrates Danish furniture design with a catalogue of 150 Danish chairs. Each chair
is presented with photographs from several angles along with design illustrations. The
photography is primarily black and white. Brief background information is given on
the designer or the architect and on the chair itself. The introduction provides a
background of modern Danish furniture design, which is known for its creative and
innovative combination of beauty with functionality. This section also discusses early
furniture design and the Danish influence on Japan.

555 **Jacob Jensen design.**
Paul Schäfer, translated from the Danish by Patricia Ryan.
Copenhagen: Rhodos, 1993. 119p.

This book features one of the country's foremost designers. Published in connection
with an exhibition at the Museum of Decorative Art in Copenhagen in 1993, the book
is part biography and part catalogue. There is brief information on the designer's
background and thoughts about his work. The bulk of the book presents the various
products Jensen has designed, the most notable being numerous products for Bang &
Olufsen, watches, furniture, telephones, and a recent Nilfisk vacuum cleaner. Jensen's
work exemplifies classic Danish functional design. A list of Jensen's exhibitions and
distinctions is provided.

556 **Contemporary Danish furniture design: a short illustrated review.**
Frederik Sieck. Copenhagen: Nyt Nordisk Press, 1990. 231p. bibliog.

A comprehensive reference work on furniture design that describes the work of some
120 designers and includes 520 black-and-white photographs. Two opening chapters
discuss the historical background for contemporary designs, and typical trends and
influences. The main part of the book, which is arranged alphabetically by designer, is
presented as a catalogue, and features typical examples of a designer's work. Brief
biographical and exhibition information is provided for each designer and each photograph is captioned. The work is not analytical and its emphasis is on the illustrations.

557 **Arne Jacobsen: architect and designer.**
Poul Erik Tøjner, Kjeld Vindum.   Copenhagen: Danish Design
Centre, 1996. 3rd ed. 140p.

An account of the achievements of one of the country's premier designers, who made
his mark in both architecture and product design. Jacobsen's major architectural
accomplishments are described in detail through profiles of the individual buildings
and their distinctive features. Jacobsen is also noted for his furniture, lamps, cutlery,
glass and tableware. Among his most famous designs are the Swan, the Egg, and the
stackable Ant chairs. His innovative ideas are also explored through interviews with
industrialists, technicians, model makers, and other architects and designers who
worked with Jacobsen. The building and product profiles are accompanied by numerous
photographs and drawings. The book also includes a chronology of significant life
events and awards. The work is presented in parallel Danish and English text.

Customs and Folklore

Folklore

558 Danish fairy tales.
Retold by Inge Hack, illustrated by Harry and Ilse Toothill.   London:
Frederick Muller, 1964; Chicago; New York: Follett Publishing, 1967.
194p.

A collection of twenty tales passed down through the centuries by word of mouth
among the peasant population. These stories, some with medieval roots, were first
recorded in writing during the late 1800s during the educational movement inspired by
N. F. S. Grundtvig. The tales reflect the outlook, customs and beliefs of their tellers,
and often contain superstition and gruesome details. It was the author's aim to bring
these alternatives to the stories of Hans Christian Andersen to the English-speaking
world. The book is imaginatively illustrated with eighteen drawings.

559 'To work, to life or to death': studies in working class lore.
Edited by Flemming Hemmersam.   Copenhagen: Society for Research
in the History of the Labour Movement in Denmark, 1996. 363p.
bibliog.

A collection of articles that address working-class and labour lore in Norway,
Denmark, and Finland. Three articles are devoted to Denmark, examining the labour
lore of the Social Democrats during the period 1870 to 1940. The research is based on
printed materials as well as objects such as flags and banners, and aims to discern the
significance of various aspects of labour lore for workers' self-understanding. One
article describes, analyses, and traces the migration and reformulations of three of
the labour movement's familiar and important quotations. The second interprets the
symbolic language of several workers' First of May songs. The third describes and
analyses workers' celebrations in terms of their origins and symbols. The opening
chapter introduces this field of scholarly research, defining its scope and terminology.

560   **Interpretation of fairy tales: Danish folklore in a European perspective.**
Bengt Holbæk.   Helsinki: Academia Scientiarum Fennica, 1987.
660p. bibliog.

This book is based on the author's PhD research, which analysed the tales collected by
Evald Tang Kristensen, primarily on Jutland, during the late 1800s. The work is
divided into three parts. Part one assesses the source material examining the historical
and cultural background of the tales, their characteristics, and their authenticity. Part
two reviews previous attempts at interpretation, and presents a new view on the
production of symbols in fairy tales. Part three analyses different types of tales. The
work also provides background information on Jutland and on Kristensen. Part of
the book is a catalogue of 127 narrators and their tales which number over 2,000.

561   **Scandinavian legends and folk-tales.**
Retold by Gwyn Jones, illustrated by Joan Kiddell-Monroe.   Oxford;
New York; Toronto: Oxford University Press, 1956. Reprinted, 1992.
222p.

A collection of stories from Denmark, Norway, Iceland and Sweden, presented in four
parts. These parts include princes and trolls; tales from the Ingle-Nook; from the land
of fire and ice; and kings and heroes. These tales stand on their own. There is no other
explanatory text or background information.

562   **Scandinavian folk belief and legend.**
Edited by Reimund Kvideland, Henning K. Sehmsdorf.   Minneapolis,
Minnesota: University of Minnesota Press, 1988. 429p. bibliog.

A comprehensive and detailed survey representing rural oral traditions and folk belief
from the mid-19th to the early 20th centuries in Denmark, the Faroe Islands, Iceland,
Norway, Sweden, and Finland. The work comprises ten parts: the human soul, the
dead and the living, healers and wise folk, witchcraft, invisible folk, the devil, trolls
and giants, buried treasure, history seen from the village, and recent urban folklore.
Over 400 folk beliefs and legends are included. Every entry is numbered, and the
collector and printed source is cited. The informative introduction places the oral
tradition in the social and economic conditions of the time, and provides a genre
analysis on dimensions such as form, content, and function. The source material and
the existing research literature are also discussed.

563   **Scandinavian folktales.**
Translated and edited by Jacqueline Simpson, illustrated by Caroline
Gowdy.   London; New York; Toronto; Auckland: Penguin Books,
1988. 242p.

A collection of primarily mythical legends from pre-industrial and medieval
Scandinavia presented in seven groups. These groups include legends of the landscape;
historical legends; morality tales; the dead; magicians, witches and shapechangers,
fairies of the homestead; and fairies of the mountains, forests and water. The introduction
provides a particularly informative discussion about the folktale genre, as it distinguishes
between the fairy tale or 'wonder tale' and the folktale or legend, describes the
defining features of a legend, and discusses the various ways that legends can be
classified. The author observes that taken together these tales provide evidence of

cultural history up to the early 20th century. Each of the book's seven parts also includes a brief introduction.

564 **Alexander and the golden bird and other Danish folk tales.**
Translated from the Danish and retold by Reginald Spink, illustrated by Carol Peel. Edinburgh: Floris Books, 1991. 111p.

A collection of tales from Danish collections originally transcribed in the late 1800s from word-of-mouth stories. Some of these tales are of local origin and others have an international character. Some are folk tales that originated in the lower classes replete with giants, 'little folk', talking animals, and magic spells. Others are the fairy tales of the upper classes peopled with kings, queens, princes, and princesses. The compiler-translator has preserved the plot and the original character of the tales, but has condensed the narrative where necessary to render them more acceptable to a modern audience. These tales should appeal to all ages.

565 **Interpreting legend: Danish storytellers and their repertoires.**
Timothy R. Tangherlini. New York; London: Garland Publishing, 1994. 373p. bibliog. (Milman Parry Studies in Oral Tradition).

A scholarly work that attempts to understand legends in their cultural contexts and within the lives of their tellers. It aims to answer the basic question 'who tells what to whom in the form of a legend and why?'. The researcher systematically examines the folk literature collected by folklorist and teacher Evald Tang Kristensen during the late 1800s and the early 20th century. This is the largest collection of folk literature in the world to be produced by a single person. The author provides a short biography of Kristensen, a description of late 19th-century rural Denmark and its people, and an analysis of the content of legend repertoires. Essentially, legends reflect both the fears and aspirations associated with the economic and social circumstances of the teller, where threat is often manifested as a supernatural being. A legend's conclusion in the form of either the triumph of the threat, or of the human community, or perhaps an unresolved ending, is also significant for its culturally relevant meaning. This study would be of interest to those in the field of oral tradition and storytelling. For another examination of Kristensen, see *Danish legends: from the collections of E. T. Kristensen* by Jacqueline Simpson (Enfield Lock, England: Hisarlik Press, 1997. 256p.).

566 **Danish folk tales.**
Collected by M. Winther, translated from the Danish by T. Sands, J. Massengale. Madison: Department of Scandinavian Studies, University of Wisconsin-Madison, 1989. 95p. (Wisconsin Introductions to Scandinavia, WITS II, no. 5).

This work is a translation of a collection originally published in 1823. It is considered to be an important contribution to the field of Scandinavian folklore due both to its early date, which makes it one of the first of these publications, and to Winther's unedited style. The introduction offers some biographical information on Mathias Winther, as well as background on the collected tales and the various forms they take. These tales are adventure stories as opposed to fantasy tales. They are written versions of orally transmitted, non-localized stories with fully developed plots. Among the tales in this collection are both masculine and feminine type adventure tales, and secular and religious legend-tales. The translators have made every effort to maintain

Winther's original form, and consider this work to be a enjoyable introduction to the genre as a whole.

Customs

567 Danish and German national symbols.
Inge Adriansen. In: *National identity and international community*. Edited by Jens Holger Schjørring. Copenhagen: The Danish Cultural Institute, 1993, p. 61-90. (Contact With Denmark).

Examines the cultural significance of some of the most important Danish national symbols, and explores how they are indicative of external cultural influence. The symbols discussed are *Mother Denmark*, the female symbol of the Danish nation; *the Girls of South Jutland*, the symbol of the lost Southern Jutland (Schleswig); and *Dannebrog*, the world's oldest national flag. The author discusses the origins of these symbols and the controversies surrounding their use. Particular mention is made of the mythical origin of *Dannebrog*, a myth that is a well-established part of the Danes' historic consciousness. The Danish national symbols are compared to similar, although not completely parallel, German symbols. The text is supplemented with several black-and-white illustrations.

568 Songs from Denmark: a collection of Danish hymns, songs and ballads in English translation.
Edited by Peter Balsev-Clausen. Copenhagen: The Danish Cultural Institute, 1988. 183p. bibliog.

Communal singing is an important characteristic of Danish culture, and the 'living community song' has long been an integral part of Danish life. This work presents the texts and melodies to eighty-three church songs, folk songs, and narrative ballads. It is not meant to be an anthology, but a representative selection of popular songs by the country's most important songwriters and composers from the Middle Ages up to the present day. Indexes of song titles are provided in English and in Danish. There are also indexes of the authors and composers, where each entry is accompanied by one line of bibliographical data. The introduction provides a brief history of popular song in Denmark.

569 Christmas in Denmark.
Chicago: World Book Encyclopedia, Inc., 1986. Reprinted, 1996. 80p.

Provides an enchanting account of the country's Christmas traditions. For example, the book describes the central role that candles play during the holiday season, the types of decorations used both in the home and in public places, and the food that is served throughout the season, especially on Christmas Eve. There are special sections with detailed instructions for making some traditional Christmas decorations; recipes for the seasonal sweets; and music and lyrics to Christmas carols, as well as the text to two Christmas fairy tales. The work is illustrated with numerous colour photographs. This book is geared toward children and teenagers, but can also be appreciated by the adult reader.

570   **Denmark.**
Nigel and Margaret Allenby Jaffé.   Skipton, England: Folk Dance
Enterprises, 1987. 140p. bibliog. (European Folk Dance Series).

An informative work for teachers, students, and those who are interested in folk dance
just for fun. This volume offers background information on many aspects of folk
dance in Denmark such as the styles, the regional costumes and colours, and the music
and musical instruments. There is also a significant chapter on the country's history
and folklore. A strength of the work is the authors' effort to go beyond description,
analysing the origins of folk dance in the lives of the people, the geography and
climate, and the holidays and customs. Included in this volume are the instructions for
performing twelve different folk dances, each with its accompanying sheet music. The
book is beautifully illustrated with over fifty photographs of regional costumes and
scenes.

571   **Ten dances from Denmark.**
Nigel and Margaret Allenby Jaffé.   Skipton, England: Folk Dance
Enterprises, 1988. 23p. (European Folk Dance Series).

Provides the instructions and the accompanying sheet music for ten Danish folk
dances. No other text or photographs are included.

572   **Defining a nation in song: Danish patriotic songs in songbooks of
the period 1832-1870.**
Hans Kuhn.   Copenhagen: C. A. Reitzels Publishers, 1990. 286p.

An interesting examination of a neglected area of social history. The author, a literary
historian, identifies the songs that helped to form and express the Danes' national
identity in the mid-19th century, where poets produced verses meant to be sung, and
ideological groups used songs to spread their message. Communally sung popular
songs were a significant part of the middle-class lifestyle and were more widespread
than literature. Thus they comprise a part of the period's collective consciousness, and
today they stand as an indication of society's mood at the time. There is a detailed
examination of the twenty-two most frequently occurring songs in the songbooks of
the period in the context of the political, social and intellectual developments of the
time. These are recorded on an accompanying audio-cassette. Eighteen others are
discussed more briefly. Chapter two comprises an annotated bibliography of the
125 source songbooks. The work assumes a basic knowledge of Danish history and
civilization, and a reading knowledge of the Danish language.

573 **Dolls in Denmark: then and now.**
Pauline Luckey. Loveland, Colorado: Oralu Corporation, 1992. 135p.
bibliog.
Tells the story of dolls, the doll industry, and doll production with a focus on history,
tradition, and folklore. The chapters discuss dolls by material such as porcelain, cellu-
loid, cloth, and plastic; folk dolls and folk costumes; the exclusively Danish Christmas
elves (*nisser*); and the Danish troll that is known worldwide. There is also information
on modern-day doll artists, and on the history and productions of two doll factories. A
final chapter presents the museums in Denmark that exhibit dolls. This author has
travelled extensively in Denmark to research this work, and the text is richly detailed.
The book is enhanced with 311 black-and-white and colour illustrations.

**Definitely Danish: Denmark and Danish Americans: history, culture,
recipes.**
See item no. 7.

Cuisine

574 Grandmother's cooking: traditional Danish dishes.
Hanne Bloch, translated from the Danish by Martha Gaber
Abrahamsen.   Copenhagen: Komma & Clausen, 1992. 64p.

This author offers the traditional Danish dishes she enjoyed as a child, but attempts to adapt them to modern eating habits, omitting the greasy and thick sauces. The emphasis of this book is on the use of seasonal ingredients, as well as high-quality ingredients, to make even the most basic dishes come out their best. The book includes over sixty recipes, some of which are not found in other cookbooks. The recipes are presented in seasonal sections. There are only a few colour photographs. A conversion table of British, American, and continental measures is provided.

575 Danish chefs and their food: Danish culinary art.
Edited by Karsten Hansen.   Ørbæk, Denmark: Tommeliden, 1998. 229p.

A collection of 213 recipes presented in seventy-one three-course menus (first course, main course and dessert) by the country's most well-known television cooks, cookbook authors, and expert chefs representing some of the best restaurants. Each entry provides a brief profile of the chef or kitchen, and the addresses and telephone numbers of restaurants. A colour photograph of every dish is also included, along with tips for presentation and serving, and wine recommendations. The book is published in English, Danish, and German versions.

576 Karoline's Kitchen.
Aarhus, Denmark: Danish Dairy Board, [n. d.]. 57p. (Available from
Danish Dairy Board, DK-8000 Aarhus C.)

The Danish Dairy Board, in the form of their test kitchen, 'Karoline's Kitchen' (*Karolines Køkken*), publishes various cookbooks featuring Danish dairy products. This cookbook is a special English translation (of one in the series) in response to tourist demand. All the recipes have been tested and approved, using Danish dairy products and other ingredients available in Denmark. There are many unique cheeses and fermented dairy products, and descriptive and nutritional information is provided for the foreign consumer. The book provides recipes for hors d'oeuvres, main courses, sauces, dressings, salads, breads, cakes, and desserts. Every recipe is accompanied by a colour photograph. Nutritional information is provided for each recipe, and it is noted if the dish is suitable for freezing.

577 A little Danish cookbook.
Janet Laurence, illustrated by Agnetha Petersen. Belfast, Ireland: The Appletree Press; Copenhagen: Paludan, 1990. 60p.

An introduction to Danish cooking that includes meats, fish, salads, and desserts. Recipes for twenty-seven of the most classic dishes are provided, such as: liver paté, open sandwiches, meatballs, spiced herring, apple pudding, and Danish pastries. Metric, imperial, and American measures have been used in all the recipes. Each recipe also gives the Danish name of the dish.

578 My favourite Danish-American recipes.
Nanna Michelsen Powell. Olathe, Kansas: Cookbook Publishers, 1991. 92p.

A recipe collection with a multicultural character, a fact which makes the title of this book a little misleading. The author was born and raised in Denmark, but the recipes were actually inspired by her travels in a military marriage. If a recipe reflects a specific culture it is labelled as such. Interspersed throughout this work are several Danish classics, such as *frikadeller* (meatballs) and 'Danish' pastry. However, within the seven sections of the book, only twenty-eight recipes were specifically labelled as Danish. All recipes have been adapted to the American kitchen in terms of measurements and ingredients. The plastic ring binding makes this a handy volume.

579 Scandinavian Christmas: recipes and traditions.
Edited by Sue Roemig. Iowa City, Iowa: Penfield Press, 1985. 40p.

A compilation of short essays and authentic recipes for various Christmas favourites from Denmark, Iceland, Finland, Norway, and Sweden. The contributors are ordinary people from in and around the Scandinavian communities of Minnesota and Iowa. There are sections on beverages and appetizers, vegetable and side dishes, breads, soups and main dishes, and desserts. The recipes are adapted to the American kitchen. A noteworthy addition to be found here is the design plan and dough recipe for making a Christmas gingerbread house.

580 Dear Danish recipes.
Compiled by Michelle Nagel Spencer. Iowa City, Iowa: Penfield Press, 1988. 160p. (Available from Stocking Stuffers by Mail, Penfield Press, 215 Brown Street, Iowa City, Iowa 52245).

A lovely recipe book that offers a little of everything: beverages, appetizers, soups and sauces, salads, sandwiches, main dishes and side dishes, breads, cookies, cakes and desserts. This is a small booklet – the pages are just $5\frac{1}{2}$ by $3\frac{1}{2}$ inches – but with easy-to-read, well-sized print. It is bound with plastic rings for handy use. A collection of Christmas recipes published between 1937 and 1943 in *Kvinden og Hjemmet* (The Woman and the Home), a Danish-American newspaper, is a special feature. Danish proverbs and prayers are interspersed throughout the book in both Danish and English. Information on Danish-American sites of interest in the United States is also included.

Sports and Recreation

581 Masculine movements: sport and masculinity in Denmark at the turn of the century.

Hans Bonde. *Scandinavian Journal of History*, vol. 21, no. 2 (1996), p. 63-89.

Combines sports studies and men's studies to examine the educative and socializing function of sport for young boys at the turn of the century. In addition to the school, the family provided the significant educational setting for youth, and was primarily a women's sphere. Sport was a means for boys to escape the 'cult of motherhood', and it served to socialize young men into dynamic and goal-directed individuals. This article is a sociological and historical analysis based on the Danish sports literature from 1880 to 1920. The author traces the development of the sports movement in Denmark and examines the significance of concepts such as body movement, speed, dynamics and strength, as well as examining the role of technology in sport and the development of ball games.

582 Denmark.

Bjarne Ibsen, Laila Ottesen. In: *Worldwide trends in youth sport.* Edited by Paul De Knop, Lars-Magnus Engström, Berit Skirstad, Maureen R. Weiss. Champaign, Illinois: Human Kinetics Publishers, 1996, p. 101-14. bibliog.

Provides a concise overview of youth sport in Denmark in the following topical areas: the organizational network including the public, voluntary and market sectors; the extent of sports participation and dropout rates, examining age and gender patterns; and promotional campaigns that particularly target departures from traditional sports and experimental programmes. A final section comments on the degree to which sport improves the health and social aspects of the lives of youth. This book chapter is part of a cross-national comparison of twenty countries. The reference list comprises almost exclusively Danish-language works.

583 **Forest recreation in Denmark from the 1970s to the 1990s.**
Frank Søndergaard Jensen.   PhD dissertation, The Royal Veterinary
and Agricultural University, Copenhagen, 1998. 166p. (Also available
from the Danish Forest and Landscape Research Institute, Skovbyrnet
16, DK-2800 Lyngby, Denmark).

This work represents a summary of the author's research. The topics examined here
include a comparison of administrative perceptions and Danes' preferences on forest
conditions; the differences in the Nordic countries' use of forests for recreation; and
patterns of forest recreation and forest preferences in Denmark in a twenty-year
period. Within this survey data there is information on the frequency of forest use and
the types of activities undertaken. This type of research is significant in that forest
recreation is an important aspect of the country's leisure culture and has received
much political and administrative attention.

584 **The Nordic world: sport in society.**
Edited by Henrik Meinander, J. A. Mangan.   London; Portland,
Oregon: Frank Cass Publishers, 1998. 213p. bibliog.

A collection of papers on the social history of sport by various scholars in the five
Nordic countries. The aim of this volume is to examine the prominence of competitive
sport in the Nordic countries during the 20th century, and to show the new directions
for research in this area. The papers address individual countries and also deal with
the region as a whole. Among the papers that relate specifically to Denmark are such
topics as the political function of gymnastics on the Danish-German border during the
period 1848-1920, and how women's involvement in sports has positively affected
women's status in general. Other topics include, for example, the Nordic countries'
role in the Olympic movement, and the relationship between sports organizations and
the welfare state. This group of studies first appeared as a special issue of *The
International Journal of the History of Sport* (vol. 14, no. 3, 1997).

585 **Danish gymnastics: what's so Danish about the Danes?**
Else Trangbæk.   *International Journal of the History of Sport*, vol. 13,
no. 2 (1996), p. 203-14.

Examines the peculiarly Danish model of gymnastics. It is noted that the model is
actually based on a Swedish form of gymnastics adopted during the democratic and
cultural modernization of the farming movement in the late 19th century. The author
discusses the symbolic value of gymnastics in the light of three central elements of
this period: the popular enlightenment of the farming community, the anti-German
collective awareness after the loss of the southern part of Jutland in 1864, and the late
industrialization of Denmark. The adoption of Swedish gymnastics in organizations
and schools was an ideologically based policy and not just a question of different
exercise systems. The plurality of modern-day Danish sports organizations is examined in
this historical context.

586   **Discipline and emancipation through sport: the pioneers in women's sport in Denmark.**
Else Trangbæk.   *Scandinavian Journal of History*, vol. 21, no. 2 (1996), p. 121-34.

Combines women's history and sports history to examine the social and political significance of sports for the female identity at the end of the 19th century. Part of the discussion focuses specifically on the work of two pioneers in the women's sport movement, Erna Juel-Hansen and Paul Petersen, and chronicles the development of women's sport in Denmark and the founding of the Women's Sports Club. The broader analysis examines the special challenges faced by women at the time of the industrial and scientific revolutions, when women were relegated to the home and constrained by definitions of femininity that emphasized bodily functions.

Libraries and Museums

587   **Royal treasures from Denmark 1709: Frederik IV in Florence.**
Mogens Bencard, Preben Mellbye-Hansen, Piero Pacini.   Livorno,
Italy: Sillabe, 1994. 227p. bibliog.

This work is both an exhibition catalogue and a look at part of the Rosenberg Palace collection. It was published for the 1994 exhibition in Italy honouring Frederik IV's visit there in 1709, and was meant to promote cultural exchange between the two countries. The exhibition comprised many of the gifts the King received during his visit, as well as some of the furnishings of the King's residences and some of his personal belongings. The text is quite extensive, with detailed chapters on Frederik IV's realm, the journey to Italy, the sojourn to Florence, and the programme of the visit there. The catalogue contains illustrations and explanatory text for ninety-eight items and works of art, the majority of which are part of the Royal Collections at Rosenberg Palace. A final chapter profiles the Rosenberg Palace. The entire work is written with parallel English and Italian text. The bibliography contains works primarily in Danish and Italian.

588   **Museumsguide Danmark.** (Museum Guide Denmark.)
Edited by Frank Birkebæk, Michael Lauenborg, Tove Borre.   Viborg,
Denmark: Museumstjenesten for Danske Museer, 1992. 242p. map.

A complete guide to all 148 state or state-subsidized museums. The guide is divided by county, and for each county section there is a map showing the location of the museums. For each museum, addresses, telephone numbers, and opening hours are given. The text offers a brief description of the museum's contents and also mentions permanent exhibitions. A photograph either of the museum or of a significant work is also provided. A pictogram key is used for other important information such as parking, restaurants, gardens, etc. This guide is extremely brief and visitors would do well to call ahead about special exhibitions or conducted tours. The work is presented with parallel Danish, English, and German text.

220

589 **Frederiksborg museum: illustrated guide.**
Povl Eller, translated from the Danish by David Hohnen.
Frederiksborg, Denmark: The Museum of National History at
Frederiksborg Castle, 1991. 6th rev. ed. 143p.
This complete guide begins with the history of this Dutch Renaissance-style castle
which became the home of King Frederik II in 1560. The history of the founding of
the Museum by the Carlsberg Foundation is also described. The visitor's guide
includes floor plans and numbered keys to the castle, the various floors, sixty-nine
rooms, and the cellars. The text takes the visitor along a normal route through all of
the rooms of the museum, and describes many of the objects exhibited in them. The
text is fairly detailed. The guide includes colour as well as black-and-white illustrations for the items considered to be the most important.

590 **The Royal Danish collections: Amalienborg, Christian VIII's
palace.**
Jørgen Hein, translated from the Danish by Martha Gaber Abrahamsen.
Copenhagen: The Royal Danish Collections, 1994. 63p.
An illustrated guide to Christian VIII's palace in the Amalienborg Palace complex
which serves as a museum to Kings Christian IX, Frederik VIII, and Christian X. The
work provides floor plans to the museum – which includes the ground and first floors –
and numerous colour plates of the various rooms and some of their more significant
contents. There is also a wealth of background information on the palace, as well as
the first three generations of the Glücksborg family covering the period 1863-1947.
Genealogical charts and a chart of Denmark's kings and the Dukes of Schleswig-
Holstein are also provided.

591 **On parchment, paper and palm leaves . . . , treasures of the Royal
Library, Denmark.**
Harald Ilsoe.   Copenhagen: The Royal Library, 1993. 364p. bibliog.
Published to celebrate the library's 200th anniversary as a public institution, this
volume presents in words and pictures a sampling of the library's rare and significant
books, manuscripts, maps, pictures, and music. The first major section of the work
chronicles the origin and growth of the collections with particular emphasis on the
library's historic core, the Library of Kings. The second major section presents a
sampling of treasures by theme. The library's collections are of varied geographical
origin, and include works not only from Denmark but also from Europe, Asia, and
North and South America. The author and compiler of the volume is an historian and a
long-time library staff member. Each section is introduced with a history of the
collection and every item is captioned. Items were chosen for this volume based on
their pictorial qualities; Danish manuscripts receive less attention.

592 **The Viking ships.**
Bent Engelbreth Jørgensen, Jan Skamby Madsen, Max Vinner.
Roskilde, Denmark: The Viking Ship Museum, 1994. 28p.
Offers a short, concise introduction to the story of the fast, seaworthy Viking ships.
The publication was initially the catalogue for a travelling exhibition, and many of the
items featured here are housed at the Viking Ship Museum in Roskilde. There is
general information on Viking ships as well as information on specific archaeological

finds. The building of a replica at the Museum's shipyard is described in detail. Navigation and sailing are also described. This work, which is printed on glossy paper, contains numerous colour photographs, drawings, and diagrams.

593 **Historical gardens of Denmark: a guide to historical gardens of museums, castles and manors.**
Edited by Jane Schul, Jette Abel, Kirsten Lund-Andersen, translated from the Danish by Anne Marie Nielsen. Frederiksberg, Denmark: The Society for the History of Gardening, 1997. 224p. map.

A comprehensive guide that aims to stimulate interest in an important cultural heritage for Danes and tourists alike. An introductory section briefly describes the types and classifications of the featured gardens. The guide is divided into fourteen county sections, and uses a pictograph key for practical information. Descriptive text is provided for each garden, along with addresses, telephone numbers, and opening times. The book is printed on glossy paper and beautifully illustrated with numerous colour photographs. Parallel text is presented in Danish, English, and German.

594 **The library system in Denmark.**
Jørgen Svane-Mikkelsen. Copenhagen: Royal School of Library and Information Science, 1997. 84p.

This is a thorough and informative book that provides a good overview of the country's library system, a system that is extensive, well functioning, and very accessible. The book describes the three primary types of libraries in the public sector – public, research, and school libraries – and how they cooperate. For each type of library, the author describes the formal structure and organization, the administration, and the major activities beyond the traditional one of lending. Cooperation and interlending among the various library sectors is also described, with special mention being made of the Danish National Bibliography. There is also a section on library associations and organizations. Library services in Greenland and the Faroe Islands are briefly covered.

Mass Media

Works about the media

595 Modern Danish television after the monopoly era.
Ib Bondebjerg. In: *Television in Scandinavia: history, politics and aesthetics.* Edited by Ib Bondebjerg, Francesco Bono. Luton, England: John Libbey Media, 1996, p. 41-69. bibliog. (Acamedia Research Monograph 20).
Examines contemporary Danish television programming during what is referred to as the 1990s mixed-culture period, which, this author observes, is characterized by strongly Americanized entertainment-oriented programming. This period is viewed in contrast to the monopoly period of information and education programming, and the public service phase. The various trends and types of programmes are described, such as reality-based news and journalistic shows, documentaries, television fiction, and children's and teenage programming. Numerous examples of these are given. The industry's 'entertainment versus culture in programming' debate is also discussed. The conclusion comments on the future of Danish national television and its survival in the face of American dominance. The bibliography contains primarily Danish-language works.

596 The structure of Danish mass media: remarks on the significance of recent developments.
Robin Cheeseman, Carsten Kyhn. *Nordicom – Information,* no. 1 (1992), p. 3-18.
Aims to provide a theoretical and analytical framework for understanding the development of the Danish mass media. The social, political, and legal developments are examined against the backdrop of a 'state versus society' framework. Throughout the discussion, a review of the various types of Danish media is presented, in terms of print media such as newspapers and periodicals; broadcast media such as national television, community radio, and local television; and 'new' media such as cable

distribution and teletext (interactive media). Relations between these types of media are analysed in an effort to determine a hierarchy of influence. A final section examines how Danish mass media is affected by the international media situation and by European Union policy developments. The theoretical aspects of this article are admittedly not well developed; the authors offer them as 'food for thought'. However, the article does contain a great deal of factual information on the Danish mass media.

597 **Small nations, big neighbor: Denmark and Quebec/Canada compare notes on American popular culture.**
Edited by Roger de la Garde, William Gilsdorf, Ilja Wechselmann.
London; Paris; Rome: John Libbey & Company, 1993. 235p.
(Acamedia Research Monograph 10).

An interesting book that examines the question of national and cultural identities in the light of the development of transnational media. It is a collection of articles by various professionals and academicians in the fields of communications, broadcasting, sociology, and literature. Its focus is on the spread and homogenization of culture from larger commercial societies to smaller ones with fewer resources. Four out of the total ten chapters are devoted to Denmark, and one other deals more generally with the Nordic countries. These chapters examine such topics as the Danish infatuation with America after 1945; how the transnational flow of television has influenced Danish culture; the cultural meaning created by American television serials; and the failure of some cross-cultural advertising in Denmark. This is a significant work in the light of recent European Union broadcasting regulations aimed at preventing a domination of American exports, leading Denmark in effect to re-regulate television broadcasting.

598 **Violence and other social problems in Denmark: media construction and reality.**
Lau Laursen. In: *Social problems in newspapers: studies around the Baltic Sea.* Edited by Mikko Lagerspetz. Helsinki: National Council for Alcohol and Drug Research, 1994, p. 83-103. (NAD Publication, no. 28).

Reports the findings of media research that traces what Danish newspapers consider to be important social problems, and compares this coverage to public discussion, legislative and administrative activities, and official statistics. Data is presented from 1,304 front-page stories, 460 editorials, and 423 commentary articles, selected over a seventeen-day period from eighteen national and regional newspapers in the first half of 1992. Stories were divided into forty-seven categories; the distribution of the top twenty is reported here. Significant findings include a high frequency of stories relating to criminality, particularly violent crime, where official statistics show little change or a decrease. There is an under-reporting of drug use, where official statistics indicate a rise. Media coverage is discussed in the framework of a theoretical perspective known as 'context constructionism'.

599 **Danish video.**
Lars Movin, translated from the Danish by Kjeld Boysen. Haderslev, Denmark: Danish Film Institute Workshop, 1992. 91p.

Offers an overview of the history, development and current trends in video production, distribution, screening, and reviewing. This survey discusses video as a medium in its various genres such as journalism, documentary, fiction, art, and experimental video. Much of the focus is on the democratization of the medium. The Danish workshop tradition that allows both amateurs and professionals access to production facilities is described, and the some of the country's most important workshops are profiled. There are also profiles of several important artists. This work aims to increase awareness of Danish video production, so that the country can continue its visionary and innovative approach, as well as become more competitive internationally.

600 **The ravens of Odin: the press in the Nordic nations.**
Robert G. Picard. Ames, Iowa: Iowa State University Press, 1998. 153p. bibliog.
Provides a contemporary view of the important newspapers of Denmark, Finland, Iceland, Norway, and Sweden. In the first half of the book, the development of the press in the modern history of the region is traced. The focus is on the 19th and 20th centuries given the importance of the press in the establishment of liberal democracy and political pluralism. The cultural, social, and political roles of the press are examined, and the style and content of press material is considered. Press accountability and protections provided to freedom of the press are also discussed. This part of the book covers the subject for the Nordic region as a whole, but the situation in individual countries is referred to. The second half of the book lists and describes, by country, the most prestigious and largest newspapers as well as the smaller provincial and political papers. The list for Denmark is not very extensive. This work is not particularly in-depth and should be considered an overview.

601 **Fundamentals in the history of Danish television.**
Henrik Søndergaard. In: *Television in Scandinavia: history, politics and aesthetics.* Edited by Ib Bondebjerg, Francesco Bono. Luton, England: John Libbey Media, 1996, p. 11-40. bibliog. (Acamedia Research Monograph 20).
Discusses the development of Danish television from its inception in the early 1950s up to the present day, with a focus on the influence of institutional factors and media politics. The work offers a three-phase chronological framework for this development: the monopoly phase, the break-up phase, and the competition phase. The author discusses the events and conflicts during each of these periods and the roles played by political groups, television stations, and advertisers. Social and cultural developments are also discussed such as television's role in post-Second World War modernization. The bibliography contains primarily Danish-language works.

Sparks of resistance: the illegal press in German occupied Denmark April 1940-August 1943.
See item no. 130.

Soap, pin-up and burlesque: commercialization and femininity in Danish television.
See item no. 285.

Newspapers

602 Aalborg Stiftstidende.
Aalborg, Denmark: Aalborg Avisselskab A/S, 1767- . daily.
This is an independent newspaper that covers the region of Northern Jutland. It has a weekday circulation of 72,000 and Sunday circulation of 87,000.

603 Aarhus Stiftstidende.
Aarhus: Aarhus Stiftstidende Fond, 1794- . daily.
This is an independent liberal newspaper that covers the region of East Jutland. It has a weekday circulation of 63,000 and a Sunday circulation of 83,000.

604 Aktuelt.
Copenhagen: Dagbladet Aktuelt A/S, 1871- . daily.
This is a national left-leaning paper with critical, in-depth coverage. It has a weekday circulation of 37,000.

605 B.T.
Copenhagen: Det Berlingske Officin, 1916- . daily.
This is a popular national tabloid paper with a weekday circulation of 148,000 and a Sunday circulation of 184,000.

606 Berlingske Tidende.
Copenhagen: Det Berlingske Officin, 1749- . daily.
This independent national paper carries national and international news, financial information, political debate, and also covers art, culture and social issues. It is considered one of the country's most prestigious papers and has a weekday circulation of 154,000 and a Sunday circulation of 201,000.

607 Bornholms Tidende.
Rønne, Denmark: Bornholms Tidende A/S, 1866- . daily.
This right-leaning newspaper covers the island of Bornholm with a weekday circulation of 14,000.

608 Børsen.
Copenhagen: Dagbladet Børsen A/S, 1896- . daily.
This is the leading newspaper for national and international financial and business news. It has a weekday circulation of 42,000.

609 Ekstra Bladet.
Copenhagen: Politikens Fond, 1904- . daily.
This national tabloid newspaper has a weekday circulation of 166,000 and a Sunday circulation of 186,000.

610 Fyens Stiftstidende.
Odense, Denmark: Den Fynske Bladfond, 1772- . daily.
This is a regional independent newspaper for the island of Funen with a weekday circulation of 66,000 and a Sunday circulation of 94,000.

611 Information.
Copenhagen: Dagbladet Information A/S, 1945- . daily.
A national newspaper, independent of political party or economic interests, that traces its history to the Nazi occupation of Denmark. It is known for serious coverage of social and political issues as well as cultural ones. It has a circulation of 22,000.

612 Jydske Vestkysten.
Copenhagen: Den Berlingske Officin A/S; Esbjerg, Denmark: Sydvestjydske Venstre Presse, 1917- . daily.
This is a regional independent newspaper for the area of southern and western Jutland with a weekday circulation of 96,000 and a Sunday circulation of 112,000.

613 Jyllands-Posten Morgenavisen.
Viby, Denmark: Jyllands-Posten Fond, 1871- . daily.
This independent national newspaper reports on all issues and areas, but is especially strong on business and economic coverage. It has a weekday circulation of 173,000 and a Sunday circulation of 269,000.

614 Midtjyllands Avis.
Silkeborg, Denmark: Silkeborg Avis A/S, 1857- . daily.
This right-leaning newspaper covers Silkeborg and central Jutland area with a daily circulation of 19,000.

615 Politiken.
Copenhagen: Politiken Fond, 1884- . daily.
This independent national newspaper is one of the country's most prestigious. It is known for significant commentary, debate, and discussion. It has a weekday circulation of 147,000 and a Sunday circulation of 199,000.

616 VT Vendsyssel Tidende.
Hjørring, Denmark: Vendsyssel Avisselskab A/S, 1872- . daily.
This is an independent newspaper for the region of Northern Jutland. It has a weekday circulation of 28,000 and a Sunday circulation of 73,000.

617 Weekendavisen.
Copenhagen: Det Berlingske Officin A/S, 1749- . weekly.
This is an independent newspaper with a focus on politics, economics, and culture. It has a circulation of 53,000.

General periodicals

618 **Danish children's literature.**
Copenhagen: Danish Literature Information Centre, 1992- . 2 times per year. (Available from Danish Literature Information Centre, Christians Brygge 1, DK-1219 Copenhagen K).

A colourfully illustrated periodical that is published as a separate supplement to *Danish Literary Magazine*. This publication, which is written in English, provides a review of current children's books in translation. Book excerpts are often included in a review. Each issue also provides a current bibliography of children's literature in translation arranged by language.

619 **The Danish economy: a quarterly bulletin.**
Copenhagen: Den Danske Bank, Economics Department, 1993- . 4 times per year. (Available from Den Danske Bank, 2-12 Holmens Kanal, DK-1092 Copenhagen K).

This publication includes regular features on Danish economic indicators, and political and economic events. There are also any number of special topics such as wages and prices, employment rates, balance of payments, inflation, investment, interest rates and exchanges, and economic forecasts. This periodical was published previously under the title *Denmark: a quarterly review*.

620 **Danish literary magazine.**
Copenhagen: Danish Literature Information Centre, 1992- . 2 times per year. (Available from Danish Literature Information Centre, Christians Brygge 1, DK-1219 Copenhagen K).

This lively periodical, published in English and written for a general audience, reports on Danish literature and the literary scene. The magazine is fully illustrated and includes interviews, profiles and portraits, as well as book excerpts and reviews. Each issue also provides current bibliographies of Danish prose, poetry, and drama in translation arranged by language.

621 **Denmark Review/Business News from Denmark.**
Copenhagen: Royal Danish Ministry of Foreign Affairs, Secretariat for Foreign Trade, 4 times per year. (Available from Royal Danish Ministry of Foreign Affairs, Secretariat for Foreign Trade, Asiatisk Plads 2, DK-1448 Copenhagen K).

A glossy magazine that features articles and company profiles related to all aspects of Danish business, industry, and services. Recent issues have included such topics as Danish-design furniture; advances in transport such as airport renovation and new bridge construction; the information technology industry; agriculture; environmental management; shipbuilding; tourism; and 'green' products.

622 **Musical Denmark.**
Copenhagen: Danish Cultural Institute, Danish Music Information
Centre, 1952- . 2 times per year. (Available from Danish Music
Information Centre, Gråbrødre Torv 16, DK-1154 Copenhagen K).
Covers all aspects of music in Denmark from an historical as well as a contemporary
perspective. This English-language magazine, which is written for the general public,
publishes articles, surveys, calendars, 'In-Briefs', and annotated lists of new Danish
recordings.

623 **Nordic Sounds.**
Frederiksberg, Denmark: Nordic Sounds, 1982- . 4 times per year.
(Available from Nordic Sounds, Christian Winthers Vej 14, DK-1860
Frederiksberg C).
This English-language magazine is a publication of the Committee for Nordic Musical
Cooperation, and covers all aspects of Nordic musical life. There are articles about the
music scene, profiles of composers, and record reviews. A select discography of
Nordic CDs is a regular feature.

Professional
Periodicals

624 **Acta Archaeologica.**
    Copenhagen: Munksgaard, 1930- . annual.
An international journal that gives priority to Nordic and Northern European studies,
but also publishes other European and Arctic research. In addition to archaeological
research, historiography and review articles are also published, but these are afforded
lesser priority. Annotated lists of books received are presented regularly. The journal
includes research in English, French, German, and Italian.

625 **Acta Sociologica: Journal of the Scandinavian Sociological**
    Association.
    Copenhagen; Oslo; Stockholm; Boston, Massachusetts: Scandinavian
    University Press, 1955- . quarterly.
The journal has a wide-ranging scope, and publishes theoretical and empirical
research articles, short notes and comments, book reviews, and review essays.

626 **Cooperation and Conflict: Nordic Journal of International Studies.**
    London; Thousand Oaks, California; New Delhi: Sage Publications,
    1965- . quarterly.
Publishes articles, reviews, and scholarly comment on international relations with a
particular emphasis on Nordic studies.

627 **Danish Yearbook of Philosophy.**
    Copenhagen: Museum Tusculanum Press, 1964- . annual.
Publishes articles primarily related to Danish philosophy, or articles by authors with
ties to Danish philosophy. Papers are published in English, German, and French.

628   **Ethnologia Scandinavica: A Journal for Nordic Ethnology.**
      Lund, Sweden: BTJ Press, 1972- . annual.

This journal publishes articles in English and German, and includes academic papers, book reviews, and reviews of new dissertations. The range of topics includes all branches of material and social culture, from both historical and contemporary perspectives.

629   **NORA: Nordic Journal of Women's Studies.**
      Oslo; Copenhagen; Stockholm; Boston, Massachusetts: Scandinavian University Press, 1993- . 2 times per year.

An interdisciplinary journal of varied scope and perspective that publishes theoretical and empirical research articles on a wide range of feminist issues.

630   **Nordic Journal of International Law.**
      Copenhagen: Academic Press, 1986- . annual.

Publishes articles and scholarly comments on various international legal issues. Recent topics have included human rights, environmental law, and issues concerning international boundaries.

631   **Nordic Journal of Linguistics.**
      Oslo; Copenhagen; Stockholm; Boston, Massachusetts: Scandinavian University Press, 1978- . 2 times per year.

A journal concerned with all aspects of linguistics with an emphasis on the Scandinavian languages. The journal publishes research papers of general theoretical and methodological interest, review articles, book reviews, and short comments.

632   **Nordic Journal of Political Economy.**
      Oslo: Editors of the Nordic Journal of Political Economy, 1995- . annual.

Publishes academic papers on political, economic, and philosophical issues relative to the Nordic welfare states.

633   **Nordiske Udkast.**
      Copenhagen: Danish Psychological Publishers, 1995- . 2 times per year.

This is a journal for critical social science which publishes in English and in the Nordic languages. Its scope is twofold, focusing on the relation between the individual and society, and the interdependent development of theory and practice. The journal publishes theoretical, empirical and methodological articles, book reviews, and discussions.

634   **Scandinavian Economic History Review & Economy and History.**
      Odense, Denmark: Odense University Press, 1981- . 3 times per year.

A publication of the Scandinavian Society for Economic and Social History. The journal publishes articles, book reviews, and essays on a wide variety of economic and financial issues relating to Scandinavia in an international as well as an historical perspective. Also included is a select annual bibliography.

635 **Scandinavian Housing and Planning Research.**
Oslo; Stockholm; Copenhagen; Oxford; Boston, Massachusetts:
Scandinavian University Press, 1984- . quarterly.

An interdisciplinary journal devoted to social science research on the physical, political, social, and economic aspects of housing and planning at local, regional and national levels. The journal publishes research articles, short notes, and book reviews.

636 **Scandinavian Journal of Design History.**
Copenhagen: Rhodos International Science and Art Publishers, 1991- . annual.

Publishes articles in all areas and periods of design history, such as the history of arts and crafts, industrial design, graphic art, interiors, fashion, and scenography. Included are original papers, reviews, short comments, and book reviews. This artistic journal is printed on glossy paper with colour and black-and-white photographs.

637 **Scandinavian Journal of Economics.**
Oxford; Malden, Massachusetts: Blackwell Publishers, 1976- . quarterly.

Publishes research articles, short papers and comments, book reviews, and dissertation abstracts on a wide range of issues related to economics and finance.

638 **Scandinavian Journal of Educational Research.**
Abingdon, England: Carfax Publishing, 1971- . quarterly.

A journal of wide-ranging scope that covers all fields of educational research and thought, with both a Scandinavian and an international emphasis. The journal publishes historical, philosophical, comparative, experimental, and survey studies, as well as scholarly discussions and short comments.

639 **The Scandinavian Journal of History.**
Oslo; Copenhagen; Stockholm; Boston, Massachusetts: Scandinavian
University Press, 1976- . quarterly.

This journal is published under the auspices of the Historical Associations of Denmark, Finland, Norway and Sweden. The publication offers articles on Scandinavian and general history, review essays covering themes in recent Scandinavian historical research, and book reviews.

640 **Scandinavian Journal of Management.**
Oxford; Tarrytown, New York: Elsevier Science, 1988- . quarterly.

A journal with a broad scope relative to all aspects of management in public and private organizations. The journal publishes empirical investigations, theoretical analyses, review articles on the state of the art in specific areas, and book reviews.

641 **Scandinavian Journal of Psychology.**
Oxford; Malden, Massachusetts: Blackwell Publishers, 1982- .
quarterly.
A journal published on behalf of the Psychological Associations of Denmark, Finland, Norway, and Sweden. The journal publishes methodological and empirical articles within any area of psychology and its related disciplines, short notes and comments, reviews of Scandinavian books, and reviews of doctoral theses in psychology in the Nordic countries.

642 **Scandinavian Journal of Social Welfare.**
Copenhagen: Munksgaard International Publishers, 1992- . quarterly.
An interdisciplinary journal that publishes articles on social work and social welfare, with both a Scandinavian and an international focus. The journal publishes empirical and theoretical articles, policy evaluations, review articles, book reviews, brief comments, and dissertation abstracts.

643 **Scandinavian Political Studies.**
Oslo; Stockholm; Copenhagen; Oxford; Boston, Massachusetts:
Scandinavian University Press, 1966- . quarterly.
Publishes empirical and theoretical analyses, essays, and book reviews on topics related to political science and government, with both a Scandinavian and an international emphasis.

644 **The Scandinavian Psychoanalytic Review.**
Copenhagen; Cambridge, Massachusetts: Munksgaard International
Publishers, 1978- . 2 times per year.
A journal published under the auspices of the Psychoanalytical Societies of Denmark, Finland, Norway, and Sweden. The journal aims to reflect the development of psychoanalysis in Scandinavia, and publishes papers and reports with a Scandinavian emphasis, and reviews of books by Scandinavian psychoanalysts.

645 **Scandinavian Review.**
New York: American Scandinavian Foundation, 1913- . quarterly.
Publishes articles, short stories, poetry, and photographic essays on various Scandinavian topics. There are also book reviews as well as information on current events, films, and music. This periodical was published as the *American-Scandinavian Review* from 1913 to 1974.

646 **Scandinavian Studies.**
Provo, Utah: Society for the Advancement of Scandinavian Study,
1928- . quarterly.
Publishes articles on Scandinavian literature, history, society, and culture, and the philological and linguistic problems of the Scandinavian languages. Papers are based on material examined in the original language.

647 **Scandinavica, An International Journal of Scandinavian Studies.**
Norwich, England: University of East Anglia, 1962- . 2 times per year.

Publishes scholarly papers, review articles, and book reviews on a wide range of topics relative to Scandinavian literature. The articles are primarily in English, but reviews can be in other European languages. Also included is a select annual bibliography of books published in the Scandinavian languages, as well as a select bibliography of books received that are published in non-Scandinavian languages.

Reference Works and Directories

Reference works

648 **European environmental yearbook.**
Directed by Achille Cutrera.   London: DocTer International U.K.,
1991. 2nd ed. 897p. bibliog.

This encyclopaedic work is subtitled 'nature conservation, protection of the environment, town and country planning in Belgium, Denmark, The Federal Republic of Germany, France, Greece, Ireland, Italy, Luxembourg, The Netherlands, Portugal, Spain, and the United Kingdom with special surveys on Australia, Japan, U.S.A. and U.S.S.R.'. It is a summary of information divided into four parts. Part one comprises country reports by experts, and covers twenty-two topics such as agriculture and the environment, cultural heritage, European Community (EC) policy, energy and nuclear safety, fauna and flora, forestry, leisure planning and recreation, parks and nature reserves, pollution, protection and management of seas and coasts, toxic and hazardous substances, and water supply and river management. These reports are short and concise, covering legislation, administrative structure, and policy issues. Part two is the four special surveys. Part three is a country-by-country index of all relevant national environmental legislation arranged chronologically. The section on Denmark lists legislation from 1805 to 1989 with an English translation of the act title. Part four is concerned with EC protocols and programmes. The bibliography is by country and contains works in all the relevant languages. This reference work is helpful for basic information and comparative study. It would be of interest to those in management and conservation of natural resources.

649 **Denmark.**
Copenhagen: The Royal Danish Ministry of Foreign Affairs,
Department of Information, 1996. 543p.

A single, encyclopaedic volume replete with tables, diagrams, illustrations, and inserts. This work is divided into six major sections: official Denmark, production and communications, conditions of life, culture, geography and the environment, and history. There is also a section on Greenland and the Faroe Islands. Printed on glossy paper with splendid colour photographs, this volume is attractive as well as being clearly written and enjoyable to read. It is a comprehensive and informative overview of the country, its people, and the ways of life.

650   Dictionary of Scandinavian history.
Edited by Byron H. Nordstrom.   Westport, Connecticut: Greenwood Press, 1986. 703p. bibliog.

Covers the history of the five Nordic countries since 1000 AD. The editor notes that some earlier events are included, but this information is based on archaeological evidence, versus written sources. Further, there are more entries on Denmark, Norway, and Sweden, and fewer on Finland, Iceland, the Faroe Islands, and Greenland. There are over 400 entries in all, and these vary considerably in length. They cover most of the Scandinavian monarchs from the late Viking Age to the present day; early and modern political figures, and military and cultural leaders; major events and periods; intellectual developments, social movements, and political parties. Five appendices provide a bibliography of primarily English-language sources; a list of monarchs, presidents, prime ministers, and governments; and a chronology of events from the Old Stone Age to 1982.

651   Cassell dictionary of Norse myth and legend.
Andy Orchard.   London: Cassell, 1998. 223p. bibliog.

A comprehensive work that covers the range of myths among the Germanic peoples of Northern Europe. The topical areas include: major sagas and legends; gods, goddesses, giants, dwarfs, and other supernatural beings; the cosmology of the Norse world; and other related topics such as amulets and runes. The work has a literary focus; much of the cited evidence consists of literary quotations from the 11th century onwards. There are 750 main entries, 300 headwords, and thousands of cross-references. Four appendices provide alphabetical lists of Odin's names and titles, dwarf names, giant names, and troll wives and giantesses. A bibliography of further reading consists of approximately 900 items which include general surveys, primary texts, translations, and secondary criticisms.

652   Medieval Scandinavia: an encyclopaedia.
Edited by Phillip Pulsiano, Kirsten Wolf.   New York; London: Garland Publishing, 1993. 768p.

This work seeks to provide a balanced presentation of an extensive knowledge area, covering the Migration Period to the Reformation for the five countries that comprise 'Norden' (Denmark, Sweden, Norway, Finland, Iceland). It is specially designed to accommodate those readers who lack knowledge of the Scandinavian languages. The alphabetical entries, which represent the work of some 250 contributors, range from 150 to 5,000 words, and comprise either a detailed discussion or a broad survey. Each entry also includes a bibliography and cross-references.

653 **The compositions of Vagn Holmboe: a catalogue of works and recordings with indexes of persons and titles.**
Paul Rapoport.   Copenhagen: Edition Wilhelm Hansen, 1996. 224p. bibliog.

This work is intended for anyone looking for basic information about Vagn Holmboe's music. It provides two comprehensive chronological catalogues, one of compositions and one of recordings. It also includes three indexes: persons and ensembles connected to Holmboe's music; a systematic register of compositions; and titles of compositions. The book is considered to be the most complete catalogue available as it provides detailed indications of orchestral scoring, indications of texts in sung works where biblical sources are identified, publication numbers, and approximate durations of scores.

654 **Historical dictionary of Denmark.**
Alastair H. Thomas.   Lanham, Maryland; Oxford: The Scarecrow Press, 1998. 533p. map. bibliog.

This reference work covers early periods, as well as modern and contemporary eras. It includes entries in a variety of areas such as rulers and monarchs of older times; politicians, political parties and trade unions of contemporary periods; economy and society; culture such as art, music, literature, and religion; the welfare state; foreign relations; and the European Union. A chronology of significant events is also included. Seven appendices provide a list of Danish monarchs; a list of prime ministers and cabinets; a breakdown of party shares of Cabinet Office; a breakdown of party shares of votes from 1890 to 1998; referendums in Denmark from 1916 to 1998; economic data for 1997; and population data from 1769 to 1990. There is also an extensive bibliography of primarily English-language sources published since 1965, divided by topic.

655 **Dictionary of Scandinavian literature.**
Edited by Virpi Zuck, Niels Ingwersen, Harald S. Naess.   New York; Westport, Connecticut: Greenwood Press, 1990. 792p.

This reference work covers Denmark, Sweden, Norway, Finland, and Iceland. All listings are in alphabetical order and are not divided by country. The book includes two main types of entries: author entries and general articles. The emphasis is on author entries, which provide brief biographical data, an analysis of the author's major works, a summary statement regarding the author's impact on the country and his/her current standing, a list of the author's works in chronological order, and a list of reference sources. The editors note a deliberate English-language bias, since the author entries also include works in English translation. Authors are included in the book if they have emerged on the literary scene in or before 1970. This reference work is aimed at students, professors in Scandinavian departments in universities, and scholars of comparative literature and related disciplines.

Scandinavian cinema: a survey of films and film-makers in Denmark, Finland, Iceland, Norway and Sweden.
See item no. 543.

Twentieth century Danish music: an annotated bibliography and research directory.
See item no. 666.

Directories

656 **Health services research in Denmark 1989-1991: a catalogue of 391
projects and a statistical analysis of health services research in
Denmark.**
Peter Bjerregaard, Finn Kamper-Jørgensen.   Copenhagen: Danish
Institute for Clinical Epidemiology, 1992. 540p.

This catalogue aims to make Danish health services research visible internationally,
and presents information on planned, ongoing, or recently completed health services
projects. The data was gathered from questionnaires to researchers and research
institutes. An introduction defines terminology, describes the data collection, and lists
the various category classifications and codes. Summary findings are reported regarding
the topics studied, research interests and objectives, and fiscal aspects. The one-page
project descriptions are sorted by main topic, name of principal investigator, and title
of project. Existing publications from the project are noted.

657 **Export directory of Denmark.**
Virum, Denmark: Krak's Publishing, 1997. 70th ed. 953p.

This comprehensive directory contains information on some 6,000 Danish exporters in
all types of industry. The opening section is a multilingual business guide to Denmark
with information on the main business contact points, foreign embassies and
consulates, Danish diplomatic and consular services abroad, and Danish commercial
associations abroad. Complete address, telephone and fax information is provided.
The directory itself is an alphabetical list of goods and services with a full index; a list
of firms; and an index of trademarks. The directory is published annually.

658 **ISO 9000 Denmark: a register of quality certified companies in
Denmark.**
Frederiksberg, Denmark: ISO 9000 Denmark, 1996. 367p.

This register provides a quality management system, that is recognized worldwide, for
qualifying products to the world market. The system backs up the existing manufacturers' self-certification, based on international standards. The work is primarily an
index of ISO 9000 certified companies listed by goods and listed alphabetically. It also
includes the names and addresses of certification bodies, and an index of DANAK
accredited bodies. DANAK refers to 'Danish Accreditation' by the Danish Agency for
Development of Trade and Industry, which is part of the Ministry for Business and
Industry. This body accredits testing and calibration laboratories, and inspection and
certification bodies, according to European standards. The register is meant for use
by Danish businesses taking part in world trade, but would also be informative for
international companies doing business with Denmark.

659 **Kompass-Denmark: register of Danish industry and commerce.**
Holte, Denmark: Kompass-Denmark Publishers, 1998/99. 38th ed.
2 vols.

The information in this register is based on interviews with leaders of the 15,000
companies mentioned. These include all manufacturers of more than local importance,
leading wholesale and haulage firms, banks, insurance companies, advertising agencies,

and other service organizations connected with trade and industry. Volume one lists products and services by alphabetical order, and then by industrial classification divided into the major industrial groups. All suppliers of a particular product or service can be found, as well as all the products supplied by any one company in the list. Volume two comprises an agencies section with the names of foreign companies represented in Denmark and their Danish agent, an alphabetical index of companies and a cross-reference to the product group in volume one, and a summary of standard company information. The text is presented in Danish, English, German, Spanish, and French.

660   **Musical Denmark Yearbook 93-94.**
Copenhagen: The Danish Cultural Institute and The Danish Music Information Centre, 1994. 168p.

This volume's primary feature is the 'Music in Denmark Key Directory' which lists the country's music publishers; record companies; music importers and distributors; recording studios; audio-visual producers; chamber music societies; professional ensembles, choirs, and operas; music boards; educational institutions and libraries; music magazines; and information on the live music scene, clubs, and tour production. In addition, this work marks the fortieth anniversary of the magazine, 'Musical Denmark'. The first part includes magazine articles about topics such as current popular singers and the state of the record industry.

Bibliographies

661 Literature from Denmark published in English between 1980 and 1991.
Lise Bostrup. Copenhagen: The Danish Literature Information Centre, 1991. 53p. (Available from Danish Literature Information Centre, Christians Brygge 1, DK-1219 Copenhagen K).

This publication provides four comprehensive lists of literature in English for the period 1980 to 1991: works by Hans Christian Andersen, works by Søren Kierkegaard, Danish literature, and Danish children's literature. The English title, the Danish title, the publisher and publication date are provided for each entry. The work also includes brief profiles of four Danish authors with works in English translation: Jens Peter Jacobsen, Dorrit Willumsen, Henrik Nordbrandt, and Peter Seeberg. The Danish Literature Information Centre currently maintains a list of 'Danish Literature in English Translation since 1981' which is updated twice a year. The list is divided by literature categories (anthologies, fiction, children's literature, etc.), and each entry notes the author, English title, Danish title, translator, illustrator, and foreign publisher.

662 Dania polyglotta: literature on Denmark in languages other than Danish & books of Danish interest published abroad. New series.
Copenhagen: The Royal Library, 1969- . annual.

This is an annual bibliography compiled by the Danish Department of the Royal Library. The works are divided by subject heading, as well as by language within the subject category. The earlier series goes by the title *Dania polyglotta: literature on Denmark in languages other than Danish* (Copenhagen: The Royal Library, 1946- . annual).

663 **Denmark in international affairs: publications in languages other than Danish 1965-1995.**
Henrik Holtermann. Copenhagen: DJØF Publishing, 1997. 232p.
A multilingual interdisciplinary bibliography that contains 3,849 citations of primary and secondary sources. There are also approximately fifty publications from 1996. The work is divided into eight major sections: general analyses and theories, security and defence, international economic relations, international law, international organizations, development assistance, relations to specific countries and regions, and Greenland and the Faroe Islands. These are further divided into subsections. The citations within each topic are alphabetized by author or editor. Citations are not grouped by language. No annotations or descriptions are provided.

664 **Søren Kierkegaard and his critics: an international bibliography of criticism.**
Compiled by Francois LaPointe. Westport, Connecticut: Greenwood Press, 1980. 430p.
This extensive and well-organized bibliography, which attempts to be as complete and accurate as possible up to 1979, is divided into two parts. Part one lists the works of Kierkegaard translated into major European languages. Part two comprises the bulk of the work, and lists books devoted exclusively to Kierkegaard, organized by language; dissertations and theses; books and articles that are general discussions of Kierkegaard's life and work; entries devoted to single works by Kierkegaard; and relevant literary, philosophical, and theological works listed by name and by subject. The appendix lists bibliographies devoted to Kierkegaard.

665 **Scandinavian mythology: an annotated bibliography.**
John Lindow. New York; London: Garland Publishing, 1988. 539p.
This work aims to provide easy access to scholarship on Scandinavian paganism. It comprises a single alphabetical listing by author's last name with a detailed index; there are no chapter divisions or subject headings. The total 3,059 entries provide annotations that are mainly descriptive rather than critical. The introduction provides a concise survey of the major research areas of the field.

666 **Twentieth century Danish music: an annotated bibliography and research directory.**
Lansing D. McLoskey. London: Greenwood Press, 1998. 149p.
This comprehensive work covers all music-related sources since 1900, with an emphasis on the post-Nielsen era (1931 to the present day). Information is also given for the Faroe Islands, but not for Greenland. Publications in all languages are included. The author notes that most material on Danish music in the 20th century exists in journals and periodicals published in Denmark and Scandinavia, but there has been a recent rise in publications in English and in other languages. The bibliography comprises books and reference sources, bibliographies and catalogues, discographies, journals and periodicals, and articles in journals and periodicals. The research directory lists information services and research facilities, music organizations and professional associations, public institutions, teaching institutions and conservatories, music publishers, record labels, orchestras and opera companies, performing ensembles and music festivals. Two appendices provide chronological and alphabetical lists of Danish composers.

667   **Carl Nielsen: a guide to research.**
Nina Miller.   New York; London: Garland Publishing, 1987. 245p.
This bibliographical reference work contains annotated entries for writings on composer Carl Nielsen published up to mid-1986, in nine languages (Danish, Norwegian, Swedish, Dutch, English, French, German, Italian and Spanish). The entries also include all existing doctoral dissertations and theses. All items have been personally examined by the author. The book is divided into the following areas: general background; Nielsen's life and works such as letters, diaries, documents, pictures, and biographies; Nielsen's own writings; and evaluations of Nielsen's music published since his death.

668   **A checklist of Danish literature after 1945: based on the holdings of the Memorial Library of the University of Wisconsin-Madison.**
Compiled by Erwin K. Welsch, Robyn Peterson, Mogens Knudsen.
Madison: University of Wisconsin General Library System, 1987.
2nd ed. 400p.
A significant checklist of the works of contemporary Danish authors, who either established their reputations or achieved prominence after the Second World War. Although the list comprises works in Danish, translated works, some of which are in English, are also noted. The list is arranged by author and includes titles up to 1984. Each entry includes title, author, and publisher. This is a significant list of authors and titles, and represents the library's holdings which have been developed to serve the university's Scandinavian Studies programme.

Discover Denmark: on Denmark and the Danes; past, present and future.
See item no. 4.

A linguist's life: an English translation of Otto Jespersen's auto-biography with notes, photos and a bibliography.
See item no. 155.

Danish emigration to U.S.A.
See item no. 183.

Nordic studies in information technology and law.
See item no. 321.

Danish literature: a short critical survey.
See item no. 486.

A history of Danish literature.
See item no. 491.

Scandinavian Economic History Review & Economy and History.
See item no. 634.

Scandinavica, An International Journal of Scandinavian Studies.
See item no. 647.

Cassell dictionary of Norse myth and legend.
See item no. 651.

Historical dictionary of Denmark.
See item no. 654.

The Faroe Islands

669 The *skinn* values of pilot whales in the Faroe Islands: an evaluation
and a corrective proposal.
Dorete Bloch, Martin Zachariassen. *North Atlantic Studies*, vol. 1,
no. 1 (1989), p. 39-61.

In a study of the status of the traditionally hunted pilot whale, these researchers
assessed the reliability of official measurement procedures which date back to 1832,
based on a regressive divided rod that measures a value known as *skinn*. It was found
that *skinn* values on the forty rods that exist today differed to such a large extent that a
measure for a large whale could be off by several *skinn*. A new hypothetical rod is
proposed that is more in line with biological parameters. This article is technical in
nature, but it also provides a glimpse into a significant and now controversial aspect of
the Faroese way of life.

670 The formation of a nation: the Faroe Islands.
Hans Jacob Debes.   In: *Ethnicity and nation building in the Nordic
world*.   Edited by Sven Tägil.   London: Hurst, 1995, p. 63-84.
bibliog.

Provides an account of the Faroese national movement from its beginnings in the early
19th century, then its breakthrough in the 1870s and 1880s, to self-rule in 1948. The
preconditions for the movement to take place are analysed in terms of geography,
history, culture, and language. The national awakening, which brought such developments as a written language, educational reforms, and the establishment of a Faroese
folk high school, is examined. The political and economic developments such as the
creation of political institutions and elections, population growth, a lack of emigration,
and a rise in the standard of living are described, as are the specific events leading up
to the national plebiscite of 1946 and the passing of the Home Rule Act in 1948. The
author sees the Faroese case as unique in that it was not a bourgeois movement, no
state was established, and a majority of the people accepted home rule status as 'a
self-governing community within the Danish state'.

The Faroe Islands

671   **Færøsk Arkitektur.** (Architecture on the Faroe Islands.)
Edited by Kim Dirckinck-Holmfeld, Susanne Møldrup, Marianne
Amundsen, translated by Peter Avondoglio, Gaber Abrahamsen.
Copenhagen: The Danish Architectural Press, 1996. 136p.
Describes in text and pictures the development of the Faroe Islands' tradition of building, from medieval stone and timber structures to contemporary buildings. It is also a
commentary on the Faroese culture and national identity as it examines the architecture in the context of the unique natural conditions and the harsh climate of the
islands. This is a significant work in that the Faroes have experienced a surge in architecture since the mid-1970s, and a new generation of architects is making its mark,
while remaining true to their culture and surroundings. Included in this volume are
portraits of the capital city, Tórshavn, which depict its old quarter, its government
administration buildings, and the cultural centre. Many individual structures are also
described, such as a traditional Faroese house and a modern interpretation. One chapter profiles individual architects. The volume is beautifully illustrated and the entire
text is presented in Danish and English.

672   **Landscape, personhood, and culture: names of places and people
in the Faeroe Islands.**
Dennis Gaffin. *Ethnos*, no. 1,2 (1993), p. 53-72. bibliog.
Examines the cultural and social significance of place-names and person names. It is
noted that names are not merely descriptive, but communicate cultural principles.
Specifically, names are analysed for how they mark economic and historical conditions,
highlight individual personalities, express social and political relationships, and
enhance local, regional, and national identities. The analysis demonstrates the coherence and tradition of Faroese culture, and its identification with the land. Numerous
examples of the complex Faroese naming system are mentioned throughout the article.

673   **The Faroes: the faraway islands.**
Anthony Jackson.   London: Robert Hale, 1991. 223p. maps. bibliog.
This work is one of the most comprehensive books written in English on this small
group of islands in the North Atlantic. The first half of the book discusses the islands'
natural history, the social history, and contemporary social and political conditions.
The lifestyle of the Faroes could be described as medieval up to the mid-19th century.
Today this is a prosperous community, although economic development varies from
village to village. The second half of the book is a tour through the islands, with
descriptions of all the villages and how to reach them. Twenty-six tourist trails are
provided, with place-names, distances, and road numbers noted on corresponding
maps. The book also includes thirty black-and-white photographs taken by the author,
and depicting seascapes, landscapes, and island life. A chronology of significant
events, and a glossary with spelling and pronunciation explanations are also provided.

674   **Socio-economic transformation and the Faroese national identity.**
Jóan Pauli Joensen. *North Atlantic Studies*, vol. 1, no. 1 (1989),
p. 14-20.
Provides an overview of some of the societal changes that led to the Faroese nationalist movement. The new ideas of a national identity during the late 1800s grew out of
the shift from a stable agrarian culture to a diversified society based on commercial
fisheries. The Faroe Islands of the 18th century were characterized by structural and

245

cultural stability in terms of technology, economy, and social relations, where the social order was based on land ownership. Many forces came together in the 19th century, such as changes in property laws, population increases and accompanying migrations to larger villages, the growth of the fishing industry, and the introduction of free trade. It is observed that the emergence of a middle class and a wage-earning working class meant the need for a new basis for identity beyond the village affiliation.

675 **Fisherman of Faroe: William Gibson Sloan.**
Fred Kelling. Göta, Faroe Islands: Leirkerid Publications, 1993. 270p. bibliog.

Relates the saga of William Gibson Sloan, a pioneer missionary from Scotland to the Faroe Islands beginning in the 1860s. The book chronicles Sloan's travels from Scotland, his sojourn in the Shetland Islands, and his preaching of the gospel to the Faroese people, as well as the opposition he experienced. The work provides a detailed account of Sloan's life – his own spiritual apprenticeship and missionary zeal, and his personal circumstances on the Faroe Islands. The story also includes profiles of other fellow 'fishermen'. Sloan's legacy on the Faroes remains. At the time of the book's publication, the assemblies of Christians in the Faroes had multiplied from a handful in Sloan's time to around thirty. In addition to this biographical saga, the book offers historical and cultural perspectives on the Faroe Islands.

676 **No nation is an island: language, culture, and national identity in the Faroe Islands.**
Tom Nauerby. Aarhus, Denmark: SNAI-North Atlantic Publications, Aarhus University Press, 237p. maps. bibliog.

Analyses the evolution of the Faroese language and the establishment of its national culture in terms of both historical and contemporary elements. The book aims to show that Faroese national identity has emerged in a process of interaction with the outside world. The introduction lays the theoretical foundation with a discussion of several paradigms of nation-building, settling on an interplay between transnational and international foundations of national identities. Subsequent chapters discuss the formation of national symbols, specifically the political dimension of the language question in the nationalist struggle at the end of the 19th century; the development of the Faroese written language, and its Danish and Icelandic influences; attitudes towards language and what they reveal about Faroese identity; and finally the hunting of pilot whales – a cultural practice that been the target of international criticism since the mid-1980s – and its status as a national symbol. The text is enhanced with numerous black-and-white photographs.

677 **The physical environment of the Faroe Islands.**
Edited by G. K. Rutherford. The Hague; Boston, Massachusetts; London: Dr W. Junk Publishers, 1982. 148p. bibliog. (Monographiae Biologicae, Volume 46).

Reports on a land classification and soil survey that was conducted in order to gain an understanding of the distribution of the soils in the Faroes which would in turn have implications for land management. The overall analysis was based on a breakdown of the landscape into areas of similarity or land systems which could be described according to their morphology, materials, and origins. This is a scientific report with contributions from nine authors. The chapters comprise a general description of the landscape, including how the Faroes were formed, and reports on the geology, flora and vegetation, animal life, insect life (specifically the Ground Beetle), the land systems, and the soils. With the exception of Chapter 9, 'Man and the physical environment', this work is not recommended for the general reader. This final chapter briefly describes such topics as the settlement of the islands, housing, industry and agriculture.

678   **The Faroe Islands.**
Liv Kjørsvik Schei, Gunnie Moberg, drawings by Tróndur Patursson.
London: John Murray Publishers, 1991. 248p. map. bibliog.
Tells the story of the Faroe Islands – their history and natural history, their people, culture, and way of life. The historical chapters highlight the early history and Viking era, more recent times after the conversion to Christianity, and the Faroese political awakening and the national movement. Other chapters are devoted to folklore, language, literature, art, dancing, the farming and fishing industries, and place-names. There are also individual chapters on Tórshavn, the capital city, and on individual islands or island clusters. The detailed text is factual as well as anecdotal. The work is enhanced with numerous black-and-white and colour photographs. A glossary of Faroese words is also included.

679   **Space and gender at the Faroe Islands.**
Elisabeth Vestergaard.   *North Atlantic Studies*, vol. 1, no. 1 (1989), p. 33-37.
Provides a description and an analysis of the spatial organization of the bygone Faroese peasant society, and its cultural classification system of male and female. The author notes that the social life of the peasant society revolved around the village whose spatial organization was divided into 'inside' and 'outside'. The gendered division of labour reflected this distinction, where women's work consisted of indoor activities, while men's activities took place out of doors. Further, women were culturally defined by sexual functions, and men by social relations. Women held an ambiguous position in society in that they were members of society, but they also were outside society, i.e., male society. Material from anthropological fieldwork provides the basis for this discussion.

680   **Faroese history and identity: national historical writing.**
Vagn Wåhlin.   *North Atlantic Studies*, vol. 1, no. 1 (1989), p. 21-32.
Proposes that Faroese history and historical writings have emphasized the 'unique' situation of Faroese society. The central position of the nationalist movement in Faroese culture has resulted in either a focus on what was common among a population that in fact comprised different villages, regions, and social classes, or a concentration on common enemies. This author argues for a break from tradition and the creation of a more modern understanding of history. It is argued that historical research could benefit from a comparative approach, one that would look to parallel societies and to internal Faroese differences, in order to bring Faroese problems into line with those of the rest of the world, especially the other North Atlantic communities.

681 **The Christmas meeting in context: the construction of a Faroese identity.**
Jonathan Wylie. *North Atlantic Studies*, vol. 1, no. 1 (1989), p. 5-13.
Provides a larger cultural perspective for the ideas put forth at the famous public meeting on 26 December 1888. The author explains that the Faroese nationalist movement 'to defend the Faroes' language and the Faroes' customs' evoked basic themes of Scandinavian culture such as the adherence to an 'ethos of egalitarian individualism' and the selection of linguistic and historical symbols of collective identity. The author suggests that the Faroese attempt to establish a collective identity separate from the rest of Scandinavia was a response to socio-economic changes, and was complicated by those changes and by the Faroes' pre-existing bilingualism. Raising the status of Faroese, the informal and primarily spoken language, was at odds with the fact that Danish was the formal language of social institutions and of contact with the outside world. This insightful article is clearly written and well organized.

682 **The Faroe Islands.**
Jonathan Wylie. Lexington, Kentucky: The University Press of Kentucky, 1987. 257p. bibliog.
This book tells the story of the Faroe Islands in an historical and anthropological account. The author traces internal developments, as well as patterns of external contact, using a variety of sources such as folktales, parliamentary records, tourist writings, poetry, old newspapers, and data on land tenure. Historically the work covers the early Norse settlement in the early 9th century, the Faroese Reformation and its aftermath – particularly the land tenure system, the agricultural reforms of the 18th century, the nationalist movement in the mid-1800s, and the sociological changes and the economic growth of the 20th century. The work also aims to define the Faroese national culture, and to show how and why the Faroese have maintained their cultural distinctiveness, and ultimately became politically distinct from Denmark. An important theme of this work is the salience of the past for the collective identity of the Faroese people, and the significance of their historiographic and literary affairs in the maintenance of national identity.

Statistical bulletin: selected statistics of the Faroe Islands.
See item no. 431.

Index

This index is a single alphabetical sequence of authors (personal and organizational), titles of publications, and subjects. Index entries refer both to main items, and to other works mentioned in the annotation to each item. Title entries are in italics. For indexing purposes, the Danish letters å, æ and ø have been treated as corresponding to the letters a, ae and o.

Map of Denmark

This map shows the more important features.

ALSO FROM CLIO PRESS

INTERNATIONAL ORGANIZATIONS SERIES

Each volume in the International Organizations Series is either devoted to one specific organization, or to a number of different organizations operating in a particular region, or engaged in a specific field of activity. The scope of the series is wide-ranging and includes intergovernmental organizations, international non-governmental organizations, and national bodies dealing with international issues. The series is aimed mainly at the English-speaker and each volume provides a selective, annotated, critical bibliography of the organization, or organizations, concerned. The bibliographies cover books, articles, pamphlets, directories, databases and theses and, wherever possible, attention is focused on material about the organizations rather than on the organizations' own publications. Notwithstanding this, the most important official publications, and guides to those publications, will be included. The views expressed in individual volumes, however, are not necessarily those of the publishers.

VOLUMES IN THE SERIES

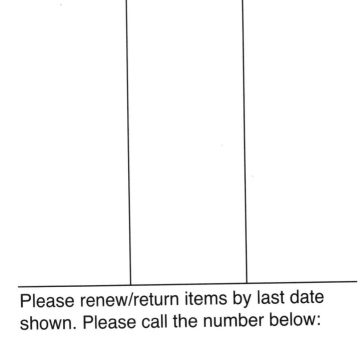

Please renew/return items by last date shown. Please call the number below:

Renewals and enquiries: 0300 123 4049

Textphone for hearing or
speech impaired users: 0300 123 4041

www.hertsdirect.org/librarycatalogue
L32